THE FOUNDING CONSERVATIVES

THE FOUNDING CONSERVATIVES

How a Group of Unsung Heroes Saved the American Revolution

DAVID LEFER

SENTINEL

SENTINEL
Published by the Penguin Group
Penguin Group (USA) Inc., 375 Hudson Street,
New York, New York 10014, USA

USA | Canada | UK | Ireland | Australia | New Zealand | India | South Africa | China

Penguin Books Ltd, Registered Offices: 80 Strand, London WC2R 0RL, England

For more information about the Penguin Group visit penguin.com

Illustration credits
Insert page 4 (top): Charles Willson Peale, *Gouverneur Morris and Robert Morris,* 1783, Pennsylvania Academy of the Fine Arts, Philadelphia; 5 (bottom): Copyright Capital Newspapers Division of The Hearst Corporation, Albany, New York; 7 (top): *Siege of Charleston* by Alonzo Chappel (print), New York Public Library, Mid-Manhattan Library, Picture Collection

ISBN 978-1-59523-069-0

Printed in the United States of America
1 3 5 7 9 10 8 6 4 2

Book design by Sabrina Bowers

For Marie-Laure Béraud, Konstantinos Tsakonas, and Michael Macari, whose histories remain

One cannot care so much about what has happened in the past and not care what is happening in one's own time. One cannot care about what is happening in one's own time without wanting to do something about it.

EDMUND WILSON

Contents

INTRODUCTION

In the fall of 1779 a small but fatal riot on the streets of Philadelphia changed the course of the Revolution and forever altered the nature of American politics. It began when hungry militiamen, enraged over the ever-rising cost of bread, seized four rich merchants. With fixed bayonets and a lone drummer beating "The Rogue's March," the mob paraded its captives around the city and then toward the house of the prosperous lawyer James Wilson. Wilson, a future U.S. Supreme Court justice, was a staunch free-market advocate and opposed the sorts of price controls demanded by radicals. The mob, he knew, was not coming in peace.

Informed that an attack was imminent, America's leading conservatives rushed to Wilson's house that afternoon to defend him. To the growing din of shouts and drum taps, they hastily barricaded the building and readied their powder. No one knows who fired the first shot, but within ten minutes the mob had rolled a cannon into firing position and was smashing through Wilson's doors with hammers and iron bars. Blood stained the street, and by the time the mob retreated, five men were dead and fourteen wounded. That America's conservative leadership even survived the Fort Wilson Riot, as it was soon called, would have a lasting impact on American politics.

The street fight had a seismic impact on public perception as well. Within a year, fear of the mob would lead to the decline of radical power and the ascendance of conservatism as the dominant political force in America for the next twenty years. Those two decades were among the most formative in American history, and during this time conservatives found themselves in a position to shape the new republic, from rewriting the state constitutions and running the government under the Articles of Confederation to drafting the Constitution and getting it ratified in the states. As the historian Samuel Eliot Morison observed in a speech entitled "The Conservative American Revolution," "Had James Wilson and his friends not defended themselves, this brawl on October 4, 1779, would have been to the American Revolution what the capture of the Bastille on July 14, 1789, was to the French Revolution." In other words, had America's first conservatives not held out that day, the nation's history might have turned out radically different.

Outside scholarly circles, most people have no idea that the American Revolution was wracked by bitter and often violent struggles between left and right. For much of the twentieth century, in fact, this notion was largely dismissed within the academic community as well. Morison's views, for example, were squarely in the minority when he described the significance of the Fort Wilson Riot in 1975.

Having taught American history for many years at both the high school and college level and having written about the subject in a previous book, I was astonished to discover this relatively unknown side of the American Revolution. I learned about it one day when one of my brightest students asked me who John Dickinson was. As far as I knew, Dickinson had played only a small role in the Revolution, but I was pleased to recall what most history textbooks say about him. "He wrote the *Letters from a Farmer in Pennsylvania,*" I replied.

"I know that," she said. "That's what it says in all the textbooks. But who was he?"

I had to admit I didn't know any more about him but promised to get back to her with more information. A quick search revealed that only one Dickinson biography had been written in the twentieth century, a book with the oxymoronic title *John Dickinson: Conservative Revolutionary.* Could one be revolutionary and conservative at the same time? I wondered. I checked the book out of the library.

I was amazed to learn that in the buildup to independence, Dickinson was the most trusted man in America and the second most famous American in the world, after Benjamin Franklin. His contemporaries credited him with single-handedly rallying the colonies in the fight against British oppression. It was only because of Dickinson, said one American in 1774, "that there was a present disposition to dispose the tyranny of Parliament."[1] Moreover, his *Letters from a Farmer in Pennsylvania,* published between 1767 and 1768, were the most eloquent defense of liberty penned in the colonies up to that point and the literary hit of the decade. Almost every colonial newspaper carried them, and they were republished in a dozen pamphlet editions soon afterward. In an age when Americans read widely and enthusiastically, there was no better path to fame than to write well. Dickinson was a virtuoso with his pen, and every political body he belonged to over the course of his long career would recognize and utilize his talent for words. So great was Dickinson's influence on American thought in the years leading to independence that historians long ago hailed him as "the penman of the American Revolution."[2]

Dickinson's accomplishments intrigued me so much that I began reading about his political allies, discovering in the process similar titles such as *Carter Braxton: A Conservative in Revolt; Revolutionary Conservative: James Duane of New York;* and *Philip Schuyler: The Origins of a Conservative Patriot.* These men were equally impressive. James Wilson, who studied law under Dickinson, was one of America's finest legal minds and drafted much of the Constitution. Robert Morris, who helped defend Wilson's home during the Fort Wilson Riot, served as America's first chief executive, established the United States Navy, and personally bankrolled the Continental Army as well as much of the American economy. John Jay crafted much of New York's constitution, served as president of Congress, and secured American economic interests while brokering the peace treaty with Britain. Philip Schuyler, an upstate New York patrician, orchestrated the military victory that changed the course of the war. Silas Deane of Connecticut secured the French aid that kept the American army alive. John Rutledge of South Carolina almost single-handedly saved the Deep South. James Duane, Gouverneur Morris, Robert Livingston, Edward Rutledge, Carter Braxton, and many others also played pivotal roles in the Revolution. Yet as consequential as these men were in their lifetimes, they have been largely forgotten today.

Then I delved into the history of conservatism, and several things struck me right away. First, Dickinson and his allies were indeed revolutionary conservatives. Hailing largely from the colonial upper classes, they were initially reluctant to embrace independence. Yet they were not Loyalists. They were among the most zealous defenders of American rights, and many fought with distinction against both British Redcoats and their own social peers who had stayed loyal to the Crown. They were committed Patriots who nonetheless wanted to preserve as much of the old social order as possible. Many of their core tenets, in fact, would be surprisingly familiar to modern conservatives: their faith in history and experience; their mistrust of theory and dogmatism; their support for venerable social institutions; their reverence for the military; their insistence on protecting property over equality; their belief in yoking the interests of the rich and powerful to the government; and their devotion to free-market capitalism.

Another thing that struck me had to do with the supposed origins of conservatism. According to almost every history of the subject, the first modern conservative was Edmund Burke, a British statesman who feared the radical excesses of the French Revolution. Yet here was a group of American revolutionaries who espoused remarkably similar beliefs. America, it seemed, had its own, legitimate conservative heritage that predated Burke by more than a decade. If conservatism was an ideology that prized tradition, how strange it seemed that so few knew of its American genesis.

An exhaustive search of the Library of Congress catalog also revealed something surprising. In the tens of thousands of entries on the American Revolution, I could not find a single book on the birth of the American right during this period. The closest hit was Morison's twenty-eight-page speech. Other than that, all I found were two works that bookended the era I was interested in. Leonard Labaree's *Conservatism in Early American History* examines American elites during the colonial era but stops before the Revolution. In *The Revolution of American Conservatism,* David Hackett Fischer investigates conservative politics in the first decades of the nineteenth century, beginning with Jefferson's electoral victory in 1800. This book aims to bridge this yawning gap.

In the course of my research, I also learned why I had heard next to nothing about the pitched ideological battles between left and right during the Revolution. Historians, it turns out, have changed the way they interpret the Revolution several times over the past two centuries. In the years following World War II, American historians made a conscious decision to downplay any hint of strife among the Founding Fathers. With the United States facing an existential and ideological threat from Soviet Communism, the "consensus" school, as it was called, deliberately emphasized Americans' underlying unity during the Revolution. The renowned historian Richard Hofstadter, who coined the term, explained that the "consensus" movement had been created as a response to the previous generation of historians, who had "put such an excessive emphasis on conflict that an antidote was needed."[3]

Consensus historians did more than just emphasize harmony in the American Revolution. They also believed that American history was fundamentally liberal. In his 1955 book *The Liberal Tradition in America,* the political scientists Louis Hartz argued that political thought in the United States had never strayed far from John Locke's liberal ideology. Hartz went so far as to deny that America had ever had a homegrown conservative tradition. For those of us who grew up in the 1960s, 1970s, and 1980s, most of the textbooks we read in school were written by historians of this generation. No wonder we viewed the founders as a monolithic cohort of like-minded men, marching in lockstep toward independence.

The idea that Americans had been divided into radical and conservative camps was far from unknown, however. At the turn of the twentieth century, scholars of the "progressive" school had viewed the Revolution largely through the lens of class conflict. To these earlier historians, social and economic forces had been as important as political ones at the birth of the republic. With the rise of the consensus school, this view largely fell from fashion.

Only in the past few decades has historiography begun swinging back toward the progressive interpretation of the Revolution, albeit with far more sophistication than a century ago. In the face of fierce opposition, historians such as Alfred Young, Edward Countryman, and Gary Nash have helped revive the notion that class conflict played a significant role in the fight for independence. Their work frequently mentions the fight between radicals and conservatives, but their focus remains on the radicalism of the American Revolution. As interest in the conflict between left and right mounts, the time has come to study America's revolutionary conservatives in their own right.

Of course, many other historical prisms offer insight into the Revolution as well. America was divided by regional differences, western land claims, population sizes, gender, age, and race. All of these divisions should be and have been studied, and the fact that this book focuses on one sort of conflict does not mean others did not exist. But I contend that the split between left and right remains one of the most important.

To me, the idea that the founders were just as politically divided as we are today holds a certain realistic appeal. It makes them seem more human. It also reminds us of the many similarities between our era and theirs. The Revolution was a time of war without end; of real estate crashes, rampant speculation, and mounting public debt; of popular outrage at bankers and merchants who grew rich while the rest of the nation struggled; of bitter disputes over taxation; and of such animosity between left and right that it frequently left Congress paralyzed for months on end. Given the turbulence of the period, it's unsurprising that the founders reacted more like us than their impassive marble likenesses would lead us to believe.

One of the trickiest parts of studying the birth of conservatism in the eighteenth century is that most of the terms we use today to describe it did not yet exist. *Conservative,* which derives from the Latin *conservare,* meaning "to guard, defend, preserve," was not coined until the early nineteenth century. According to the *Oxford English Dictionary,* it was first coined in England in 1830 to replace the older *Tory,* but this is one of those rare cases when the OED gets something wrong. America, not Britain, deserves credit for inventing the word. Jacob Wagner, a Massachusetts federalist, first used *conservative* in its modern political sense in a letter dated May 13, 1808.[4] Even using *right-wing* to talk about American politics in the 1770s and 1780s is anachronistic, since the terms *left* and *right* referred to the seating arrangement of France's National Assembly at the start of the French Revolution in 1789.

But while *conservative* did not attain its current meaning until several decades after independence, the ideas behind the word came into existence *avant la lettre* in those early years of revolutionary turmoil. For lack of better terms, radicals repeatedly called their enemies "aristocrats" and "monarchists." These epithets, however, were propaganda more than political reality. The fact was, America's founding conservatives supported neither aristocracy nor monarchy, even if they admired features of these institutions. Rather, they represented a new of type of political creed based on a reverence for tradition.

Modern conservatism can be defined not as any specific set of policies but as a philosophical approach to one of the defining features of the modern world: accelerating change. Conservatives do not oppose all change, as reactionaries do. They understand both its inevitability and the futility of trying to turn back the clock. Their aim, instead, is to prevent change from galloping out of control by preserving custom, defending inherited institutions, and championing prudence. Conservatism is in this sense continually evolving and inherently unyielding.

This book makes three main arguments. First, the founding conservatives saved the American Revolution. Though most of them have been forgotten today, collectively they were as important to the creation of the United States as Washington, Jefferson, and Adams. Second, the founding conservatives brought modern capitalism to America. While the New World was no stranger to the concept of profit making—one scholar has quipped that it arrived aboard the *Mayflower*—conservatives were the first advocates of banking, corporations, and large-scale industry in America. And third, we should no longer look to Britain for the origins of American conservatism. Modern conservatism, I argue, was born at the moment of independence. While our tradition parallels Britain's—both drew inspiration from English Whig thought of the late seventeenth and early eighteenth centuries—America's conservative heritage reflects our nation's unique history and culture.

The founding conservatives did not always concur with one another; nor did they all focus on the same issues. Some of them were social conservatives, who fought to preserve stability amid revolutionary upheaval. Others were economic conservatives, who labored to build mighty financial engines that would turn America into a powerful commercial empire. Still others were political conservatives, who mistrusted popular power and clamored for greater executive authority to keep democratic forces in check. These men were united by common political concerns, but they did not form an organized political party with rigid positions. And their disagreements, minor as they were, reveal that America's conservative tradition is a rich and multifaceted one. There was no single conservatism at the birth of the republic.

The founding conservatives learned several important lessons as the Revolution progressed. The first was that compromise was essential. Which is not to say they were pushovers. They haggled, argued, and fought (literally at times) for their beliefs. But had they not bent for the good of the nation at several critical junctures, they would have quickly become irrelevant. By remaining flexible, they were able to continue exerting a powerful influence over the course of events. The second lesson they gleaned was that in a democratic society, the upper classes cannot hold on to power by appealing only to tradition. New political realities were overturning customary voting patterns in the 1770s and 1780s. The right adapted by persuading the masses that their economic interests were aligned and by promising to deliver greater prosperity than the left.

These two lessons remain as relevant today as they were during the Revolution. Above all, the fundamental question of conservatism—one that is especially germane to modern conservatives—was formed and articulated in the early years of the Revolution: how does one preserve cherished values and traditions in the face of social upheaval? The founding conservatives' attempt to answer this question represents their most enduring gift to the present. At a time when many on the right are questioning what they stand for and searching for a winning electoral strategy, there is no better place to look than at the wealth and diversity of ideas that animated America's first conservatives.

Learning about them has given me personal insights as well. Although I have voted Democrat in most major elections, researching this book has given me a new appreciation for conservatism. The old saw that conservatives support existing evils while liberals want to replace them with new ones has more than a little truth to it. Social and political structures that have evolved organically over hundreds of years must be accorded a certain respect. They may not be perfect, but they have stood the test of time. In this light, conservatives' fondness for tradition makes tremendous sense.

America's conservative legacy is a proud and perdurable one. The founding conservatives may have disagreed with the revolutionary radicals, but ultimately they knew they were on the same side. They created their brand of politics as a careful response to both radicals and reactionaries. As the historian Clinton Rossiter puts it, conservatives "struggle against those who would hurry ahead to Utopia or back to Eden." Politicians today who know only how to obstruct and never how to compromise cannot justifiably claim to be part of America's founding conservative tradition.

The most intriguing character I encountered during the years I spent researching and writing this book was surely the first one, for in the space of two years John Dickinson performed one of the most remarkable political transformations in American history. He began the summer of 1774 as the darling of the American left and ended the summer of 1776 as the leader of America's first conservatives. What makes his political conversion so fascinating is that he did not in fact alter any of his principles. Dickinson, as always, stood firm. It was America in those turbulent years that changed around him.[5]

The key to making sense of Dickinson's politics lies in his deep familiarity with English history and jurisprudence. As a law student at London's Middle Temple in the 1750s, he immersed himself in the works of England's great political thinkers and the workings of its government. What he learned led him to prize liberty and fear the creeping expansion of royal power. If his extensive reading on the life and death of republics taught him anything, it was that free men needed to remain ever vigilant to the threat of tyranny. When governmental authority starts to swell, Dickinson wrote, there comes a point beyond which "there is no means in nature for altering its course but violence, and I think a moderate acquaintance with English history will teach one this truth."[6]

Violence, by which Dickinson meant civil war and revolution, was the great risk. If corruption continued to flourish in Britain, if the Crown's armies became a mechanism for oppression, then freedom and the rule of law would fall into jeopardy. A moderate acquaintance with English history had taught him that much. To understand Dickinson's response to the rising threat to American liberty and to understand the birth of conservatism in general, we too must look to the past.

CHAPTER 1

COURT AND COUNTRY

On a bitterly cold day at the end of January 1649, Charles I of England had his head chopped off. The King wore two shirts to the execution block so that his shivering would not be mistaken for fear. Had he known how vastly his kingdom was about to transform, all the clothing in England would not have stopped his shivers. Charles Stuart's death marked the end of the English Civil War, but one of the most tumultuous centuries in British history was just beginning. Two revolutionary forces, republicanism and capitalism, were being unleashed, and the social, political, and economic changes they wrought would divide Britain and render it more powerful than ever before.

England's century of turmoil began in 1642 with the eruption of its civil war, a paroxysm of bloodshed that tore the nation in two. In the eyes of many, Charles I had committed two unpardonable sins. The first was to flirt with Catholicism in a country that had largely rejected the religious authority of Rome. The second was to attempt to establish absolute power. Specifically, he disbanded Parliament when it insisted on claiming more political rights. Monarchs, Charles earnestly believed, possessed a divine right to rule. The problem was that without Parliament he could never raise enough money to fight wars abroad or quash uprisings at home. Caught between his need for ever more cash and his refusal to meet Parliament's demands, the King responded with a series of autocratic measures and new taxation. With liberty and property seemingly under attack, Parliament rebelled, and years of open warfare broke out. The fighting remained inconclusive until Oliver Cromwell, a Parliamentary cavalry officer with an iron will and an unshakable faith that God marched by his side, defeated the royalist forces. Charles was soon captured, and just before he was brought to trial, Cromwell purged Parliament of anyone hoping to spare the King's life.

Standing atop a black-clad scaffold in central London, Charles was allowed one last speech. Defiantly, he told the assembled onlookers that the people's freedom consisted of having a government, not of having a share in it. He remained convinced of his innocence and of the folly of a government without a monarch. Charles then turned politely to one of his executioners to ask if some neck hairs might interfere with the beheading. The executioner helped tuck the stray wisps beneath Charles's white satin cap. Then he swung a heavy axe through the King's neck. Lifting the severed head, a second executioner cried, "Behold the head of a traitor."[1] Many in the crowd reportedly groaned, less from the sight of dripping blood than from the audacity of what had just been done.

With the destruction of the monarchy, and the House of Lords a few weeks later, Parliament's victorious forces looked forward to a golden age of republicanism. The ideal republic or commonwealth, as imagined by James Harrington in his *Commonwealth of Oceana* of 1656, would be a virtuous society composed of independent men who banded together for the common defense. It would be mostly agrarian, with no extremes of wealth or poverty and widespread ownership of land. Harrington's work was initially banned, but after dedicating it to Cromwell, he was finally granted access to a printing press. Harrington hoped his dedication would do more than just get him published; he prayed it would inspire the new Lord Protector to uphold the great and ancient traditions of republicanism.

Founded in classical Greece and Rome, republicanism is best understood as a political spirit rather than as a specific type of a government.[2] The word comes to us from the ancient world. Derived from the Latin *res publica*, literally meaning "public thing," a republic is a constitutional system in which the government (the *res*) is primarily concerned with the good of the whole (the *publica*).[3] Republics aren't necessarily hostile to monarchy, despite the fact that England's proved fatal to Charles. John Milton, who was a high official in Cromwell's government before he became a famous poet, said he hated "only tyrants," not kings.[4] A king who respected the proper limits of his position could play a stabilizing role in a balanced constitutional system. A tyrant, on the other hand, destroys the liberty of his subjects in order to consolidate power. History, under the republican view, was a never-ending struggle between liberty and power. And too often power won.

Republicans believed that the death of the Roman Republic in 46 B.C. was due largely to Julius Caesar's unquenchable thirst for power. In February of that year he smashed the last of the resistance to his rule, and in April the stern and incorruptible Marcus Porcius Cato chose to kill himself rather than live under Caesar's tyranny. According to Plutarch, Cato tried stabbing himself, but after realizing he had missed his vital organs, he tore open his belly with his bare hands. Cato's superhuman dedication to Rome's ancient government made him a heroic figure to British republicans. They fought back tears of admiration every time they heard him demand "liberty or death" in Joseph Addison's famous 1712 play *Cato, a Tragedy*. Such sentiment was not mere melodrama. On the eve of the American Revolution, Patrick Henry spoke in dead earnest when he uttered his memorable variation on Cato's line, "Give me liberty, or give me death."

By the time barbarians sacked Rome in the early fifth century, the crumbling empire had lost all traces of its former republican self. Yet the light of liberty was not extinguished. Many came to believe that the very Germans rampaging through Italy had become Rome's true heirs. With their elected monarch, egalitarian society, and just code of law, these Teutonic tribes seemed to embody all the ideals of classical republicanism. Tacitus, John Dickinson's favorite Roman author, praised the Goths' nobility and independence and saw in them everything his own countrymen had lost. And so republicanism departed sunny Greece and Rome for northern Europe's dark forests.

It might have stayed there had English republicans not been desperate to find a source of republican virtue in their own age. They discovered it, of course, in themselves. According to eighteenth-century historians, the Anglo-Saxons who settled England hailed from none other than the same Germanic tribes that had conquered Rome. They brought with them their free and democratic political institutions, establishing an unbroken line between Britain's political institutions and those of classical antiquity.[5] For five hundred years, this view held, England enjoyed untrammeled liberty, widespread ownership of property, and a constitution that constrained the power of government.[6] England's idyllic kingdom came to an end only in 1066, when William the Conqueror forced feudalism and despotism upon the English. The French, in other words, destroyed Anglo-Saxon freedom, and the English began a centuries-long struggle to regain it.

Modern scholarship does not totally support the eighteenth-century view of history, which is commonly referred to as the Whig interpretation. What historians can confirm is that after languishing for a thousand years after the fall of Rome, republicanism reemerged in Renaissance Florence and then in Civil War England. From there it vaulted across the Atlantic, where its impact on American thought can only be described as seismic. Republicanism, scholars now believe, was the single greatest factor driving Americans into armed resistance in the 1770s.[7] Surprisingly, the full significance of these ideas was uncovered only in the past few decades, but their rediscovery has fundamentally altered the study of the American past.

The basic tenets of republicanism are easy to grasp. The first is that all governments—whether aristocracies, monarchies, or republics—follow a cycle of birth, death, and then rebirth as a new form of government. This cycle was the original meaning of the word *revolution*, a natural wheeling through the different forms of government.[8] As far back as the ancient world, republics were considered the most prosperous type of society. The trouble was that their success carried the seeds of their own demise. Prosperity inevitably brought luxury and corruption, which eventually transformed republics into dictatorships. In time these tyrannies too decayed, starting the process over again.

Only one thing could help preserve a republic from inevitable decay, and that was virtue. Derived from the Latin *vir*, or man, the word *virtue* had a very different connotation in the seventeenth and eighteenth centuries. It implied manliness as well as selflessness, an ability to fight for the state, and a willingness to place its interests above one's own.[9] What now implies chastity once stood for virility, a word that shares the same root. For British republicans, the citizen-soldiers of Sparta and Rome exemplified this ideal. And they considered Britain's own citizen militias a bulwark for liberty.

Martial virtue was deeply intertwined with another key concept of republicanism: the ownership of land. The right to keep and bear arms was prized in the English constitution precisely because men were expected to defend their property.[10] Land ownership in turn served as the foundation for all political power. Only men whose wealth came from owning land were worthy of holding power because they alone were deemed capable of rising above self-interest. They were, in a word, independent. Artisans, laborers, and merchants—in fact, all who depended on trade—lacked independence precisely because they owed their livelihood to others. Commerce, accordingly, was held in deep suspicion. Almost three thousand years after the founding of Sparta, republicans still praised its legendary lawgiver, Lycurgus, for banning luxury, moneymaking, and gold and silver coinage. The "Jewish humour," as Harrington dubbed commerce, subverted the state.[11] For republicans in every age, virtue and commerce had no business together.

Since all republics eventually decayed, republicans were ever alert for the slightest sign of corruption. Corruption involved more than just the ubiquitous bribery that was endemic in Britain in the mid-eighteenth century. It implied a wholesale seizure of power by the government and a citizenry that had become passive and oblivious to the loss of its rights. As men became fond of luxury, they grew "effeminate" and lost their manly virtue. Professional armies were especially insidious, it was thought, because they weakened men's martial spirit and easily became tools for oppression. Corruption was the malefic handmaiden of tyranny.

If the aftermath of England's civil war had taught Britons anything, it was that tyranny was far from unthinkable in their sceptered isle. Soon after Charles I's decapitation, Cromwell had used his army to wipe out all remaining resistance, even among the very groups that had helped him gain power. If the Lord Protector had been merciless toward the King, he was equally so in stamping out a growing radicalism among the lower classes. Levellers, who could be immediately recognized by the sea-green ribbons they wore on their clothing, called for near-universal suffrage and equality of the sexes. Diggers, an even more radical splinter group, advocated the abolition of private property and the creation of classless socialist communes.[12] Many of these radicals had, in fact, served in the army, but their attempts to secure greater political rights brought them imprisonment, exile, or death. While the clampdown on radicalism was largely welcomed by the elites, Cromwell's reliance on military force to control the government turned many against him. His death in 1658 led England to conclude that perhaps monarchy had not been so onerous after all. Two years later Parliament swept Cromwell's son from power and restored to the throne the beheaded King's son, Charles II.

After so many years of warfare, it came as a great relief when the new King's reign proved relatively boring. Charles was a bon vivant, more interested in cavorting with his multiple mistresses—with whom he acknowledged sharing a dozen illegitimate children—than in bending the nation to his will. Yet England's political upheavals were far from over. Charles's ambivalent feelings toward Catholicism divided the nation into two rival factions: Whigs, who supported republicanism, and Tories, who backed the prerogative of the king. In 1685 Charles's more ambitious younger brother took the throne and ended all hope of maintaining the sybaritic spirit of the previous two and a half decades. James II's autocratic manner reopened old wounds. His artless attempts to reassert absolute power and his open espousal of Catholicism led

Whigs and Tories to put aside their differences. It was time, they agreed, for the King to go.

On November 5, 1688, Parliament welcomed William of Orange into the seaside town of Torbay in southwestern England. The Dutch prince had several things going for him. He was married to the King's daughter. He was Protestant. And he happened to be traveling with a large army. James fled to France, aggrieved as a father-in-law but grateful his head remained on his shoulders. Though he had not officially abdicated, Parliament seized upon his abrupt absence to crown the Dutch invader William III of England. The nation dubbed this sudden swap of monarchs the "Glorious Revolution." It was indeed glorious: carnage from another civil war had been averted, and William recognized both the sovereignty of Parliament and a Bill of Rights guaranteeing constitutional liberty. The key to maintaining a harmonious republic, the English decided, was to establish a balanced "constitution," which, unlike America's later written document, referred simply to the nation's amalgam of ancient laws and traditions. When the king, the aristocracy, and the commoners held one another in check, no one branch of government could monopolize power and threaten the others. It was, as George III would later say, "the most beautiful combination that ever was framed."[13] Parliament had found a king it could live with. William had acquired a large nation he could use to prosecute his wars on the Continent.

Along with his army, William brought something even more formidable to England—a series of Dutch financial innovations that we now call capitalism. Capitalism needs to be understood as more than just making money. Commerce is as old as human history, as Lycurgus's decision to ban it in the ninth century B.C. shows. Modern capitalism, on the other hand, was invented in the early seventeenth century as a way of pooling money to limit risk in large-scale investments. If there was one thing that distinguished this new financial system from anything that had come before, it was the sheer scale on which it operated. Capitalism was big and systematic in its approach to making money.[14]

In 1602 the Dutch East India Company became the world's first multinational corporation as well as the first company to sell shares of its stock. The company established trading posts in Asia, Africa, and America, bringing Dutch consumers new luxuries from around the globe. It founded new colonies and a private military force that rivaled those of foreign nations. In Amsterdam the East India Company founded the world's first stock exchange, where its shares and later others were traded. To help finance these ventures, the Dutch founded the Bank of Amsterdam in 1609, which by the middle of the seventeenth century had become the most powerful bank in Europe.

William lost no time importing these financial institutions into his new kingdom. In the process of adapting them, though, the English made two novel changes that enabled them to unseat the Dutch as Europe's financial powerhouse. They created the world's first national bank, and they established a funded national debt.[15] In so doing they cemented the relationship between private interest and national power in a way that had never before been attempted. Linking the interests of the elite to those of the government, many believed, would finally assure social stability.

In 1694 the King and Parliament granted a group of rich London merchants an exclusive charter to accept deposits and issue currency. In exchange, the newly founded Bank of England agreed to supply the government with large loans on a regular basis. The deal benefited both sides. Investors in the bank could literally print their own money, and with a government-guaranteed stream of interest payments coming their way, they discovered a lucrative new way of investing. Holders of public and private securities began trading them, leading to a profusion of new commercial and financial houses in London. For the government, these innovations were equally advantageous. As long as it maintained good credit, the ministry now possessed a virtually inexhaustible source of funds for military operations. What this arrangement amounted to was a remarkable secret weapon: capitalism, the British realized, won wars.

It also made them rich. The English could now battle the French for decades, absorb Scotland, and in the words of the historian J. G. A. Pocock, "pursue empire in the Atlantic, the Mediterranean, and India"—all without going bankrupt.[16] In the span of a century, Britain's Financial Revolution, as historians call it, transformed an impoverished war-torn island into the mightiest military and economic power in the world. But not everyone benefited from capitalism. The collusion between private interests and the government led to the creation of powerful monopolies and fomented an increasing disparity of wealth in England.

The tremendous energies unleashed by capitalism proved every bit as disruptive as the republican beliefs of the mid-seventeenth century. Suddenly money, self-interest, and luxury were being lauded as virtues. In 1714 Bernard de Mandeville, a Dutch physician who had immigrated to England, wrote an infamous book whose subtitle alone provoked mass outrage. *The Fable of the Bees: Or, Private Vices, Public Benefits* describes a thriving bee colony that collapses as soon as it decides to begin acting selflessly and virtuously. Mandeville's belief that vice is more beneficial to society than self-sacrifice was so inflammatory that he was eventually prosecuted for his writing. His book, though, was a publishing success, an indication of the growing appeal of his ideas. Voltaire was among those who picked up on this theme. He praised the greed he witnessed at the London Stock Exchange and accused the world of hypocrisy when it disparaged moneymaking. "'Beware of luxury,' said Cato to the Romans," Voltaire wrote mockingly. "Luxury has been declaimed against for the space of two thousand years . . . and yet it has always been liked."[17]

Soon a succession of influential thinkers began challenging traditional notions of republicanism. David Hume and Adam Smith, two of the brightest luminaries in Scotland, still praised the classical ideal, but they didn't think it was very practical. Human beings were motivated primarily by self-interest, Hume argued in his 1752 essay "On Commerce," and any government that refused to take into account this basic truth would probably fail. In his *Theory of Moral Sentiments* of 1759, Smith devised the most sophisticated theory yet to explain the advantages of self-interest. An "invisible hand," he argued, secretly guided the actions of the individual. "By pursuing his own interest," Smith said, "he frequently promotes that of the society more effectually than when he really intends to promote it."[18]

These ideas did more than violate the basic principles of republicanism. They also caused a major political rift. As the Financial Revolution gained steam, power began shifting away from its traditional base in the landed aristocracy and toward a new class of "moneyed men" and the government's growing bureaucracy. The result: Britain underwent its final and, from the American point of view, most important upheaval in its century of tumult.

By the second decade of the eighteenth century, the feud that had been raging between Tories and Whigs since the days of Charles II ended in a decisive Whig victory. With even the monarchy recognizing the sovereignty of Parliament, old Tory arguments about the supremacy of the king had little relevance. The Whigs quickly established total dominance over British politics, but political harmony remained elusive. Almost as soon as they had secured power, these eighteenth-century republicans split into two rival camps: the Court party, which supported the economic revolution of the late seventeenth century; and the Country party, which yearned nostalgically for the pure republicanism of the mid-seventeenth century. The rhetorical battle between these groups was heated, and it lit the fuse leading directly to the American Revolution.

In 1721 Robert Walpole, leader of the Court party, became Britain's first lord of the Treasury. By taking over much of the executive authority once enjoyed by the king, he effectively created a new position. He is now considered Britain's first prime minister, a term of abuse that was coined by his enemies and that he rejected. Fat and charming, Walpole had a genius for staying in power, which he achieved by skillfully and liberally doling out favors, offices, and bribes. He owed his success to more than just his corrupt politics, however. By consolidating the gains of the Financial Revolution, he ensured Britain's continued economic growth. His conservative outlook was summed up by his motto *quieta non movere,* which translates roughly as "Things are fine as they are."[19] The British public evidently thought so too. For all the corruption it saw (or chose not to see), it clearly enjoyed the fruits of Court policy. Voters would return Walpole and his successors, the Pelham brothers, Henry and Thomas, to office for the next half-century.

The Court didn't take its electoral success for granted. It actively wooed the public, using sophisticated public relations techniques just as skillfully as modern politicians do. One of the most effective ways of molding public opinion in the eighteenth century was to lay claim to the classical republican heritage. Cato, who had long been praised for his defiance to power, made a poor figurehead for a ruling party. The ensuing public relations battle to replace him with his fellow senator Marcus Tullius Cicero lasted fifteen years. Court publicists went so far as to commission numerous biographies of Cicero, most of which were thinly veiled comparisons to Walpole. Cicero personified the Court approach. Unlike the grim, uncompromising Cato, he preached a pragmatic wisdom. He argued that choosing the lesser evil is often the best course and that moderation and prudence are the highest political values.

As Whig, the Court party was descended from the republican tradition, but as the party in power, it could no longer embrace the rhetoric of opposition. Practical realities of governing were now more important than ideological consistency. Court support for capitalism, standing armies, a large government bureaucracy, banking, corporations, and a national debt all reflected its pragmatism and the "nonutopian nature" of its politics, in the words of the historian Reed Browning.[20] Yes, power could lead to tyranny, but it was necessary for effective government. Commerce might threaten virtue, but money was needed to maintain the empire. A standing army jeopardized liberty, but citizen militias were simply not a realistic alternative for fighting foreign wars. And a little corruption never hurt anyone. As Walpole's paid supporters pointed out, it had brought order and stability to British society for the first time in nearly a century.[21]

Where the Court saw simple pragmatism, Country Whigs saw immediate danger. England's opposition party was ultraorthodox in its republicanism and apocalyptic in its predictions. Its unrelenting message was that the government's growing power was paving the way to tyranny. Walpole's great nemesis, the frustrated and brilliant Viscount Bolingbroke, saw England as heading for the same shoals that had sunk all the ancient republics. "The fate of Rome," he warned, "will be renewed . . . in Britain."[22] He called for a return to virtue and simple government, which he naturally believed should be led by landed aristocrats like himself.

Though the Country party never actually managed to win many elections in England, it achieved immense influence by developing a systematic and extensive literature of opposition.[23] Nowhere was its impact greater than in America. Almost everything Americans learned about republicanism and the Whig tradition came from this body of writing, and in the years leading up to the American Revolution, it taught them to mistrust practically every action taken by the British government. Edmund Burke, a former classmate of Dickinson's, warned Parliament that the American colonists read voraciously and knew their rights. "I have been told by an eminent bookseller," he said, "that in no branch of his business . . . were so many books as those on the law exported to the plantations."[24] Americans were going so far as to build their own printing presses, Burke added. And they were publishing the great works of the Country Whig canon.

The most popular political work in America before the Farmer's *Letters* was a series of essays written under the pseudonym Cato.[25] Inspired by the devastating economic crisis of 1720, which was sparked by massive fraud on the London stock market, *Cato's Letters* lambasted capitalistic greed, attacked business monopolies, and warned of the growing gap between rich and poor. Its authors, the London journalists John Trenchard and Thomas Gordon, became the leading critics of Walpole's administration and his "government by money."[26] Their equally influential newspaper, *The Independent Whig*, was so popular in the colonies that Isaac Norris, John Dickinson's father-in-law, spared no expense to have his bookseller send him the latest edition from London every week. Gordon's translation of Tacitus became a cornerstone of the Founding Fathers' political education.[27] What distinguished Gordon's English version from the original was the extensive notes that turned the Roman historian into a mouthpiece for Whig ideas.

While the influence of Country ideology on America was vast, Court thought had little immediate impact. The Court was a party of action rather than rhetoric. It published no great tracts or treatises justifying its policies.

There were, however, "subtle influences whereby these ideas came to America," writes the historian Lance Banning.[28] David Hume's work was one such conduit. Americans who had lived or studied in Britain were another.

Some historians argue that Country Whigs were the conservatives of mid-eighteenth-century Britain, because they were traditionalists in their adherence to classical republicanism. But just a century earlier orthodox republicans had been England's radicals, an indication that their traditionalism was far newer than they liked to admit. Moreover, by the eve of the American Revolution, Court ideas had become even more firmly entrenched in British society than had Country ones. As defenders of the established order, Court Whigs could lay equal claim to the mantle of conservatism. Yet modern conservatism comprises more than mere respect for tradition or an adherence to the establishment. It was born from a rich admixture of Court and Country ideas that was still fluid in the mid-eighteenth century. Only after being tempered in the crucible of the American Revolution would it start to coalesce.

CHAPTER 2

NONE SHALL MAKE THEM AFRAID

Born in 1732, the same year as George Washington, John Dickinson spent his boyhood on his father's lush Delaware plantation, Poplar Hall. In addition to growing tobacco, Dickinson's father, Samuel, was a well-known lawyer and judge. He oversaw his son's education attentively, hiring several private tutors and discussing Dickinson's favorite topics, Latin and history, over long conversations at the dinner table. Dickinson's mother, Mary, came from a prominent Quaker family with a steadfast belief in public service. "From my infancy," Dickinson later wrote, "I was taught to love humanity and liberty."[1] At the age of eighteen, he decided to follow his father into the legal profession. The "certainty and quiet" of the law, he felt, suited his temperament.[2] Colonial America had no formal law schools, so most who wished to become lawyers began by clerking with an older attorney. The sons of America's elite traveled to England to study law. Dickinson did both. After spending three years in Philadelphia working for a prominent attorney, he sailed for England in the last week of October 1753.

It was a rough crossing, and the young man spent most of the long voyage curled in the bunk of his stuffy cabin wracked with fever and nausea. It is fair to say that in this condition John Dickinson probably had the worst twenty-first birthday of any Founding Father. Two months later he arrived in the British capital, as happy to stand on dry land as he was to begin his studies at London's famous Middle Temple. Founded in the fourteenth century, the Middle Temple was one of the three Inns of Court where British lawyers had trained since the early Middle Ages. It was designed to awe, with parts of the Temple modeled on the Church of the Holy Sepulcher erected by the crusaders in Jerusalem. With its hammer-beam roof, brightly colored heraldic glass, and ornately carved oak screen, the main hall maintained the feel of a medieval college, but it was the school's extensive library that was its crown jewel.[3]

A quiet, scholastic world of its own, the Middle Temple was sandwiched between two of the busiest commercial thoroughfares in London. On one side flowed the Thames River, choked with the imperial capital's shipping. On the other side lay Fleet Street, home to many of the city's lawyers, writers, and merchants. The surrounding neighborhood, which Dickinson described as full of "noise, dirt and business," was a seamless fusion of the ancient and modern.[4] For a young provincial, nothing could have been more exciting.

Despite its illustrious reputation, the education at the Middle Temple was actually mediocre. There were no classes and only one formal requirement: students had to spend three years in residence, a condition so lax it could be satisfied simply by dining at one of the Inns of Court six times a semester. As one of Dickinson's American classmates, a rich Maryland Catholic named Charles Carroll, complained:

> Nothing can be more absurd than the usual manner of young gentlemen's studying the law. . . . They are soon disgusted with the difficulties and dryness of the study, the law books are thrown aside, dissipation succeeds to study, immorality to virtue, one night plunges them into ruin, misery, and disease.[5]

For an ambitious young man like Dickinson, lack of formal oversight was no excuse for debauchery. As for the "vicious pleasures of London," he told his parents, "I know not what they are." And if he did know, he reassured them, he would "never think of them."[6]

His parents needn't have worried. The young man's deepest passion was for his studies, which suited his intellect more than he had imagined possible. Like history, Dickinson's other favorite subject, law depended on precedent, but it also required and rewarded ingenuity. Above all, the law served a practical and noble purpose in society. It was the guardian of justice, prudence, and liberty—the civic virtues Dickinson valued most highly.

Dickinson adhered to a rigorous schedule, rising at five in the morning, studying eight hours, and dining at four o'clock. He immersed himself in the works of the great political philosophers and legal theorists of his day and of antiquity. The influence of classical thought on British law was profound, and he pored over Roman authors such as Cicero and Tacitus, the renowned defenders of ancient republican virtue. One of Dickinson's prized possessions was a translation of Tacitus's works, purchased his final year in London. Housed today in a Philadelphia library, the five volumes still bear the hundreds of folds Dickinson made to mark key passages.[7] For more contemporary insight into English jurisprudence, he read Sir Edward Coke, the renowned seventeenth-century jurist; Paul de Rapin's fourteen-volume history of England, which cautioned against granting too much power to the king or Parliament; and his beloved Bolingbroke, the incorruptible eighteenth-century republican. "I fly to books" was a common line in his letters home.[8]

Yet Dickinson also recognized that reading constituted only part of his legal training. If he wanted to become a successful lawyer, or statesman for that matter, he had to learn the art of persuasion. "All the law of Coke and the eloquence of Cicero can never influence men who don't understand you," he wrote. Along with like-minded classmates, he regularly attended the great legal and political forums of London, Chancery Court, the King's Bench, Whitehall, and Parliament, writing down the proceedings verbatim and studying them when he returned to his rented rooms. He paid special attention to great orators of the day, trying to divine the secrets of their rhetorical brilliance. "I have heard some of the greatest men in England, perhaps the world," he wrote home.[9] His field trips gave him a ringside seat to two of the fiercest political battles of the decade, making his exposure to these debates all the more formative.

The first controversy erupted in March 1754, when the death of Prime Minister Henry Pelham led to tumultuous nationwide elections. Pelham's older brother, the Duke of Newcastle, took over as the new prime minister, but it took six months to sort out some seventy hotly contested seats in Parliament, proof, Dickinson said, "of the corruption of the age." He was stunned at the pervasive fraud he witnessed. Over £1 million was spent securing votes in London alone. "Bribery is so common," he wrote, "that it is thought there is not a borough in England where it is not practiced." So bankrupt was Britain's civil society that "it is grown a vice here to be virtuous." He feared for England's survival and placed the blame on squarely rampant luxury and the loss of "old-fashioned religion." As he told his father, it is the "utter disregard of virtue which is the unfailing cause of the destruction of empires."[10]

The fate of the empire was very much on Dickinson's mind two years later, when he witnessed the second major political blowup of the decade. On April 18, 1756, France invaded the British-held island of Minorca in the Mediterranean. It was a minor loss that quickly escalated in the world's first truly global conflict, the Seven Years War. Known in America as the French and Indian War, the conflagration would eventually involve every major European power, touch five continents, and leave roughly one million dead. In a letter to his father, Dickinson predicted the conflict would soon engulf America. It was a remarkable insight for a twenty-three-year-old. But neither he nor anyone else at the time could have predicted that two decades later the impending war would trigger a fatal crisis between Britain and her colonies.

British politicians were in agreement over George II's decision to declare war, but they were far from united on how to fight it. At the heart of the controversy lay the Duke of Newcastle's decision to use professional foreign mercenaries rather than citizen militiamen to defend Britain from French invasion. A militia bill passed unanimously in the House of Commons, only to be blocked by the prime minister. The uproar was immediate. "The Ministry," Dickinson declared, "have given great offense."[11] Not only were the thousands of German mercenaries landing in Britain a threat to the liberties of all Englishmen; their deployment also set a dangerous constitutional precedent by inexorably expanding the government's power.

Dickinson's education encompassed far more than mere jurisprudence. He attended the theater, dined in high society, attended receptions with the King, and visited the famous Vauxhall Gardens, whose elegance took his breath away. With orchestras hidden in groves, a Chinese temple, and beautiful walks bounded by statues and paintings, the gardens represented the pinnacle of British grandeur. At dusk, Dickinson said, "a thousand lamps that hang on the branches of the trees are lighted up and raise another day."[12] Nothing in America could match what he saw in England. "More is learnt of mankind here in a month," he wrote, "than can be in a year in any other part of the world."[13]

Yet Dickinson was never tempted to settle in England. After so many years abroad, he had become desperately homesick. America might have lacked Britain's wealth and refinement. It might have been largely unsettled, "yet that wilderness to me is more pleasing than this charming garden," he wrote from London. In America "life is a stream pure and unruffled, here an ocean briny and tempestuous. There we enjoy life, here we spend it."[14]

Dickinson's years abroad aroused a deep ambivalence toward the mother country. More than ever he was devoted to the republican ideals of freedom and virtue, and yet he appreciated the dynamism of British capitalism. He was disgusted by the corruption he witnessed—the fixed elections, the bribery—and yet he saw the benefits of imperial power. For most Americans schooled in the classical republicanism of the Country Whigs, corruption and power were forever inseparable. [Dickinson's time in England, however, led him to a startling conclusion that formed the foundation of his conservative politics: great nations, he realized, must possess both virtue and power. This was Dickinson's vision for America.] Only in America, he believed, was such a republican empire possible. Britain might have been beyond salvation, but

America still beckoned as the last great hope for liberty. "Notwithstanding all the diversions of England," he wrote home, "I shall return to America with rapture."[15]

On February 8, 1757, more than three years after arriving in England, John Dickinson received his law degree, and that fall he moved to Philadelphia to put into practice everything he had learned abroad. He was "flattered" to discover just how lucrative his British legal training was. "Money flows in," he told his mother.[16] But he was not content simply enjoying the comfortable life afforded by his high income. His true calling, he believed, lay in public service. In 1759 Dickinson was elected to the relatively sedate Delaware Assembly, and in 1763 he took a seat in the far more raucous Pennsylvania Assembly. American colonists could not know it at the time, but 1763 was a pivotal year in American history. The end of the French and Indian War that year would ignite a chain reaction of discontent that set America and Britain on a collision course. Faced with crushing debt from years of fighting, Britain began eyeing its American colonies as a fat new source of revenue. Dickinson too was about to face a personal watershed, one that would define his career. Within the next eighteen months he would become bitter enemies with the two most powerful men in Pennsylvania politics.

Like many great antagonists, John Dickinson and Joseph Galloway resembled each other. Both were rich, accomplished lawyers who married well and enjoyed an exalted status in Pennsylvania society. Both were gentleman farmers who hailed from prominent Quaker families, though Galloway had converted to Anglicanism to win British favor. Portraits show Galloway as alert and genteel, with a lean physique and deep eyes. Just two years older than Dickinson, he enjoyed a significant head start in politics, having never left America for his legal studies. His upper-class connections were of tremendous use to his political partner, the bespectacled, homey, and keenly resourceful Benjamin Franklin. Though a quarter century older than Galloway and already wealthy, Franklin was lowborn, and entrée into elite Philadelphia circles had proven difficult for the fifteenth child of a Boston candlemaker.

For nearly a decade Franklin and Galloway had been feuding with the proprietor of Pennsylvania and Delaware. Unlike most of the other colonies, which were controlled by the king, Pennsylvania and Delaware were governed by the aristocratic Penn family, headed by Thomas Penn. As a reward for the Penn family's service to the monarchy after the restoration, Charles II had granted

William Penn, Thomas's father, a vast territory in the New World, which the new proprietor named Penn's Woods, or Pennsylvania. Where William had been an enthusiastic promoter of democracy and religious tolerance, his son was interested primarily in squeezing as much money from his colonies as possible. Acting increasingly like a feudal lord, Thomas Penn demanded special tax exemptions and ordered his appointed governor to thwart the Assembly whenever it suited his family's financial interests.

Outraged by the threat to the colony's traditions of self-government, Dickinson joined a growing chorus denouncing Penn. But he was not prepared to accept what Galloway and Franklin had in mind next. In March 1764 they launched a massive public relations campaign to oust the Penns and transform Pennsylvania into a royal province. Inundating Philadelphia with petitions, pamphlets, and newspaper articles, Galloway and Franklin painted a golden picture of the freedom and prosperity that would follow if the recently crowned George III controlled Pennsylvania. What they didn't say, but tacitly assumed, was that with the proprietors out of the way, they would be the ones in charge.

Dickinson was no fan of the Penn family, but his education in England instantly turned him against this scheme. Replacing the tyranny of the Penns with the tyranny of the king would solve none of Pennsylvania's problems. The rights of Pennsylvanians, he believed, would be less secure after a sudden shift in government. As the historian Edward Countryman observes, "John Dickinson had the genuine conservative's acute awareness that one thing leads to another."[17]

When the Pennsylvania Assembly met on May 24, 1764, to debate petitioning King George to turn Pennsylvania into a royal colony, Galloway arrived brimming with confidence that his motion would easily pass. So he was stupefied when Dickinson, who had only recently fulminated against Thomas Penn, rose to oppose it. Galloway grew increasingly outraged as he watched legislators paying attention to Dickinson's finely reasoned arguments.

"[It is] not the proper time to attempt the change in our government," Dickinson argued, "neither the proper season nor the proper method." In such matters prudence was essential. Rushing into such a momentous decision would likely shift power from the Assembly, "the proper guardian of the public liberties, to other hands."[18] The British were simply not to be trusted, Dickinson said, and he listed all the threats to liberty that royal control would bring. The Crown was likely to garrison a permanent army in Pennsylvania, violating the precept against standing armies. It would threaten the province's cherished religious freedom by establishing the Church of England and requiring citizens to pay a tithe.[19] In fact, Dickinson pointed out, rumors were already circulating that Britain's new prime minister, George Grenville, was planning new taxes on sugar and stamps in the colonies. At the end of the debate, Galloway's petition was approved, but Dickinson's opposition had been sufficient to create a deep rift in the legislature. The real fight began after the Assembly voted to adjourn until September.

Throughout the summer Dickinson traded nasty barbs with Galloway and Franklin. When Galloway's attacks grew personal, however, the normally calm Dickinson snapped. After Galloway charged him with being motivated solely by "a restless thirst after promotion," Dickinson challenged his opponent to a duel. This was a common response for an eighteenth-century gentleman who felt his honor had been impugned. Then Dickinson followed with a low blow. With all the fury of an underpaid copyeditor, he began mocking Galloway's "continual breaches of the rules of grammar; his utter ignorance of the English language; the pompous obscurity and sputtering prolixity reigning through every part of his piece; and his innumerable and feeble tautologies."[20]

Galloway considered the attack on his sentence structure a greater affront than a challenge to fight to the death. The next time the two men crossed paths outside the Assembly, Galloway accosted Dickinson. Was he indeed the author of the grammatical diatribe?

"Yes, sir," Dickinson replied.

Without warning Galloway lunged, trying to seize Dickinson's prominent nose and swinging his walking stick at his head. Dickinson parried the blow with his own cane and struck back at Galloway, giving him a "fair knock on the head."[21] For several minutes the two legislators thrashed each other with their sticks until they were forcibly pulled apart.

If Dickinson's and Galloway's printed assaults had been nasty before, they grew doubly so after the fight. Word of the "torrent of low scurrility" issuing from Pennsylvania presses was reaching Britain. "In the name of goodness," wrote one London resident to a friend in Philadelphia, "stop your pamphleteer's mouths."[22] Dickinson's attacks proved effective, however, in tarnishing his antagonists' reputations.

Two weeks later in the October 1 elections, Philadelphia voters turned Galloway and Franklin out of office. It was only a brief setback, though. Many of their allies retained their seats. The following month Franklin was appointed Pennsylvania's colonial agent in London, where he would spend the next four years advocating in vain that Pennsylvania become a royal colony.

Galloway, who enjoyed the backing of Philadelphia merchants, was reelected the following year and in 1766 won the speakership of the Assembly. He would wait patiently to exact his revenge.

Dickinson's warnings about the dangers of royal government soon proved correct. Only a week before his fight with Galloway, Americans learned that the British were planning to impose taxes on sugar. Just a few months later news of the Stamp Act arrived. This new tax was one of a dozen tariffs Parliament instituted to pay off Britain's enormous war debts. All commercially used paper would now require a special taxed stamp. Not only were ordinary items like liquor licenses, playing cards, and almanacs to be taxed, but so were newspapers, legal documents, and pamphlets, arousing the ire of America's professional classes. Penalties for evasion ranged from heavy fines to death.

From New Hampshire to Georgia, the colonies erupted in protest. In pamphlets, legislative resolutions, and mass meetings, Americans made their unhappiness known. They organized militias to block the distribution of stamps and committees of correspondence to maintain contact with one another. For the first time the phrase "no taxation without representation" began to circulate. According to the historians Edmund and Helen Morgan, the Stamp Act crisis was the "prologue to revolution."[23]

Not all colonists supported the protests, though, and America soon split into two rival camps—Whigs and Tories. The terms had evolved significantly since their birth in late seventeenth-century England and in some ways had reversed in meaning. Tories in eighteenth-century America now backed Parliament and its right to legislate in the colonies. American Whigs, on the other hand, supported colonial rights and largely embraced the old Country Whig fear of government power.

For Tories like Galloway, the Whig reaction to the Stamp Act was dangerous for two reasons. First, he worried the protests would ruin his chance to convert Pennsylvania into a royal colony. Second, he feared that the growing unruliness of his fellow Americans was threatening social stability. When Philadelphia mobs began attacking supporters of the Stamp Act, he organized the Association for the Preservation of the Peace, a Tory self-defense group of eight hundred "sober inhabitants."[24] He also defended Parliament's right to tax America, in print. In an anonymous pamphlet signed simply "Americanus," he argued that Britain had incurred great costs defending America and deserved to be recompensed.

In October 1765 nine colonies voted to send representatives to a Stamp Act Congress in New York City to devise a collective colonial response. Galloway tried everything he could to prevent Pennsylvania from sending delegates, but Dickinson outmaneuvered him and was chosen to attend. For many delegates, it was their first time on a national stage, and they were electrified by the chance to intermingle with some of the most talented men in America. Caesar Rodney of Delaware commented that the delegates constituted "an assembly of the greatest ability I ever yet saw."[25] Amid this crowd, the thirty-three-year-old Dickinson shone above them all. He arrived in New York on October 6 and quickly impressed the other delegates with his industry and ingenuity. Over the next eleven days, he drafted almost all the major documents to come out of the Congress, including a Declaration of Rights and Grievances and a petition to the Crown. His extensive legal training enabled him to tackle, as few other Americans could, the complex constitutional issues at the heart of the controversy.

Combined with a devastating economic boycott of British goods, the political protests in America sparked fierce debate in Parliament. Not all in the British government supported the Stamp Act, and by the end of 1765 there was considerable support for repealing it. Edmund Burke, now the colonial agent for New York in London, was instrumental in its repeal. The Irish-born Burke was a stalwart defender of American rights. Riding on the coattails of the Marquis of Rockingham, who had just pushed Grenville from power, Burke was elected to Parliament just in time to help forge a compromise. Like Dickinson, Burke had a practical bent when it came to politics. Overturning the Stamp Act, he believed, was right because it was prudent. Whatever the underlying principles, he said, Parliament had to accept that the American boycott of all British goods was causing "the most distressful circumstances that could well be imagined; our manufactures at a stand, commerce almost totally annihilated, provisions extravagantly dear, and numerous populace unemployed."[26]

On January 14, 1766, the day Parliament opened debate on repealing the Stamp Act, Burke took his seat for the first time. Over the next few weeks, he would speak in favor of repeal multiple times. He voted to accept the Stamp Act Congress's petition, penned largely by Dickinson, but was outvoted. In March, however, Burke crafted a means of reconciling with America. It was a masterful stroke that balanced the desires of the colonists with the authority of Parliament. Parliament would repeal the Stamp Act but at the same time declare that it retained the right to legislate for the American colonies "in all cases whatsoever." Retaining a right did not mean that it had to be acted upon,

Burke reasoned. The Declaratory Act, as it became known, seemed to satisfy both sides for the moment.

In April news of the Stamp Act's repeal arrived in America. Whigs throughout the colonies rejoiced, but their relief was temporary. Burke and Rockingham's ministry would soon fall, replaced by one determined to solve Britain's financial problems through colonial taxation.

On December 2, 1767, Joseph Galloway choked with rage when he opened his copy of *The Pennsylvania Chronicle and Universal Advertiser,* a newspaper he had recently helped found. The *Chronicle* had published a letter attacking the recently passed Townshend Duties. According to the letter's anonymous author, these new taxes were a thinly veiled attempt to enslave America. As the *Chronicle*'s editor, William Goddard, well knew, his boss could not have disagreed more. "I don't well see how the public weal of the province can be affected by it," Galloway had written to Franklin a couple of months before.[27] If anything, the Assembly speaker saw the new duties as an "abundant favor" to the colonies.[28]

Confronting his editor, Galloway demanded to know why he had published the "damned ridiculous!" letter and who had written it. Goddard refused to divulge the author's name, and despite Galloway's protests, he insisted that the letters addressed a topic of widespread interest. The two men broke all ties after a second letter was printed, and over the next ten weeks the *Chronicle* published ten more letters. When Philadelphia's other two papers began printing the mysterious letters, Galloway knew they would soon spread throughout the colonies. Eventually nineteen of the colonies' twenty-three papers carried the letters.

Speculation over the identity of the author was rampant. Riveted by the anonymous author's eloquent broadsides against the Townshend Duties, Americans read and reread them for clues. From the start it was clear that the author knew history. The first letter was dated November 5, 1767, which was, the author noted, the seventy-ninth anniversary of William III's landing at Torbay, an occasion that "gave liberty to all Englishmen."

The *Letters* began simply:

> My dear Countrymen,
>
> I am a Farmer, settled . . . near the banks of the river Delaware, in the province of Pennsylvania. I . . . have been engaged in the busy scenes of life, but am now convinced that a man may be as happy with-

out bustle as with it. My farm is small, my servants are few, and good; I have a little money at interest; I wish for no more; . . . I am completing the number of days allotted to me by divine goodness.[29]

The folksy introduction is especially fascinating when we consider how essentially dishonest it was. The "Farmer" of these *Letters* was of course Dickinson. By portraying his life as quiet, pastoral, and independent, he was invoking, as all popular American politicians must, the republican ideal. What he chose not to reveal was that he was not actually a country farmer but one of the richest lawyers in the colonies who lived in the largest, busiest city in North America. Philadelphia was in fact one of the most populous cities in the entire British Empire. But with this brief introduction, Dickinson, known thereafter as the Farmer, cemented his reputation for virtue and gained the trust of almost all his fellow Americans. As misleading as his pseudonym was, it was also ingenious.

Once he had won his readers' confidence, he could then explain why the Townshend Duties were so terribly dangerous. This was no easy feat, because Charles Townshend, Britain's cunning chancellor of the Exchequer, had deliberately designed these taxes to be as insignificant as possible. Light duties were imposed on a series of basic items that the colonies could not make themselves: silk, lead, glass, and paint. At the same time, Townshend significantly reduced taxes on tea to encourage Americans to buy officially imported tea rather than contraband, which would now cost more.

Parliament had several motives in passing these duties, all of which the Farmer attacked. First, Parliament wanted Americans to pay for the cost of stationing British troops in the New World. For Dickinson, this was tantamount to demanding Americans pay for the means of their oppression. Second, the British wanted to use the new taxes to pay the salaries of colonial governors and other British officials. Traditionally, Crown appointees had been paid by American legislatures, whom they needed to placate if they wanted to collect their salaries. Without this check on British power, Dickinson believed, colonial legislatures would be hard pressed to protect American rights. Finally, Parliament wanted to establish a precedent, however small, that confirmed its right to tax the colonies. In other words, Dickinson warned, the Townshend Duties would serve as a legal wedge opening the door to ever more taxes.

The *Letters* went beyond merely emphasizing the inherent dangers of the new taxes, however. They also articulated for the first time the difference between constitutional and unconstitutional taxation. Since the days of the

Anglo-Saxons, Dickinson argued, the British constitution had protected property. By taxing Americans without regard for their wishes or welfare, the British were violating this basic principle. Dickinson conceded just one right to Parliament. It could impose taxes to regulate trade for the good of the whole empire—even if those taxes proved more burdensome in the end. What was at stake was not the amount of money Americans had to pay, he said, but the underlying constitutional principle.

With this argument Dickinson was coming to a new conception of sovereignty. In effect, he was saying that different parts of government could be sovereign within their own spheres. To the British government the idea that it could regulate only some affairs in America and not others was outlandish. "Extremely wild" was how Lord Hillsborough, Britain's secretary of state for the colonies, described the Farmer's *Letters*.[30] Dickinson's argument was especially difficult for the British to understand because it seemed to violate the fundamental principle of *imperium in imperio* (sovereignty within sovereignty). According to eighteenth-century political theory, sovereignty could not be divided. As Galloway put it, Parliament either could or could not legislate for America. He saw no middle ground. Dickinson, however, was ahead of his time. Two decades later his view of sovereignty would play a central role in the American Constitutional Convention and serve as the basis for America's federal system of government. Only in the nineteenth century would the British adopt Dickinson's system to govern their empire. They would have done well to listen to him earlier.

The force of Dickinson's writing came from its simplicity and erudition. His clean ringing phrases inspired ordinary Americans. His sophisticated legal reasoning, Latin quotations, and historical allusions appealed to the jurists and philosophers of the day. What the colonists valued so much was Dickinson's ability to speak to and about power. He articulated their grievances to the British and in doing so clarified their own thinking.

One of the things that made his *Letters* so persuasive was their emphasis on reason and moderation. As passionate as Dickinson was in defending American rights, he was no firebrand.

Spirited and unremitting protest was essential, he argued, and he urged Americans to boycott British goods, petition the King, and hold mass rallies. But he also counseled his countrymen against doing anything rash. "The cause of liberty is a cause of too much dignity to be sullied by turbulence and tumult," he wrote in one of the *Letters*. "Those who engage in it should breathe a sedate yet fervent spirit."[31] Since one of Dickinson's main goals was to preserve constitutional liberty, he would support only constitutional means to fend off attacks on that liberty. The wrong sort of protest, the Farmer warned his fellow Americans, could undermine the very thing they were fighting for.

In many ways, Dickinson embodied his philosophy of moderation. He strove to emulate the stoic composure of the ancient Greeks and Romans, possessing an unyielding belief in prudence and restraint. "I am truly moderate," he declared.[32] Too much of anything had to be avoided:

> Too much writing—too much reading—too much eating—too much drinking—too much working—too much exercise—too much idleness—too much loving—too much continence—too much law, or physics, or religion—all equally throw us from the balance of real pleasure.[33]

The only time Dickinson seemed to lack moderation was when he was extolling its virtues.

At the heart of the Farmer's *Letters* was a short, logical argument that neatly summarized American discontent. Dickinson believed "that we cannot be happy without being free; that we cannot be free without being secure in our property; that we cannot be secure in our property, if, without our consent, others may, as by right, take it away; that taxes imposed on us by Parliament, do thus take it away."[34]

Property in itself was not important to Dickinson, so much as the security of that property. It's an important distinction and one that lies at the heart of the conservative vision Dickinson was slowly articulating. [The protection of property was the "foundation" of all other rights, he declared. * Americans believed that "their property, acquired with so much pain and hazard, should be disposed of by none but themselves—or, to use the beautiful and emphatic language of the sacred scriptures, 'that they should sit every man under his vine, and under his fig tree, and NONE SHOULD MAKE THEM AFRAID.'"[35]]

Dickinson believed that the freest society was one where people could enjoy their property without the fear that it would be arbitrarily taken. The fact that he quoted from Micah 4:4 rather than a classical or legal passage is significant. For all his awesome knowledge of English jurisprudence, history, and politics, Dickinson also saw the Bible as a key source for civic rights. As the historian Forrest McDonald points out, Dickinson differed from many other Founding Fathers in emphasizing that divine law, not reason alone, served as a basis for these rights.[36]

* * *

In late May 1768, seven months after the Farmer's *Letters* were first published, John Dickinson was finally unmasked as their author. He was immediately celebrated throughout the colonies. The College of New Jersey at Princeton awarded him an honorary doctorate. Artists and sculptors vied to produce his likeness. According to the *Pennsylvania Chronicle,* the image of "the beloved Farmer of Philadelphia" was a favorite at a visiting waxworks exhibit from Boston.[37] As Americans geared up to challenge the British military, a new naval vessel was christened the *John Dickinson.* On the ship's figurehead, the Farmer's noble face stood watch over American waters.

Nor was Dickinson's appeal limited to the American side of the Atlantic. British political thinkers studied his writings closely, praising them as a powerful defense of the hereditary rights of Englishmen. French philosophes swooned over Dickinson's works, believing them to be an elegant justification of the rights of man. In Paris, Jean-Jacques Rousseau and Denis Diderot saw his writings translated into French. Dickinson, declared Voltaire, was the "American Cicero."[38]

One person, at least, did not lay laurels at Dickinson's feet.

Galloway had long harbored suspicions that his nemesis had penned the Farmer's *Letters.* With their author's identity now revealed, he could openly attack him. Calling Dickinson "a monster," Galloway thought the *Letters* amounted to sedition. He especially objected to Dickinson's call for renewed economic sanctions against Britain. Using his powers as speaker of the Pennsylvania Assembly, he did everything he could to interfere with the proposed new boycott. Dickinson mocked Galloway's "submissive behavior," but Galloway's job was made easier by the fact that many Philadelphia merchants did not see the Townshend Duties as a serious menace.[39] Once again in control of the *Pennsylvania Chronicle,* he ran editorials charging that the embargo was a radical New England trick aimed at ruining Pennsylvania's trade.

[Outside Pennsylvania, however, the economic blockade was increasingly effective. On March 5, 1770, the day of the Boston Massacre, Britain's prime minister presented a motion for a partial repeal of the Townshend Duties. All taxes were dropped, with the exception of the one on tea.] Once again Americans rejoiced, especially colonial merchants, who instantly dropped the boycott in their eagerness to resume making money. Dickinson remained skeptical. There would be no true peace, he believed, until Britain dropped all the unconstitutional taxes. In the meantime there was little to do but tend to his thriving legal practice, where he was helped by a brilliant new law clerk, a young Scottish immigrant named James Wilson.

Dickinson had no doubt that more trouble was on the way. "My countrymen have been provoked," he wrote, "but not quite enough. Thanks to the excellent spirit of the administration, I doubt not the proper measures will be pursued for provoking them still more." Until that moment, he would continue to act as America's sentinel, the "calm friend of freedom who faithfully watches and calls out new danger."[40]

CHAPTER 3

THE RISE OF RADICALISM

On the cold, wet evening of December 16, 1773, some one hundred men dressed as Mohawks stormed three heavy merchant ships moored at Griffin's Wharf in Boston. To conceal their identities, the men had caked their faces with coal dust obtained at a local blacksmith's. Their names were hidden, too, even from each other, but their mission was hardly secret. Lining the waterfront, two thousand onlookers, shivering in damp woolen clothes, cheered on the attack with shouts of "huzzah!" and "Boston Harbor a teapot tonight!" Aboard the *Dartmouth,* George Robert Hewes, a local cobbler who left the only eyewitness account of the event, asked the ship's captain for keys to the hatches and a dozen candles to light the holds. The captain complied but begged the raiders not to damage the ship or its rigging.

Wielding clubs and tomahawks, the raiders smashed open 342 chests of tea over the next three hours. The contents were then dumped into the icy water below. No one was seriously injured in the assault, though a few looters caught sneaking tea into their pockets were themselves pitched into the water. At first light, boats full of "Indians" threaded between British warships to hack at chests that had stayed afloat. By midmorning, ninety thousand pounds of tea lay at the bottom of the harbor, enough, according to legend, to turn the water a rich Darjeeling brown for the next three days. In total, the Boston Tea Party destroyed almost £10,000 of British East India Company property, worth roughly a million dollars today. To some, the attack was a courageous act of patriotism; to others, it was an outrageous case of vandalism.

While the Boston Tea Party marked a new level of destructiveness in the conflict with Britain, popular violence was nothing new in the colonies. For years urban mobs had held rallies, hanged and burned British officials in effigy, and threatened them in person when they could. They tarred and feathered their enemies, plundered and tore down their houses—including that of

Lieutenant Governor Thomas Hutchinson of Massachusetts—and demolished government offices. When the occasional radical leader was arrested, threats of more violence usually secured his release. A warning from the mob led many a public official to resign his post before trying to enforce an unpopular law.

The rioting that punctuated colonial life was not just political. It served also as a way to protect the community. Mobs routinely ran smallpox carriers out of town, shut down brothels, and banned entertainment deemed inappropriate. In 1766 a New York City crowd attacked the opening performance at the Chapel Street Theater, shouting that it was "highly improper that such entertainments should be exhibited at this time of public distress, when great numbers of poor people can scarce find subsistence." Under a hail of "brick bats, sticks and bottles and glasses," the audience members fled the theater, only to have their "caps, hats, wigs, cardinals, and cloak tails" seized on their way out.[1] The mob then demolished the entire building, igniting the broken boards to build a giant bonfire.

But the most important function of the popular violence was economic. Whenever food prices rose too steeply, lower-class mobs seized bread and other basic provisions, a practice dubbed "the moral economy of crowds" by the historian Edward Thompson.[2] Merchants who charged more than what was traditionally considered a "just price" put their shops and livelihoods in peril. Nor could merchants count on help from the government if attacked. When the authorities intervened, it was inevitably on the side of the poor. Royal officials routinely implemented price controls and ensured the fair distribution of staples.

Popular uprisings were seen as an important social safety valve, a way for the common people to obtain redress and vent frustration.[3] Even the recently homeless Hutchinson conceded their legitimacy, up to a point. "Mobs," he said, "a sort of them at least, are constitutional."[4] They had rules of etiquette and tacit lines they generally did not cross. When it suited their purposes, the upper classes themselves enjoyed taking part in a good riot. The bloody brawls that broke out in Boston every November 5 in commemoration of "Pope's Day" were tolerated precisely because they did not threaten the status quo. This order of affairs, however, was about to change dramatically.

By the late 1760s, popular protests began reflecting a new and more desperate struggle that was taking place in America. Hunger, joblessness, and meager wages, exacerbated by series of economic crises, had led to a new sense of frustration among the lower classes. And social unrest was only exacerbated by a growing stratification of colonial society.[5] By the second half of the eighteenth century, America's upper classes were increasingly monopolizing elected office and commanding a growing proportion of colonial wealth. For the common people, fierce yearnings for greater equality soon became linked to the protests against Britain.[6]

In newspapers, pamphlets, and public demonstrations, the growing call for equality was heard throughout the colonies. Barred from voting and holding political office by property qualifications, the lower orders began demanding new political freedoms. Why should the working classes not have "an equal right of electing and being elected?" asked the Philadelphia artisan "Brother Chip." "Are there no . . . men well acquainted with the constitution and laws of their country among the tradesmen and mechanics?" According to "Brutus" of New York, those "mercantile dons" who claimed "that the mechanics have no right to give their sentiments" were "flagrantly wrong."[7]

For many, greater political freedom meant little without accompanying economic reform. Financial inequality lay at the root of most of the revolts that swept through the colonies in the 1760s. The great Leveler Uprising of 1766 broke out after the semifeudal landlords of New York's Hudson Valley evicted hundreds of tenant farmers who refused to pay higher rents. Organizing themselves into armed peasant militias, the farmers retook their old lands. The revolt quickly spread to the great estates of Dutchess, Westchester, and Albany Counties. In April two thousand insurgents marched to the foot of the King's Bridge separating Manhattan from Westchester. Poised upon the edge of the city, they called on the "poor people" to tear down the houses of the rich. If anyone tried to stop them, the mob promised to "kick their arses as long as we see fit."[8] Two hundred British soldiers armed with cannon finally suppressed the farmers before they could do more damage. At his trial for treason, William Pendergast, the rebellion's leader, argued that he "pitied poor people who were turned out of possession." After all, he said, "it was hard that they were not allowed to have property."[9]

Among the working classes, criticism of the rich began to crescendo. "Our great merchants," complained a Philadelphia "Tradesman," were "making great fortunes at the expense of the people." If current trends continued, he warned, merchants would "soon have the whole wealth of the province in their hands," and the people would be reduced to the level of impoverished coolies. Society needed to be reformed so that "all ranks and conditions would come in for their just share of the wealth."[10] John Adams, no plebeian himself, agreed wholeheartedly. "The dons, the bashaws, the grandees, the patricians, the sachems, the nabobs, call them . . . what you please, foam and curse," he said. "The decree is gone forth . . . that a more equal liberty must be established in America."[11] So potent was the idea of equality, according the historian Gordon Wood, that it became "the most radical and most powerful ideological force let loose in the Revolution."[12]

Just how radical was the American Revolution? More than a century ago the Progressive historian Carl Becker declared that the Revolution involved two distinct struggles. First, there was "the contest for home rule," by which he meant the fight between Britain and America. Second, it involved a battle over "who should rule at home," that is, the elites or the common people.[13] While the Revolution clearly involved a struggle between Britain and her colonies, the notion that it also involved a battle between radicals and conservatives over control of American society proved so controversial that it sparked one of the most heated scholarly debates of the twentieth century.

Some historians went so far as to insist that so little changed during the American Revolution that it was a mistake even to call the event a revolution. Moreover, the word *radical,* which derives from the Latin *radix,* meaning "root, base, foundation," provoked endless debate, with the term coming in and out of fashion several times over the past hundred years. Like *conservative, radical* was not coined in its modern sense until the nineteenth century. Some historians have proposed substituting the term *popular,* but *radical* continues to be used largely because it has proven to be such a useful anachronism.[14] It helps make unfamiliar eighteenth-century political concepts intelligible to us today.

The great historiographic debate was finally settled in recent decades when those denying there had been any social aspect to the Revolution gave up in light of new research. It could no longer be questioned whether the American Revolution had been radical—only to what extent.[15] Combining strains of Country Whig thought, Leveller beliefs from the English Civil War, and evangelical doctrines of Scottish Presbyterianism, radicalism spread rapidly among artisans and laborers in just about every large American town and city.[16] Just as they had a century before, these forces encouraged disobedience to the Crown and challenged the rule of the upper classes. They upended traditional beliefs in deference and ignited a political awakening among the lower and middle classes. The most tangible by-product of the egalitarian fervor sweeping the colonies was an organized political movement that aimed to reform society and redistribute power, usually through legislative means, occasionally through violence.

Ultimately, the Revolution was far more dynamic and complex than the simple class conflict described by Progressive historians. It involved every group in American society, including women, teenagers, blacks, and American Indians. And in recent years, scholars have studied how the revolutionary upheavals in American society affected these groups. Yet the ideological divide first noted by early twentieth-century historians remains a useful lens for viewing the conflict.

Certainly, America's upper classes looked on with alarm. As the fight for American rights began merging with the struggle for political equality, many elites recognized that the conflict with Britain was a powder keg best handled gingerly. Then the Boston Tea Party took a match to it.

The Tea Party was in many ways a direct response to one of the world's first recorded acts of corporate welfare, the Tea Act of 1773. Hoping to aid the struggling British East India Company, Parliament had granted the giant corporation an exclusive monopoly to sell its tea in the colonies. To its supporters, the act seemed like a stroke of genius. It would prop up a teetering corporation, whose stockholders included the King, and it would raise revenue for the government. Best yet, it would reduce the price Americans paid for tea by as much as 25 percent. But in that lower price lay a three-penny tax left over from the Townshend Duties. Parliament was attempting one last gambit to assert its right to tax America.

Which was exactly what worried American Whigs. By accepting the Tea Act, Americans would be setting a legal precedent, one that could potentially lead Parliament to enact similar legislation in other industries. The act also infuriated American merchants because it allowed the East India Company to sell directly to consumers, cutting them out as middlemen and closing a lucrative stream of income. Successful smugglers, like John Hancock of Boston, were especially indignant. The new law would make it impossible for them to beat official prices, numbering their days in business. Profit as well as principle was at stake.

As seven ships laden with dutied tea set sail from England that fall, American Patriots mobilized for resistance. The arrival of the *Dartmouth* in late November led to a dangerous impasse. Boston radicals would not let the tea be unloaded. Hutchinson, now the colony's governor and still irked by the obliteration of his home, refused to let the ships leave port. British law mandated that customs officials could seize a ship's cargo if it remained unloaded for more than twenty days, and both sides knew the clock was ticking.

Historians have long suspected that Samuel Adams was the chief instigator behind the Tea Party, but no one has ever been able to prove it.[17] Born in 1722, Adams attended Harvard like many other young Boston gentlemen. Unlike most of his classmates, he never earned much money. He did have a passion for political rebellion, however, and his master's thesis was titled "Whether it be lawful to resist the Supreme Magistrate, if the Commonwealth cannot be otherwise preserved." Even at the age of twenty-two, he was contemplating the legal mechanics of independence. He gravitated toward radical politics while holding a succession of local offices, including fire warden and tax collector, and in the 1760s he helped organize numerous protests and boycotts against the British. By the time of the Tea Party, he had become one of the leaders of the American protest movement.

Prematurely gray, trembling of voice, and palsied in one hand, Adams was a far less eloquent speaker than his younger cousin John. Sam, however, had a genius for the backroom deal that the more earnest John never possessed. Some would later accuse Sam Adams of fomenting nearly all of the civil unrest leading to the Revolution. This was an exaggeration, but there was no denying that he was a consummate politician and a master manipulator of public opinion. "Damn that Adams," said Governor Francis Bernard. "Every dip of his pen stings like a horned snake."[18]

Calling Adams a radical was partly a simple matter of personality. His impetuous temperament led him to pursue increasingly violent measures against Great Britain. As militant as Dickinson was in opposing British attacks on American liberty, the Farmer's insistence on prudence and calm reflected a far more conservative disposition. Though historians disagree over when Adams first sought independence—some say as early as 1768, others put it as late as 1775—his actions undoubtedly escalated the crisis between America and Britain significantly.

Yet there was more to Adams's politics than mere rabble-rousing. Austere, rigid, and ever alert for tyranny, Adams was above all a radical republican, a Country Whig to the bone. His ideal society, he proclaimed, was a "Christian Sparta," with the accent on "Sparta" rather than "Christian."[19] He praised the self-sacrifice of the ancients and applauded their economic equality. Like the Minute Men, Americans, he believed, had to stand ready to defend their rights at a moment's notice. His republicanism, however, lacked the elitist quality that had distinguished Lord Bolingbroke's a few decades earlier. Adams's politics had a distinctly democratic flavor that reflected his New England roots. Like many New Englanders, he mistrusted almost all concentrations of executive power, and Governor Hutchinson was among those he despised most.

On December 16, the last day before Hutchinson would be empowered to unload the tea, Adams led an all-day rally at the cavernous Old South Church. More than seven thousand people braved the rain and cold to listen to impassioned speeches denouncing British government, the Tea Act, and Governor Hutchinson. Throughout the day Adams sent emissaries to the governor trying to convince him to let the tea-laden ships leave without unloading their cargo.

When word came that the governor still would not back down, Adams adjourned the meeting. Banging his gavel three times, he announced that "*this* meeting" could do no more to protect American rights. Uproar ensued. Someone in the rear of the balcony shouted, "Boston harbor a teapot tonight!" Another cried, "Hurrah for Griffin's Wharf." A third: "The Mohawks are come! Every man to his tent." The commotion grew so loud, it could be heard three blocks away. Minutes later the "Indians" struck.

American reaction to the Tea Party was sharply divided. While John Adams cheered the attack as "the grandest event," Benjamin Franklin labeled it "an act of violent Injustice."[20] All it had done was provoke "the torrent of clamor against us."[21] Particularly appalling to Franklin and others of a more conservative bent had been the eagerness "to destroy private property."[22] Dickinson suggested that the Bostonians "pay for the tea," fearing that the protests could spiral out of control and result in widespread social upheaval. New Englanders, he believed, had a tendency to forget that. "By rushing forward contrary to the maxims of discipline," he wrote to Josiah Quincy of Massachusetts, they had betrayed "the common cause." When tea ships approached Philadelphia, he made sure his city's demonstrations were far more orderly.

Dickinson's highest priority was to prevent the tea ships' cargo from being sold anywhere else in the colonies. Writing anonymously, he published a series of devastating assaults on the legal basis of the Tea Act. What most alarmed him was the subtlety of a tax hidden in lower prices. The British government, he believed, was trying to hoodwink Americans. "It is something of a consolation to be overcome by a lion," Dickinson fumed, "but to be devoured by rats is intolerable." He exhorted his countrymen not to allow "the ruin of American freedom and liberty." And he called on them to "resolve therefore, nobly resolve, and publish to the world your resolutions, that no man will receive the tea, no man will let his stores, or suffer the vessel that brings it to moor at his wharf." Anyone who did so "should be deemed an enemy to his country."[23]

Dickinson signed these essays "Rusticus," but readers soon recognized his distinctive style, and word spread excitedly throughout the colonial press that the Farmer had once again taken up his pen in the cause of American rights. Dickinson did not stop with words. In October 1773 he helped organize a town meeting in Philadelphia that attracted thousands of protesters. In December news arrived that the *Polly Ayres,* a merchant ship carrying British tea, was approaching the city. Every river pilot near Philadelphia was issued a letter addressed to the captain of the *Polly Ayres* warning him against trying to unload his cargo. On Christmas Day the ship pulled into port. When protests broke out, the captain agreed to return to England with his tea undelivered. Dickinson was victorious. Most important, he had achieved his goal through legal means. "It is not only the cause," he reminded his fellow Americans, "but our Manner of conducting it, that will establish Character."[24]

Whig protesters in other American cities managed to block the sale of tea with relatively little violence. In Charleston, South Carolina, the tea was unloaded but then locked in the customs house and not removed until several years later, when a new revolutionary government sold it to help fund the war effort. In New York, a few crates of tea were destroyed on one ship that tried to slip past the embargo, but the captain of a second ship carrying tea was persuaded to turn back, seen off by the largest crowds "ever known in this city" and a band playing "God Save the King."[25] Had Boston's tactics been similar to those employed in Philadelphia, Charleston, or even New York, a resolution to the conflict with Britain might have been found and revolution potentially averted. Parliament's next actions, however, played right into the Whigs' darkest conspiracy theories.

As much as Dickinson had lamented the violence of the Boston Tea Party, he was outraged by Britain's response to it. Parliament targeted Massachusetts with a series of severe punitive measures. Officially called the Coercive Acts, they were so offensive to Americans that they were soon dubbed the Intolerable Acts in the colonies. Two of the stipulations were drastic. First, Parliament ordered the Port of Boston closed to all shipping until the East India Company was reimbursed, a provision that quickly crippled the Massachusetts economy. Second, it revoked the colony's ancient charter and turned it into a royal colony. Overnight, the people of Massachusetts were essentially deprived of their livelihoods, stripped of their constitutional protections, and placed under martial law.

Other provisions further provoked fears that the government would not rest until it had trampled over every basic constitutional right. One of the most inflammatory punishments was to enlarge the colony of Canada so that it now encompassed western lands previously claimed by American land speculators. This measure outraged America's budding capitalist investors. Additionally, Americans charged with high crimes could now be sent to England for trial. Sam Adams's name was high on the potential list. Across the continent Americans erupted in fury, but they were far from united on how to deal with the crisis.

On Thursday, May 19, 1774, the Boston silversmith Paul Revere galloped into Philadelphia bearing a letter from his province asking for aid and proposing a "solemn League and Covenant" to unite the colonies. Like the rest of Americans, Philadelphians were split over how to react. Rich merchants and pacifist Quakers, who tended to side with Parliament, opposed helping Massachusetts. New England, they felt, had only itself to blame for its troubles. But poorer craftsmen and mechanics, the same groups clamoring for greater equality, supported aiding Massachusetts. Their growing power convinced the city's leaders that some sort of plan was needed. Accordingly, a mass meeting was called for the following evening at the City Tavern on Second Street, an enormous three-story building that John Adams dubbed "the most genteel tavern in America."[26]

Radicals knew they stood no chance of obtaining a vote in support of Boston without Dickinson's backing. "No person in Pennsylvania ever approached [him] as a rival in personal influence," wrote Joseph Reed.[27] What worried radical leaders most was the Farmer's widely known criticism of the Boston Tea Party. On Friday morning, radical leaders rode out of the city and up into the country to visit Dickinson's famous home, Fairhill. Though they were going to discuss politics, the trip also had the air of a pilgrimage.

Dickinson's estate was the most splendid in Pennsylvania and by some accounts the most beautiful home in the colonies. Nothing was more impressive to travelers on the road to Philadelphia than a glimpse of the estate's perfectly proportioned hip roofs and dormer windows rising high above the surrounding countryside. Perched on a hilltop surrounded by abundant orchards, groves, and gardens, Fairhill reflected the civilized tastes and incandescent mind of its celebrated occupant. It was understated but elegant, its ordered beauty the epitome of Georgian neoclassical design.

Soaring above the home's central turret was an enormous gilded weathercock that connected, via a ten-foot shaft, to a compass in the stairway below. Used to track commercial fleets coming into port, such devices were common in merchant houses throughout the Atlantic world.[28] The glinting landmark was visible as far away as Philadelphia's bustling wharves three miles to the south. Along the Delaware River, which rippled past Fairhill to the east, ships used it to note the direction of the winds.

Built in 1717 by his wife Mary's grandfather, Fairhill was originally intended to be a simple farm. After taking up residence some fifty years later, Dickinson launched a renovation that transformed the home into something at once more refined and more spiritual. Under the Farmer's management, Fairhill became just the sort of "philosopher's garden" that Pennsylvania's founder, William Penn, envisioned for his colony, a place where one "reads and contemplates the power, wisdom, and goodness of God."[29]

With its partially sunken English basement, Fairhill seemed to rise out of the earth. The black and white marble entrance hall led to four large symmetrical parlors wainscoted in oak and red cedar polished with wax. A narrow staircase in the rear led to the second story and to the famous compass. Two dependencies flanked the house, a bathing house on one side and one of the finest libraries in the colonies on the other, where Dickinson spent many hours immersed in the great works of history. Attached to the library was the first greenhouse in Philadelphia, where oranges and lemons could be picked in wintertime. In the summer the house was shaded by the first weeping willows in North America, a gift from Benjamin Franklin to Dickinson's wife's family years before. All around the mansion bloomed a profusion of plants, some specially imported from Europe and the southern colonies. And threading between the manicured courts and parterres were well-groomed gravel paths inviting strollers to indulge in peaceful meditation.

Visitors were inevitably stunned. Stopping to visit after a tour of the South in 1773, Josiah Quincy, Jr., of Massachusetts exclaimed that Fairhill was superior to any of the great plantations he had just seen. He was spellbound by Dickinson's good taste and good fortune, by "the antique look of his house, his gardens, green house, bathing house, grotto, study, fishponds, fields, meadows, . . . his paintings, antiquities, improvements, etc., in short his whole life."[30] Silas Deane of Connecticut found Fairhill an oasis of green amid the endless yellow wheatfields that "crowd into the very squares of the city."[31] As Dickinson well knew, the peaceful surroundings were the perfect setting for cooling radical zeal.

After a long day of negotiation, the radicals persuaded Dickinson to help them. In exchange, they pledged to curb their more extreme demands. That evening some two to three hundred people crowded into the candlelit City Tavern. Revere's letter was read to the crowd, and the city's leading radicals took the stage calling for immediate support for Massachusetts. So stifling was the heat from the close-pressed bodies that one radical fainted in the middle of his speech. Reactionary leaders then took the floor opposing any action whatsoever.

At last Dickinson stood to speak. As agreed earlier at Fairhill, he took a moderate position designed to win support for Massachusetts. He proposed that the governor call a special session of the Assembly to discuss the issue and suggested establishing a committee of correspondence to communicate with the other colonies. In contrast to the extremists who had just spoken, the Farmer seemed to argue "with great coolness, calmness, moderation, and good sense," as one observer wrote. All of his proposals were agreed upon with "great relief."[32]

Dickinson and the radicals fully expected the governor to deny their request, which would allow them to create a special assembly of the people independent of the Galloway-controlled legislature. Before departing, the crowd appointed a nineteen-man committee chaired by Dickinson to write a letter of sympathy to Boston. The letter provided little comfort to Boston firebrands who had been hoping for more concrete aid, but it was the best Philadelphians could muster for the moment. Dickinson's next move was to join the growing calls for a Continental Congress.

CHAPTER 4

THE VIEW FROM ABOVE

On May 19, 1774, a rich twenty-two-year-old by the name of Gouverneur Morris peered over the balcony at the Merchants' Coffee House in lower Manhattan and realized his world was about to change. Hundreds of New Yorkers from both sides of the political spectrum had gathered in the famous meeting place on the southeast corner of Wall and Water Streets to argue about the recent news from Boston. To Morris's right "ranged all the people of property."[1] On the left stood New York's radicals: the laborers, mechanics, stevedores, and sailors who were led by a group of "upstart merchants," as the gentry described them, "a number of demagogues . . . not distinguished by birth or breeding."[2] The Coffee House was a fitting location for a mass protest sparked by tea, but to Morris the angry debate below was entirely out of place. What had started as a meeting over how to respond to the Coercive Acts had quickly degenerated, to his mind, into a quarrel "about the future forms of our government, whether it should be founded upon aristocratic or democratic principles."[3]

Morris favored the aristocrats. Charming and rakish, he was, along with George Washington, one of the most physically imposing of the Founding Fathers. Well over six feet at a time when most men were far shorter, Morris occasionally posed as a stand-in for sculptors trying to carve Washington's robust torso. Unlike the stern and taciturn Virginian, however, Morris enjoyed dressing in fine silks and lace and was an inveterate seducer of women. The fact that he would lose his leg a few years later in a carriage accident and be fitted with a wooden peg would only serve to enhance his rakish reputation with the ladies. "Gouverneur Morris kept us in a continual smile," said one female admirer.[4] He was cynical, self-interested, and witty. And he could turn a phrase like no one else.

Born to rich, landowning parents, Morris was christened with his mother's maiden name. The Gouverneurs were French Huguenots who had fled Catholic France after the government began to hunt down Protestants; they had landed in America in the mid-seventeenth century. In French the name meant "governor," and early on he was groomed for command. "It is my desire," said his father, Lewis, "that my son Gouverneur Morris have the best education that is to be had in Europe or America."[5] Only a rich man could harbor such aspirations in the late eighteenth century. At a time when the average American man's entire wealth amounted to only £47.50, higher education cost £150 a year.

Tutored by a Swiss émigré, Gouverneur learned to speak French at a young age and became so fluent that he later wrote political essays and poems in that language. The rest of his education was typical of young eighteenth-century gentlemen. He studied Hebrew, Latin, and Greek but discovered his greatest talent lay in mathematics, a skill that served him well when he turned his attention to government finances. Only twelve years old when he enrolled in King's College (later Columbia) in New York, he was by far the school's youngest student, but he excelled in his studies and spent several extra years earning a master's degree. Before graduating, he also began an apprenticeship with a New York lawyer, and in October 1771 he earned his law license. He was not yet twenty.

With his prolific web of family and social connections, Morris quickly began earning a good income. He became an accomplished defense attorney, assisted in real estate transactions, and speculated in land. He showed little interest in politics other than as a spectator, and after the Boston Tea Party he traveled to Philadelphia to partake in patriotic celebrations and stay "up all night making merry."[6] But as the political situation deteriorated, he started to take notice. He was less concerned with the struggle for American rights than with the lower classes' clamoring for greater equality. He was shocked by what he witnessed at the Merchants' Coffee House in May 1774.

Newly emboldened, New York's lower classes were increasingly challenging the aristocracy's assumption that they ought to rule. "The mob begins to think and reason," Morris wrote a few days later. "Poor reptiles! . . . They bask in the sunshine, and ere noon they will bite. . . . The gentry begin to fear."[7] If anything led him to rethink his neutrality toward the conflict with Britain, it was the mob's aggressive demand for rights. He came to believe it was crucial for elites like him to join in the fight for colonial rights in order to keep it under control.

Morris was, according to the historian Merrill Jensen, the first person to recognize that America's link to Britain had traditionally kept the upper classes in power. "If the disputes with Great Britain continue," he wrote, "we shall be under the worst of all possible dominions; we shall be under the domination of a riotous mob." Coined only a few decades before, the word *mob* came from the Latin *mobile vulgus,* meaning "fickle crowd." Mobs, in other words, were considered dangerously volatile. If New York's mobs continued to gather strength, Morris worried, he might well have to say, "Farewell aristocracy."[8]

New York's aristocrats were far from ready to cede power. They had profited handily under British rule and were unwilling to challenge its authority.[9] Overwhelmingly Anglican in religion, they were among the most culturally British of all Americans, and many in the surrounding countryside were steadfast in their support of the Crown. While the patricians had presided over New York for the better part of a century, they were but a dwindling portion of the population. The city itself was one of the most diverse in the colonies, its pushy inhabitants ever eager to make a shilling. To more earnest New Englanders, the fast-paced atmosphere could be daunting. "They talk very loud, very fast, and altogether," complained John Adams as he traveled through a few months later.[10] He was slightly mollified by the exquisite meal he enjoyed overlooking the Hudson.

Not everyone in New York was raking it in. The growing gap between rich and poor had caused a recent spike in crime. Muggings were at an all-time high. In response, the governing council had voted to spend more money on streetlamps and night patrols, but the new jail was already overflowing with felons. In the meantime, riots continued to plague the city.

New York in the spring of 1774 was thus ripe for a showdown between the classes, and the news from Boston provided the perfect pretext. Two days before Morris attended the Coffee House debate, Paul Revere had galloped into town to deliver his letter demanding a total and immediate boycott of British goods. It was the moment radicals had been waiting for. That day they called for an embargo. They then proposed a slate of twenty-five men, all from their own ranks, to form a committee of correspondence that would seize control of the protest movement. Ruing the business losses that an embargo would entail, the upper classes were dead set against this plan. Yet so powerful had the lower classes become that the elites were careful not to block radical proposals outright. They adopted instead a strategy of subtle delay and vague promises.

One of the first orders of business at the May 19 meeting was deciding who could vote during it. While radicals insisted that "every man whose liberties were concerned" had a right to participate, the upper classes countered that "none but Freeholders and Freemen" should vote—in other words, people who could prove they had money.[11] The elites carried the point and in doing so regained control of the meeting. Rather than acceding to the committee of twenty-five, they proposed a larger committee of fifty-one men. They allowed commoners to participate but made sure they themselves held a majority. For the moment, the upper classes had the upper hand. Nevertheless, in order to secure the cooperation of New York's mechanics in this deal, they had to concede that they could be dismissed "if they misbehaved."[12]

The split between the upper and lower classes was not the only fault line threatening to shatter New York. A deep fissure also ran through its upper classes. Many of the colony's wellborn were royalists, including Oliver DeLancey, William Bayard, and Roger Morris (no relation to Gouverneur). Also known as Tories or Loyalists, this group were those who sided with the Crown. They were in many respects far-right reactionaries, unwilling to countenance any social change. And they worried that the rise of the lower classes would result in the complete destruction of society. As Charles Inglis, the rector of Trinity Church in Manhattan, argued in *The True Interest of America Impartially Stated,* the mob lacked the virtue necessary to govern themselves in a republic. Without the controlling influence of monarchy, "all our property throughout the continent would be unhinged; the greatest confusion, and the most violent convulsions would take place."[13] It was a belief held by Loyalists throughout the colonies. James Chalmers of Maryland feared the chaos of a democracy would inevitably lead to the rise of a military dictator in America like Oliver Cromwell. The lower classes would start by passing laws restricting wealth, after which "a war will ensue between creditors and their debtors," he warned, "which will eventually end in a general . . . abolition of debts which has more than once happened in other states on occasions similar."[14]

The Patriot side, however, had grandees of its own. Like others who supported American rights, they disagreed with British policy, but they did not necessarily join in the call for greater equality at home, as lower-class Patriots did. For the moment, the best way to describe this group is that they were moderates. Why they joined the fight against Britain when many of their own families and closest friends had declared their allegiance to it is a question that no scholar has ever conclusively answered but that many have pondered. Gouverneur Morris, for example, moved increasingly toward the Patriots, even as most of his family remained solidly Tory.

The historians Edwin Burrows and Mike Wallace have proposed a series of possible explanations for why certain members of the upper classes joined the American cause, from national pride and a confidence that the upper classes would be able to reassert control, to a sense of duty to the Whig beliefs of their forefathers.[15] But there is another explanation for this historical conundrum. America's Patriot gentry were motivated also by a desire to preserve social order, in a time of unprecedented social upheaval. Standing in the way of inexorable change was not merely unproductive, they realized; it was also suicidal. Though they did not yet have a name, they were bound by a common ideology.

In New York City this nascent political movement was dominated by a quartet of close-knit friends. In addition to Gouverneur Morris, it included James Duane, Robert R. Livingston, and John Jay, who had just been appointed a member of the Committee of Fifty-one. In upstate New York, the older and phenomenally wealthy Philip Schuyler would become the doyen of the movement. All would soon play pivotal roles in the birth of the nation, but Jay was destined to become the most prominent among them.

Like Morris, Jay also graduated from King's College, where he was a serious and socially isolated student. His father believed him to be "a youth remarkably sedate," but by the time he finished his legal training in 1768, he had blossomed into a man about town.[16] As president of the city's Dancing Assembly, he became the darling of New York high society. As a member of the Moot, an exclusive club for lawyers, he met with Morris, Livingston, Duane, and others every Saturday at the popular Fraunces Tavern to debate pressing legal issues of the day.

Also descended from a wealthy Huguenot family, Jay fervently supported religious freedom, except when it came to Catholics. Painted in London in 1783, he had a slender, high forehead and a large, sharp nose. Many found Jay arrogant, and toward his social inferiors he could verge on authoritarian. To his equals, he came across as a man of great integrity and discretion. He was, according to Carl Becker, the perfect embodiment of a "boldly cautious spirit."[17] As fervently as he supported American rights, it seemed only natural to him that "the people who own the country ought to govern it."[18]

The richest of New York's moderates was Jay's closest friend, Robert R. Livingston. Tall and thin, Livingston was not handsome, but he was described as graceful. One of the few people permitted to visit Jay's rooms while the two were students at King's College, Livingston later became Jay's law partner for several years. Their lives became further intertwined when Jay married Livingston's first cousin, Sarah. Livingston complemented the intense and punctilious Jay. He described himself as having "a spice of melancholy" in his nature, and he preferred long, quiet walks around his country estate to the rough-and-tumble of New York politics.[19]

Livingston hailed from one of America's most aristocratic families but also one of the most unoriginal when it came to names. Historians typically refer to him as Robert R. Livingston to distinguish him from his father, grandfather, and great-grandfather, all of whom were also named Robert, as well as from his first cousin once removed, Robert Livingston, Jr. The middle initial used to tell him apart from the others stood, of course, for Robert. It was a large family and had spread its tendrils through most of New York's gentry.

James Duane, for example, had married another of Livingston's first cousins, Maria. A successful lawyer, banker, and politician, Duane would have made a mighty feudal lord had he been born several hundred years earlier. He owned a 36,000-acre estate in upstate New York, employed 235 tenant farmers and laborers, and had founded a town called, needless to say, Duanesburgh. He also had little sympathy for radical revolutionaries. In 1766 he helped the Livingstons prosecute angry tenant farmers who had marched in the Leveler Uprising.

Duane's reputation for political intrigue was enhanced by his soft, deep voice. To New Englanders, he was a "swivel-eyed genius" and a "man of artifice."[20] The feeling was mutual. "I fear these people will spread over the whole Continent," Duane said of New Englanders. "They will [overthrow] the political and religious principles—if candor and truth are religious principles—of their neighbors."[21] He used his considerable brilliance in the courtroom to defend New York's establishment from peasant uprisings, religious dissent, and democracy. Like many elites of the day, he denounced the growing egalitarianism. "God forbid that we should ever be so miserable as to sink into a republic!" he said soon after New York's Tea Party.[22]

As much as he reviled radicals, Duane was the first moderate to recognize the need to sound like them. If moderates had any hope of staying relevant, he realized, they would have to adopt the language of revolution. Accordingly, when he and Jay were appointed to help write the rules for the Committee of Fifty-one, they made sure to denounce British tyranny in republican-sounding language, without committing to anything specific. It was a masterpiece of rhetorical dexterity.

Moderates could temporize only so long, however. With the threat of violence mounting by the day, they devised one last strategy to forestall an embargo. The decision to enact a boycott, they said quite honestly, was too difficult for them to make. "What ought to be done in a situation so critical," Duane wrote, "while it employs the anxious thoughts of every generous mind, is very hard to determine."[23] What was required was a Continental Congress to decide the issue.

At another tumultuous Coffee House meeting on May 23, Jay, Duane, and two others wrote to Boston proposing a colonywide assembly to pass "some unanimous resolutions formed in this fatal emergency, not only respecting your deplorable circumstances, but for the security of our common rights."[24] Moderates quickly rallied to the idea. The plan, they believed, would allow for further delay. In the meantime, it was hoped, cooler heads might prevail. Rich merchants still hoped some resolution might be found before trade was interrupted.

Radicals were pleased by the proposal as well, since they had been floating similar ideas for a while. The problem, however, was deciding on criteria for attendance at the assembly. Radicals and moderates proposed their own slates of delegates. After three weeks of tense negotiations, New York's radicals finally agreed to support the moderate candidates, with one important caveat: the Committee of Fifty-one had to stipulate that an embargo would likely "prove the most efficacious means to procure a redress of grievances."[25] New York's moderates acquiesced, carefully avoiding any promise that they would actually support a boycott. The tenuous accord in place, Jay, Duane, and three other delegates began preparing for the trip to Philadelphia. They had no doubt that they would dominate the proceedings there, just as they had in New York.

Philadelphia was the self-evident choice for the Continental Congress. It was the geographic center of the colonies, the largest city on the continent, and the second most populous municipality in the entire British Empire, after London. Bounded by the Schuylkill in the west and the Delaware in the east, Philadelphia was, wrote the rich merchant Robert Morris, "to the United States what the heart is to the human body in circulating the blood."[26] Mercantile houses lined the bustling waterfront where wharves jutted into the Delaware. Wagons choked the streets, which were laid out in America's first urban grid. Away from the water, the streets were numbered along a north-south axis. Intersecting these were streets named for native trees—Chestnut, Walnut, Spruce, and Pine.

The city's vast wealth also made Philadelphia an ideal choice for moderates, who felt they could count on a sympathetic populace for support. The city's reputation for calm further assuaged fears that radicals might seize control. As the Philadelphia attorney Joseph Reed pointed out, "There have been no mobs, no insults to individuals, no injury to private property."[27]

Enthusiasm for a Continental Congress swept rapidly through the colonies that summer. On June 15, Dickinson published an anonymous letter backing the plan. Like many Philadelphians, he believed that a colonywide meeting would be more prudent than a sudden ban on all trade with Britain. Boston and Virginia soon followed in support, and by the end of the summer, every colony except Georgia, the newest colony and farthest away, had agreed to send a delegation.

It would be the first intercolonial assembly since the Stamp Act Congress almost a decade earlier. Dickinson, along with Christopher Gadsden and John Rutledge of South Carolina, was one of the few who had also attended that earlier assembly in New York, and he had done more than anyone else since then to keep America's spirits alive. For delegates on both sides of the political spectrum, no other man's participation was more eagerly anticipated than Dickinson's.

Philadelphians were in general pleased to host the congress, but like New Yorkers, they remained deeply divided over how far to escalate the conflict. To demonstrate solidarity with Massachusetts against Britain's Coercive Acts, Patriot leaders declared June 1 a day of mourning. Throughout the city, the bells of Christ Church tolled for American liberty. It was a reverberation that no royalist could escape hearing.

At a meeting a week later a familiar vexing question arose: how to choose the congressional delegates. Philadelphia mechanics, who were in touch with their New York brethren, feared that they too would be marginalized. A committee of mechanics formally petitioned the Farmer for help, viewing him as their champion: "You we revere and you we depend upon," they wrote. "Your love of the [Whig] cause will readily pardon our Freedom and Fears."[28] But couched within their entreaty was a veiled threat. Should royalists hinder the common people, they warned, rioting might erupt. Dickinson pleaded for patience. "Nothing can ruin us but our violence," he had written in May to Boston. Any "blood or tumults" had to be eschewed.[29] If not, he feared, the first fatality might be the Patriot cause itself.

Dickinson's solution for selecting Pennsylvania's delegates was to hold a special provincial convention. At a series of ten- to twelve-hour meetings over the next few days, he helped hammer out the details for a convention. The first step was to hold a rally more massive than any held before, over which Dickinson agreed to preside, along with the merchant Thomas Willing, in the Pennsylvania State House Yard.

Surrounded by a seven-foot wall and accessed through a giant wooden gate twice that size on Walnut Street, the yard served a variety of public purposes. On one side stood the observation platform and orrery built by David Rittenhouse, the Philadelphia clockmaker and accomplished amateur astronomer, as part of an international effort to measure the transit of Venus across the face of the sun in 1769. Nearby piles of cannonballs and barrels of gunpowder were stacked for the militia. On June 18 a crowd of eight thousand pressed into the courtyard. Its first order of business was to denounce the Coercive Acts. It then declared its support for a special convention to be held on Friday, July 15. To coordinate Patriot activities over the next month, a new committee of correspondence was chosen, with Dickinson leading the list of forty-three names. The mechanics were not disappointed. All Tories were deliberately excluded.

Now was the moment to set into motion the ruse Dickinson had earlier devised with radical leaders. A special convention was a bold move. To win popular support, he believed Patriots had to make a show of first going through existing channels. Nine hundred citizens signed a petition asking Governor Penn to convene the Assembly so that it could choose Pennsylvania's congressional delegates. It was fully expected that the governor would turn them down, justifying holding a convention.

But then the plan hit a major snag. Joseph Galloway, speaker of the Assembly and de facto leader of the opposition, had been observing his old adversary's machinations and now made a surprise move. He backed Dickinson's plan and also petitioned the governor to call the Assembly. Penn, who now felt safer trusting the man who had spent years trying to oust him from office, complied.

On June 28, using Indian uprisings as a pretext, the governor called for the Assembly to meet on July 18. It was a setback, but proponents of the convention decided to push forward anyway. For Dickinson, it was essential that representatives from western counties be included in the convention. Poorer Pennsylvanians living on the frontier were far more likely to support active resistance to Britain, and their inclusion would boost the number of Whigs at the convention. Taking to the saddle, Dickinson spent several days touring Pennsylvania's backcountry meeting with local politicians and advising them on setting up committees of correspondence.

In the two weeks leading up to the convention, Dickinson retreated to his book-lined study to work out a set of resolves that he planned to present. Covered with scarlet begonia and cords of ivy climbing over the windows, Fairhill's library was an idyllic place to work. Connected to the building was an ornate glass beehive, its deep thrum drowning out all sound save that of a quill scratching against paper.

Dickinson's output during this fortnight was as prodigious as the bees'. When the seventy-five delegates to the convention met in Carpenters' Hall across from the State House at four p.m. on July 15, they discovered that Dickinson had already written out most of the major questions facing them, as well as the best possible responses. One statement was deemed so eloquent that the convention agreed to publish it independently. "An Essay on the Constitutional Powers of Great Britain" justified Whig resistance to British policy on simple but compelling grounds. Since "the happiness of the people is the end . . . of the Constitution," Dickinson reasoned, legislation that added "to the misery of the people" had no "rightful or legal power." In other words, laws that hurt the colonies could legally be rejected. The convention did make major revisions to Dickinson's work, but his efforts provided the intellectual backbone to many of the final resolutions. Before the convention adjourned on July 22, it officially recognized Dickinson for the "laudable application of his eminent abilities to the services of his country."

"I will try," Dickinson replied with a courtesy elaborate even by eighteenth-century standards, "during the remainder of my life, to remember my duty to our common country, and if it be possible, to render myself worthy of the honor for which I now stand so deeply indebted."[30]

With just over a month left to bolster support for the Continental Congress, the convention decided to make one last-minute change before adjourning. Rather than choosing the delegates itself, it decided to take a chance and let the Assembly select them. It was just what Galloway had been waiting for. With the legislature now in session, he ruled that only Assembly members were eligible to become delegates. Dickinson, who had not held public office for several years, was suddenly barred from the congress he had labored so mightily to create.

CHAPTER 5

DELICACY AND CAUTION

On the last day of August 1774, four magnificent horses bore John Dickinson down into the oppressive heat of Philadelphia to meet the newly arrived delegation from Massachusetts.[1] He was weak from a flare-up of gout, but he threw himself into the task of meeting as many of the new congressmen as possible. Some already knew him personally, many had corresponded with him, and all knew him by reputation. His lack of official status at the Continental Congress did nothing to dim his influence. Dickinson would offer them advice and warn them against Galloway and, if they were lucky, invite them to Fairhill.

Of all the delegates slowly arriving from throughout the colonies, Dickinson was most eager to meet the group from Massachusetts. For one thing, the colony's predicament would be the main topic of debate in Congress. For another, Dickinson wanted to come to some sort of understanding with the New Englanders. He didn't doubt they were good Whigs, but he feared they might be a touch too eager to stir up trouble. They had, after all, precipitated the current crisis, so it was vital for Dickinson to know whether they were reasonable men or radicals ready to plunge the continent into war.

The Massachusetts contingent was equally eager to meet Dickinson. John Adams, whose fascination with him bordered on obsessive, yearned for an introduction. For years Adams had meticulously noted every moment when his path crossed Dickinson's, no matter how obliquely. In 1769 he recorded in his diary that Dickinson's brother was visiting Boston. In 1771 he described his joy at discovering a copy of the Farmer's *Letters* in his room at a Connecticut inn. In July 1774 he rhapsodized in a letter to his wife, Abigail, about a conversation he and a friend had had about one of the *Letters.* Along the arduous journey from his home in Braintree, Massachusetts, to Philadelphia, a four-hundred-mile route that took him through five colonies and fifty towns, Adams must have tried to picture meeting Dickinson. Like many Americans, he had almost certainly already seen a portrait of him.

Dickinson's appearance, said one acquaintance, combined a "severe simplicity" with "a neatness and elegance peculiarly in keeping with it." His eyes were a bright and penetrating blue, his hair was as "white as snow," and his large beaked nose poked sharply out of his long, smooth face.[2] All who met Dickinson were struck by his height. His perfect posture and incredible thinness, often exacerbated by recurring attacks of gout, made him seem even taller. While his manners were "unostentatious," he was not unsophisticated. His extensive travels had made him "familiar with society in its most polished forms."[3] By all accounts he moved as he spoke, with poise and grace. In other words, he was the exact opposite of John Adams.

Adams was dining with Samuel Ward, the former governor of Rhode Island, when Dickinson's opulent coach clattered to a halt outside Ward's lodgings. Dickinson exchanged courtesies with the men, inquiring after the health of their families and doing his best to charm them. In his diary that evening Adams eagerly recounted the meeting:

> He is a shadow, tall, but slender as a reed, pale as ashes. One would think at first sight that he could not live a month. Yet upon a more attentive inspection, he looks as if the springs of life were strong enough to last many years.[4]

It was a dramatic moment for Adams, for Dickinson represented all he hoped to attain. Adams had gone to Philadelphia in the hope of fulfilling his destiny. Three days after his election to the Massachusetts delegation, he confided to the pages of his diary, "I feel myself unequal to this business."[5] Here would be assembled the most erudite and accomplished of all Americans, a gathering of wealth and power and prestige into whose ranks Adams one day hoped to ascend.

It wasn't that Adams thought he didn't belong. It was that thus far in his life he had done little to achieve the sort of recognition he felt he ultimately deserved. At forty-three, he had never before left New England. He was largely unknown and keenly unhappy about it.

"Why have I not genius to start some new thought?" he wrote in his diary at age twenty-three. "Some thing that will surprise the world. New, grand, wild, yet regular thought that may raise me at once to fame."[6] He was, according to the historian Edmund S. Morgan, "one of the vainest men who ever lived," with an "almost psychopathic yearning to be thought a great man by everybody."[7]

Adams's hunger for recognition had the perverse effect of making him resentful toward anyone who he feared might overshadow him. As a result he had developed an almost pathological genius for unkind words. Unlike his cousin Sam, however, Adams could not always control when he used them. Those who worked closely with him frequently found him unbearable. Franklin later wrote that Adams "means well for his Country, is always an honest man, often a wise one, but sometimes, and in some things, absolutely out of his senses."[8] Part of Adams's irascibility stemmed from what the historian Bernard Bailyn termed his "feeling of gracelessness and social clumsiness."[9] Adams never felt comfortable with other people, fearing he was somehow physically inadequate. Dickinson was tall and refined, Jefferson tall and graceful, and Washington tall and heroic. Adams was balding, barrel-shaped, and heavy-lidded. He told a friend he resembled "a short, thick Archbishop of Canterbury."[10]

It would be unjust to say that a hunger for greatness was all that motivated him. Adams sincerely loved his homeland, which to him meant Massachusetts, and he was well aware of the dangers it faced. By itself Massachusetts could never defend itself against the British. Adams's job, as he saw it, was to make the plight of his colony America's collective concern. This was no small undertaking; perpetually at the back of his mind was the fear that the other colonies would abandon Massachusetts to deal with Britain on its own. Like his cousin Sam, John Adams had not yet crossed the psychological Rubicon, as the historian Neil York terms it, in favor of independence. But the fact that many suspected the New Englanders of harboring hopes for independence did not help his cause.

The Massachusetts delegation was well aware it had image problems. "We have numberless prejudices to remove here," John Adams remarked.[11] Even before the Massachusetts delegation reached Philadelphia, a contingent from Pennsylvania, headed by the eminent Philadelphia physician Benjamin Rush, rode to the outskirts of the city to warn them about Galloway and urge them to mind their behavior.

Slender and delicate, with lively blue eyes and a prominent nose, Rush stood five foot nine. As the most prominent doctor in the colonies, his practice was booming, and in his spare time he published scientific papers on a variety of medical subjects, eventually becoming one of the eighteenth century's greatest experts on mental illness.

An excitable and intellectually curious man, the Scottish-educated doctor was rapidly swept up in the growing revolutionary fervor, sympathizing with Boston's plight far more than others of his social circle. He took an immediate liking to John Adams, seeing in the grumpy New Englander a man of good sense. Climbing into their carriage to ride back to the city, Rush immediately invited the Adams cousins to his home on Water Street, where they admired the view of the Delaware out his rear windows. Until they found longer-term accommodations, both Adamses lodged with Rush.

John Adams quickly heeded Rush's warnings. They only confirmed the sort of political strategy he suspected he would need to employ in order to control Congress. "We have been obliged to act with great delicacy and caution," he wrote. "We have been obliged to keep ourselves from out of sight, and to feel pulses, and to sound out depths." Rather than fight it out in the open, the New Englanders would subtly "insinuate our sentiments, designs, and desires by means of other person, sometimes of one province, and sometimes of another."[12] Men like Rush would do nicely for this scheme.

By September 1 almost all of the delegates had arrived in Philadelphia. They had traveled by ferry and wagon, crossing treacherous rivers and dusty rutted roads, sleeping in bug-infested inns and eating little they found appetizing. Their food and lodging improved considerably once they reached the city, but for those who had never before been there, Philadelphia came as a shock of cosmopolitan contrasts and vivid sights and sounds.

The delegates encountered all manner of people as they settled into their new lodgings. Philadelphia was home to rich Quaker merchants and poor laborers living in squalor. There were Indians, slaves, Jews, and immigrants from around the globe. A French visitor noted that the ladies were "very well shaped," but he deplored their "lack of grace" and "very bad curtsies." What really vexed him was that "they pride themselves on a scrupulous fidelity towards their husbands."[13]

In the heart of Philadelphia stood the State House, a red brick Georgian-style building that had been the home of the province's government since 1732. Its bell tower rose nearly 170 feet, making it the tallest structure in the city. Tolling on the hour was its famous bell, ordered by Dickinson's father-in-law from London years before, which had a curious propensity for developing cracks no matter how many times it was recast. The biblical inscription on its rim served to remind the delegates of their solemn duty: "Proclaim liberty throughout the land, unto all the inhabitants thereof."

Even before Congress officially opened, intensive lobbying had begun. The first order of business was to find an official place to meet. Speaker Galloway proposed the Pennsylvania State House and pushed hard for his choice.

With the Assembly meeting just down the hallway, he would be considered the host and doyen; his views would gain proportionally greater weight.

It was a prospect Dickinson feared. With vigorous behind-the-scenes politicking, he and Sam Adams managed to persuade a majority of delegates to vote for an alternative site: Carpenters' Hall, diagonally across from the State House. The victory was symbolic, but it was also a tacit declaration that Congress was not willing to be dominated by Galloway. An "interest . . . out of doors," the speaker wrote, referring to Dickinson, had wrecked his plans.[14] In the meantime, Sam Adams persuaded Congress to appoint Charles Thomson, a local radical leader whom Galloway had deliberately excluded from Congress, as permanent secretary to the body.

At ten o'clock in the morning on September 5, the fifty-five representatives gathered for the first time. The first day's proceedings were spent largely in the reading of credentials, but the next day proved far more productive. Despite the oppressive heat, made more unbearable by woolen clothing, the delegates were excited to get down to business. Their greatest hope was to persuade Parliament to rescind the Coercive Acts. The question was how to accomplish this: through aggression, appeasement, or some combination of the two. Almost immediately Congress split over this question.

On one side were those hoping to adopt a more conciliatory approach to the conflict. It was this group, led by Duane and Galloway, that comprised the bulk of America's moderates. These men, Galloway later wrote, "intended candidly and clearly to define American rights, and explicitly and dutifully to petition for the remedy which would redress grievances." But Galloway had an additional goal that was not shared by all on the right. He also wished "to form a more solid and constitutional union between the two countries."[15] In this he was opposed not just by the radicals but also by such men as Dickinson, who argued that except for regulating imperial trade, America should run its own affairs.

On the other side were those eager to provoke Great Britain. Congressional radicals were dominated by an unusual coalition. Sam Adams, who led the democratic New Englanders, found staunch support in one of the most aristocratic delegations to Congress, the gentlemen of Virginia. Rich, athletic outdoorsmen, the Virginians were, as the historian Garry Wills describes them, accompanied everywhere by their liveried slaves.[16] Their leader was Richard Henry Lee, a magnificent horseman who kept one hand wrapped in a black silk handkerchief, having blown off some fingers in a hunting accident. With his thick mane of hair and military bearing, Lee provided a panache that Massachusetts's radicals both lacked and yearned for. In later years a clearly biased Galloway would accuse the Lee-Adams alliance of wishing from the start "to delude the people from their allegiance, to throw the subsisting governments into anarchy, to incite the ignorant and vulgar to arms, and with those arms to establish American independence."[17] This was hyperbole, since no congressmen in 1774 openly advocated independence, even if a few privately contemplated it. But Galloway was undeniably correct in asserting that the delegates were deeply divided.

The depth of the split was laid bare on the second day of Congress, when Patrick Henry, a fiery former preacher from Virginia, announced that "government is at an end" and that the colonies had been thrown back into a "state of nature."[18] Nothing could have been more abhorrent to moderates than the idea that all social and political bonds had been broken. On the contrary, they argued, the existing royal governments and colonial legislatures still functioned. As John Jay cautioned in response, America must wait "before we undertake to frame a new constitution."[19]

To be sure, the rift between left and right was not the only axis of division. Just as occurs today, many factors affected political decision making in that first Congress. Regional loyalties, colony size, and personal friendships frequently trumped ideological considerations. The lone representative who finally showed up from Georgia puzzled many by always voting with Connecticut, until it was discovered that he had once lived there. Yet the existence of other divisions in Congress does not mean ideological divisions were unimportant. As the historian H. James Henderson has shown in his detailed study of voting patterns, partisan trends emerged in Congress early on.[20] In other words, like-minded men gravitated together to pursue common goals.

Within these factions, opinion was far from monolithic. As the historian Neil York points out, the Founding Fathers were highly flexible in their beliefs, naturally seeking consensus across partisan lines.[21] Since modern political parties did not yet exist in 1774, it was far easier for moderate delegates to disagree with each other over certain issues. In matters of substance, however, they were very much in accord.

The first major battle between left and right broke out the moment Richard Henry Lee proposed natural law as one of the central foundations for American rights. The Massachusetts contingent immediately backed him, with John Adams "very strenuous for retaining and insisting on it."[22] Many moderates, on the other hand, saw an appeal to natural rights as a slippery slope. Natural law, they feared, could be used to justify any course of action, up to and including independence. Instead, moderates argued, American rights must be based on established legal precedent. John Rutledge of South Carolina for one thought their claims were "well founded on the British constitution, and not on the law of nature."[23] Parliament would likely scoff at the notion of natural rights, but it could not reject an appeal to English law. Moreover, the colonies themselves were bound by British legal traditions. "They had," Rutledge pointed out, "no right to elect a king," nor could they "set up what constitution they please[d]."[24]

Tall, grave, and dignified, Rutledge was, after George Washington, the most Olympian of the Founding Fathers. A French diplomat described him as one of the most eloquent men in American government, "but also the proudest and most imperious."[25] With his fierce dark eyes, a firm-set mouth, and a broad forehead Rutledge clearly looked like someone who didn't suffer fools gladly, and he frequently unleashed his volcanic temper on his enemies and inferiors. To those whom he respected, however, he was the epitome of southern courtesy and charm. The finest lawyer in South Carolina, he had studied law at the Middle Temple in London just a few years after Dickinson. The scion of an already wealthy family, he had grown even richer through his courtroom skills. But as the crisis with Britain came to a head, he increasingly let his legal practice suffer in order to spend more time fighting for colonial rights.

In many ways Rutledge was as devoted to preserving South Carolina's traditional order as he was to defending American liberty at large. A member of Charleston's elite, he had no intention of letting the fight with Britain endanger the dominance of his class. Although he had actively participated in blocking the sale of British tea, he had also parried demands by Charleston's radical mechanics and artisans for a total boycott of British trade. Soon after Rutledge was elected to the Continental Congress, a worried merchant asked him what could be done to prevent South Carolina's delegates from siding with the radicals. Rutledge's response: "Hang them."[26]

Upon arriving in Philadelphia, Rutledge immediately gravitated toward those who counseled restraint. Galloway, who found him "a gentleman of amiable character," was grateful to have him at his side. Rutledge's "sentiments and mine differ in no one particular," he wrote. The Southerner "has looked into the arguments of both sides more fully than any I have met with, and seems to be aware of all the consequences which may attend rash and imprudent measures."[27] Even Patrick Henry, who disagreed with Rutledge's political views, could not help praising his eloquence, noting that "he shone with a superior luster." John Adams, of course, disliked Rutledge instantly, finding "nothing of the profound, sagacious, brilliant, or sparkling in him." If anything, Adams said, he "maintains an air of reserve, design and cunning—like Duane and Galloway."[28]

In attacking those who would rely exclusively on natural law, Duane and Galloway fully backed Rutledge. The British constitution, Duane argued in a long speech, was the true bulwark for the colonists' liberties. It was "their birth right and inalienable inheritance."[29] It was imperative, he said, to place American rights on "some solid and constitutional principle which will preserve us from violations."[30] To do otherwise would imperil their cause. Galloway openly mocked his opponents, adding, "I have looked for our rights in the law of nature, but could not find them [there]."[31]

Not all the moderates supported Rutledge, Duane, and Galloway. John Jay was willing to consider including natural rights. In the end, a compromise was reached. American rights were deemed to rest both on "the immutable laws of nature" and on "the principles of the English constitution, and the [colonial] charters or compacts."[32] By relying on both tradition and reason, the delegates devised a uniquely American conception of the law, one that would also have a lasting impact on American legal theory. It embedded the idea of American exceptionalism, the idea that America's destiny is different from that of other nations, in one of the earliest acts of America's first national government.

On September 16 Paul Revere once again galloped into Philadelphia with news from his beleaguered province—British warships had begun shelling Boston. The fighting had started. Secured in his saddlebags, he carried a set of fiery anti-British resolutions that had been adopted by Suffolk County, Massachusetts. The Suffolk Resolves, as they became known, had already been adopted across New England, and they tore Congress in two. The Resolves were more extreme than any document presented thus far. Not only did they declare the Coercive Acts unconstitutional, a position Dickinson had long held, but they also called for armed defense against the British, self-government for Massachusetts, and a complete boycott of British goods. Radical delegates moved immediately to endorse the Resolves. Galloway and his allies battled hard to oppose them, but with wartime fervor sweeping through Carpenters' Hall, they had to concede defeat the next day. Congress minced no words in adopting the Resolves on September 17, assailing the "unjust, cruel, and oppressive acts of the British Parliament."[33]

"This is one of the happiest Days in my Life," John Adams wrote in his diary. "This day convinced me that America will support Massachusetts or perish with her."[34]

To many on the right, the Suffolk Resolves were tantamount to "a declaration of war."[35] According to the *Pennsylvania Journal*, "The only apology which could be made for the conduct of the Continental Congress in adopting the Suffolk Resolves was that they came into their vote immediately after drinking thirty-two bumpers of Madeira [wine]."[36] Galloway considered leaving Congress, but Duane talked him out of it. So convinced were both men that the Resolves amounted to treason that they gave each other written proofs that they had voted against it. They realized immediately that the vote had abruptly and permanently altered the dynamic in Congress. Those on the right had taken their seats assuming they would run the show, but events were rapidly overtaking them. In the span of twenty-four hours, their long-standing efforts to stave off a trade embargo had failed. "God knows how the contest will end," John Jay wrote fearfully to a Tory friend. "I sincerely wish it may terminate in a lasting union with Great Britain."[37] If moderates wished to rein in the growing radical momentum, they would have to react quickly.

On September 28 Galloway proposed an audacious plan to bind the colonies closer to Britain. Similar to Ben Franklin's Albany Plan, which had been proposed and rejected at the start of the French and Indian War, Galloway's Plan of Union would have created an American president-general appointed by the Crown to govern the colonies and a national legislature to be elected every three years by the colonial legislatures. Though many moderates privately expressed reservations over the proposal, they believed it also accomplished something vital: it provided for a stronger national government.[38] As a result, a core group of like-minded moderates decided to back Galloway, including Jay, Duane, and John Rutledge's fiery younger brother, Edward, another graduate of London's Middle Temple.

What radicals hated most was that the plan conceded to Parliament many of the points they had been fighting for. It seemingly brought British corruption to American shores. "We shall liberate our constituents from a corrupt House of Commons," Patrick Henry cried, only to throw "them into the arms of an American Legislature that may be bribed."[39] At a time when Britain was increasingly coming to be viewed as a foreign invader, the last thing the radicals wanted were closer ties. Furthermore, the plan could split the colonies if only some provinces moved to adopt it. "Among all the difficulties in the way of effective and united action in 1774," wrote John Adams, "no more alarming one happened than the plan . . . presented . . . by Mr. Joseph Galloway."[40]

With the Adams-Lee faction working in Congress and Dickinson operating behind the scenes, Galloway's plan was tabled by a vote of six colonies to five. For the moment the threat had been neutralized, but it had not been defeated. Galloway's repeated attempts to force reconsideration of his plan were dashed, however, when Revere's one-man courier service returned to Philadelphia with more shocking news: General Gage was fortifying British positions in Boston with cannons. Against all precedent, a British standing army was arming itself against British subjects. On October 22 Sam Adams and Richard Henry Lee seized the occasion to have all record of the Plan of Union expunged from the congressional record. So thoroughly did they wipe out all traces of the proposal that no copy of the plan survives today, just a few passing references in letters. "Measures of independence and sedition," Galloway later wrote, "were . . . preferred to those of harmony and reconciliation."[41]

Dickinson's help in defeating Galloway's plan had been crucial. Though he was largely sympathetic to the moderate side, he was undoubtedly motivated at least in part by his animosity toward Galloway. Far more likely, however, was that Dickinson saw closer ties to Britain as a greater threat than boon to American liberty. For all of the suspicions he harbored, he remained unwavering in his support for New England. In a private meeting he assured both Sam and John Adams that any defensive measures Massachusetts took against the British would receive the full support of the other colonies. Sam paid him the highest compliment he could think of, calling him "a true Bostonian." Adams's praise was all the more remarkable considering that he generally saw Pennsylvania Quakers as "puling pusillanimous cowards."[42]

The Adams cousins had clearly made a favorable impression on Dickinson as well, because a week after the opening of Congress, Dickinson invited John, along with several other delegates, to dine at Fairhill. The guests welcomed the respite from Philadelphia, which at the moment was plagued by an infestation of mosquitoes and horseflies. A chance to escape the city's smallpox and dysentery outbreaks was also appreciated. Adams's impressions of Fairhill were vivid. He loved the river views and surrounding countryside. A fellow bibliophile, he was particularly impressed by Dickinson's extensive book collection. Most of all he was happy to have such a formidable ally in the fight against Galloway. "Mr. Dickinson," he wrote, "has an excellent heart and the cause of his country lies near it." Twelve days later Adams spent another "most delightful afternoon" with Dickinson.[43]

So it was with jubilation that Adams greeted Dickinson's arrival in Congress. With military tensions mounting in Boston, popular sentiment began shifting against Britain throughout the continent. At the start of October, Pennsylvania held new elections, and Whigs won a series of stunning victories. Tories lost their Assembly majority, and Galloway was turned out as speaker. In the space of a few weeks the man who had once ruled supreme in

Pennsylvania had lost most of his power; in half a year he would disappear entirely from the American political scene. In the end, his attempts to bar Dickinson from Congress proved "a myopic achievement," in the words of the historian Jack Rakove.[44] Dickinson would likely have helped stem the swelling tide of radicalism had he been allowed to participate in Congress from the start.

Having won a spot in the Assembly, Dickinson at long last took his seat in Congress in mid-October. "The spirit and principles of liberty here are greatly cherished," John Adams wrote home. "The elections of last week prove this. Mr. Dickinson was chosen."[45] As always, Dickinson was well prepared to wield his pen when he took his seat. In the thirteen days Congress remained in session, he drafted two major documents. His "Address to the Inhabitants of Quebec" invited British Canadians to join the Continental Congress, denounced the Quebec Act (which gave increased freedoms to Roman Catholics) and most important, neatly and elegantly summarized American rights. His second task was to edit a petition to His Majesty, King George III, that had been drafted in part by John Adams, along with Patrick Henry and Richard Henry Lee. It was Adams's first experience working with Dickinson as a fellow delegate, and instantly there was friction. The "draft brought in by the original committee," Dickinson explained to a friend, "was written in language of asperity very little according to the conciliatory disposition of Congress."[46] He rewrote the petition in a more moderate manner, overruling Adams, who insisted on keeping the first draft's truculent tone.

It was a seemingly small disagreement, but to Adams it was more than the natural pique a writer feels toward an overzealous editor; Dickinson's interference was nothing short of apostasy. As Adams saw it, the Farmer had threatened the New England cause. Perhaps more dangerously, he had demonstrated his potential to stand in Adams's way.

Dickinson had good reason for not bending to Adams. Because the document was meant to address the King, whom most Americans still considered their ally against Parliament, Dickinson took pains to avoid giving offense. He explained American grievances against parliamentary abuses from the point of view of a British subject wishing to preserve British rights. In this respect, his argument was essentially traditionalist. Americans, he said, were only resisting "innovations" that infringed on their traditional freedoms. With the greatest politeness, he concluded, "As your Majesty enjoys the signal distinction of reigning over freemen, we apprehend the language of freemen can not be displeasing."[47]

Congress approved all of Dickinson's changes to the petition to the King the day before it adjourned on October 26. Most of the delegates were exceedingly pleased with the revised petition. Like Dickinson, they hoped that a firm but respectful defense would lead to both reconciliation and greater freedoms. Should no progress occur over the coming months, a second Continental Congress was scheduled for the following spring. But a majority of congressmen departed Philadelphia expecting the conflict to be resolved before then. At a gala banquet at the City Tavern to celebrate the end of Congress, five hundred guests raised thirty-five toasts, including one to the King. Optimism reigned supreme.

Moderates were less sanguine. As a Maryland merchant wrote a few months later, "Adams, with his crew, and the haughty sultans of the South juggled the whole conclave of the delegates."[48] Duane was already in secret contact with British authorities in a last-ditch effort to defuse the conflict. The British, however, remained adamant that Boston must pay for the tea. That, he knew, would never happen. If anything, Duane feared, New Englanders would launch an attack on the British Army.

For John Adams and the radicals, Congress had been a stunning success. Massachusetts would not be abandoned in its fight with Britain. And Adams's own deepest desire had been fulfilled: "I left Congress and Philadelphia in October 1774, with a reputation, much higher than ever I enjoyed before or since."[49] One thing had soured for him, though. His formerly high opinion of the Farmer was forever altered. Six weeks after enjoying his last dinner at Fairhill, Adams was now convinced that "Mr. Dickinson is very modest, delicate, and timid."[50]

Dickinson's mood was uncharacteristically dark. While he had been pleased with his work in Congress, he had little hope a resolution would be found. "Reconciliation depends upon the passing moment," he wrote to his former guest at Fairhill, Josiah Quincy of Massachusetts, "and the opportunity will in a short time, be irrevocably past, as the days beyond the flood."[51] The future of America would be decided in Massachusetts, and he did not know which to fear more, the rashness of the New Englanders or the stupidity of the British. As much as it would have heartened him in the past, his victory over Galloway did little to cheer him. After years of battle, Dickinson had finally vanquished his old foe, but somehow, he sensed, a new and far more formidable opponent was about to take his place.

CHAPTER 6

THE OLIVE BRANCH AND THE LIGHTNING BOLT

On April 19, 1775, the stench of gunpowder and dead men filled the air between Boston and Concord, Massachusetts. Hundreds had been killed and many more were wounded. The fighting began just after sunrise, when seven hundred Redcoats, sent from Boston to seize munitions and arrest radicals, found their passage blocked in the town of Lexington. A small group of militiamen stood in a line before them. No one knows who opened fire first, but within minutes the Americans were running for their lives.

What stunned the British soldiers most was the fact that they had been challenged at all. Their mission to destroy militia stockpiles in Concord was supposed to have been secret, but American spies had received advance warning of the raid. The day before, the Americans had hidden much of the weaponry and sent Paul Revere on his famous midnight ride. All along the route from Boston to Concord, Revere and other riders had alerted militiamen that the British were coming. The resistance the Redcoats had encountered in Lexington was only a small taste of things to come.

In Concord the British soldiers destroyed what matériel they could find, but as they marched back to Boston, they encountered increasingly stiff resistance. Skirmish after skirmish depleted their ammunition. Wave after wave of fresh militiamen harassed them from behind. Americans took up sniper positions behind stone walls and in attic windows.

The British were already nearing total exhaustion. They had set out in the middle of the previous night and were now running out of water. With many of their officers killed or wounded, discipline began to crumble. Enraged troops began moving house to house, shooting and bayoneting anyone they found. They killed a farmer standing in his doorway and executed two drunks in a tavern, where the soldiers promptly got drunk.

The tide of battle shifted in midafternoon, when thousands upon thousands of militiamen began turning up. In the end the British escaped total annihilation only by beating a rapid retreat all the way back to Boston. By the end of the day, sixteen thousand militiamen were encircling the city. America was at war.

The Second Continental Congress, which met for the first time three weeks later, found itself in charge of a war it had not authorized and did not know how to run. It was exactly what moderates had feared might happen after the first Congress. James Duane of New York had warned the previous fall that radicals might become emboldened by their political victories. "My principal alarm," he had written, "is that those measures will inflame the ardor of our friends in Boston and precipitate an attack on the King's troops."[1]

As it turned out, the British made the first move by marching on Concord, but Duane worried that any conflict between the unprepared colonists and the vastly superior forces of Britain was bound to be "disgraceful and ruinous" for both sides. He did concede that the "wicked" and "oppressive" British government bore ultimate responsibility for the "innocent blood" spilled at Lexington and Concord. As a result, the other colonies were bound to stand with Massachusetts "by the most solemn of engagements."

How exactly Congress should honor that solemn engagement, however, was far from clear. Many of Duane's friends believed Congress should not be involved at all. The New York Assembly refused to choose any delegates, electing to send its own petition seeking reconciliation to the King and Parliament. Duane thought this was the wrong approach and decided to attend anyway. The presence of moderates like him, he believed, would be critical if radicals were to be kept in check. "Every emotion of intemperate zeal, every sally of anger and passion," he wrote, had to be avoided.[2] Given the attitude of the New Englanders, this would be no simple task.

As John Adams rode from his farm in Braintree, Massachusetts, to Philadelphia, he was unsure how his fellow colonists would greet him. Massachusetts, after all, had just plunged the continent into war. He was relieved to discover that no one blamed New Englanders for the fighting. If anything, "the accounts of the battles are exaggerated in our favor," he wrote home.[3]

At the outskirts of Philadelphia, Adams and the other Massachusetts delegates were welcomed by a crowd of five hundred and escorted into town by a cavalcade of mounted officers. A regiment of riflemen and a military band accompanied them. Adams found the city transformed. It was now infused with the "military spirit which runs through the continent." Thousands of militiamen drilled in the streets daily, and many prominent gentlemen had become officers. Dickinson, Adams noted with some jealousy, had become a colonel. "Oh that I was a soldier!" he wrote to his wife.[4] He began studying "military books" in the event that he became one. Perhaps the most gratifying part of Adams's return to Philadelphia was that he was now well known to the other delegates, many of whom had been reappointed from the First Congress.

Notable new arrivals included John Hancock, a rich Boston smuggler; James Wilson, Dickinson's eloquent, bespectacled former law clerk; Thomas Jefferson, a tall, red-headed Virginian whose elegance was matched only by his taciturnity; and Benjamin Franklin, back in America for the first time in eight years and cured of his anglophilia after the king's Privy Council had publicly humiliated him for his role in leaking private letters written by Massachusetts's governor. One glaring absence was Joseph Galloway. Though elected to Congress, the Pennsylvania speaker chose not to attend and retreated to his country estate, where he continued to pen attacks on Dickinson. Galloway's self-recusal paved the way for Dickinson to become the most influential man in Congress. It also removed any lingering objections to moving from Carpenters' Hall to the State House; there Congress would meet, with a few interruptions, for the next nine years.

As a token of respect, the Pennsylvania legislature moved to one of the smaller upstairs rooms, allowing Congress use of the first-floor Assembly Room, a commodious chamber with twenty-foot ceilings, marble fireplaces, and a crystal chandelier. The room that was to become Congress's home was filled with several score Windsor chairs arranged in a semicircle around the president's high-backed seat, which was elevated on a small dais. As before, delegates from New England sat on the left, the middle colonies in the center, and the South on the right. In the warm summer months, tall windows let in long shafts of sunlight as well as ravenous black flies, forcing the delegates to choose between stifling heat and itchy red welts. But deciding whether or not to open the windows was one of the least difficult choices Congress faced.

From day one, Congress realized it had two essential questions to confront: how would it conduct the war, and where would it find the resources to do so? As usual, Dickinson arrived in the State House with a plan. To implement it, he knew he would need allies, and he found a staunch one in Duane. The two men had a natural affinity for each other. They represented the richest and most diverse colonies in America. And both wished to minimize the disturbances of war while still defending American rights. The Dickinson-Duane "system," which John Adams found objectionable, quickly came to dominate Congress.[5] What was needed, Dickinson and Duane insisted, was a balanced approach to the conflict. Congress must pursue peace if possible but fight for freedom if necessary. Preparations for war, Dickinson declared, "must go *pari passu* [hand in hand] with measures of reconciliation."[6]

Radicals, on the other hand, focused exclusively on making war. First, the colonies would need soldiers. At the end of the first week, Richard Henry Lee of Virginia introduced a motion calling for the creation of a national army. To his great surprise, John Rutledge, the prominent South Carolina moderate, seconded him. But Rutledge did so with an ulterior motive. Before the issue of an army was resolved, the Carolinian said, he had a question he first wanted answered, "such as do we aim at independency? Or do we only ask for a restoration of rights and putting of us on our old footing?"[7]

By broaching the taboo subject of independence, Rutledge accomplished two important things. He forced radicals to declare themselves against independence, something moderates suspected they secretly desired. He also combatted Tory propaganda that had dubbed Congress "a mad, blind monster" bent on declaring "total independency."[8] An open renunciation of independence at the outset of Congress would allay many fears.

When Robert Livingston voiced his support for Rutledge, arguing that Congress had to decide on its ends before voting on the means, John Adams immediately rose to object. The previous Congress, he insisted, had already settled the issue. There was no reason to take a vote. Privately, however, Adams was decidedly in favor of independence, even if he thought the colonies were "not ripe for it."[9] Above all, he wanted to avoid negotiation "like death."

"Powder and artillery," he wrote, "are the most efficacious, sure and infallible conciliatory measures we can adopt."[10]

Two weeks of furious debate erupted out of Lee's motion and Rutledge's question. Accusations of cowardice and treachery darted back and forth. The arguments grew so acrimonious during one session that half of Congress stormed out in protest. Moderates themselves were far from unified over how to proceed. Dickinson had argued for "a vigorous preparation for war" and "a vigorous prosecution of it." But when he also proposed conceding the regulation of trade to Parliament and paying for the tea destroyed in Boston, Silas Deane noted that he argued "smoothly and sophistically on the subject and gives rather disgust." Rutledge himself "treat[ed] Dickinson's plan with the utmost contempt."[11]

The dilemma facing moderates was tricky to resolve. They were advocating military action against British forces while simultaneously claiming loyalty to the Crown. The only way to rationalize this position was to believe that George III was being deliberately misled by corrupt ministers. It was up to Congress to convince the King that America was merely defending its rights under the British constitution. Accordingly, concessions and negotiations were vital for this plan to succeed.

For radicals, the moderate approach was the height of folly. As John Adams saw it, the entire British government, including the King, had "been now for many years gradually trained and disciplined by corruption." The only way to cure this "cancer" was by "cutting it out entire."[12] Like his fellow radicals, he claimed to remain "as fond of reconciliation as any man," but one crucial factor differentiated moderates from "the party in favor of energetic action," as Franklin called it. For men like John Adams, Sam Adams, and Richard Henry Lee, the problem was not simply that the British government was corrupt. It was that the entire nation was so riddled with iniquity that "there was no degree of vice, folly, or corruption" to which it would not stoop, as Sam Adams wrote.[13] Dickinson, on the other hand, always took pains to distinguish between the wicked prime minister, "Mr. Grenville," and "the generous, sensible and humane nation, to whom we may apply."[14] Having lived in England, as many moderates had, Dickinson saw something that no radical could quite believe. For all the corruption he had witnessed firsthand as a student, he knew the British government and its admirable legal system still worked. They were not to be cast off lightly.

So great was Dickinson's persuasive power that by the end of May Congress rejected any suggestion of independence and largely adopted his moderate approach. In a series of resolutions authored largely by Dickinson, Congress declared that "these colonies immediately be put in a state of defense." At the same time it expressed a fervent wish for "a restoration of the harmony formerly subsisting between" the mother country and the colonies.[15] As the historian Charles Stillé writes, Dickinson and his allies "worked quietly and effectively,—the olive-branch in one hand, and 'the lightning of Jove' in the other."[16]

In order to defend the continent, Duane proposed the creation of two standing armies, one in Massachusetts and one in New York. To lead the new Continental Army, the delegates appointed George Washington, who had arrived in Congress dressed in his old militia uniform. The towering Virginian was ordered to depart immediately for Boston, where he needed to transform the unpaid volunteers surrounding the city into a professional army capable of sustained campaigning. Washington was an ideal candidate to lead America's war effort. His character was impeccable and his personality indomitable. As impassive and stately as a marble bust, Washington was one of few men in history able to live up to his idealized image of himself. And though sympathetic to the moderates, he managed to transcend ideological differences. Massachusetts radicals especially liked the idea of placing a Virginian in charge of the war. No longer would the fight be seen as New England's alone.

The choice for Washington's second in command, on the other hand, pleased few on the left. An aristocratic New Yorker, Philip Schuyler was a close ally of the moderates. Some radicals hinted that New Englanders might mutiny if forced to serve under him. Nevertheless Schuyler was commissioned one of four major generals in the new Continental Army. His task was almost as formidable as Washington's: preventing a British invasion from the north. At the start of June, Congress had resolved not to attack Canada. But when word came at the end of the month that the British military commander of Canada was preparing a strike force, Schuyler was ordered to seize Fort Saint Jean and the city of Montreal. Canada, Congress hoped, could be turned into a fourteenth colony and would then join the fight against Britain. How Schuyler would accomplish this objective, with little money or ammunition, Congress left up to him.

With defensive preparations under way, Congress now turned to the second part of the moderate plan. At the end of May, John Jay of New York stood to propose a second petition to the King. The one from the previous autumn had been ignored. The purpose was to beseech George III to come to the aid of his American subjects. The petition would request a cease-fire in Boston, ask that the Coercive Acts be repealed, and call for the immediate start of negotiations between Britain and the colonies. Dickinson passionately seconded this olive branch to the King. Many suspected a second petition would fail just as the first had, but the Farmer's great reputation persuaded the delegates to lean in favor. It was more than John Adams could bear.

"I was opposed to it, of course," he wrote.[17]

Rising to his feet, Adams launched into a long condemnation of the proposed measure. Sending it would be both inconsistent and futile. Taking up arms and then sending a petition was in fact absurd.[18] The moment Adams sat down, another New England radical, John Sullivan of New Hampshire, stood to oppose the petition, arguing with "wit, reasoning and fluency," according to Adams. Throughout Sullivan's denunciation, Adams kept his eyes fixed on Dickinson, studying the emotions shuddering across his face. "I was much delighted and Mr. Dickinson was very much terrified at what he said," Adams reported. He was thrilled when he saw that Dickinson "began to tremble for his cause."

Adams's gloating was interrupted just at that moment, much to his annoyance, when he was called out to the State House yard on other business. He donned his hat and headed out the door. Dickinson darted out after him, caught up with him in the yard, and accosted him with "as rough and haughty [a manner] as if I had been a school boy and he the master."

Dickinson was practically in a frenzy. "What is the reason, Mr. Adams, that you New Englandmen oppose our measures of reconciliation?" he exclaimed. "Look, Ye! If you don't concur with us, in our pacific system, I, and a number of us, will break off from you in New England, and we will carry on the opposition by ourselves in our own way."

Adams held his temper. "Mr. Dickinson," he responded, "there are many things that I can very cheerfully sacrifice to harmony and even to unanimity." He eyed Dickinson coolly. "But I am not to be threatened into an express adoption or approbation of measures which my judgment reprobates. Congress must judge, and if they pronounce against me, I must submit, as if they determine against you, you ought to acquiesce."[19]

In the end it was Adams who had to acquiesce. Jefferson later wrote that the motion passed mainly out of deference to Dickinson, who did not want "to go too fast."[20] There is some truth in this. But it is also true that Dickinson simply outmaneuvered Adams through shrewd and ruthless behind-the-scenes politicking. Moderates, Adams wrote, "addressed themselves with great art and assiduity to all the members of Congress whom they could influence," including, to his shock, members of his own Massachusetts delegation. The key, however, was the Deep South. "The balance," Dickinson admitted, "lay with South Carolina." "Accordingly," Adams wrote, "all their efforts were employed to convert the delegates from that state."[21] In the end, Dickinson's cultivation of the Rutledge brothers proved decisive. With South Carolina's backing, the New York–Pennsylvania bloc was able to defeat the Massachusetts-Virginia alliance.

The task of composing the Olive Branch Petition, as it became known, was assigned to a committee, which included Dickinson, Jay, Rutledge, Franklin, and Thomas Johnson of Maryland. Jay wrote the first draft, but Dickinson took out his editor's quill and rewrote most of it. Jay's draft, for example, had specifically stated that America did not seek independence. Dickinson cut this line, leaving Congress's options more vague and more threatening. He further removed many of the concessions Jay had included. Still, Dickinson recognized that for the address to have any chance of success, he would have to write with the humility of a loyal subject. "To the King's Most Excellent Majesty," he began, "Most Gracious Sovereign . . ." He blamed the King's ministers for the present troubles. And he assured the King that Americans remained loyal to "your Majesty's person, family, and government," praying "ardently" for reconciliation.[22]

Dickinson presented his draft to Congress on July 5. Four days later the petition was entrusted to Richard Penn, Pennsylvania's lieutenant governor, who was departing for England. A duplicate was sent aboard another ship the next day to ensure the document's arrival. No one knew when or if George III would reply. Like most delegates, Dickinson had little hope the petition would avert all-out war. It would, however, delay it.

What Dickinson really sought with the Olive Branch Petition was time. America needed more time to prepare its defenses and more time to unify. "Procrastination is preservation," he wrote. As ever, history guided his thinking. From classical times to the present, in instance upon instance, Dickinson observed how rashness had always led to disaster. "It is a melancholy employment to peruse those various instances of recorded history in which the best causes have been ruined by an excess of virtuous zeal."[23] For all of his own extensive reading, Adams had missed this important lesson.

Delay was the key to consolidating public opinion, which remained sharply divided. Any rush to war and independence, moderates believed, would splinter the colonies. And if the provinces went their separate ways, all American rights would be imperiled. In this sense, Dickinson saw the Olive Branch Petition as a vital tactical maneuver. If the British accepted it, America would secure its liberties without further bloodshed. "If they reject this application with contempt," he wrote, ". . . such treatment will confirm the minds of our countrymen to endure all the misfortunes that may attend the contest."[24] A rejection, in other words, would unite Americans as never before.

As calm as he had remained during his confrontation with Dickinson, Adams now could not stop ruminating about it. In the interest of harmony, he had signed the Olive Branch Petition along with the rest of the Massachusetts delegation, but the more he thought about it, the more vexed he grew. In his diary he began jotting down any rumor that could blacken his opponent's reputation. He blamed Dickinson for the British capture of Charlestown, Massachusetts. He slandered him in his letters. "A certain great fortune and piddling genius . . . has given a silly cast to our whole doings," Adams wrote to General James Warren.[25] To his wife, he said that Dickinson only "pretended to be very valiant."[26]

Unfortunately for Adams, some of his private invective did not remain so. In August 1775, British forces intercepted some of his letters when they captured a courier crossing the Hudson. They were only too pleased to learn of discord within Congress and published Adams's letters. Newspapers carrying the letters soon reached Philadelphia. Adams later tried to explain himself by saying he had simply been "irritated with the unpoliteness of Mr. Dickinson and more mortified with his success in Congress."[27] Dickinson said nothing publicly about Adams's comments, but on a copy of a newspaper that ran the intercepted letter, he wrote, "Letter from John Adams of Massachusetts Bay in which he abuses me for opposing the violent measures of himself and others in Congress."[28]

For a while, Adams became "an object of nearly universal scorn and detestation." He had insulted Pennsylvania's favorite son. Benjamin Rush noted that Adams would "walk the streets of Philadelphia alone."[29] Adams claimed not to care. "I rather rejoiced in this as a fortunate Circumstance," he claimed.[30] Sooner or later, he wrote, everyone else would come around to his way of thinking.

In mid-September Adams ran into Dickinson on Chestnut Street heading to the State House. They passed "near enough to touch elbows." As customary, Adams bowed and doffed his hat, curious what Dickinson would do. But the Pennsylvanian "passed without moving his hat, head, or hands."[31] From then on, Adams vowed, he would pass Dickinson in the same "haughty" manner. The two men never spoke to each other in private again.

Adams might have been temporarily ostracized from Philadelphia society, but he turned out to be right about one important thing. Others were coming around to his way of thinking. While Dickinson had won this particular battle, he had expended precious political capital to fight it. And though the Olive Branch Petition had passed unanimously, most delegates had felt little real enthusiasm for it. Whisperers began to question Dickinson's devotion and valor.

Well into the nineteenth century, Adams would assert that Dickinson's Quakerism had led him to oppose violence—that and the fact that he had been browbeaten by his mother and wife, both of whom were devout pacifists. "Johnny, you will be hanged," Adams claimed Dickinson's mother would tell him, "your estate forfeited and confiscated, you will leave your excellent wife a widow, and your charming children, orphans, beggars, and infamous." If he had had such a mother, Adams wrote in his *Autobiography,* it would have unmanned him, or at least made "me the most miserable man alive."[32]

However accurate his assumptions about Dickinson's family life, Adams could not have been more wrong about his opponent's beliefs. While Quaker constitutional thought clearly exerted an influence on him, Dickinson was not a Quaker, and he was not a pacifist.[33] In fact, he was not a Quaker precisely because he was not a pacifist. For years he had been on poor terms with Philadelphia's Society of Friends for this reason. (It was also the cause of many a family quarrel.) "I am on all proper occasions an advocate for the lawfulness of defensive war," Dickinson wrote. "This principle has prevented me from union with Friends."[34]

It was not conflict that Dickinson abhorred, but ignorance born of ideological fanaticism. At a time when prudence was required, radicals were assuming that virtuous American militiamen would handily defeat corrupt British mercenaries. But war with Britain would not be quick or easy, he knew. Virtue and patriotism, though laudable, would not by themselves defeat the most powerful military in the world. Boston might have been encircled, but General Thomas Gage still had twenty regiments of Regulars at his command and a fleet bristling with cannons at anchor in Boston Harbor.

For all his misgivings, Dickinson was ready to sacrifice his life and property if that was the only way to secure American freedom. "Our towns are but brick and stone, and mortar and wood," he wrote; "they, perhaps, may be destroyed; they are only the hairs of our heads; if sheared ever so close, they will grow again. We compare them not with our rights and liberties."[35]

His commitment was unquestionable. In addition to serving as commander of Philadelphia's First Battalion of Associators, he also chaired the city's Committee of Public Safety, responsible for raising troops and building fortifications. He oversaw the construction of a fleet of naval riverboats and supervised the installation of defensive positions along the Delaware. He pushed through a system of universal enlistment for all males between the ages of sixteen and fifty. He instituted fines for any man refusing to "associate" for the common defense, including Quaker conscientious objectors. As Dickinson knew, the money from these fines would not be incidental. Benjamin Rush estimated that 75 percent of the taxes raised for the war came from noncombatants and Tories.

In Congress, Dickinson affirmed his support for the war yet again by taking up his pen. The "Declaration Setting Forth the Causes and Necessities of Taking Up Arms" explained America's reasons for fighting and boosted enthusiasm for the war effort. The committee assigned to compose the Declaration first appointed John Rutledge to the task, but when his draft was deemed unsatisfactory, young Thomas Jefferson was asked to rewrite it. It was the first major address Jefferson crafted for Congress, and he took it seriously. Though this second draft was excellent in many ways, the committee still found it lacking. It was then that Dickinson was asked to step in.

Like most young writers, Jefferson was touchy about letting an older editor leave fingerprints all over his clean prose. When he saw Dickinson's heavy corrections, he grew so incensed that the Farmer decided just to throw away his draft and start from scratch. The resulting document was a thorough mix of the two writers' style and content. Parsing out who wrote what, however, proved next to impossible, and over the next 175 years, scholars argued relentlessly over which Founding Father deserved more credit for the Declaration. The debate was further confused by something Jefferson wrote when he was seventy-eight years old, long after Dickinson had passed away.

According to Jefferson, his original draft had been far more bellicose. Dickinson, however, had objected and softened the tone. In the final version, Jefferson claimed, the first part was Dickinson's but the last four and a half paragraphs were his. For much of the nineteenth century, historians heaped praise upon the parts supposedly written by Jefferson and criticized Dickinson's feckless prose. Some even claimed the difference in styles was so distinct that they could tell where in the middle of the paragraph Dickinson had stopped writing and Jefferson had begun.

Except that none of what Jefferson remembered was true. Only at the end of the nineteenth century was a draft in Dickinson's own handwriting discovered, and only in the middle of the twentieth did scholars piece together who had written which parts. Some of the fiercest language turns out to have been Dickinson's, and his threats of independence were far more blunt. Jefferson did have some cause to be annoyed by Dickinson's edits: the older writer had rendered a number of straightforward sentences more complicated than need be. But many of the Declaration's boldest phrases, long ascribed to Jefferson, turned out to be Dickinson's: "Our cause is just. Our union is perfect. Our internal resources are great, and, if necessary, foreign assistance is attainable." As the historian Julian P. Boyd comments, "This is not the language of one who is intent upon watering down or weakening the declaration of a just cause; it is daring and threatening, and its rhythm and terseness admirably suited to the purpose at hand."[36]

As much as he had chafed at working with Dickinson, Jefferson learned much about the art of political polemics through their collaboration. Rather than address the Declaration to the King, as he had in the Olive Branch Petition, Dickinson explained America's actions out of "obligations of respect to the rest of the world." A year later Jefferson would borrow and slightly alter this phrase in another Declaration, just as he did the list of grievances Dickinson included.

Whoever deserves the final authorial credit—and it is often difficult to determine whose influence was greatest when multiple writers are involved—the effect was clear and resounding:

> With hearts fortified . . . we most solemnly, before God and the world, declare that . . . the arms which we have been compelled by our enemies to assume, we will in defiance of every hazard, with unabating firmness and perseverance employ for the preservation of our liberties; being, with one mind, resolved to die freemen rather than live as slaves.

Even Adams had to admit it was a "spirited manifesto."

Congress issued the Declaration for Taking Up Arms one day after the Olive Branch Petition. Two weeks later the document arrived at Washington's headquarters outside Boston. Morale had been plummeting since the start of the siege. In increasing numbers, troops were deserting due to disease, boredom, and the approaching harvest season. Many of the New England militiamen ringing Boston had expected to fight a few short battles and then go home, but they found themselves becoming enmeshed in a protracted war. The Declaration could not have arrived at a better moment. It explained why they had to keep fighting. And it showed them that the rest of America stood with them. Far off in Philadelphia, delegates from every colony were working to secure American freedom.

Upon its arrival, Washington ordered the Declaration read aloud throughout the sprawling American encampment. General Israel Putnam, a hero of the recent battle at Bunker Hill, marched his Connecticut volunteers in parade formation to nearby Prospect Hill to hear a reading. As they listened, the militiamen stood on the very road the British had taken to Lexington and Concord just three months before.

"Huzza! Huzza! Huzza!" they cried after hearing the Declaration's ringing conclusion. A single loud "Amen" followed.

Above the militiamen a signal gun fired, and Connecticut's new standard, just arrived, rose and unfurled itself before the cheering troops. One side bore the words "An Appeal to Heaven!" in large golden letters. The reverse showed

Connecticut's armorial sigil, a plain white shield with three grape vines atop a scroll with the words *Qui Transtulit Sustinet*—"He who is transplanted sustains."[37] That day and for the rest of the summer, Dickinson's and Jefferson's words, which had retraced the same four hundred miles John Adams had traveled two months before, played no small role in sustaining America's fledgling army.

CHAPTER 7

PATRIOTISM AND PROFIT

Tankards aloft, the one hundred members of Philadelphia's St. George Society were in midtoast "to England and Country" when an express courier burst into their banquet hall with news of the battles at Lexington and Concord. No tidings could have been more appalling to the Sons of St. George, who considered themselves the most devoted of British subjects. They had founded their society several years before to aid English immigrants to Philadelphia. Dues went toward freeing Englishmen from debtors' prison and funding frequent revels at waterfront taverns. Every April 23 the society held its most lavish feast of the year in honor of St. George, England's patron saint. During the Renaissance St. George's Day had been more popular than Christmas, but by the late eighteenth century only the most ardent English nationalists still adorned their lapels with the customary red rose. In Philadelphia the St. George Society celebrated by throwing a rowdy and very liquid dinner in the famous Long Room at the City Tavern.

The news from Boston froze every man in his place. Then chairs clattered, tables tipped, and dishes crashed to the floor as the members poured into the street swearing allegiance to the Crown and clamoring for arms. Among the few who remained behind was Robert Morris, the society's cofounder and master of ceremonies. Throughout the uproar, the story goes, Morris's mug remained poised halfway to his lips, but when the hall was finally emptied, he lowered his drink and came to a fateful decision. As deep as his love for England was, Morris realized, America was now his home. Unlike his friends in the St. George Society, he would never take up arms against the colonies.

An Englishman by birth, a Presbyterian by creed, and a merchant by trade, Robert Morris bore all the hallmarks of a Tory. Yet his sense that America was in the right exerted a powerful influence over his thinking. "I sided with this country because their claims are founded in justice," he wrote shortly after the brouhaha at the City Tavern. And he wished his Loyalist friends "would consider it well before they act against it."[1] There turned out to be little the Tories could do against America. Very soon after the St. George's Day uproar, they learned to keep their views to themselves if they knew what was good for them.

Morris's support for the Patriot cause was not based solely on his sense of justice, however. He also harbored deep feelings of gratitude toward his adopted country. A poor boy from Liverpool, Morris had found unimaginable opportunities in America. At the age of thirteen he had followed his father to Pennsylvania, where he was soon orphaned. With only a meager inheritance, he apprenticed himself to the Philadelphia merchant Charles Willing, where he began by sweeping floors, won a promotion to clerk, and proved so adept at making money that he was soon named full partner along with Charles's son, Thomas. When he was only fifteen, Morris cornered the Philadelphia flour market, inducing a sudden shortage and reaping huge profits in the resulting price surge. By the mid-1770s the firm of Willing and Morris formed the heart of a growing multinational business empire, and Morris was poised to become the most powerful merchant on the continent. From his waterfront office at the southern end of Front Street, he oversaw a fleet of ships and a web of business connections that crisscrossed the globe.

Like most merchants, Morris knew that the trade boycott advocated by radicals would be bad for business in the short term. But he also understood the extent to which his prosperity depended on free trade, one of the main liberties under attack by Parliament. In the long run, any threat to American rights endangered his business interests. If played right, he suspected, the conflict with Britain might also prove lucrative. Morris was no radical. He ardently wished for reconciliation with the mother country, but it must also be admitted that a certain sense of enlightened self-interest informed his decision to back America.

Well over six feet tall, blunt-featured, and jowly, Morris would be considered a large man even by today's standards. At the center of his doughy face shone two bright blue eyes, an indication of the piercing intelligence that helped him sniff out profit in so many far-flung places. He was a man of sizable appetites as well as girth, and the pleasure he took in luxury was evident. He dressed in the finest silks and woolens, spent lavishly on entertainment, and was one of only eighty-four men in all of Philadelphia to own a horse-drawn carriage. Republican austerity had no appeal for him.

In addition to maintaining a splendid home in the city, Morris also owned The Hills, a beautiful estate several miles north, on a rise overlooking the

Schuylkill. It impressed all with its gardens, greenhouses, and ornamental fish-filled ponds. The frequent parties Morris threw there overflowed with guests and bottles of claret. Where Dickinson's Fairhill evoked a sense of serenity and reverence, The Hills inspired appetite and inebriation. Many a business deal was struck over the sumptuous dinners Morris would serve. "I dine at The Hills every Sunday," he wrote. "Thus you see I continue my old practice of mixing business and pleasure and have ever found them useful to each other."[2]

For Morris, doing business was more than a vocation. It was a calling of the highest honor. "I declare that the character of a real merchant, a generous, open and honest merchant, is a character I am proud of," he said. "It is the profession to which I have been bred from my earliest youth, the station in which it has pleased God to place me."[3] He rejected the radical republican notion that making money harmed society. Rather, he argued, the active pursuit of self-interest benefited all. "It seems to me," he wrote, that "the present opportunity of improving our fortunes ought not to be lost, especially as the very means of doing it will contribute to the service of our country at the same time."[4] Profit, in short, was patriotic.

The outbreak of war posed practical as well as ideological problems for supporters of American rights. Almost all essential materials were in short supply: medicine, cloth, tools, and, most important of all, weaponry and gunpowder. Parliament's ban on selling munitions to the colonies had left America virtually defenseless. Most of the meager supplies the colonists possessed had been seized in raids on British positions, but skirmishing had depleted much of these dwindling stores. Desperate measures were needed to address the shortage. At his headquarters in Cambridge, Washington secretly ordered his powder barrels filled with sawdust to hide the severity of the situation from his own troops. In Philadelphia, Franklin suggested equipping soldiers with bows and arrows, pointing out that four arrows could be loosed in the time it took to reload a single musket. American military commanders determined that this was not one of the Philadelphia inventor's cleverest ideas.

Tackling the gunpowder problem was no easy matter. With no central procurement system in place, colonial governments had to rely on private merchants to secure vital war supplies. Merchants, however, could only find matériel abroad, and the hazards posed by the Royal Navy were formidable. British frigates patrolled the high seas and lurked off foreign ports ready to board American ships. Captured smugglers placed both their vessels and their necks at risk. Still, many merchants were willing to undertake this gamble. Securing a lucrative military contract was one of the few ways they could circumvent Congress's strict trade embargo. And once they had a ship under sail, nothing could prevent them from doing other business on the side.

In Pennsylvania the need for weaponry grew pressing. With Congress now meeting again in Philadelphia, the city had become a strategic military target. No one knew when British forces might attack. Soon after it started meeting, the Second Continental Congress called upon the province to raise eight companies of "expert riflemen" to defend the city. They would join the numerous militia companies that had sprung up spontaneously after news of Lexington and Concord. On the last day of June, the Pennsylvania Assembly established a Committee of Public Safety to build defenses, organize the colony's ad hoc militias, and help "procure any quantity of powder . . . with the utmost expedition."[5]

Since the committee's actions constituted a hanging offense, proceedings were conducted in utmost secrecy. The twenty-five-man committee, which included Franklin, Morris, and Dickinson, began meeting six days a week in the State House Assembly Room. With Congress using the same room later in the morning, meetings had to start at six a.m. Unsurprisingly, attendance was sparse; fewer than half the members showed up even for the first meeting. Out of deference to his age, Franklin was chosen president, but the elder statesman often preferred sleeping in. Running the proceedings was left largely to Morris, who was elected vice president, and to Dickinson, another early riser. Only Morris, however, possessed the skills and contacts needed to secure large quantities of gunpowder. He knew just the man to whom he could entrust the entire operation. As vice president, he hired himself to be the committee's chief contractor. In the process, he discovered he had a gift for espionage as well as for profit.

Morris's first step was to mobilize his enormous network of commercial agents across Europe and throughout the Caribbean. He used every ruse he could think of. Local officials were bribed, British spies evaded, and ships issued false papers and forged manifests. The initial costs for these covert operations were borne by Morris and his financial partners, but they expected to be well compensated for their efforts. In early August he and another merchant submitted invoices to the committee for £25,000. It was a staggering amount of money, but Morris delivered. By the end of the month, he and his partners were able to smuggle more than two and a half tons of gunpowder into Pennsylvania.

Morris's talents soon attracted the attention of Congress. In September he was enlisted to obtain gunpowder for Continental forces. He proved just as deft in supplying the nation as he had his province. As ship after ship sailed into Philadelphia laden with powder, Morris sent a steady stream of wagons out of the city to Washington's forces in Cambridge and General Schuyler's troops in Albany, who were preparing to invade Canada. By the time Philadelphia's leaves began to change color, Morris had for all intents and purposes become America's chief weapons supplier. Single-handedly he secured more gunpowder for the Continental Army than all the other colonial merchants and public safety committees combined.

Morris lost ships as well. Some were captured; some mutinied; some simply disappeared. When in the fall of 1775 Congress awarded him its largest munitions contract yet, the Philadelphia merchant insisted that the government cover the cost of insurance. Franklin, signing on behalf of Congress, readily agreed to this condition, and Morris was advanced £80,000 to smuggle thirty thousand pounds of gunpowder from Europe. With powder selling at £14 a barrel, he stood to make a profit of over £12,000. Morris had been well off before the outbreak of fighting. If he succeeded in delivering this powder, he would in a single stroke become one of the richest men in America.

When word of this contract reached Congress, radicals erupted in fury. Specifically, they demanded to know whether the insurance Morris had asked for would cover just the loss of the powder or the entire voyage along with his profits. Neither Morris nor Franklin was present to explain the details, but Thomas Willing, serving as a Pennsylvania delegate, defended his business partner. Morris was above all a "man of reason and generosity," he assured his fellow delegates. If the terms of the contract were deemed objectionable, Morris would undoubtedly accede to any changes.

Willing's assurances did little to mollify the opposition, however. Eliphalet Dyer of Connecticut objected that the real problem was less the insurance than the size of Morris's potential profits. Earning such an enormous sum from a patriotic cause struck him as wrong. "There are not ten men in the colony I come from," he declared, "who are worth so much as will be made clear by this contract."

Morris's supporters struck back. George Ross, a colleague from the Pennsylvania Committee of Public Safety, asked Dyer, "What does this matter to the present debate, whether Connecticut men are worth much or no?" Before Dyer could answer, he continued, "It proves that there are no men there whose capital or credit are equal to such contracts. That is all."[6]

As the debate heated up, other moderates rose to defend Morris. If America was to stand any chance against Britain, they argued, all its resources had to be brought to bear. This included mobilizing its merchants, who were entitled to make a profit given the risks they ran in securing powder. The moderates persuaded Congress on this point, for two days later Willing and Morris were awarded yet another contract for powder and arms.

Yet the deeper question raised by this debate remained unresolved—namely, what was the propriety of profit? The dispute between the opposing factions in Congress was a direct continuation of the clash between Court and Country in England half a century before. And it was a disagreement that would continue to pit left against right in America for decades to come. For congressional radicals, who held rigidly to Country ideology, excess profit was an affront to the republican spirit of self-sacrifice. For moderates, as for the Court Whigs before them, recognizing the centrality of self-interest was just simple realism.

Few represented the radical view better than Richard Henry Lee. "The Spirit of Commerce," he declared, "is a Spirit of Avarice." It wasn't that Lee objected to profit per se; he was after all a wealthy plantation owner. What he and other radicals opposed was large-scale capitalism. The unfettered pursuit of property endangered republics because it so easily grew out of control. "Whenever the power is given," Lee said, "the will certainly follows to monopolize, to engross, and to take every possible advantage."[7] He scoffed at the claim that self-interest could be good for society. "I know there are Mandevilles," he wrote, "who laugh at virtue, and with vain ostentatious display of words will deduce from vice, public good! . . . He who increases in wealth in such times as the present, must be an enemy to his country, be his pretensions what they may."[8]

The radical position was not merely theoretical. Throughout the colonies, ad hoc committees were springing up to establish price controls, prevent monopolies, and threaten violence against anyone who made more money than was deemed acceptable. Attempts to regulate the economy were bound to succeed, radicals believed, because Americans, as a virtuous people, would gladly sacrifice their self-interest for the good of the state. Such views were not confined to the lower classes. Henry Laurens, one of the few South Carolina aristocrats to side with New England radicals, declared, "Reduce us all to poverty and cut off or wisely restrict that bane of patriotism, Commerce, and we shall soon become patriots, but how hard is it for a rich or covetous man to enter heartily into the kingdom of patriotism."[9]

For the American right, this view was profoundly wrong. "Public virtue is not so active as private love of gain," John Jay countered. Far from making America stronger, he believed, the radical position would hinder the war effort and damage the economy. "Shall we shut the door against private enterprise?" he asked. Entrepreneurship was what America needed, not legislative interference. Only by unleashing the power of free enterprise would the colonies overcome the shortage of military supplies. "We have more to expect from the enterprise, activity and industry of private adventurers," Jay wrote, "than from the lukewarmness of assemblies."[10]

Perhaps the most eloquent defense of the free market was delivered by Lee's longtime nemesis, Carter Braxton. For more than a generation, the aristocratic Braxtons and upstart Lees had feuded over Virginia politics. And for more than a decade, Carter Braxton had battled Richard Henry Lee in the colony's House of Burgesses. A ruddy-faced planter who had wiled away his youth in London, Braxton had the elegant manners and bored demeanor of many highborn Virginians. Many of his family members were Loyalists, but throughout the mounting crisis with Britain, Braxton fought ardently for American rights.

Braxton was a close business associate of Morris's, and his attacks on radical economics were every bit as fierce as the Pennsylvanian's. His "Address to the Convention of the Colony and Ancient Dominion of Virginia" of 1776 was a comprehensive refutation of Lee's ideas, which he saw as influenced by the "leveling" tendencies of New England. Above all, Braxton believed, the radical position was profoundly naïve. Its assumption that human beings could somehow suppress their own interest was Utopian, "a mere creature of a warm imagination."[11] The hard reality, he wrote, was that men enjoyed making money.

"A disinterested attachment to the public good, exclusive and independent of all private and selfish interest," he declared, "never characterized the mass of the people of any state." The key to man's happiness in fact was self-interest, when "he acts for himself, and with a view of promoting his own particular welfare." Radical republicans could not abide this idea and hence proposed laws meant to curb wealth and luxury. "To this species of government," he continued, "everything that looks like elegance and refinement is inimical however necessary to the introduction of manufacturers, and the cultivation of arts and sciences."

In countries with fewer natural resources, Braxton conceded, the harsh strictures of classical republicanism might work, but they ran counter to the acquisitive spirit of America. Americans would forever demand, he said, the right to enjoy the fruits of their labor "unrestrained by any ideal principle of governments" and to acquire property "without regarding the whimsical impropriety of being richer than their neighbors." Fearing the effect Braxton's treatise might have on Virginia politics, Lee immediately branded it "a contemptible little tract." Patrick Henry attacked it as showing "too great a bias to aristocracy." As a sign of just how dangerous Braxton's Virginian enemies viewed his essay, they enlisted John Adams to pen a fierce rebuttal as well. Braxton's ideas, Adams fulminated, were simply "too absurd to be considered twice."[12]

One of the main reasons Robert Morris came to oppose Britain was its heavy-handed attempt to control American commerce. Now similar efforts were under way in America, and Morris was not about to let his fellow colonists infringe on his right to make money. "I assert boldly that commerce ought to be free as the air," he said.[13] When Congress proposed creating a Chamber of Commerce to regulate American trade and manufacturing, Morris was outraged. "Do they mean to combine the jarring interests of these states into commercial systems that will adapt the minds of their respective traders?" he asked one congressman. "It is impossible. Do they mean to lay restrictions and form regulations? They are pernicious."

Like Adam Smith and David Hume, Morris believed that the market would regulate itself. Like John Jay and Carter Braxton, he believed that private enterprise, not government regulation, would solve America's supply problems. "Our traders are remarkable for their spirit and daily forming those enterprises you wish for," Morris wrote. "Their own interest and the public good go hand in hand and they need no other prompter or tutor." There simply was no conflict between public and private interest, as radicals insisted.

Throughout the colonies, local militias, which were heavily dominated by the lower classes, began enforcing restrictions on commerce. As vice president of the Committee of Public Safety, Morris had already had several run-ins with radical militiamen. Despite being authorized by the Assembly to organize Pennsylvania's militia companies, the committee ran into a surprising amount of resistance not from Tories but from the militias themselves. Only "the people," radicals declared, had the right to issue orders, not a committee dominated by the city's elite. Radical militiamen objected to military regulations and to low pay. And they insisted on appointing their own officers, a long-standing practice among New England militias. To the upper classes, this was yet another pernicious sign of Massachusetts leveling and a practice that Washington was in the process of furiously stamping out among Continental troops.

The militia's propensity to direct violence against the upper classes as well as at the British was becoming a growing concern for Morris. After a local attorney with Tory leanings named Isaac Hunt appeared before the Committee of Public Safety to defend a merchant accused of violating trade restrictions, a mob of radical militiamen seized him from his home and paraded him around town in a cart while people hurled rocks at him. Hunt meekly apologized to the crowd and was eventually let go before worse harm could come to him. The militiamen then descended on the home of another well-known Tory, Dr. John Kearsley, who was an old friend of Morris's from the St. George Society. Far rasher than Hunt, Kearsley thrust a pistol out his window and threatened to kill any man who entered his house. The militiamen slashed his hand with a bayonet, beat him up, and pushed him into their cart, intending to tar and feather him after parading him through the streets. While the disheveled doctor bled profusely and shouted himself hoarse, a drummer marched along tapping the lightly mocking beat of "The Rogue's March." Eventually, the mob freed Kearsley out of pity, but when he returned home, he found all his windows smashed.

Enraged, Kearsley promptly wrote several letters to the British ministry promising to raise five thousand Loyalist troops to fight the Patriots and begging for reinforcements. He also sent detailed plans of the Delaware, indicating safe landing points for British troops. When the letters were discovered sewn into a woman's garment aboard a ship bound for London, the old doctor was arrested and brought before the Committee of Public Safety. Morris, as acting chairman, had to sentence his old friend to prison. Kearsley was also expelled from the St. George Society and had all his lands confiscated. The sentence was soon commuted to exile in the frontier town of Carlisle, where the doctor went insane and died shortly thereafter.

The incident may well have been a tipping point for Morris, because within days he decided he had to do more to counter the growing tide of radicalism. In October he decided to run for a seat in the Pennsylvania Assembly. He had never before stood for elected office—in the past he had been content to let Willing stand as their firm's public face. Morris's lack of political experience was not held against him, though, and he proved popular with voters. Even radicals could not deny his contributions to the American cause.

Soon after taking his seat in the Assembly, Morris was elected to Congress, which immediately made the most of his organizational talents. Within weeks he was appointed to three of its most important committees: the Committee of Trade, also known as the Secret Committee; the Committee for Secret

Correspondence, the forerunner of the U.S. State Department; and the Marine Committee, which oversaw the construction of America's first navy. Combined, these three assignments made Morris one of the most powerful men in Congress. He was soon running American finances, foreign affairs, and naval warfare. The work was so dangerous and so clandestine that no other congressman was privy to as much secret information as Morris. "I well know," wrote his business partner John Langdon, "that almost the whole of the business must pass through your hands."[14]

Morris's work for the Secret Committee, which soon elected him chairman, overlapped with his activities on the Pennsylvania Public Safety Committee. Now, however, he was in charge of weapons acquisitions for the entire Continental Army. His hand was everywhere, signing contracts for muskets, cartridges, and gunpowder; consolidating military supply networks; selling booty seized by American privateers. With money in short supply and many foreign merchants unwilling to accept Continental currency, Morris established elaborate bartering schemes that traded American tobacco, rice, indigo, and lumber for weapons.

Still, massive amounts of money were needed to fuel this trade, and only private merchants had the wherewithal to funnel large sums around the Atlantic. Since discretion was paramount, Morris awarded government contracts only to trusted businessmen, namely his friends and trading partners. He trusted no firm more than his own, which was one of the few on the continent capable of meeting the army's needs. Between 1775 and 1777 almost a quarter of all payments from Congress went through Willing and Morris, some $483,000 out of more than $2 million. Morris always endeavored to make a handsome return, even on supplies that were essential to the army. "I have agreed for the medicines at prices that will yield us fine profits," he wrote to the merchant William Bingham. "The profits on these adventures when they do arrive will equal one's most sanguine wishes."[15]

Morris did more than just take advantage of wartime shortages. On occasion he induced them. He proposed one such scheme to his fellow merchant John Bradford. "What think you of buying up in your state all such prize goods (not perishable) as sell cheap and laying them by awhile," Morris wrote. "This year's fares must be nearly over and it's a long time to the next crop of West Indian produce."[16] Another time he urged the merchant Jonathan Hudson to "hurry them [the goods] back as soon as possible," since scarcity would certainly "raise prices in Carolina."[17] Morris later assured Hudson that "we have nothing to do but make money as fast as we can."[18]At the same time, he never lost sight of his duty to the American cause. Throughout his correspondence,

Morris emphasized the principle that he and his fellow merchants could "sell for immense profits and at the same time be most useful to America."

Nowhere was the intersection of Morris's business interests and national security more apparent than in the creation of the Continental Navy. He had already worked extensively with Dickinson on strengthening Pennsylvania's maritime defenses. All along the Delaware, they had overseen the construction of fortresses and launched a provincial navy made of sleek, oar-driven boats with large cannons fixed to the bow. To hinder the passage of enemy ships, they had ordered lines of sharpened spikes sunk into the river bottom; only trusted river pilots were told their secret locations.

Morris's lobbying for a navy stemmed as much from his desire to protect American shipping as from his wish to defend the coastline from the British fleet. He also saw the need for ships capable of delivering secret correspondence to American agents throughout Europe, many of whom, of course, doubled as his own in commercial matters. Based on Morris's recommendations, Congress decided to build five ships and appointed him to a new naval committee. No one else on the committee possessed the depth of Morris's shipping experience, and within a matter of months, he essentially became the first commander of the American navy. In addition to overseeing its construction and operations, he began shepherding the careers of promising young commanders such as John Paul Jones and John Barry.

In searching for a suitable candidate for America's first warship, Morris looked no further than his own docks. In September he bought the *Black Prince* from Willing and Morris and began transforming the merchant ship into a fighting vessel. He then began buying and retrofitting other ships and ordered the construction of a dozen more. Since his firm was so heavily involved in the process, his waterside offices soon doubled as the headquarters of the new Continental Navy. With his warehouse brimming with valuable rigging, weaponry, and provisions, soldiers of the Continental Army stood guard outside.

If radicals felt uncomfortable with Morris's immense profits, their discomfort doubled as the concentration of power in the hands of one man increased. They had already begun blackening Morris's reputation while he worked as a private contractor to Congress. Now that he largely monopolized American defense, finance, and diplomacy, accusations of malfeasance multiplied. In Congress, Richard Henry Lee led the charge against Morris's practice of cornering the market. "No person living detests more than I do the pernicious practice of engrossing, especially the necessities of life," the Virginian wrote to Patrick Henry. "'Tis begotten of avarice or inhumanity and deserves every kind of discouragement. I have spoken to Mr. Morris."[19]

What evidence of corruption Richard Henry Lee presented was supplied largely by his younger brother Arthur. "Mr. Morris might have paid for all his private purchases out of the public treasury," the younger Lee declared.[20] He could not have had any actual proof of embezzlement, since he resided in London at the time, but he was relentless in his campaign against Morris. Based on Lee's whisperings, Henry Laurens openly accused Morris of writing off a cargo of tobacco that had been confiscated by the British by shifting it from a private to a public ledger, a charge that proved false upon investigation. Nevertheless these attacks began to wear Morris down. While it was difficult for radicals to prove their charges, Morris found it difficult to prove his innocence, largely because he kept the bookkeeping entries for the government and his own firm deliberately jumbled together. For security reasons, all military transactions had to be disguised as commercial ones. But some of the confusion also stemmed from slipshod accounting. A detailed examination of his records has led some historians to conclude that he never repaid the government for some $80,000 in loans. It remains unclear whether this discrepancy was simple oversight or outright misappropriation. To the end, Morris maintained his probity. Nor would these attacks make him quit. "I shall," he wrote his friend Silas Deane, "continue to discharge my duty faithfully to the public and pursue my private fortune by all such honorable and fair means."[21]

One thing Morris could not do was prevent his jobs from taking their physical toll on him. With the possible exception of Dickinson, no man in Congress worked so hard. By February 1776, Morris was complaining of failing eyesight, brought about from being "harassed the whole time by much public business, of which . . . more than one man's share falls to my lot."[22] Ironically, Dickinson's great enemy was one of the few radicals who recognized Morris's great worth. "You ask me what you are to think of Robert Morris?" John Adams wrote to a fellow delegate. "I'll tell you what I think of him. I think he has a masterly understanding, an open temper and an honest heart." The New Englander was forced to concede that "he has vast designs in the mercantile way, and no doubt pursues mercantile ends, which are always gain; but he is an excellent member of our body."[23]

Part of the stress Morris was feeling was due to the staggering difficulty of what he was trying to accomplish. Like Dickinson, he sought to defend American rights while staving off the radical push for independence. And it did not help that George III was playing directly into the radicals' hands. On November 1, 1775, Congress learned that the King had rejected the Olive Branch Petition. In fact, George refused to receive any document from the American Congress. The colonies, he declared before Parliament, were now in "open and avowed rebellion."[24]

Tall and handsome with soft blue eyes, George preferred a quiet life on his farm with his wife and fifteen children to the intrigues and squabbles of his ministers at court. (The fact that he remained faithful to his wife also never ceased to shock.) But the King's response to American demands was anything but mild. Only military force, he asserted, would bring the colonists to heel. A "desperate conspiracy" was afoot in America, he was convinced, just as radicals were certain that a cabal of British ministers was plotting against American liberties. In fact, George believed, Congress was "preparing for a general revolt . . . carried on for the purpose of establishing an independent empire"—moderate calls for reconciliation notwithstanding.[25] If anything was responsible for the widening split with Britain, it was runaway conspiracy theories on both sides of the Atlantic.

On a wet, chilly afternoon in February 1776, Morris received word that one of his merchant vessels had just arrived from Bristol. British officials had temporarily detained the ship after discovering a letter addressed to a Philadelphia merchant, but eventually the ship was allowed to depart after the captain swore he was bound for Cork. The ship's most precious cargo escaped detection: hidden at the bottom of a bread barrel, "placed in a careless manner, as if for the ship's use," were several letters addressed to Morris.[26]

The news these letters bore was alarming. In order to punish the colonies, Morris's correspondents informed him, Parliament had just passed the American Prohibitory Act. This measure went far beyond targeting the rebellion in New England. According to the act's terms, all American ships sailing for Britain and the British West Indies would be seized as of January 1, 1776. Then, starting March 1, all American ships entering the colonies would be seized, and beginning June 1, all foreign ships would be as well. For a people utterly dependent upon international commerce, there could be no more brutal form of economic warfare, and of all the actions taken against the colonies, none did more to turn the public against Britain. As John Adams put it, the act "throws thirteen colonies out of the royal protection . . . and makes us independent in spite of our supplications and entreaties."[27]

In addition to a copy of the act, Morris's correspondence included other dismaying intelligence. Most frightening was the revelation that the Crown was raising an invasion force of twenty-six thousand men, among whom were large numbers of foreign mercenaries. To many, it was confirmation that George III had become a tyrant. Morris also learned where the British planned to attack. Two of the landing sites, Boston and Virginia, were to be expected. But when it was learned that New York and South Carolina were also to be attacked, the American right began to despair. Along with the middle provinces, these two colonies were bastions of moderate sentiment.

The following day Morris brought his correspondence to the State House to share with his fellow delegates. Silence reigned as Congress heard the Prohibitory Act read aloud. Only one hope for accommodation remained. Congress had also just received word that Britain's prime minister, Lord North, was sending peace commissioners to negotiate on behalf of the Crown. For moderates, it was a final thread of hope at a time when the basic fabric of government and society appeared to be unraveling. Boosting their optimism was news that the minority faction in Parliament, led by the Marquis of Rockingham and Dickinson's old classmate, Edmund Burke, would continue to argue for American rights so long as the colonies shunned independence. At all costs, moderates believed, both British aggression and radical agitation had to be resisted, because the "commissioners are certainly coming out to treat."[28]

CHAPTER 8

YIELDING TO THE TORRENT

While browsing in Robert Aitken's Philadelphia bookstore in early 1775, Dr. Benjamin Rush struck up a conversation with a shabbily dressed Englishman with a magnetic personality. Blue-eyed, with wavy hair and a nose afflicted by a touch of rosacea, Thomas Paine had arrived in the colonies just a year before. True to American tradition, he had wasted no time reinventing himself. In England he had worked as a corset maker, a privateer, a preacher, a servant, and a customs official. In these numerous occupations, he had never made much money, and what little he earned he preferred spending on philosophy lectures rather than on new clothes. When the thirty-eight-year-old arrived in Philadelphia, however, he possessed something more valuable than pounds sterling: a letter of introduction from Benjamin Franklin, whom he had met in London. Impressed by his high connections and eloquence, Aitken had hired Paine to work at his bookshop and to edit his *Pennsylvania Magazine* for £50 a year.

Rush and Paine immediately hit it off. Though the doctor deplored Paine's lack of religion, he admired his politics, especially after reading an essay Paine wrote attacking slavery. He also thought Paine might be able to help with something that had been troubling him. In late 1775 Rush began composing an essay urging Americans to back independence. Paine, he decided, was far better suited to the task. As a stranger to Philadelphia, the Englishman had relatively little reputation to lose.

"I suggested to him that he had nothing to fear from the popular odium to which such a publication might expose him," Rush wrote, "for he could live anywhere." The doctor, however, had too many personal and professional ties to the city, "where a great majority of the citizens and some of my friends were hostile to a separation of our country from Great Britain."

As Paine churned out pages, he would go to Rush's house to read them aloud and ask for suggestions. For his personal safety, Rush urged Paine to avoid two words—"independence and republicanism."[1] The good doctor had little else to add but advised him to show the composition to Franklin, who had recently returned to America, and probably also to Samuel Adams. Rush's most significant contribution was the title. Paine had wanted to name his long essay "Plain Truth." Rush thought "Common Sense" had a nicer ring.

When it was finally published in January 1776, *Common Sense* did more to electrify Americans than any piece of writing since the *Letters from a Farmer in Pennsylvania*. Paine's simple style connected with common Americans in a way that Dickinson's learned elocutions never had. He stated forthrightly and clearly what few colonists outside New England dared to say. (He also ignored Rush's warning about the words *independence* and *republicanism*.) He argued that Parliament was not the real problem America faced. It was the King himself, and the sooner America got rid of him, the better. All of English law and history supported this seemingly radical conclusion.

"'Tis the Republican and not the monarchical part of the constitution of England which Englishmen glory in," he wrote. "It is easy to see that when republican virtue fails, slavery ensues. Why is the constitution of England sickly? But because monarchy hath poisoned the republic."[2]

Paine signed his essay only "an Englishman," but he did not remain anonymous long. Far from being targeted by angry mobs, as Rush had feared, he became an instant celebrity. Within months more than one hundred thousand copies had been printed and circulated throughout the colonies. It is no exaggeration to say that Paine's ideas were discussed in almost every coffeehouse, home, and church in America.

Yet the fact remained that large numbers of Americans opposed independence. At the same moment Paine was composing *Common Sense,* six colonies were specifically instructing their delegates not to vote for independence, Dickinson himself drafting Pennsylvania's resolution. Nearly half of the colonies, in other words, continued to resist the radical agenda.

Nowhere was the debate over *Common Sense* fiercer than within the ranks of the American right. Until 1776 the main conflict had been merely over how far to press the case for American rights. All moderates had opposed independence, even as they attacked British policy. Loyalists also opposed independence and fully backed the Crown. Both sides had hitherto agreed that the benefits of continued British rule outweighed its drawbacks. For a century and a half, England had protected the colonies and kept the peace among them. Its political institutions had provided social stability, and its trade networks had generated unprecedented prosperity. At a stroke, independence would undermine many of the social, legal, and economic pillars of American life. The publication of *Common Sense,* however, fractured all sense of right-wing accord.

What alarmed many elites was that resistance to Britain was degenerating into revolution. Much as they wished to defend American rights, they could not countenance the massive social upheaval independence would bring. "This convulsion has, indeed, brought all the dregs to the top," wrote a worried James Allen of Pennsylvania.[3] As a result, Paine's essay created almost as many new Tories as it did radicals.

Back in late 1775, for example, Allen had cursed George III as a monarch "as despotic as any prince in Europe." Yet a few months later he found himself defecting to the Loyalists. "I love the cause of liberty," he explained, "but cannot heartily join the prosecution of measures totally foreign to the original plan of resistance. The madness of the multitude is but one degree better than submission to the Tea Act."[4]

The great divide at the heart of the American right boiled down to a central problem of modern politics: how does one deal with change? In a world that had known little of it for centuries, learning how to deal with social upheaval was painful for many. In their approach to change, Tories were essentially reactionary. They clung to the status quo, hoping to turn back the clock. But in refusing to accept the inevitable, they were sowing the seeds of their irrelevance. For all practical purposes, they had ceased to play any active role in shaping American political thought.

The remaining moderates, on the other hand, took a far more pragmatic approach. Some sort of compromise, they believed, was essential. They did not like the turmoil they were witnessing any better than the Tories did, but they realized that if all the elites abandoned the fight against Britain, the radicals would take over entirely. And that threatened a total breakdown of American society. "Licentiousness is the natural effect of a civil discord," warned James Duane, "and it can only be guarded against" if "men of property and rank" stay in charge.[5] Keeping these men in the fight would not be easy. As Robert Livingston noted, "two thirds of our gentlemen fell off early in this controversy."[6]

By early 1776 men like Dickinson, Morris, Wilson, Jay, Livingston, Braxton, and the Rutledge brothers were coming to a profound realization: revolution was coming, and there was nothing they could do about it. They could stand in its way and be knocked aside; or they could hold on tight and guide it as best they could. It was a stark choice, but as they now began to understand, their role was no longer to oppose independence categorically. It was to uphold order and conserve tradition amid unprecedented upheaval.

Accepting the inevitability of change was more than a simple survival strategy. It also represented a major breakthrough in political thought and a remarkable insight into the nature of modernity. Clearly, these men did not invent political expediency. Rather, they created what might be called obstructive compromise: accepting just enough change in order to keep it firmly under control.

No one articulated this new philosophy better than Robert Livingston, who advocated "the propriety of swimming with a stream which it is impossible to stem." As he advised his fellow remaining moderates, they would have to "yield to the torrent if they hope to direct its course."[7]

Now what they needed most of all was time: time to establish American political and social institutions before the old British ones were swept away; time to strengthen and build the army; time to establish a proper government; time to unite a still deeply divided populace. The critical difference between radicals and the remaining moderates was no longer over whether to declare independence but when. They would make sure the moment came as slowly as possible.

Truth be told, these men were hardly "moderate" anymore. With the Tories out of the picture, they now represented the far right of America's political spectrum. As the historian Charles Page Smith points out, there was more than a little irony to this situation: "The extreme right wing had been displaced and the conservatives were the old radicals—men like Dickinson, Cushing, and Willing."[8] One final crucible remained, however, before they could truly be called America's founding conservatives. For now John Adams's name for them—"Mr. Dickinson and his party"[9]—would have to suffice.

While radicals were predicting a quick and easy victory, Dickinson and his allies knew the coming war would be calamitous, whether or not America won. How would a nation with no organized government, no money, no foreign allies, no navy, and no weapons defeat the mightiest military machine in the world? Lives would be lost, property destroyed, and liberties trampled. Robert Morris had personal concerns as well. "A revolution, war, the dissolution of government, the creating of it anew, cruelty, rapine, and devastation in the midst of our very bowels," he wrote to Franklin. "These, sir, are circumstances by no means favorable to finance."[10]

As the right saw it, declaring independence too soon was just as perilous as not declaring it at all. Independence was "a delusive bait which men inconsiderately catch at, without knowing the hook to which it is affixed," Carter Braxton warned. "It is an object to be wished for by every American, when it can be attained with safety and honor. That this is not the moment I will prove."[11]

But simply trying to delay independence was not much of a strategy. What was needed was a systematic plan to bolster American strength abroad and at home. In a letter to his uncle, Braxton outlined four crucial issues that needed to be addressed before independence could safely be declared. First, he wrote, Congress needed to hear from the peace delegation that George III was sending to America. Many wanted "to await the terms to be offered by Commissioners." While it was unlikely anything substantive would be proposed, Braxton thought it essential to hear them out before formally separating with Britain.[12] Then "America with one united voice," Braxton wrote, could justifiably declare independence.

The second critical problem that needed to be addressed was America's lack of foreign allies. While radicals argued that such alliances could be found after independence, Dickinson and his faction declared it the height of folly to break with Britain without support from a major European power. The colonies simply lacked the resources to win a war.

Securing a foreign ally would not be easy. Any country backing the colonies risked a war with Britain. France, America's best hope for support, had little desire to meddle in what it saw as an internal British matter. And with English spies lurking everywhere, even the appearance of consideration for the colonies carried risks. What America needed, therefore, was a secret representative at the French court, and Robert Morris knew just the man—someone who could negotiate for French diplomatic support, secure weapons, and, needless to say, engage in private business for the benefit of Willing and Morris.

In early March 1776, Morris selected Silas Deane, a Connecticut Yankee who had served in the First Continental Congress. New England radicals had made sure Deane was not returned to the Second Congress after he had shown too much sympathy for the moderates, but the contacts and friendships he had made in Philadelphia, especially with Morris, allowed him to stay involved in the war effort and to profit handsomely in business. Deane's mission was kept so secret that few congressmen outside the Secret Committee initially knew of his commission, which was to "go to France, there to transact such business, commercial and political, as we have committed to his care, in behalf and by authority of the Congress of the Thirteen United Colonies."[13]

When news of the appointment finally leaked out, radicals erupted in fury. Here, they said, was yet one more sign that merchants were putting their own interests ahead of the nation's. They were especially disgusted that Deane would receive a commission of five percent on all remittances. When Morris began soliciting Congress for letters of introduction and character testimonials for Deane to take to France, Sam and John Adams refused to help. Their plans to antagonize Deane, however, were just beginning.

In order to mislead British spies, Morris supplied Deane with false papers stating he was a merchant from Bermuda. Just to make sure the cover story was watertight, Morris actually sent Deane off to Bermuda in April 1776, then hired a ship there to take him across the Atlantic. The crew were told their destination was England. Only when the ship had made it safely across the Atlantic did Deane order a change of course for Spain. From there he made his way overland to France. In July he finally reached his destination, where he set about purchasing clothing and muskets for twenty-five thousand men, opening what he thought were secret negotiations with the French (though his own secretary would turn out to be a British spy), and doing whatever else he thought necessary to help the war effort.

Yet as important as it was to secure a foreign alliance, caution remained essential. Many on the right feared that America might escape British domination only to find itself under the thumb of another European power. "Would such a blind, precipitate measure as this be justified by prudence," Braxton asked, "first to throw off our Connection with Great Britain and then give ourselves up to the Arms of France?" After all, he pointed out, the French court was already "so famous for intrigues and deception" that it would without a doubt "avail herself of our situation" and try to take advantage of the colonies. That was why signing a deal before declaring independence was so vital. Much better terms could be negotiated at this point. Afterward America would become totally dependent on France.

The third danger posed by a rush to independence was the specter of civil war among the colonies. Festering territorial disagreements between them were already turning deadly, especially between New England and the middle colonies. In December 1775, for example, Pennsylvania had sent detachments of militia to attack Connecticut farmers who were occupying the Wyoming Valley in the northern part of the province. Connecticut then sent in hundreds of armed forces to protect its settlers. The situation continued to deteriorate, and a few years later the Pennsylvania militia attacked again, leaving scores of settlers injured. Throughout the colonies, in fact, conflicts were erupting wherever provinces disputed territorial rights. In Vermont,

New York landowners such as James Duane clashed with New England farmers who were occupying land claimed by the New Yorkers. Similar territorial strains in Maryland and Virginia also threatened to tear the colonies apart.

Without a central authority to arbitrate these claims, many feared that America would splinter into rival regional powers. Until now, the British government had kept a lid on these simmering tensions, usually siding with the middle colonies. Many on the right suspected that New England's alacrity to throw off Britain's yoke stemmed in part from a desire to gain territory at its neighbors' expense. If such territorial disputes were not carefully addressed, Braxton warned, "the Continent would be torn in pieces by intestine Wars and Convulsions."

The fourth and final danger America faced was a general lack of unity. In late 1775 Dickinson, who was urging the colonies "to keep up the appearance of an unbroken harmony," was alarmed when New Jersey proposed sending its own peace petition to the King. Spurred by its Loyalist governor, William Franklin, the illegitimate son of Ben, the New Jersey legislature was now threatening to break ranks with the other colonies. Such moves, Dickinson saw, were dangerous. If the colonies did not stand united, Britain would pick off the rebellious ones one by one, guaranteeing the establishment of tyranny in all of them. On December 5, 1775, Jay and Dickinson rode the seventy miles from Philadelphia to Perth Amboy, New Jersey's provincial capital, where "they harangued the House for about an hour."

"Petitions [are] not now the means," declared Jay, who refused to present a similar New York plan for reconciliation to Congress. "Vigor and unanimity [are] the only means." The time for separate petitions was gone. Only a "petition of United America presented by Congress ought to be relied on." In the end, wrote an irritated Governor Franklin, the two congressmen "persuaded [him] to drop the design."[14]

The surest way to ensure American unity, Dickinson and his party now believed, was to form a single nation and found a central government. They had previously opposed such proposals, arguing that a rush to nationhood would actually create more havoc than harmony. But by mid-1776 it was clear that the creation of a confederation of states was now every bit as important as a formal declaration of independence.

"A grand Continental League must be formed and a superintending power also," Carter Braxton wrote. "When these necessary Steps are taken and I see a Coalition formed sufficient to withstand the power of Britain or any other, then am I for an independent State and all its Consequences, as then I think they will produce happiness to America. It is a true saying of a wit—we must hang together or separately."[15]

The right's arguments for delay persuaded many in Congress. In the resulting stalemate, it became clear that any declaration of independence would be put off by at least half a year, and perhaps by longer. The radicals were horrified. To men like Sam and John Adams and their Virginia allies, social upheaval was of little importance. "Was there ever a revolution brought about, especially as important as this, without great internal tumults & violent convulsions?" asked Sam Adams.[16] Even his cousin John, who was far more traditionalist in his disposition, could not wait to reengineer American society. In a letter to Richard Henry Lee, he approved strongly of a group of revolutionaries "pulling down tyrannies at a single exertion, and erecting such new fabrics as it thinks best calculated to promote its happiness."[17] Never would Dickinson and his allies dream of tearing down the old and replacing it with the new so blithely.

So fevered was the radicals' rush to independence that they began threatening to break up the colonies. If the middle colonies would not join them, Sam Adams warned, New England might form a separate confederation to fight Britain on its own. "Judas Iscariot," as the Philadelphia lawyer Edward Tilghman called Sam Adams, "made a motion" in which "whole colonies threatened to leave Congress."[18]

With the animosity between the Adams and Dickinson factions crescendoing, radicals decided the only way they could win was to play dirty. What open debate had failed to accomplish, innuendo and backroom machinations would get done. In February Arthur Lee, who was still in London, began spreading rumors that the New Yorkers Jay, Duane, and Livingston were spying for the British.[19] Soon afterward his brother Richard Henry Lee started spreading rumors that Jay's well-regarded "Address to the British People" had actually been composed by Jay's father-in-law.

Just how seriously eighteenth-century gentlemen took their literary reputations was made clear by Jay's relatively mild response to Arthur Lee's allegations. But when he heard that Richard Henry Lee had impugned his honor as an author, Jay marched up to him in the State House yard and shook him by the buttons on his jacket, insisting that the Virginian admit to spreading lies. Jefferson, who was quietly standing nearby, stepped between the two men saying he had heard the rumors too, but not from Lee. Jay relaxed his grip and stormed off.

As influential as the New York delegates were in delaying independence, it was clear to radicals that Dickinson posed the real problem. If they wanted to accelerate the split with Britain, they would have to destroy his clout within the Pennsylvania government. Dickinson's reputation remained unassailable: in mid-February he had marched through Philadelphia at the head of four militia battalions, ascended to a rostrum, and praised the soldiers' courage and sense of duty. Even John Adams had been impressed, writing his wife that Dickinson's action "becomes his character and sets a fine example, is much talked of and applauded."[20] If Dickinson could not be touched, then Pennsylvania's government itself would have to be demolished. The only question was how.

On May 6, 1776, Philadelphia buzzed with the news that two British men-of-war, the forty-four-gun *Liverpool* and the twenty-two-gun *Roebuck,* had passed through the mouth of the Delaware and were heading toward Philadelphia. Their combined firepower would easily level the city. The resulting frenzy was too good an opportunity to pass up. Rising before Congress, John Adams demanded that all colonies that had ordered their delegates not to vote for independence now be required to "repeal or suspend those instructions for a time." The motion failed, but anxiety continued to mount.

The next day the distant thunder of cannon fire could be heard throughout the city. Thirteen Pennsylvania galleys, all armed and organized by Dickinson and Morris, had emerged from the shallows to engage the enemy vessels with "courage and conduct," as an American prisoner aboard the *Roebuck* reported. "The *Roebuck* received many shots betwixt wind and water; some went through, some in her quarter, and was much raked fore and aft."[21] Its rigging shredded, the warship was run aground and quickly surrounded. But under the looming protection of the *Liverpool,* it managed to free itself. The next day both men-of-war resumed their course toward Philadelphia, chased by the Pennsylvania galleys.

Thousands of people swarmed the riverfront, as the explosions grew closer and the acrid scent of gunpowder choked the air. By dusk the battle sounds were deafening. Observers counted sixty blasts in seven minutes. And then abrupt silence: the British ships had tacked and sailed away. The cheering that erupted probably was not as euphoric as might have been expected. Until then, the war had always been distant, confined to Massachusetts and cold northern woods. Now Philadelphia was on the front lines, and the gravity of that fact began to sink in. A mightier British force might sail up the Delaware anytime, and then Philadelphia might not be so lucky.

Something changed in the city that day, and the Adams-Lee junto could sense it. It was the moment they had been waiting for. They now set into motion the coup that they had been planning within the Pennsylvania government. "It was a measure which I had invariably pursued for a whole year," John Adams wrote.[22]

If they could overthrow the Pennsylvania Assembly, Dickinson's power base, and replace it with a radical government, independence would be theirs. Pennsylvania was the keystone to revolution for many reasons. Not only was it the most populous colony, but it was also the political and financial capital of America. As Pennsylvania went, so went all the middle colonies.

In a series of behind-the-scenes maneuvers, the Adams-Lee faction coordinated with Pennsylvania radicals to oust the Pennsylvania Assembly. It would then be, as Richard Henry Lee wrote, "adieu to Proprietary influence and timid senseless politics."[23] A new radical-led government would thereupon order Pennsylvania's congressional delegates to vote for independence.

On May 10, two days after the naval battle on the Delaware, Adams got himself appointed to a committee assigned "to prepare a resolution recommending to the people of the States to institute governments." He then made sure the committee "requested me to draft a resolve."[24] In itself, the resolution was not inflammatory. That was part of Adams's plan. It simply recommended the creation of new governments in any colonies "where no government sufficient to the exigencies of their affairs have been hitherto established."[25]

Since Pennsylvania already had a stable, functioning government, Dickinson voted for Adams's resolution. The colony's Charter of Privileges of 1701 was still in effect, protecting rights of its citizens and granting the Assembly sole legislative authority. Pennsylvania's government was so "sufficient to the exigencies" of the situation, in fact, that it was supplying more troops and matériel to the war effort than any other. Dickinson had no reason to see any threat in the resolution.

On May 13 Adams sprang his trap. With the help of Richard Henry Lee, he submitted a preamble to his resolution that made Dickinson and his allies shudder. Adams read aloud before Congress: "It is necessary that the exercise of every kind of authority under the said Crown should be totally suppressed, and all powers of government exerted under the authority of the people of the colonies."[26]

It took just moments for these words to sink in. If Adams's preamble passed, any colonial government deriving its power from the Crown would be legally nullified—including Pennsylvania's, whose charter had been granted by William III.

"Why all this haste? Why this urging? Why this driving?" shouted James Duane in the ensuing fracas. "I do protest . . . this piece of mechanism, this preamble."[27]

Congress, he said, had no more right to pass this preamble than did Parliament. It had no authority to meddle in the internal affairs of the colonies. New York, which he represented, still held out hope that the peace commissioners would arrive. Silently, he was dumbstruck by how masterfully the Adamses and Lees had manipulated Congress. "I suppose," he added ruefully, "the votes have been numbered and there is to be a majority."[28]

Duane was correct. Votes had been carefully counted beforehand, and the radicals had enough to win. It was at this juncture that James Wilson of Pennsylvania rose to speak, delivering one of the most eloquent defenses of conservative principle in the Continental Congress.

"In this Province," he said when all had quieted down, "if that preamble passes, there will be an immediate dissolution of every kind of authority; the people will be instantly in a state of nature. Why then precipitate this measure? Before we are prepared to build the new house, why should we pull down the old one, and expose ourselves to all the inclemencies of the season?"[29]

Wilson urged that the preamble not be included with the resolution just yet. The Pennsylvania Assembly had given clear instructions (he didn't need to add, written by Dickinson) that its delegates were not to vote for independence. All government, he said, derived its power from the people, and the members of Congress remained its servants. He and the other representatives had been "sent here to act under a delegated authority. If we exceed it, voluntarily, we deserve neither excuse nor justification."

Even the most hardened radicals were forced to consider his arguments. Congress now voted to delay publishing the preamble until a new Pennsylvania Assembly took its seats two days later.

When word leaked out about how close Congress had come to passing the preamble, Philadelphia radicals rioted. Within hours assaults on Wilson's character were published throughout town. In speeches and rants he was denounced as a traitor. Angry mobs threatened murder and mayhem. The viciousness of the attacks shocked even the advocates of independence in Congress, and his fellow delegates felt obliged to unanimously sign a "Defense of Wilson," attesting to his patriotism and probity.

On Wednesday, May 15, news came that by a two-vote majority, the Pennsylvania Assembly had voted to maintain its previous instructions to its delegates. Nothing could now hold back the flood. By a vote of six to four, Congress passed the preamble, causing the entire Maryland delegation to storm out and refuse to return for several days.

"This Day the Congress has passed the most important Resolution that ever was taken in America," John Adams wrote.[30] It is difficult to think of another instance in American history of a man from one state interfering so brazenly with the political balance of another. Caesar Rodney of Delaware saw all too clearly what Adams's preamble portended: "Most of those here who are termed the cool considerate men think it amounts to a declaration of independence."[31]

On Monday, May 20, under light rain and gloomy skies, a crowd of four thousand people, one of the largest ever to gather in Philadelphia, squeezed into the brick-lined State House yard. Hour after hour they listened to speeches advocating independence. As evening fell, lit torches guttered and smoked in the drizzle.

Over the hubbub, the meeting's moderator, Daniel Roberdeau, called for a new state government, his voice so stentorian it could be heard a quarter mile away. Three deafening cheers erupted, rattling the State House windows. When Roberdeau read Dickinson's directive barring Pennsylvania's delegates from voting for independence, the crowd roared in anger. A series of resolutions attacking the Assembly were now read aloud and passed by the meeting. One man who voted against a measure was immediately "abused and insulted," whereupon he immediately "thought it prudent to vote with the multitude."[32] The crowd's next step was even more radical: it declared Pennsylvania's existing government henceforth dissolved and called for a constitutional convention to create a new one.

To their great consternation, the members of Pennsylvania's Assembly awoke to discover they had been rendered supererogatory overnight. Even if they continued to legislate until a constitutional convention could be called, the Assembly was now a lame duck. Within days many legislators simply stopped showing up, and the Assembly had trouble achieving a quorum from then on.

Dickinson and his allies countered with an "Address and Remonstrance" of their own. They pointed out that Monday's mass meeting had had no legal authority and that Congress's preamble was merely a recommendation, not a decree. Seventy-five years of law and tradition were not to be discarded lightly. What radicals were trying to do, they argued, amounted to a repudiation of "our birthright, in the charter and wise laws of Pennsylvania."[33]

They were hardly alone in this view. Some six thousand people immediately signed the "Remonstrance," provoking a war of pamphlets, editorials, and rebuttals. The debate was fought not only with words. When two supporters of the Assembly were caught in Lancaster and York with copies of the Remonstrance, crowds seized them and built a bonfire out of their pamphlets. One man escaped; the other was imprisoned as a Tory.

The Assembly's last hope lay in exploiting the ambiguity of Adams's language in the preamble. Assembly leaders secretly decided to ask Congress to clarify a key question: if the Pennsylvania government renounced all traces of royal authority, would it be allowed to retain its own authority? When Benjamin Rush learned of this gambit, he quickly recognized the danger it posed. If successful, the Assembly might yet thwart the radicals. In a note to Richard Henry Lee, he warned that the Assembly's request for clarification "shows a design to enslave the people of Pennsylvania," and he urged his friend "not to desert us in this trying exigency."[34] Along with his letter, he enclosed a copy of the petition for Lee to circulate among his colleagues.

The next day Sam and John Adams met with Philadelphia's radical leaders to devise a plan. Any objection to the petition would sound better coming from local interests rather than from another colony. Philadelphia radicals then submitted a "Memorial" imploring Congress to reject the Assembly's request for clarification. "This situation of our province," they wrote, "requires vigor and harmony in the direction of both civil and military affairs, but these can never be obtained when a people no longer confide in their rulers." With the Adamses and Lees politicking in the background, Congress simply ignored the Assembly's request.

Without a quorum, it was difficult for Pennsylvania's Assembly to do much at all, but in mid-June it finally formed a committee, comprising Dickinson, Morris, and several others, to write new instructions for its delegates. On June 15 Dickinson and Morris told the remaining legislators that "the situation in public affairs is so greatly altered, that we now think ourselves justifiable in removing the restrictions."[35] The last vote the Assembly ever took was to adjourn until August, but it never met again. With a constitutional convention scheduled for June 18, it was only a matter of time until Pennsylvania radicals seized total control. Though John Adams did not share their fervor for democracy, he was giddy at the thought that he had bested his enemies and that separation from Britain was at hand.

"Every post and every day," he wrote, "rolls in upon us independence like a torrent."[36]

CHAPTER 9

THE CRUCIBLE OF CONSERVATISM

With bright light streaming through the tall windows behind him, Richard Henry Lee stood before Congress on Friday, June 7, 1776, clutching a piece of paper that would change the "natural course and order of things."[1] A week earlier word had arrived that the Virginia convention in Williamsburg had voted to instruct its delegates to declare independence.

"Resolved," Lee began reading in his high drawl, "that these United Colonies are, and of right ought to be, free and independent States, that they are absolved from all allegiance to the British Crown, and that all political connection between them and the State of Great Britain is, and ought to be totally dissolved."

It is impossible not to imagine John Adams grinning as he listened to the Virginian. Congress was poised to vote on independence, and the radicals thought they had the votes to push it through. Right away Adams stood to second the motion. Other pressing business kept the delegates from discussing the measure until the next day, but at ten o'clock sharp on Saturday, Congress reconvened and resolved itself into a committee of the whole, a parliamentary trick allowing the delegates to debate without taking a binding vote.

Dickinson, Wilson, Edward Rutledge, and Robert Livingston immediately opposed the resolution with familiar arguments. They were "friends to the measures themselves and saw the impossibility that we should ever be united with Great Britain," they said, "yet they were against adopting them at this time."[2]

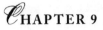

For one thing, anxiety over the military situation was at an all-time high. Two weeks before, word had come that the American army in Canada was disintegrating. Just over a week before, Washington had spent two days with Congress discussing the dire situation in New York. He had only seven thousand men with which to defend the city against the rumored seventeen thousand Hessian troops aboard the approaching British armada. Charleston too was in danger, according to reports. And news was circulating of Tories raising armies in Delaware, New York, and New Jersey, and of Indians plundering and scalping along the frontier.

Dickinson's greatest concern remained America's lack of unity. Only four colonies had specifically ordered their delegates to vote for independence: Massachusetts, Virginia, Rhode Island, and North Carolina. But other colonies continued to oppose it or to give no specific instructions regarding the question. The colonies that had been directed to vote for independence, he argued, had no right to declare it on behalf of the others.

The fact was, "The people in the Middle Colonies . . . were not yet ripe for bidding adieu to British connection." They were "fast ripening," but too precipitous a declaration of independence would cause Pennsylvania to "secede from the union," and nothing would be more calamitous to the American cause. The only "wise and proper" course, they concluded, was to resist taking "any capital step until the voice of the people drove us into it."[3]

Leading the counterattack were Lee and Adams. Independence, they argued, already existed. "The question [is] not whether, by a declaration of independence, we should make ourselves what we are not, but whether we should declare a fact that already exists."[4] In any case, further allegiance to the Crown was impossible. The King had declared the colonies out of his protection and was waging war against them at that very moment. Even James II, deposed in 1688, had never declared his people out of his protection. To wait for unanimity would be a vain attempt, they argued, "since it is impossible that all men should ever become of one sentiment on any question."[5]

By seven o'clock that night with debate proceeding by candlelight, the issue remained far from resolved. Since Congress did not meet on Sunday, arguments would have to be resumed on Monday. It was a restless Sabbath for Dickinson and his allies. Not only was the political momentum against them, but their allies in Congress were also fast dwindling, many having returned to their home colonies to stem the rising tide of radicalism. John De Hart, an important ally from New Jersey, had returned to combat what he saw as growing "leveling principles." John Rutledge had returned to South Carolina several months before to help set up a new government, and John Jay was back in New York to do the same. As a leading member of the New York Provincial Congress, Jay also had to devise measures against the colony's sizable Tory population.

"I wish you had been here," Edward Rutledge wrote to Jay the day after

Lee's motion. Surely, he said, the New Yorker would have cast his vote with "the sensible part of the house."[6]

Too busy to return to Pennsylvania, Jay did what he could from New York. Prompted in part by James Duane, who warned of the "orators from Virginia with Colonel Henry at their head," Jay drafted a declaration blocking New York's delegation from voting on independence. "The good people of this colony have not, in the opinion of this congress, authorized this congress, or the delegates of this colony, in the Continental Congress, to declare this colony to be and continue independent of the crown of Great Britain."[7] The resolution passed the New York Provincial Congress unanimously. If independence were to occur, Jay believed, it would be only because "our country was prompted and impelled to independence by necessity and not by choice."[8]

Rutledge, meanwhile, warned that an immediate declaration of independence was tantamount to "giving our enemy notice of our intentions before we had taken any steps to execute them."[9] Even a slight delay might help bolster America's resolve and its defensive capacity. It might also help keep the radicals in check a little bit longer.

For much of the previous year, Edward Rutledge had been outspoken in his denunciation of Great Britain, leading radicals to consider him an ally. He had, for instance, supported John Adams's preamble. But though he was far more of a firebrand than his older brother, Rutledge nonetheless believed deeply in the fundamental importance of prudence and tradition. The more he saw the extent of radical maneuvering to engineer independence, the closer he grew to Dickinson and his allies. He became especially fond of his young colleagues from New York.

By late spring Rutledge was railing against the "overruling influence" and "low cunning" of the Massachusetts delegates. He decried their efforts to declare independence before other crucial steps had been taken. "A man must have the impudence of a New Englander to propose in our present disjointed state any treaty (honorable to us) to a nation now at peace," he wrote. In the end, radicals were making America look "ridiculous in the eyes of foreign powers by attempting to bring them into a union with us before we had united with each other."

At the heart of his alienation from the radicals lay a fundamental rejection of their reckless tactics. Even if many radical leaders belonged to the upper classes, their power rested on "captivating . . . the lower class of mankind." Nothing could be more unscrupulous than their willingness to ally themselves with "men without character and without fortune" in order to achieve immediate independence—as the coup they had fomented in Pennsylvania demonstrated. Should they realize their goals, Rutledge feared, it would "occasion such a fluctuation of property as to introduce the greatest disorder."[10]

Matters were not helped by the fact that the young southern gentleman shared his rooming house with much of the New England delegation. There he was offended daily by the democratic and puritanical ways of John and Sam Adams, John Hancock, Robert Treat Paine, and Elbridge Gerry. When "those louts" proposed outlawing duels in the Continental Army, Rutledge nearly challenged them all to one himself.

Adams, with typical malice, had few kind words to say about Rutledge, whom he labeled "excessively vain, excessively weak, and excessively variable and unsteady—jejune, inane, puerile." Adams even mocked his looks and bearing. "He shrugs his shoulders, distorts his body, nods and wriggles with his head, and looks about with his eyes, from side to side, and speaks through his nose."[11] Most unfairly, he attacked Rutledge's debating style as "ungraceful," but the younger man was not to be underestimated. An accomplished litigator himself and the de facto leader of the South Carolina delegation, Rutledge was quite capable of swaying Congress with his eloquence, sensibility, and clout.

In preparation for the resumption of debate on Monday, Rutledge planned to introduce a motion of his own to counter Lee's. "I mean to move that it should be postponed for 3 weeks or a month," he wrote to Jay, who had become a close friend. "I don't know whether I shall succeed in this motion; I think not, it is at least doubtful. However I must do what is right in my own eyes, and consequences must take care of themselves."[12]

To convince radicals to cooperate, Rutledge came up with a shrewd idea. Three days before, Lee had acknowledged the usefulness of establishing foreign alliances and a confederation of the colonies. Rutledge used these concessions as a way to buttress his own motion. Standing before Congress on Monday, he urged one last delay, during which time Congress would set up three committees: one to draw up a declaration of independence, one to work on an alliance with France, and one to prepare for a system of articles for confederation.

Rutledge's proposal turned out to be persuasive, even to Adams. Congress now agreed to postpone debate on independence until July 1. "Three greatest measures of all were carried," Adams wrote. "Three committees were appointed." Adams was pleased to be placed on the committee on independence, along with Livingston, Franklin, Jefferson, and Roger Sherman of Connecticut. Jefferson, it was decided, would write the actual Declaration of Independence, but Adams would help edit it thoroughly. Five other delegates were chosen to work on an alliance with France or Spain. And Dickinson took charge of the committee drawing up the Articles of Confederation.

With so little time to spare, Rutledge begged Jay to come back to Philadelphia. "I know full well that your presence must be . . . useful at New York, but I am sincerely convinced that it will be absolutely necessary in this city." He knew just how skillful Jay would be in parrying the radicals' arguments during the final debates over independence, the Articles of Confederation, and a treaty with a European power. "Whether we shall be able effectually to oppose the first, and infuse wisdom into the others will depend in great measure upon the exertions of the honest and sensible members," Rutledge wrote at the end of June.[13]

Jay replied that he wished he could return, but weighty matters detained him in New York. "We have a government, you know, to form; and God only knows what it will resemble." With so many Loyalists at large and the British fleet approaching, he also had to contend with continual "plots, conspiracies, and chimeras dire."[14]

Privately, many on the right continued to hope for some last-minute peace accord before the final break occurred. "Where the plague are these commissioners," wrote an anguished Robert Morris. "If they are to come what is it that detains them?"[15]

The three-week delay proved useful to both sides. Radicals shored up support for independence during this time. And in doing so they justified conservative arguments that America needed more time to unify. While there had been a real possibility that the colonies would split apart on June 7, now a majority supported separation from Britain. By June 28, Delaware, Connecticut, New Hampshire, Pennsylvania, New Jersey, and Maryland had authorized their delegates to vote for independence. The problem for the radicals was that granting delegates permission to vote for independence was not the same as instructing them to do so. No one knew how individual congressmen would actually vote.

Pennsylvania remained the keystone to independence. And the key to Pennsylvania was Dickinson's former law student, James Wilson. Tall and muscular with a ruddy face and a mild burr, Wilson had left Scotland for America eleven years before. He was born the poor son of a farmer, but his bearing struck many as aristocratic. His dress was so impeccable and his posture so straight that his enemies accused him of haughtiness. A friend offered a different explanation for Wilson's habit of peering down at people through his thick, round glasses. His "'lofty carriage' is very likely the effect of habit; for I know by experience that a man who wears spectacles must keep his head erect to see through them with ease, and to prevent them from falling off his nose."[16]

From an early age, Wilson's tremendous intellect had opened doors for him. At age fifteen he won a scholarship to St. Andrews, one of the oldest universities in the British Isles, where he studied the classics, mathematics, and the great authors of the Scottish Enlightenment. Some scholars suggest he also attended the Universities of Glasgow and Edinburgh, where he may have studied with Adam Smith. A devout Calvinist, he intended to enter the ministry, but when his father died, Wilson left school to support his mother and younger siblings by serving as a tutor with a noble family. By 1765, over the objections of his family, he decided to leave Scotland, where he would always be of "common rank in life." America offered opportunity he would never find at home.

Wilson arrived in the New World and was immediately caught up in the fervor surrounding the Stamp Act crisis. Instantly, he was an American. After receiving a master's degree from the College of Philadelphia the following year, he applied to study law with Dickinson, even though he was broke. A cousin helped out by selling him a farm for an IOU. Wilson then sold the farm to Dickinson to cover the cost of tuition and room and board.

Industrious to the core, Wilson soaked up the Farmer's brilliance. Dickinson had him read everything they could find on the constitutional crisis with Britain along with the works of his fellow Scot, David Hume, the oeuvre of French political philosopher Montesquieu, and the great theorists of the English Civil War, Sidney, Harrington, and Locke.

Wilson's education was practical as well. In his notebooks, he assiduously copied records of land disputes, which comprised about 80 percent of a Pennsylvania lawyer's work, as well as legal definitions, pleadings, replevins, torts, and assumpsits. On the first page of his first notebook, he transcribed two quotations from Cicero. The first attested to his ambition: "The house of the lawyer is the oracle of the whole city." The second revealed a conservative outlook remarkably similar to his teacher's: "A lawyer is a man who knows how to give advice and apply in the most cautious manner those laws and that constitution that private men are directed by in a state."[17]

After less than a year, Dickinson declared his student graduated. He began courting the rich and beautiful Rachel Bird and in the process neglected writing home to his mother. As his fame and prosperity grew, she feared her son was becoming too preoccupied with worldly matters. "You will find," she admonished him in a letter, "the best things ever you did will yield you no comfort in a dying hour, none but Christ."[18] But Wilson's path now lay in the law, not in the Lord. He began traveling the countryside extensively on horseback representing clients in a wide variety of cases. In the process he became an eloquent pleader. Within a decade he would be pleading just as eloquently for his new country.

In January 1775, Wilson was chosen to be a member of the provincial convention along with Dickinson, and in May he was elected to the Continental Congress, where he began working closely with Robert Morris. Despite his close connections to the right, John Adams was impressed. Writing to his wife, Adams described him as a "young gentleman from Pennsylvania . . . whose fortitude, rectitude, and abilities too greatly outshine his master's."[19] All who met him were astounded by his genius for legal and political theory, James Madison calling him "justly distinguished for his intellectual powers."[20] And his rhetorical brilliance distinguished him as quickly in Congress as it had in courtrooms. "He produced greater orations than any other man I have heard," his friend Alexander Graydon wrote.[21]

Wilson retained an enormous respect, bordering on reverence, for his former law instructor. On constitutional and economic matters, he remained firmly in the Dickinson camp. But he had begun to disagree on the question of independence, and John Adams could sense it. Starting in early 1776, Adams and his Virginia cohorts applied continual pressure on Wilson to side with them. Dickinson in turn did all he could to keep Wilson from straying. The "two Johns, Adams and Dickinson," as Wilson's biographer Charles Page Smith writes, "contended for his political soul."

Wilson remained determined to make up his own mind over independence. He feared, as all conservatives did, the social turmoil that would result from independence, and he refused to support such a momentous change until a clear majority of Pennsylvania citizens supported it. But by the end of June, he had come to agree with Adams. Announcing he had sensed a shift in mood among his constituents, Wilson now said he would vote for independence. Given the high esteem his colleagues had for him, this change of heart had an immediate impact on many other congressional holdouts. It remained unclear what effect it would have on the other members of the Pennsylvania delegation.

As the number of hours until the final debate dwindled, only Franklin and Morris stood openly in favor of independence. John Morton, a gentleman farmer and jurist aligned with Dickinson, remained undecided. Joining Dickinson and Morris in opposing independence were Charles Willing, Morris's business partner; Charles Humphreys, a Quaker miller and pacifist; and Andrew Allen, a lawyer who had initially supported the American cause but was increasingly troubled by the radicalism sweeping Pennsylvania.

Among the other colonies, South Carolina remained opposed, Delaware was split, and New York, following Jay's instructions, continued to balk. What would happen on Monday, July 1, was anybody's guess.

At nine o'clock in the morning, some fifty-one delegates assembled in the State House for what John Adams, who had risen excitedly before dawn, called "the greatest debate of all."[22] The day was hot, damp, and dreary. To the discomfort of all, all of the windows and doors were shut to guard against eavesdropping British spies. The first order of business involved reading letters. Several generals described battlefield conditions, constitutional conventions in New Jersey and New Hampshire reported on their progress, and Maryland's new resolution permitting its delegates to vote for independence was read. Six thousand dollars for purchasing war supplies was then approved for Virginia.

At ten o'clock, all were ready for the final showdown over independence, and few had any doubt about which two heavyweights would soon face off. With a heavy bang of his gavel, John Hancock called for quiet as Lee's June 7 resolution was read once again. Congress then resolved itself into a committee of the whole to carry out debate, with Benjamin Harris of Virginia assuming the chair.

It was now midmorning. Looking deathly pale and tired, Dickinson rose. He had slept little the past few nights, having worked feverishly on a final speech. In draft after draft, he edited, scratched out, and inserted new points until the final form was almost illegible.[23] Revolution now seemed unavoidable, but Dickinson was prepared to argue the conservative position one last time.

"The consequences in the motion now lying before you are of such magnitude that I tremble under the oppressing honor of sharing in its determination," Dickinson began. "I feel myself unequal to the burden assigned me. . . . My conduct, this day, I expect will give the finishing blow to my once too great, and . . . now too diminished popularity." Nevertheless he felt compelled to proceed. He would now expend a decade's worth of goodwill and political capital, because he felt it was the right thing to do. "Silence would be guilt," he said. "I must speak, though I should lose my life, though I should lose the affections of my country."[24]

He began to speak of that highest of conservative value—prudence. All gentlemen, he conceded, "agree that prudence is required in forming our decision." Where they disagreed was over how to define it. His notion of prudence, he said, differed fundamentally from that of the radicals, who wanted to "brave the storm in a skiff made of paper."[25]

For more than two hours Dickinson warned of the blood, chaos, and economic ruin that war would bring. He outlined one last time the main points he and his allies had been making over the previous six months. More than a declaration of independence, America needed foreign allies and signed treaties, not vague promises from abroad. Internal land disputes needed to be reconciled and civil war avoided. And still, he argued, the population remained too divided. The struggle with Britain could be decided only militarily; rhetoric and declarations would not decide the ultimate victor. Above all, America needed battlefield victories along with soldiers and supplies for sustained campaigning. "The war will be carried on with more severity," he warned. "The burning of towns, the setting loose of Indians on our frontiers has not yet been done."

Congress needed to think long and hard before voting for separation.

> People are changeable. In bitterness of soul they may complain against our rashness and ask why we did not apply first to foreign powers, why we did not settle difference among ourselves, why we did not take care to secure unsettled lands for easing their burdens . . . Why we did not wait till we were better prepared. . . . When our Enemies are pressing us so vigorously, when we are in so wretched a state of preparation, when sentiment and designs of our expected friends are so unknown to us, I am alarmed at this Declaration being so vehemently presented.[26]

If somehow he were to come into possession of a "Doomsday Book of America," as Dickinson put it, it would show that one day, several more decades hence, America would divide into two nations, a North and a South. With that he took his seat.

For a long time no one spoke, all reflecting on Dickinson's sober words. Rain started to pelt the windows. In his notes later that day, Adams made a rare kind remark about Dickinson: "He conducted the debate not only with great ingenuity and eloquence, but with equal politeness and candor."[27]

Finally, Adams stood.[28] Responding to Dickinson in a soft voice, he said, "This is the first time of my Life that I have ever wished for the talents and eloquence of the ancient orators of Greece and Rome, for I am very sure that none of them ever had before him a question of more importance to his country and to the world."

Continuing, Adams emphasized how just the American cause was and how advantageous a split with Great Britain would be. He delineated all of the scorn and neglect George III had shown the colonies and lambasted his tyrannical decision to use foreign mercenaries against his own people. Now was the proper moment to separate from Britain, he concluded. It was clear "from the voice of the people, from the necessity of the measure in order to obtain foreign assistance, from a regard to consistency, and from the prospects of glory and happiness which opened beyond the war, to a free and independent people."[29]

After he had finished, a newly arrived delegation from New Jersey asked to hear the main arguments for independence again. Tired from speaking, Adams tried to remain seated, but Edward Rutledge approached him laughing. "Nobody will speak but you on this subject. You have all the topics so ready that you must satisfy the gentlemen from New Jersey."

Adams was reluctant, replying that he would feel like "an actor or gladiator, for the entertainment of the audience." He would just be repeating himself. "Nothing new can be advanced by me." But he rose again and set forth the arguments for independence. Exhausted and perspiring, he finally sat down for good. He had been on his feet for more than two hours and had delivered the speech of his life. Thomas Jefferson later wrote that Adams was "not graceful nor elegant, nor remarkably fluent" but spoke "with a power of thought and expression that moved us from our seats."

Debate would continue for nine more hours, turning the day into the longest session yet of the Continental Congress. By candlelight that evening, the delegates were ready to vote. Congress was still acting as a committee of the whole, so the outcome would not be binding. The vote came out nine to two in favor of independence, with only Pennsylvania and South Carolina opposed. Delaware was split, and New York was obliged to abstain until it received new instructions.

Rutledge then asked to postpone the final vote on independence until the next day. Though his colleagues disapproved of the resolution, he thought they "would then join in it for the sake of unanimity."[30] The request was granted. It was a difficult night for the southern holdouts. Rutledge wrestled with his conscience and debated the issues with his colleagues. In the end, the importance of unanimity outweighed other considerations. Sometime in the early hours, the South Carolina delegation agreed to formally vote for independence the next day.

Delaware too would soon vote for independence. Word had been sent to Caesar Rodney that his tie-breaking vote was urgently needed. Riding eighty miles through thunder and lightning to reach Philadelphia the next morning, he arrived just in time to break the deadlock in the Delaware delegation.

Now it all came down to Pennsylvania. John Morton had decided to join Wilson and Franklin in voting for independence, but that still left Dickinson, Morris, Willing, and Humphreys against it. Andrew Allen, meanwhile, was so sickened by the idea that he left Congress that day, joined the Loyalists, and soon made his way to the British lines. Even without Allen, Dickinson still had the votes to keep Pennsylvania from supporting independence. But if ever American rights were to be safeguarded, if ever American citizens were to feel unafraid to sit under their vines and under their fig trees, the colonies had to declare their independence unanimously.

Throughout the night, Dickinson and Morris wrestled with this dilemma. They still believed independence to be a mistake, and as contrarians they felt it their duty to vote their conscience. But neither could they oppose independence any longer. They were ardent patriots as much as prudent realists, and they always placed the good of their country before their personal politics. "It is the duty of every individual to act his part in whatever station his country may call him to in hours of difficulty, danger, and distress," Morris said. Although "the councils of America have taken a different course from my judgment and wishes . . . I think that the individual who declines the service of his country because its councils are not conformable to his ideas makes but a bad subject."[31]

At the end of a long, ruminative vigil, Dickinson and Morris hit upon the only honorable solution they could find. The next day, Tuesday, July 2, amid a torrential downpour and thunderclaps, they returned to the State House for the formal vote on independence. But rather than taking their seats with the rest of the Pennsylvania delegation, they withdrew "behind the bar" and were officially marked absent. They could only watch with mixed feelings as Pennsylvania now said "yea" to separation by a single vote: Wilson, Franklin, and Morton against Willing and Humphreys. By abstaining, Dickinson and Morris had rigged the vote in favor of independence.

Delaware now cast its votes in favor of Lee's resolution, as did South Carolina. The final vote was twelve colonies in favor, with only New York continuing to abstain. Independence was thus technically achieved "without a single dissenting" vote.[32] The next few days were spent arguing over the actual text of Jefferson's Declaration of Independence. Southerners objected to his attacks on the slave trade, and on July 4, with the offending sections removed, the final draft was approved. New York soon sent word that it too supported the Declaration. Congress would not get around to signing the document until August, when Robert Morris, after due consideration, finally decided to affix his name to it. Dickinson never signed the Declaration of Independence. He had more practical ways of proving his patriotism.

The historian Forrest McDonald has argued that had Dickinson been more receptive to independence in June 1776, he would no doubt have been the one chosen to write the Declaration of Independence. What would a Dickinson Declaration have looked like? To be sure, it would have been very different from Jefferson's. Instead of basing American rights on the laws of nature, it would have relied on English constitutional history and legal precedent.[33] Instead of invoking self-evident truths, it would likely have cited biblical example. It would, in sum, have been a significantly more conservative document. Within a few years, it would also have been just the sort of work John Adams favored.

Only two days after his debate with Dickinson, Adams began to come around to his opponent's way of thinking. In a letter to his wife on July 3, he wrote, "The delay of this Declaration to this time has many great advantages attending it. . . . Time had been given for the people maturely to consider the great question of independence, and to ripen their judgment, dissipate their fears, and allure their hopes. . . . This will cement the union, and avoid those heats, and perhaps convulsions, which might have been occasioned by such a Declaration six months ago."[34]

By 1813 Adams had completely repented of his earlier hastiness and political machinations. "I was in a great error, no doubt," he said, "and am ashamed to confess it, for those things were necessary to give popularity to our cause, both at home and abroad."[35]

But in 1776 few could see the good that Dickinson had done. His enemies were quick to seize upon the absence of his signature. Ezra Stiles, a Connecticut minister and future president of Yale University, prophesied that by not signing the Declaration, Dickinson "now goes into oblivion or a dishonorable reminiscence with posterity."[36] Others speculated that like Andrew Allen, Joseph Galloway, and so many others, he would join the Tories. More than any other delegate who had balked at independence, Dickinson was singled out and subjected to the harshest of vitriol. He shrugged off these attacks.

A month after independence, he addressed his adversaries. "What can be more evident than that I have acted on principle?" he asked.[37] He had no intention of joining the enemy. Like Morris, he would stand by America. "When a determination was reached upon [independence] against my opinion, I regarded that determination as the voice of my country," he wrote. "That voice proclaimed her destiny, in which I was resolved by every impulse of my soul to share, and to stand or fall with her in that scheme of freedom she had chosen."[38]

By consenting to stand or fall with freedom, Dickinson, Morris, Rutledge, Jay, Braxton, and all their allies became America's first true conservatives. They had passed through the final crucible. Change was inevitable, they knew, but by fighting so hard to keep it in check, they had saved America from being torn apart. Nor were they bitter about separating from Great Britain. As they saw it, they had not lost the battle over independence so much as they had ensured that the fledgling nation would now survive long enough to mount a credible challenge to British arms and found a new republican form of government. They still had much work to do.

For Dickinson, pressing matters were at hand. The rebellion that had been largely confined to Massachusetts was about to engulf a continent. On July 4, 1776, the day Congress formally approved the Declaration of Independence, 113 hulking British transports suddenly appeared off the coast of New Jersey. The brand-new state begged Congress for help. Dickinson, a colonel in the First Battalion of Associators, became the first commander to lead his men out of the city and begin a week-long march to join General Washington's forces outside New York. In doing so, he also became one of the few congressmen to march off to war, something neither John nor Sam Adams ever undertook. Somehow, during that same tumultuous week, he also found time to draft the Articles of Confederation. In the first article, Dickinson legally christened the new nation: "The Name of this Confederacy shall be 'The United States of America.'" Even as he lifted his sword to fight for his country, he continued to wield his pen in its defense.

CHAPTER 10

THE PHILOSOPHER IN ACTION

An Irishman who called himself "an Englishman" was the best friend America had in Parliament. Ever since the Stamp Act crisis, Edmund Burke had vigorously defended colonial rights against the actions of the British government. As the New York Assembly's agent in London, he was, in fact, paid to advance the interest of Americans. But his fondness for the inhabitants of the New World was based on more than mere remuneration. He stood in awe of their bold defense of their constitutional rights.

"The fierce spirit of liberty is stronger in the English colonies than in any other people of the earth," Burke told Parliament. Americans, he felt, embodied the best of English civic virtue. In their "veins the blood of freedom circulates."

He wished only that Englishmen in England would stand up to arbitrary power with as much resolve. As chief aide to the leader of the Whig party, Burke was committed to upholding England's ancient constitution. A self-described "true but severe friend to monarchy," he was convinced that George III exerted a corrupting influence on Parliament, in violation of the accord reached after the Glorious Revolution of 1688. If his support for American rights antagonized the King, so much the better.

The son of a wealthy Protestant attorney, Burke was born in Dublin in 1729. Though his mother was a Roman Catholic, he was raised as an Anglican. At the age of fifteen, he enrolled in Trinity College in Dublin. Five years later he moved to London to study law at the Middle Temple, but it is unclear whether he met Dickinson during this time. Burke soon gave up his legal studies to travel through the Continent. Writing about history and politics was what he really loved. He became an early member of "The Club," a London literary society that included Adam Smith and Samuel Johnson. After publishing several well-regarded works, he became private secretary to a number of influential politicians.

Soon after entering the political arena, Burke fell in with the Marquis of Rockingham, around whom parliamentary opposition to Tory power had coalesced. Rockingham immediately realized the young man's brilliance and began to defer to his judgment. As the Earl of Buckinghamshire noted, Burke had become not "Lord Rockingham's right hand only but both his hands."[1] Burke, in turn, revered Rockingham for his principled defense of English liberty. Though the marquis had no gift for expression, his ideas were noble. Burke helped give them clarity and strength.

As the most gifted orator among the opposition, Burke soon became Rockingham's voice as well. In 1765 the marquis arranged for Burke's election to the House of Commons. With his soft, chubby face, strong, prominent nose, and fiery red hair, Burke struck an imposing figure as he harangued his Tory MPs from the opposition bench. One of his first speeches, on the Stamp Act, "filled the town with wonder."[2]

As Burke saw it, American protests to the Stamp Act were entirely justified, and Prime Minister George Grenville's bungling was just making the situation worse. When George III replaced Grenville with Rockingham, Burke now had the power to put his ideas into action. In 1766 he devised an ingenious and pragmatic solution to the impasse. Parliament would revoke the Stamp Act. At the same time, it would proclaim Parliament's theoretical right to tax the colonies, mollifying the Tory party. Asserting sovereignty was fine, Burke felt, as long as Parliament did not act upon it in a way that threatened to envelop the empire in civil war.

Incensed that the colonies had evaded taxation, George III promptly cashiered Rockingham. Subsequent prime ministers ignored Burke's advice on the prudent use of power, provoking the inexorable decline in relations with America. Once again Burke and the Rockingham Whigs were exiled to the political wilderness.

As the crisis continued to mount, Burke struggled to change Britain's course. In his April 1774 speech "On American Taxation," he urged the British government to repeal the Townshend Duties on tea. Parliament, he said, should never have abandoned the "ancient policy" of not taxing America and needed to follow a policy of moderation and compromise. It had "shaken the pillars of a commercial empire that circled the whole globe," all for the sake of some negligible taxes.

The Rockingham ministry's actions of 1766, he declared, should serve as a model for dealing with the colonies. In pursuing its ill-considered policy, Lord North, the new prime minister, was ignoring both history and experience. He had "blustered like tragic tyrants here; and then went mumping with a fore leg in America, canting, and whining."[3]

Rising to object to Burke's invocation of history, one of North's ministers argued that Parliament was sitting to discuss the present, not the past.

Burke responded acidly, "He asserts that retrospect is not wise; and that the proper, the only proper subject of enquiry is, 'not how we got into this difficulty, but how we are to get out of it.' In other words, we are, according to him, to consult our invention, and to reject our experience." Like Dickinson, Burke was a devoted student of history, and nothing irked him more than a statesman who ignored its lessons. Those who did would be stuck in "the unpitied calamity of being repeatedly caught in the same snare."[4]

Burke warned of dire consequences if the House continued on its present path. "Again and again," he exhorted his fellow MPs, "revert to your old principles—seek peace and ensue it—leave America, if she has taxable matter in her, to tax herself. . . . Leave Americans as they anciently stood." To Burke, no principle of government was more important than tradition. "Do not burden them by taxes; you were not used to do so from the beginning. Let this be your reason for not taxing."

Most dangerous of all, he concluded, was governing based on abstract theories. These should be left to schools of metaphysics, "for there only they may be discussed with safety. But if, intemperately, unwisely, fatally, you sophisticate and poison the very source of government, by urging subtle deductions and consequences odious to those you govern, . . . you will teach [the colonists] by these means to call that sovereignty itself into question."[5]

Burke's motion to rescind the Tea Tax failed 182 to 49, and the magnitude of the defeat was seen by many as reason enough to drop support for American rights. But Burke refused to be silenced, leading some to start questioning his loyalty.

In March 1775 he delivered another ringing defense of the colonies in an address later published as "On Conciliation with America." (The speech was considered so eloquent that it was required reading in all American public schools from 1898 to 1933.) At the very moment when Americans were debating whether to hold a Second Continental Congress, Burke was urging Parliament not to punish all of Boston for the disruptive actions of Tea Partiers. True, "the conduct of the Americans cannot be justified," he admitted, "but the folly and impolicy of the provocation deserves the fullest arraignment."[6] What was needed now was compromise, not obduracy, and he called for an immediate repeal of the Coercive Acts.

"Conciliation failing, force remains; but, force failing, no further hope of reconciliation is left," he said. "Power and authority are sometimes bought by kindness; but they can never be begged as alms by an impoverished and defeated violence."[7] Magnanimity was vital in keeping the British Empire together, he argued, because "a great empire and little minds go ill together."[8]

Without a gentler approach, he concluded, America would inevitably break away. "Let the colonies keep the idea of their civil rights associated with your government—they will cling and grapple to you, and no force under heaven will be of power to tear them from their allegiance. But let it once be understood that these two things may exist without any mutual relation—the esteem is gone, the cohesion is loosened, and everything hastens to decay and dissolution."[9]

Burke addressed the Palace of Westminster for three hours, but again his motion went down in defeat, this time 270 to 78. At least, he wrote afterward, he had one consolation. At every stage of the conflict, "I have steadily opposed measures that have produced the confusion, and may bring on the destruction of this empire. . . . If I cannot give peace to my country, I give it to my conscience."[10] Four weeks after Parliament rejected his resolution, fighting broke out in Lexington and Concord.

Unlike the North ministry, which foresaw a quick military solution, Burke predicted a long, drawn-out struggle. The pyrrhic victory at Bunker Hill troubled him especially. Such early victories were dangerous, because they would lead Britain "to throw all moderation behind us and plunge ourselves into a war which cannot be ended by many such battles, though they should terminate in so many victories."[11]

He stood amazed by American resilience. As war continued to spread through New England, Burke wrote to Rockingham in August 1775, "The spirit of America is incredible. God knows they are very inferior in all human resources. But a remote and difficult country and such a spirit as now animates them may do strange things. Our victories can only complete our ruin."[12]

One of Burke's main concerns about the war was that it would make the Crown more powerful than ever. By building an enormous war machine, George III would gain the means to trample civil rights at home as well as overseas. American freedom thus stood as the bulwark for England's. If the colonies lost, he feared, the British Army would become accustomed to keeping "an English people in a state of abject subjection." And this would prove "fatal to the liberties of England itself."[13]

Despite his esteem for America, Burke denied it had a right to declare independence. Writing to his network of American correspondents, including James Duane, he urged them not to throw off British authority. "All the true friends to the colonies, the only true friends they had had, or ever can have in England," he wrote to the New York Assembly, "have laid and will lay down the proper subordination of America, as a fundamental, incontrovertible maxim."[14] American moderates clung to Burke's words in the hope that such "true friends" would eventually succeed in persuading Parliament to back down. But Burke's attempts at moderation were meeting with limited success.

In mid-November, frustrated by declining support from his own party, Burke submitted a "Bill for composing the present Troubles in America." The longer the war continued, he told Parliament, the greater the chance France or Spain would enter on the American side. This "may be considered not only as probable but in a manner certain." And if America gained a European ally, it would not only end all hope for victory; it would also prove ruinously expensive.

Just a few weeks earlier George III, enthroned and surrounded by peers in crimson robes, had told Parliament that America aimed at independence. Yet, Burke now asked, had Parliament considered practically how it would prevent the colonies from breaking away—how, for example, "a standing army of 26,000 men and 70 ships of war, could be constantly kept up in America"? If the colonies were determined to break away, Britain could do little about it. "After all our struggles," he said, "our hold in America is, and must be, her good inclination. If this fails, all fails."[15]

When a friend of the King countered that "the greater disposition Great Britain showed towards conciliation, the more obstinate, rebellious, and insolent America would become," Burke dismissed this as preposterous. "We whip the child until it cries, and then we whip it for crying," he commented.[16] Like all his previous motions, this one was defeated as well, 210 to 105. Adding to Burke's sense of failure, the House of Commons proceeded to pass the Prohibitory Act, blockading all American ports. With that the 1775 session of Parliament came to an end, along with Burke's hopes for reconciliation.

When Jefferson's Declaration of Independence reached England the following year, Burke realized the colonies had been irrevocably lost, and he placed the blame squarely on the British government's imprudence. The best option now, he argued, was a negotiated peace, not more bloodshed. This is not to say he welcomed American independence. Like most Britons, he would have preferred to see the colonies remain part of the empire. He also had little respect for Jefferson's appeal to natural rights to justify American independence.

American rights, Burke believed, were based solely in "the chartered rights of Englishmen." Deriving them from "natural" rights, as radicals did, set a dangerous precedent. Any course of action could be justified by an appeal to natural rights, for without historical or constitutional checks, he believed, liberty was prone to run amok. Like Dickinson, Burke was a man who hated extremes, "because extremes," he declared in April 1777, "as we all know . . . are destructive both to virtue and enjoyment. Liberty, too, must be limited in order to be possessed."[17]

With hostility to America growing and no sign that Lord North would change course anytime soon, Burke and the Rockingham Whigs decided to withdraw from Parliament, temporarily and strategically, to protest the war. In the meantime, despite a real fear of impeachment, Burke continued to agitate for peace. Locked in a bitter struggle with George III, Burke would spend the next five years trying to bring it about.

Burke's exalted reputation today stems not from any single, unified theory he developed, but rather from the potpourri of essays, letters, and speeches he left along with the great deeds of statesmanship and moral courage he performed as a politician. Burke was no "speculative philosopher." The best way to describe himself, he said, was as a "philosopher in action."[18]

Which isn't meant to imply that Burke was all action and no philosophy. A basic familiarity with his ideas is crucial to understanding not only Burke but also the roots of conservatism itself. At heart, Burke was a Whig, and guiding him was the traditional Whig hostility to arbitrary power wherever he found it, whether in a monarch or among the masses. He prized the gifts of the Glorious Revolution and staunchly defended the constitutional balance it had established. "Our constitution stands on a nice equipoise," he proclaimed, "with deep precipices and deep waters upon all sides of it."[19] His political heritage was thus not dissimilar to that of America's founding conservatives. Both had inherited a large part of their political beliefs from the Court Whigs.

Growing up in the age of Walpole and the Pelhams, Britain's first prime ministers, Burke imbibed many of that era's prevailing notions about government and society. In his own writings a generation later, he borrowed liberally from the thinkers of the 1730s, 1740s, and 1750s. Lord Hardwicke, England's preeminent jurist while Burke was a student, was especially influential. It was he who had established the doctrine of the "ancient constitution" that Burke cherished so deeply. "Much that we call Burkean is in fact Walpolean in origin," writes the historian Reed Browning.[20] Burke's genius was in his ability to expand upon these ideas and electrify audiences with his gift for eloquence and "polished *gravitas*."[21]

As with Dickinson, the Court Whigs inspired Burke with a love of Cicero, whom he quoted frequently to buttress his arguments. So indebted was he to the Roman statesman's ideas that he has been called "Cicero's latter-day disciple."[22] Above all, Burke championed Cicero's classical view of prudence, calling it "the first of all virtues, as well as the supreme director of them all."[23] This precept governed his tactics throughout the American crisis. Compromise, for Burke, meant working with political reality and shunning theoretical dogma.

He certainly did not blindly follow the tenets of classical republicanism. He did subscribe to the classical definition of virtue—"I love a manly, moral, regulated liberty," he declared—but he did not believe self-sacrifice could serve as the basis for good government. Like his close friends Adam Smith and David Hume, he rejected the belief that men could be totally altruistic. Smith, in fact, told Burke "that he was the only man, who . . . thought on these topics exactly as he did."[24]

The landed gentry may have possessed a greater degree of selfless virtue than the lower classes, Burke thought, but even the aristocracy was not immune from corruption, as he had seen all too often in Parliament. "When I see in any of these detached gentlemen of our times the angelic purity, power, and beneficence, I shall admit them to be angels," he said. "In the mean time we are born only to be men." But if the individual was not capable of angelic behavior, something greater was needed to steady society.

Burke's solution was in what he called "establishments," or "social prominences," in the words of the political philosopher Harvey Mansfield. These are prominent institutions in the social landscape that have grown and thrived over time: the Church, universities, the mercantile interest, the nobility, the military, and at times even the monarchy.[25] These social institutions, Burke argued, played a vital role in securing liberty by keeping all forms of absolute power in check. By serving as storehouses of power outside conventional legislative authority, they guarded against violent change.

Burke was practically Darwinian in his justification of "establishments." Their usefulness, he believed, derived from the fact that they had evolved through complex historical processes. Though they might not be perfect, their continued existence over hundreds of years proved their fitness to survive. Jettisoning them for something newer and theoretically better was not guaranteed to improve things. It was actually quite likely to make them worse.

By attacking long-standing institutions, a leveling democracy, Burke argued, "perverts the natural order of things."[26]

In order to perpetuate themselves, social and governmental institutions relied on something Burke called "prescription." This concept, borrowed from Roman law, holds that title to property derives from long, continuous use. Conversely, legal title can be lost after long disuse.

Burke's most original contribution to political thought was in extending the idea of "prescription" beyond its original use and applying it to abstract notions of liberty and sovereignty. Just as property was legitimized through long use, he was saying, so was political authority.

What this implied was that legal rights did not need any theoretical justification in order to be valid. The fact that they had existed since time immemorial was all the legitimacy they required. "Our constitution is a prescriptive constitution," he argued; "it is a constitution whose sole authority is that it has existed time out of mind."[27]

Property law thus became the foundation for all of constitutional law. It gave, said Burke, "the most solid of all titles, not only to property, but, which is to secure that property, to government."[28] Extending this idea further, he argued that liberties did not derive from natural rights, as Jefferson had asserted in the Declaration of Independence. Rather, they represented an "entailed inheritance," passed down from one generation to the next with attachments and codicils in place.[29] Freedom, in other words, always came with restrictions on who could inherit it.*

Burke's faith in traditionalism led him to regard prejudice and superstition as both necessary and laudable. Prejudice represented society's "latent wisdom," permitting it to function smoothly. Since not every belief could be reasoned out from first theoretical principles, people were far better off relying on traditional beliefs, which were always "of ready application in the emergency."[30] Ultimately, tradition played a far more crucial role in society than

---

* Burke played a leading part in establishing prescription as British legal doctrine with the passage of the Nullum Tempus Act of 1769, which limited the right of the Crown to reclaim property that had been privately owned for more than sixty years. Burke denied that the act accomplished anything new. Rather, he wrote, it merely described a state of affairs that had already long existed. Just to be safe, he scrupulously avoided pointing out that prescription had become law through legislative statute and not through prescription itself. *Selected Letters of Edmund Burke,* ed. Harvey Mansfield (Chicago: University of Chicago Press, 1984), p. 20.

did any governmental decree. As Burke pithily put it, "Manners are of more importance than laws."[31]

Accordingly, Burke believed government needed to be limited. "It is in the power of government to prevent much evil; it can do very little positive good in this, or perhaps in anything else."[32] Like Robert Morris, he was especially opposed to government interference in commerce. The moment that government tries to do so, he cautioned, "the principles of market will be subverted."[33] Instead of empowering government regulators with little direct knowledge of a business, "it is better to leave all [contractual] dealing . . . entirely to the persons mutually concerned in the matter."[34]

In the 1790s, for example, Burke fought against laws that would have set wages based on the price of grain. Nothing could have been more foolish, he thought. It would have let justices of the peace decide economic matters, which were best left to employers and employees. While politicians were hoping these laws would lower food prices, in the end they would probably cause prices to rise.

At a fundamental level, such government interference harmed society by failing to appreciate the role the rich played in accumulating capital. Such money could then be used to better the lives of the poor. Inevitably, attacking the wealthy was counterproductive. "The throats of the rich ought not to be cut, nor their magazines plundered," Burke explained, "because, in their persons they are trustees for those who labor, and their boards are the banking houses of these latter. . . . When the poor rise to destroy the rich, they act as wisely for their own purposes as when they burnt mills, and throw corn into the river, to make bread cheap."[35]

Underpinning all of Burke's thought on tradition, prescription, and prejudice was a legal doctrine developed two millennia before. Influenced again by Cicero, Burke argued that all human law derived from divine law.* By this he meant "a principle of a superior law, which it is not in the power of any community, or of the whole race of man, to alter,—I mean the will of Him who gave us our nature, and in giving impressed an invariable law upon it."[36] Natural law, in other words, reflected God's will, which manifested itself through the unfolding of history. By honoring ancient political and social institutions, Burke was saying, men were actually adhering to His law.

---

* Cicero said, "Law is the highest reason implanted in Nature, which commands what ought to be done and forbids the opposite." *De Legibus* 1.6.18, trans. Clinton Walker Keyes (New York: G. P. Putnam's Sons, 1928), p. 317.

[Custom and tradition thus took on a religious significance for Burke. And they provided the best means for knowing the divine. Ultimately, he believed, "Religion is the basis of civil society." If society was unequal, if power was distributed unevenly and governing institutions were imperfect, it was all part of God's plan, which human beings could know only imperfectly.

This wasn't to say society could never be altered. Burke's greatest conservative insight, which paralleled conservative thought in America, was that change was inevitable. "We must all obey the great law of change," he wrote. "It is the most powerful law of nature." At the same time, he added a crucial caveat. "All we can do and that human wisdom can do is to provide that the change shall proceed by insensible degrees."[37] Like Dickinson, battling on the other side of the Atlantic, Burke devoted himself to preventing violent change. His fight for American rights was in this regard quite conservative. It was to prevent the King from abruptly altering traditional relations between Britain and its colonies.]

Edmund Burke did not establish American conservatism. Rather, both he and America's founding conservatives drew upon the same political traditions and arrived at similar conclusions. Their insights differed, however, in several regards. First, America had no established church. So American conservatives, who hailed from an array of religious backgrounds, became far more supportive of religious liberty. Second, Burke's contention that the landed gentry were essential for keeping the moneyed interest in check was not applicable to the United States. America had no great aristocratic estates similar to Britain's. It did, however, have a robust and unbridled commercial tradition, making American conservatism the torchbearer for a far more dynamic form of capitalism.

On a more fundamental level, the issue of natural rights exposed a wide rift between Burke and American conservatives. James Wilson, one of Burke's most incisive critics among American conservatives, rejected the Englishman's contention that individuals gave up their rights upon entering society. Although both men relied heavily on natural law theory, Wilson believed Burke overemphasized the role institutions played in establishing these rights. "Must our rights be removed from the stable foundation of nature, and placed on the precarious and fluctuating basis of human institutions?" he asked. "Such seems to be the sentiment of Mr. Burke."[38]

Our rights, Wilson argued, rested on something more permanent than social conventions, even those that had existed since time immemorial. They were based directly on divine law. As opposed to Burke, who believed that society served as an intermediary between individuals and their God-given rights, American conservatives argued for a far closer relationship between the two. They recognized the usefulness of institutions for maintaining social order, but they lacked Burke's reverence for them. As Wilson pointed out, ancient injustices were just as likely to be passed down through the ages as beneficial traditions.

Burke's contention that man had to sacrifice part of his liberty in order to establish good government was "fallacious," Wilson insisted.[39] What people gave up upon entering society was not their liberty, but their right to make and enforce the law themselves. "Under civil society," he said, "man is not only made for, but made by the government: he is nothing but what society frames: he can claim nothing but what the society provides."[40] Burke had it backwards, American conservatives argued. "Man does not exist for the sake of government, but government is instituted for the sake of man."[41]

Much of Burke's later reputation as the founder of modern conservatism came from his "Reflections on the Revolution in France," published in November 1790.[42] As ardent as he had been in his support for American liberties during the 1770s, he recoiled at the social upheaval he saw taking place in France in the 1790s. Unlike the American Revolution and England's Glorious Revolution, which had been "carefully formed upon analogical precedent, authority, and example," the French Revolution called for a wholesale destruction of ancient traditions and social institutions.[43] Such a radical break with the past, Burke was convinced, could only end in despotism.

Thus it was that an Englishman who was an Irishman commenting on a revolution in France was dubbed the father of conservatism in America. Meanwhile a decade and a half before the French experience, American conservatives had confronted a radical revolution that had erupted in their very midst. And unlike Burke, they needed to find an immediate and practical way to deal with it if they hoped to survive.

CHAPTER 11

ON THE BRINK OF A PRECIPICE

Three loud huzzahs greeted the Declaration of Independence when it was first read to the crowd of Philadelphians gathered in the State House yard on July 8, 1776. Throughout the city, church bells began pealing and mobs set about removing all vestiges of royal authority, first prying the King's arms off the walls of the State House and then proceeding to ransack the rest of Philadelphia. By evening bonfires were ablaze on almost every corner.

Many in Philadelphia were also excited by the prospect of voting for the first time, and elections for the upcoming Pennsylvania Constitutional Convention saw particularly high turnout that day. During the previous month, the radical-led Provincial Conference had expanded the electorate to an unprecedented extent, revoking a long-standing law that restricted the franchise to men with estates of more than fifty acres or who owned more than £50. Propertyless men, who had clamored for years for the right to vote, went to the polls in droves. In pubs and taverns across the state, men raised toasts to the new nation and to new-found political privilege.

All did not revel that day. Voting was barred to anyone refusing to take an oath renouncing allegiance to the King. As a result, a large portion of the population, still hoping for some form of reconciliation, was blocked from voting. In addition, most of the city's Quakers, who opposed taking oaths on religious grounds, were also excluded. And nothing pleased radicals more than the idea of disenfranchising these two groups.

Both Quakers and those who favored reconciliation were among Philadelphia's most affluent citizens, and one of the radicals' primary goals was to remove the rich from power. Greater democracy, it seemed, was only for the lower classes. "A government made for the common good should be framed by men who can have no interest besides the common interest of mankind," wrote the radical leader James Cannon in late June. "Great and overgrown rich men will be improper to be trusted."[1]

Throughout the summer, radicals sharpened their rhetoric against the rich. Cannon, a Scottish immigrant and mathematics professor at the College of Philadelphia, denounced the city's "aristocratical junto," which was bent on "straining every nerve to frustrate our virtuous endeavors and to make the common and middle class of people their beasts of burden."[2] Despite his academic credentials, he was decidedly anti-intellectual when it came to politics. He urged the lower classes to elect "no lawyers or other professional characters called educated or learned men, but to select men uneducated with unsophisticated understandings."[3]

Among those joining Cannon in these attacks on wealth were Timothy Matlack and Thomas Young. Matlack, the son of a brewer who had been "torn to pieces" by creditors, harbored an instinctive hatred of the rich. Before the Revolution, he had gained renown around Philadelphia for his success with gambling, horse racing, and cockfighting. He had achieved considerable glory in 1770 when his prize bantam had savaged roosters belonging to the New York patrician James Delancey.

Young, a physician from upstate New York who was a close ally of Sam Adams and an organizer of the Boston Tea Party, was equally outspoken against the rich. In the years before independence, he had warned that "men of some rank" wanted to create in America "the system of lord and vassal, or principal and dependent common in Europe."[4] In 1775 the growing conflict between rich and poor drew him south to Philadelphia, where he confirmed his reputation as a "flaming zealot."[5]

The constitutional convention that began on July 15 elected Benjamin Franklin its president, but it was Cannon, Matlack, and Young who largely controlled the proceedings. The unsophisticated farmers who composed the bulk of the delegates were easily awed by their radical zealotry and their vision of "a new democratic era modeled on the Roman Republic," in the words of one historian.[6] Firmly in power, radical leaders saw the convention as the perfect forum for pushing through social and economic reforms. They also wanted to delay any actual debate over a new constitution. Now that they commanded all executive and legislative power in Pennsylvania, they wanted to keep the convention in session as long as possible. Elections, which might return conservatives to power, would be called the moment the constitution was completed.

One of the convention's first acts was to vote itself new powers. Within days it limited freedom of speech and of the press, regulated prices, and founded jails for those who violated these new laws. The convention also began disarming all men who didn't belong to Pennsylvania militia detachments. Since radicals dominated most of the state's associator companies, this move quickly secured them a monopoly on violence. To further their control over the military, a new council of safety was also established.

The war against Britain posed the most serious threat to radical control. With fighting raging in New York, Congress ordered Pennsylvania to send more troops to aid Washington at the front. As useful as militia companies were for suppressing dissent, they were no substitute for professional soldiers. The summer growing season was at high peak, and the farmers who composed the bulk of the militia soon began deserting in droves to tend to their fields. To be sure, terror at the prospect of facing British Redcoats was no small factor as well. In late summer three militia battalions mutinied and marched on Philadelphia, while numerous others refused to muster at all. Many officers, chafing under the leadership of men with no military background, also began refusing orders issued by the radical Council of Safety.

As the chaos mounted, emboldened Tories marched through Philadelphia in open defiance of independence. Adding to the convention's woes, members of the old Pennsylvania Assembly began meeting again in late September. Still lacking a quorum, the Assembly nevertheless voted to suspend the constitutional convention, ordered disobedience to all radical authority, and voted to extend the former royal governor's salary for another year.

Cannon, Matlack, and Young realized there was no time to lose. They needed to draft a new constitution to put their government on solid legal footing. Finally approved on September 28, the Pennsylvania constitution of 1776 embodied the "leveling spirit" of the day and served as the cornerstone of radical power for the next decade and a half. Perhaps the document's most radical feature was the creation of a unicameral legislature. Flying in the face of centuries of political theory, which mandated a balanced government, Pennsylvania now vested all authority in a single legislative body with no executive oversight and no upper house to check its power. To the radicals, upper houses, like the House of Lords in England or the colonial senates before the Revolution, smacked too much of the very aristocracy they wanted to purge from America.

Pennsylvania's new government overturned tradition in many other ways as well. Elections would be held yearly, and every man over twenty-one who had lived in the state for two years and who paid taxes now had the right to vote. The doors to high office, formerly closed to all but the rich and highborn, were now flung open to the majority of citizens. Property qualifications for assemblymen, who could serve four years out of every seven, were abandoned. Instead, the only requirement for holding office was to be "noted for wisdom and virtue."[7]

In what was probably the closest attempt at direct democracy since the days of Pericles, no laws could be enacted until they had first been "printed for the consideration of the people" and then approved by voters. Bills passed in one legislative session, in other words, could not be enacted into law until the next session, so that the public could weigh in. It was argued that this would serve as a far better check on government than a second house; in practice this provision did little but slow crucial decisions in the midst of war.

Instead of a single governor, the constitution created a twelve-man Supreme Executive Council. One-third of the council members were to be rotated out of office every year in order to avoid "the danger of establishing an inconvenient aristocracy."[8] To further weaken the executive, the council also lacked a veto.

A Council of Censors was also established in order to verify the government's obedience to the radical constitution. Composed of two members from each county in Pennsylvania, the censors were to meet every seven years to change or repeal laws, impeach officeholders, and censure those who had violated the constitution. The censors were also given the power to call for a new constitutional convention, which was the sole means for altering the new constitution.

The delegates took aim at the rich as well. They abolished debtors' prison and even considered outlawing any large concentration of wealth, which the government would break up when one reached a certain limit. The so-called "Agrarian" provision held that "an enormous proportion of property vested in a few individuals is dangerous to the rights, and destructive of the common happiness, of mankind; and therefore every free state hath a right by its laws to discourage the possession of such property."[9] Although this clause was narrowly rejected in the end, the fact that it was even considered reveals the depths to which radicals wanted to enforce social and economic equality.

One of the most controversial parts of the constitution was its requirement that voters swear an oath affirming they believed in "God the Father and in Jesus Christ His eternal son" and that the Holy Scriptures were divinely inspired. Benjamin Rush, one of the most fervent supporters of the radical cause, was aghast. A devout Christian himself, he vociferously opposed the religious oath. No man, he said, "whose morals were good should be exempted because he would not take that declaration." Many on the right thought the oath took the Lord's name in vain. "The Christian religion is not treated with the proper respect" by the constitution, complained one.

Although the final version of the constitution was approved unanimously, there had been, in fact, considerable opposition to it among the delegates. Cannon, Matlack, and Young devised yet another scheme to stymie their enemies. Before a final vote was taken, the radical majority required all the delegates to swear an oath that they would not undertake "directly or indirectly . . . any acts or things prejudicial or injurious to the constitution or government . . . as established by the convention."[10] At a stroke, any delegate who disagreed with the new constitution was now barred from voting against it.

Radicals then pushed through their craftiest ruse yet. In order to hold on to power after the upcoming elections, they mandated that all citizens had to take this same oath before voting. Now, not only would Tories and Quakers be disenfranchised, but anyone opposing the radical constitution, including a sizable number of Patriots marching off to fight the British, was henceforth legally shackled from doing anything about it. As one conservative commented upon hearing the news, "We are on the brink of a precipice."[11]

Conservatives had every reason to fear the spread of radical politics outside Pennsylvania. Every state was wrestling to some extent with calls for greater equality among the lower classes. In the meantime, Cannon, Matlack, and Young were doing everything they could to promote social revolution in America. In 1777 Young passed copies of Pennsylvania's constitution to representatives of Vermont, who had come to Congress to lobby for statehood. In an open letter to the Vermont delegation, he outlined the virtues of Pennsylvania's constitution and urged them to adopt a similar model. "With very little alteration," Young wrote, a Vermont constitution based on Pennsylvania's would "come as near as anything yet concerted by mankind."[12]

When it was finally passed in July, the Vermont constitution was every bit as radical as Pennsylvania's. It established a unicameral legislature, granted every man the right to vote, mandated free education, and prohibited slavery. Although the state would not be formally admitted to the Union for more than a decade, it was for all intents and purposes already a fourteenth state.

Having participated in the tenant uprisings in the Hudson Valley in the 1760s, Young was already hostile to New York's great landlords, who laid claim to vast tracts of land in Vermont. For him and his close friend Ethan Allen, independence from the upper classes was every bit as important as independence from Britain. The land, Young argued, belonged to the men who worked it, not to the king or the "gentlemen in the province of New York."[13] It was Young, in fact, who coined the name "Vermont," deriving the word from Allen's militia company, the Green Mountain Boys.

Georgia too adopted a form of government modeled on Pennsylvania's. In its controversial constitution of 1777, radicals pushed through a unicameral legislature and nearly universal suffrage. A copy of the Pennsylvania constitution had been brought to Georgia by one of the state's delegates to the Continental Congress, Button Gwinnett, who had become enamored of Pennsylvania's radical politics while serving in Philadelphia. After signing the Declaration of Independence, Gwinnett returned home to pen the first draft of Georgia's new constitution.

Fighting over the new constitution grew so fierce that numerous duels, as well as less chivalrous forms of bloodshed, broke out between radicals and conservatives. Several men were murdered in the aftermath, including Gwinnett, who was shot by a rival politician he had charged with treason.

In a letter to the Continental Congress, the Georgia conservative John Wereat complained that radicals were resorting to character assassination, labeling with "the hateful name of Tory . . . every man who is not of their party." The source of all of Georgia's troubles, he wrote, lay squarely with the new radical constitution. With an increase in the franchise, "neither liberty nor property are secure."[14] As one scholar writes, "The fabric of an ordered society dominated by the 'best part of the community,' which Wereat and other conservative Whigs had tried to preserve in the midst of revolution, lay in tatters."[15]

For conservatives across America, the constitutions of Pennsylvania, Vermont, and Georgia represented a democratic despotism every bit as insidious as the monarchy of King George. All power needed to be restrained, and by concentrating all of it in the hands of the people, the rights of the individual were sure to be infringed. "All single governments are tyrannies," wrote James Wilson, "whether be lodged in one man—a few men—or a large body."[16] Without checks and balances, he said, liberty, "like a structure of ice, would instantly dissolve before the fire of oppression and despotic sway."[17]

Benjamin Rush, for his part, found himself increasingly disturbed by Pennsylvania's radical constitution. He had had such high hopes for Pennsylvania's new government, but now he concluded that the state was under the control of a "mobocracy."[18] His shock that radicals had secured essentially unlimited power for themselves was matched only by his regret that he had supported them in the first place. "The time is remembered with shame and indignation," wrote America's first neoconservative.[19]

To Rush, the radical constitution that had just passed was as bad as any oriental dictatorship. "The government of Turkey is not more to be dreaded than the government of Pennsylvania," he wrote in his *Observations Upon the Present Government of Pennsylvania.* "Where is the man who can insure himself a moment's safety from a body of men invested with absolute power?"[20]

While Wilson was busy organizing political opposition to the unicameral legislature, Rush penned a series of devastating essays against it. Together they began to articulate a uniquely American and essentially modern conception of legislative power. Rush attacked the radical idea that inequalities in wealth had "introduced natural distinctions of rank in Pennsylvania, as certain as the artificial distinctions of men in Europe." Radicals, he argued, could not legislate away these imbalances by creating a single legislative body.

"Where there is wealth, there will be power," Rush wrote, echoing the thought of Harrington. "The rich have always been an overmatch for the poor in all contests for power." An upper house in Pennsylvania would never be aristocratic, he wrote. America was by nature democratic, and the power of any upper house would derive from the people just as much as any lower house. "Who would believe that the same fountain of pure water should send forth, at the same time, wholesome and deadly streams?"[21] But as Rush also pointed out, although "all power is *derived* from the people," it is not "*seated* in the people."[22]

Different branches of government did not represent different classes in society, as they did in Britain. Rather all branches derived directly from the people, even if the people were not in direct control of government, as radicals wanted. This new conception of government, Gordon Wood writes, "not only destroyed conventional theory of mixed government but it necessarily involved a major adjustment in the conception of representation; for it was now somehow possible for the people, simply through the electoral process, to have two different agents speaking for them at the same time."[23]

Many Patriots found themselves in Rush's position, disillusioned with the radicals' Machiavellian tactics but uncertain how to proceed. The new constitution, as one contemporary put it, "split the Whigs to pieces." And anger at Cannon, Matlack, and Young was immense. "Tim Matlack and a number of other violent wrongheaded people of the inferior class have been the chief promoters of this wild scheme," wrote another Philadelphia gentleman.[24]

Even John Adams, who had done so much to foment the coup that had led to the new constitution, was aghast when he first read a copy of it. "Good God!" he told Rush. "The people of Pennsylvania in two years will be glad to petition the crown of Britain for reconciliation in order to be delivered from the tyranny of their constitution."[25] Adams, however, was wrong again. Those who opposed the constitution never wavered in their support of American independence once it was accomplished.

In the weeks following the convention, a coalition of former adversaries began to form around Wilson and Dickinson, who had since returned from the front. Calling themselves "Republicans," this new party included moderate Whigs, Quakers, German immigrants, and disgruntled radicals. It was a clever bit of propaganda, for Pennsylvania's conservative Republicans were among the least republican men in the state. A number of Tories also joined the effort to overturn the constitution, leading radicals to brand all Republicans, or anti-Constitutionalists as they were also called, "traitors." Whatever their political background, the men who formed America's first organized conservative party were united by one desire: to regain control of Pennsylvania politics.

On October 17, Wilson organized a group of "respectable citizens" at Philosophy Hall to protest the constitution. They objected to the "sundry improper and unconstitutional rules laid down by the last convention" and issued a series of thirty-one resolves opposing the constitution, which was full of "strange innovations" and was too great a departure from the traditional form of government "to which the people have been accustomed."[26]

On October 21 an even greater crowd of fifteen hundred met in the State House yard to hear Wilson and Dickinson debate Cannon, Matlack, and Young over the constitution. Conservatives and radicals argued into the night and met again the next evening. Wilson and Dickinson proved so eloquent that the crowd voted overwhelmingly to adopt the thirty-one resolves attacking the constitution.

A proposal to institute an alternative, less restrictive oath also won acclamation. Over the next few weeks, debate about the alternative oath raged in the press. Radical writers pilloried the idea, arguing that conservatives opposed the oath because it represented "a mighty stumbling block in the way of our gentry." Another writer stated that conservatives opposed the constitution because "they will not be governed by leather aprons."[27]

But when elections for the new Assembly were held on November 5, only the radical oath was administered. Quakers and Tories were obliged to sit out, leaving the anticonstitutionalists to battle the radicals on their own. They had their work cut out for them. If conservatives wished to revise the constitution, they needed to win over voters who wanted the same thing. But anyone allowed to vote had already sworn to support the constitution. And that constitution, radicals swore, "would be enforced by fixed bayonets."[28]

In time radicals would only make the test oath stronger. In September 1778 radicals required all delegates to Congress to take test oaths. To further cement their hold on power, they then passed a law stating that anyone wishing to vote had to produce a certificate proving he had taken the oath before June 1, 1778. One newspaper claimed that the new law disenfranchised 80 percent of the male population over age eighteen.

In Philadelphia the results of the November 5 elections were not too bad for the anticonstitutionalists. Robert Morris was elected from the city, and John Dickinson from the county. In the rest of the state, however, conservatives faced electoral disaster. Aided by the test oath, no more than two thousand out of fifty thousand eligible voters were allowed to go to the polls, according to anticonstitutionalist sources. Those voters who did turn out responded enthusiastically to radical arguments that the "great men" of the state wanted to reduce the common people to slavery.

One hope remained for the conservatives. When the new Assembly took its seats on November 28, radicals had a clear majority, but the anticonstitutionalists had won just enough votes to prevent a quorum. Standing before the Assembly, Dickinson offered a compromise to keep the government running. "We will consent to the choice of a speaker, to sit with other members, and to pass such acts as the emergency of public affairs may require," he promised, "provided that the other members will agree to call a free convention for a full and fair representation of the freemen of Pennsylvania . . . for the purpose of revising the constitution formed by the late convention."[29]

The deal was quickly brokered. Conservatives agreed to pass emergency legislation and elect a speaker. In exchange radicals agreed to call a new convention in January to revise the constitution. But the moment conservatives allowed the new Assembly to be called to order and a new speaker to be elected, radicals broke their word. No new convention would be called after all. In a fury, a host of other conservative Assemblymen, including the entire delegation from Bedford County, withdrew from the government in protest.

Dickinson, disgusted by "the behavior of some persons that day" whom previously he "had for a long time esteemed," retired from Pennsylvania politics altogether and returned to his Delaware plantation to bide his time.[30] Always a stickler for legal niceties, he felt he had no legitimate means for overturning the radical government. Rush, increasingly ashamed of his recent camaraderie with Cannon, Matlack, and Young, tried to renew his ties with Dickinson. In December 1776 he begged his old friend to return to Philadelphia and run again for the Assembly. "It becomes us to unite in heart and hand in repelling the common enemy," Rush wrote. "The eyes of the whole city are fixed upon you."[31]

Dickinson's tactical retreat quickly proved an effective means for combating the radicals. Across the state conservatives launched a campaign of civil disobedience. In addition to a mass boycott of the Assembly, which now lacked a quorum, conservative government clerks started refusing to turn over papers and records, leading to their arrest. Conservative lawyers refused to argue cases, grinding court proceedings to a halt. One anticonstitutionalist, George Campbell, who had been appointed prothonotary of Philadelphia County, told the Executive Council in March 1777 that he could not swear an oath to the new constitution. He would swear that he renounced royal authority and that he supported the United States and the government of Pennsylvania, but as long as the words "as established by the late constitution" remained in the oath, he would not take it.

Renewing their calls for a new constitutional convention, conservatives declared the radicals incapable of governing. A pamphlet war broke out in full fury. Letters for and against the idea of a new convention flooded the newspapers. Now was no time to switch governments, wrote James Cannon. At a time when "the drums beat to arms," one should not sow discord. Anticonstitutionalists who refused to take their seats in the Assembly, he said, were unfaithful to the Revolution. Writing under the moniker "Common Sense," Thomas Paine argued that the conservative reaction was clearly a case of "sour grapes."

As relentlessly as "Common Sense" churned out tracts attacking the anticonstitutionalists, he was matched by an equally prolific nemesis. Writing under the pseudonym "Addison," James Wilson decried the test oath, which targeted "Whigs, who should disapprove of the constitution." It was clear, Addison wrote, that "those who directed this measure, must have been secretly of the opinion that the constitution would be disagreeable to a majority of the Whigs in the state." So focused was he on defeating the radicals that Wilson began neglecting his legal practice, which had become one of the largest in America. The political arena, he found, held even more appeal than the courtroom.

By late 1776 the struggle between anticonstitutionalists and radicals was eclipsing the larger war against the British. Riots were now a regular occurrence in Pennsylvania, and the lives and property of both sides came under frequent attack. Needless to say, the ability of Pennsylvania's government to wage war was severely hampered.

So far Pennsylvania had escaped the worst of the fighting, but danger was fast approaching from the north. Rumor had it that General Howe, who had nearly destroyed all of Washington's forces in New York, was on the march. Pennsylvania's dysfunctional government made the threat of invasion especially grave. The political chaos had already prevented the Continental Army from getting all the support it needed in New York. Had it not been for Washington's resolve and a large portion of luck, the American Revolution might have been nipped in the bud.

Fed up with the Pennsylvania Assembly's inability to furnish the Continental Army with adequate troops or supplies, Congress threatened to take over the state. Washington was particularly frustrated by Pennsylvania's inability to secure provisions that might fall into enemy hands.

By early December the situation had deteriorated further. With British forces seventeen miles from Philadelphia, the Council of Safety announced that Howe's army "may be hourly expected." Shops and schools were closed and thousands began fleeing the city, fearing the approaching Hessian troops as well as a growing epidemic of smallpox and camp fever. Hundreds of dead were buried in shallow pits near the Walnut Street Prison. "The city was for days the greatest scene of distress that you can conceive," wrote Robert Morris; "everybody but Quakers were removing their families and effects, and now it looks dismal and melancholy."[32]

On December 10, with radical militia companies failing to muster sufficient numbers to defend the city, Congress declared martial law. Two days later Congress itself joined the stream of refugees leaving Philadelphia for Baltimore. The trip was difficult. In the freezing temperatures, the rutted Post Road joining the two cities was as hard as iron and clogged with all manner of carts and wagons. Prosperous farms and enormous flocks of grazing sheep lined the road, a stark reminder of the rich prize Philadelphia would be in British hands. Bundled in furs and jostled in their carriages, fleeing Patriots could smell flax in the air as farmers shredded stalks to dry in the cold.

A series of dramatic victories by Washington, first at Trenton on December 26 and then at Princeton on January 3, thwarted Britain's invasion plans for the moment. Hundreds of captured Hessians were paraded through the streets of Philadelphia, soon joined by thousands of returning refugees. As both armies settled in for the winter, life returned to normal in the Quaker City. In March 1777 Congress returned, but with the spring thaw came a renewed threat.

In April, with indications of an impending attack, both the Assembly and the Council of Safety fled, plunging the capital into chaos. Congress sent word that if the Assembly "did not agree to act," the national government "would take the government of Pennsylvania into their hands."[33] A congressional committee met with leaders of the state government to try to restore some order, but it was apparent that "the executive authority of the commonwealth . . . is incapable of any exertion adequate to the present crisis."[34] Congress then asked members of Pennsylvania's Board of War, the Navy Board, and the Executive Council to run the state as a quasidictatorship until order could be restored.

Outraged radicals bridled at congressional interference, which they declared a conservative scheme to discredit them and force a new convention. They fumed that anticonstitutionalists were using the press "to keep up a continual heat."[35] Conservatives countered that Congress had to interfere in Pennsylvania "in order to save it from anarchy and ruin."[36] Two tasks were essential in wartime, conservatives said: raising revenue to pay for the war and raising men to fight in it. Radicals had failed at both. Any money they had raised had gone straight to the pockets of their political allies.

Forty-two anticonstitutionalists, led by Wilson, Rush, and Morris, petitioned the president of the Executive Council and the Board of War, which was dominated by conservatives, to call a new constitutional convention. To demonstrate their reasonableness, they were willing to postpone it indefinitely, as long as a convention was promised sometime in the future. They would even support the Pennsylvania government, especially in matters of defense and public safety.

The petition left radicals in a quandary. They knew their government was not up to the task of prosecuting a war. But if they did nothing, Congress would usurp all their power. By the summer of 1777, it seemed that a new constitutional convention was in the offing. Under Wilson's leadership, conservatives had finally developed enough momentum to overthrow the radical regime.

That was the moment 256 British warships carrying an invasion force of fifteen thousand landed in Maryland and began to march on Philadelphia. With that, all plans for a new convention came undone. Wilson remarked bitterly, "The very critical situation of public affairs is of much advantage to the assembly and their friends."[37]

Dickinson might not have resigned his colonelcy in the Pennsylvania Associators had the Assembly not appointed two notorious radicals as brigadier generals. "I resolved in the first place never to be accountable to such men for any military command," Dickinson commented.[38] Yet he remained as committed as ever to fight for his country. After departing for his Delaware estate, he enlisted as a private in the Delaware militia. As British troops crossed into Pennsylvania, Dickinson's company advanced to Brandywine Creek, where Dickinson proudly served "with a musket upon my shoulder during the whole tour of duty."[39] He spent much of his time crisscrossing the countryside hunting for ammunition for American forces, and numerous accounts attest to his bravery. Knowing his worth, Delaware's chief executive tried to appoint him to the rank of brigadier general, but Private Dickinson refused the honor. Titles meant little to him at this point.

On September 11, 1777, with fog covering the British approach, Washington found his defenses along the Brandywine badly outflanked. The Continental Army fought valiantly, but after suffering a thousand casualties, it had no choice but to retreat. The road to Philadelphia now lay open to the British. Once again pandemonium reigned in the city, and Congress hurriedly decamped to Lancaster, Pennsylvania. Howe marched into Philadelphia on September 26.

As American and British forces continued to clash over the next few months, Howe issued orders to burn down the great estates along the road to Philadelphia, fearing they might shelter American snipers. On November 22, Fairhill was put to the torch. It had been specially singled out as "that damned rebel Dickinson's house."[40] Amid the crackling flames, the central turret collapsed and the golden weathercock liquefied. The perfectly proportioned windows shattered and the graceful hip roofs caved in as torch-bearing Redcoats backed away from the roaring heat and choking smoke. The woods were trampled and the gardens, paeans to the elegance and order of a departed age, torn up.

It was Dickinson's old enemy, Joseph Galloway, now running a spy ring for the British and helping Howe administer Philadelphia, who kept the old house from total obliteration. Arriving at the scene, his face shining in the red glare, he asked the soldiers not to burn the dependencies, including the library. The estate, he said, had been entailed to Dickinson's young nephew. Perhaps he felt some compunction over destroying the property of a child; perhaps he simply regretted the loss of such a beautiful home. Most of Dickinson's prized books were thus saved from the flames, and after the war they would serve as the nucleus for the library at the newly founded Dickinson College. Years later a smaller house would be rebuilt on the site, but Fairhill would never again be America's glory.

CHAPTER 12

COOL AND DO MISCHIEF

In colonial times Charleston, South Carolina, was a triangular city thrusting into Charleston Harbor at the confluence of the Cooper and Ashley Rivers. The harbor was one of the best and busiest on the Atlantic, a refuge for ships from the violence of the nearby ocean and a golden port of call for seekers of fortune. The names of the colony's ships reflected its pursuit of riches: the *Endeavour,* the *Enterprize,* the *Industry,* and the *Success,* among others.

Entering the harbor was not easy. Ships had first to navigate across the Charleston Bar, a series of underwater shoals eight miles to the southeast of the city. Once inside the harbor, rip currents and tidal changes endangered smaller vessels.

Once safely ashore, a white man found a land of opportunity, with money ready to be made in the professions, through trade, and on the backs of slaves. Even as relations with Great Britain deteriorated, Charleston's prosperity led to a building boom that reshaped the city in only a few years. As the printer of the *South-Carolina Gazette* wrote to Benjamin Franklin in 1768, "I do not suppose there is a colony on this continent so flourishing and promising as South Carolina at present. Private and public works are everywhere carrying on with spirit."[1]

Broad Street, a pearl of the British Empire, spanned the base of the Charleston triangle, hitting the water at each end. At the eastern end stood the perfectly proportioned Exchange Building, completed in 1771 in the popular Palladian style. All who arrived by sea passed through the open arcade in the Great Hall and emerged upon the elegant thoroughfare. A few blocks down, at the bustling intersection of Broad and Meeting Streets, stood the magnificent new State House, built in 1756. Catercorner to the State House was St. Michael's Church, erected five years later. On adjacent corners stood the Beef

Market and a new Watch House, which required an unplanned extra story to house the offices of the treasurer, the country comptroller, and the powder receiver.

South Carolina paid homage to those who prospered and those who ruled. Statues of venerated men stood in public squares. In the nearby Harlston Village, east-west streets received the names of royal officials, including the colony's impetuous young governor, Charles Greville Montagu, and his more diplomatic lieutenant governor, William Bull II. North-south streets were named after prominent Patriots, including the wealthy radical Christopher Gadsden and John Rutledge—an indication that, like today, one's politics, left or right, could not be determined by money alone.

One of the most spectacular private works anywhere in the colonies, in fact, was a wharf built by Gadsden. In June 1774 Gadsden wrote his friend Sam Adams in Boston that he and his slaves had spent seven years completing the longest wharf in America, able to dock thirty of the largest ships simultaneously. Canals were dredged to further enable commerce through the colony, and more were planned.

South Carolina's dazzling prosperity made it a tempting target for the revenue-hungry British. When Britain began squeezing America for more money, the colony was among the hardest hit. Overzealous British customs officials began arbitrarily seizing American ships; to cover themselves legally, the British relieved American sheriffs, judges, and other government officials of their positions and replaced them with Englishmen whose first allegiance was to the Crown.

Democratic Massachusetts has long been regarded as the lodestar of the American rebellion, but aristocratic South Carolina played just as pivotal a role in leading the fight against Britain. It was in fact the very first colony to choose delegates for the Stamp Act Congress, including Gadsden (then forty-five) and Rutledge (then twenty-six). It had clashed with the royal governor after voting to help pay the legal fees of the English radical leader John Wilkes, who had been arrested for criticizing Parliament.

Again Rutledge played a pivotal role. "In rousing the Assembly and the people to resist," wrote the South Carolina revolutionary David Ramsay, "John Rutledge kindled a spark which has never since been extinguished."[2] By 1776 hostility to the British government was well established in South Carolina. So too was a sense of gilded gentility and an iron devotion to the social hierarchy. Any revolution that attempted to oust South Carolina's elites would meet spirited resistance.

* * *

In the winter of 1776, John Rutledge returned to South Carolina to help with the province's military preparations. He hoped to go back to Philadelphia later, but after his election that spring to his colony's Provincial Congress, he decided not to rejoin the Continental Congress for "many weighty reasons." In addition to building up the colony's defenses, he also wanted to help draft a new constitution. The province had had no legitimate government ever since the colonial governor fled aboard a British warship in September 1775, an act, Rutledge wrote, designed to "loosen the bands of government and create anarchy and confusion in the colonies."[3]

Creating a new government was not something South Carolina wanted to undertake lightly—especially after Gadsden had shocked the Provincial Congress by calling for independence and presenting the legislators with a copy of *Common Sense.* His actions "came like an explosion of thunder upon the members of Congress," wrote one legislator.[4] Conservatives were mollified, however, when Rutledge assured his fellow delegates that he "was willing to ride post, by day and night to Philadelphia, in order to assist, in re-uniting Great Britain and America."[5]* Any new constitution would be only temporary, Rutledge wrote in the document's preamble, lasting "until an accommodation of the unhappy differences between Great-Britain and America could be obtained (an event which, traduced and treated as rebels, we still earnestly desire)."[6]

It took Rutledge a bit over three weeks to draft the lion's share of the new constitution; when finished, it was a model of conservative political thought. While other states were eviscerating the executive branch, viewing it as a source of tyranny, South Carolina conferred enormous power upon its president. (Rutledge consciously avoided the term *governor,* implying that the royal governor could return upon reconciliation with Britain.) The president had absolute veto power, was considered a part of the legislature, and received a sizable salary of £9,000 a year. He served as commander in chief of South Carolina's armed forces and was authorized to act largely without restrictions in matters of war and peace. Additionally, no term limits were set on the office. The bicameral legislature that Rutledge outlined had the power to appoint judges and military officers, rather than allowing these positions to be elected, and property qualifications for all officeholders were actually tight-

---

* Riding post was a painful punishment meted out by colonial mobs. Victims were forced to straddle sharp fence posts while being paraded through town.

ened. All together, wrote one radical ruefully, the new constitution departed "as little as possible from ancient forms and names."[7]

On March 26 the Provincial Congress turned itself into the General Assembly and elected Rutledge president and commander in chief of South Carolina. Flattered and humbled by the appointment, he promised the Assembly: "My most fervent prayer, to the omnipotent ruler of the universe, is that under his gracious providence, the liberties of America may be for ever preserved."[8]

Flanked by the Charleston Militia and the Provincial Regiment of Artillery and following the sheriff of Charleston, who brandished the official sword of state, Rutledge was conveyed up Broad Street from the State House to the Exchange Building, where the preamble and part of the new constitution was read. Throngs cheered wildly as Rutledge was sworn in, and the festivities concluded with "thirteen discharges from the cannon of the artillery—a *feu de joye* from the line of troops—and the cannon of the *Prosper* ship-of-war, and other armed vessels in the harbor."[9]

Lest the new legislature forget that it was but an interim government, Rutledge addressed both houses in mid-April on their proper roles. "And now gentlemen," he said, "let me intreat [*sic*] that you will, in your several parishes and districts, use your influence and authority to keep peace and good order, and procure strict observance of and read obedience to the law." Rutledge left no doubt he meant British law. He urged legislators to remind their constituents of their ancient rights as British subjects, their right to be tried by a jury, to be taxed only by their consent through their representatives, and to be governed by laws overseen by competent judges. In the end, he believed, a lasting peace with Britain would be forged when American rights were honored.

Until that time, however, America had to prepare for battle. One of Rutledge's first orders of business was to oversee the strengthening of coastal fortifications, for news had arrived that the British were preparing to set sail from New York and invade the South. No one knew if their target was Virginia or the Carolinas, but Rutledge needed to prepare for the worst. Charleston had already witnessed the might of the Royal Navy when South Carolina and British ships exchanged fire in the harbor in November 1775.

On the last day of May, Rutledge received intelligence that the long-dreaded invasion fleet had been spotted twenty miles north of the Charleston Bar. The following day fifty enemy ships, both men-of-war and troop transports, filled the harbor with bristling masts and billowing sails. "The sight of these vessels alarmed us very much," wrote Colonel William Moultrie; "all was hurry and confusion."[10]

With alarm guns sounding through the city, Rutledge sent express couriers to every parish calling for militia reinforcements. Hasty fortifications were thrown up, and lead was stripped from church windows to cast musket balls, in perilously short supply as usual. Rutledge and his privy council hastened to inspect all the city's military preparations. "The President was as diligent, as active as a man could be," wrote Henry Laurens, a rich plantation owner and a future president of the Continental Congress.[11]

The city's most important defenses lay out on the water. Two forts defended Charleston Harbor, Fort Johnson on James Island to the south and a new fort under construction on Sullivan's Island to the north. Fort Johnson was well protected. The new fort represented a serious problem, however. Only two of its four walls had been completed, and the remaining two were only a few feet high. One of Rutledge's main concerns now was completing the fort before the British attacked.

Leading a force of more than three thousand Redcoats, General Henry Clinton had been selected to attack Charleston for several strategic reasons. He had been encouraged by reports of strong Loyalist activity, which he hoped would help him oust the Patriot government. And he knew that the fortifications on Sullivan's Island were incomplete. If he could seize the island, Charleston Harbor, and with it the city's rich shipping trade, would be his.

Learning of the impending attack, Congress appointed Major General Charles Lee to take command of the Southern Department of the war. Lee, a former British officer, was a veteran of the French and Indian War and, according to Washington, "the first officer in military knowledge and experience we have in the whole army."[12] Thin and bony with a long, hooked nose, he had a violent temper that even Washington feared. On June 4 Rutledge got word that Lee, hastening down from Wilmington, would arrive imminently. "I wish you and a powerful reinforcement were now here," the president wrote him. "For God's sake, lose not a moment. . . . Bring us all the forces you can collect to cope with this armament, either from North Carolina, Virginia, or any part of this province you pass through."[13]

Two days later Lee and nineteen hundred Virginia and North Carolina Continentals arrived in Charleston, where "his presence gave us great spirits," wrote Rutledge.[14] Because South Carolina had rejected Continental Army regulations, Lee had no legal authority over the troops Rutledge had been mustering for Charleston's defense. As the state's commander in chief, however, Rutledge understood the risks of a divided command and promptly handed control of his troops over to Lee. But it didn't take him long to start questioning Lee's orders.

Visiting the half-finished fortifications on Sullivan's Island, Lee despaired of defending the position. He also had little faith in Colonel Moultrie, who was in command of the incomplete battlements. Ordering the island to be abandoned, Lee declared that the fort "could not hold out half an hour and that the platform was but a slaughtering-stage."[15]

Rutledge was furious when he learned of Lee's order. Moultrie had assured him the fort could be held, and Rutledge knew how vital it was to Charleston's defense. "While a soldier remained alive to defend it," Rutledge said, "he would never give his sanction to such an order." To Moultrie, he wrote with typical bravado, "General Lee wishes you to evacuate the fort. You will not do so without an order from me. I would sooner cut off my right hand than write one!"[16]

In the face of Rutledge's intransigence, Lee capitulated and aided Moultrie in finishing defensive works as quickly as possible. To minimize potential losses, he reduced the number of defenders by more than two-thirds to 345. He also made sure Moultrie understood the central weakness of his position. If British men-of-war swung into the island's cove, their guns would enfilade the fort, shredding its occupants to pieces.

It was fortunate for the Americans that General Clinton delayed his attack for three more weeks, giving them precious time to strengthen their positions. Lee declared Clinton "to be a [damned] fool," but the British general was waiting for reinforcements that never came.[17] Finally on June 28, he struck, launching a two-pronged attack on Sullivan's Island. In an attempt to exploit Moultrie's weakness, Clinton landed British forces on a nearby sand bank called Long Island. From there the Redcoats tried to wade through the water and launch a land assault on Sullivan Island's unprotected rear. Deep water and valiant resistance fended off the attack.

At the same time, Clinton sent the fleet in to shell the fort. Three ships attempted the exact maneuver Lee had feared, swinging around the unfinished side of the fort to pound it from the rear. "Almighty Providence confounded the plan," wrote William Henry Drayton, a rich South Carolina radical.[18] The warships got caught and tangled on the Middle Ground Shoal, where they grounded.*

At eleven in the morning, the remaining men-of-war dropped anchor three to four hundred yards from the island and prepared to bombard the soft palmetto logs protecting the front of the fort. Seeing the attack about to com-

* The Middle Ground Shoal was the future site of Fort Sumter, flashpoint of the American Civil War.

mence, Lee tried to get to the fort himself, but the small boat he was in could not push past the fierce wind and tide, stranding him, ineffectual, in the middle of the water and forcing him to retreat to the American defenses at Haddrell's Point across the harbor.

"They immediately commenced the most furious fire that I ever heard or saw," Lee wrote to Washington. "I confess I was in pain from the little confidence I reposed in our troops, the officers being all boys, and the men raw recruits."[19]

The battle now devolved into a duel of flying lead. Lee was agonized by the knowledge that the Americans on the island had next to no ammunition, and he was certain it would mean the death of all its defenders. Finally able to get through later in the day, the general was astonished instead by "the cool courage they displayed." Despite the deafening roar of British cannons, morale remained high. Those who were mortally wounded exhorted their comrades "never to abandon the standard of liberty." Men who lost limbs refused to desert their posts. "Upon the whole, they acted like Romans in the third century," Lee reported to Washington.[20]

For twelve full hours, the British blasted the fort "without intermission." The Americans returned fire as best they could with their dwindling ammunition. Back at Haddrell's Point, Lee watched the rate of American fire slowing and sent orders telling Moultrie to abandon his position and spike his cannons if his gunpowder ran out.

Moultrie instead sent word pleading for more powder. Not realizing Lee had returned to Haddrell's Point, he sent his message to Charleston, where Rutledge received it. The president immediately sent the beleaguered Moultrie what he could, five hundred pounds of powder, with more on the way the next day. With the delivery, Rutledge included a short pencil-written note on a slip of paper, "Honor and victory, my good Sir, to you and our worthy countrymen with you. P.S. Do not make too free with your cannon. Cool, and do mischief."

Rutledge's powder reached its destination at five in the afternoon, just as Moultrie was about to run out. It saved the day. While British shot was splintering the fort, American cannons were wreaking havoc aboard the exposed British vessels, cracking wood, shredding rigging, and blowing bodies apart. By the evening, the British had had enough and retreated.

In the end, ten Americans were killed and twenty-two wounded, many of whom lost legs or arms. It was an important sacrifice for the American cause. Moultrie's defense and Rutledge's faith in him saved the Port of Charleston.

Had Clinton succeeded, it would probably have closed the port for three or four years.

The following day Rutledge sent another fifteen hundred pounds of powder along with a hogshead of rum, the latter being even more gratefully received than the former. On July 4, as the delegates were approving the Declaration of Independence in Philadelphia, Rutledge visited the fort. He greeted the officers, reviewed the militiamen, and "addressed them with an energy of feeling that I had never before experienced, and if ever I had pretension to eloquence, it was at that moment."[21] In honor of Moultrie's defense, the fortress was named after him.

It was no time, however, for Rutledge to relax his guard. At the same time the British were launching their attack, the Cherokees began their own invasion of South Carolina all along the frontier. Numerous settlements were destroyed, their inhabitants killed or scattered. As the violence spread rapidly from Georgia to Virginia, furious Patriots blamed British agents for deliberately stirring up the trouble. Shortly after the battle at Charleston, Rutledge raised eleven hundred men to march against the Cherokees and "carry on a war against them, unless they will submit to reasonable terms."[22]

The Declaration of Independence arrived in Charleston on August 2 and was officially proclaimed on August 5 in a grand procession. Young and old, men and women, the people gathered around Charleston's Liberty Tree, an ancient live oak under whose spreading branches Patriots had been meeting to discuss political questions for over a decade, to listen to the document read aloud. The Declaration generally met with great approval, but many marked the occasion with solemnity rather than jubilation. Henry Laurens reflected the feelings of many Charleston conservatives when he dressed in black for the reading. His son had just passed away, but it was independence, he said, that gave him "much more pain."[23]

By the end of 1776, the Rutledge family's influence was felt in almost every part of South Carolina politics. Rutledge, of course, was the president and commander in chief. His brother Hugh was speaker of the legislature's upper house, the Legislative Council, a member of the president's Privy Council, and an admiralty judge. Edward Rutledge, the leading South Carolina delegate at the Continental Congress, was soon to return home to become an artillery officer and a representative in the General Assembly for Charleston. Their brother Thomas was a member of the General Assembly for St. Helena. And various in-laws and marriage connections further cemented the family's hold on power. The constitution, which Rutledge had done so much to craft, buttressed his kinship network's hold on state politics.

Wealthy radicals like Gadsden and Drayton began to resent this setup, and they soon set about searching for a way to break Rutledge's hold. The solution to their problems lay in America's newly declared independence. Indeed, independence posed a serious problem for Rutledge's constitution. The fact that the document declared itself to be only temporary seemed increasingly incompatible with America's status as a new nation. Since there was no going back to Britain, calls for a new constitution began to grow.

The notion was popular with almost everyone outside Charleston's gentry. Urban radicals, poorer planters, religious dissenters, frontier settlers, and everyone else who simply hated the Rutledges wanted to revise the constitution to reflect American independence and to reduce the power of the president. These groups also wanted a larger share of power for themselves. Thus in October 1776, Gadsden led the revolt in the General Assembly, introducing a motion for a new constitution. A committee was quickly formed to study the idea.

Compared to the Pennsylvania constitution, the committee's proposed changes were far from radical; money would still play a prominent role in determining political representation. On the other hand, the new constitution would greatly strengthen democracy in South Carolina. The Legislative Council would be renamed the Senate and would be elected by the general population, instead of being appointed by the lower house. The General Assembly would be elected every two years, and greater political representation would be given to the population outside Charleston.

Executive power was also sharply curtailed. The president, now to be called governor, was no longer to be considered part of the legislature. His veto power was removed, as were his abilities to declare war and peace and to enter into treaties without the consent of the legislature. The position was now subject to term limits, with the governor being ineligible for office for six years after the completion of a term. The legislature also eliminated the governor's salary and ruled that neither his brother, father, nor son could serve on the Privy Council. The last item was aimed squarely at removing Hugh Rutledge from his position.

One of the most prominent and popular changes in the new constitution was the disestablishment of the Anglican Church. Although Rutledge did not oppose this provision, he felt the issue would be better handled by a change in statutory law, not by a constitutional revision.

Addressing the General Assembly in December 1776, Rutledge made no mention of the proposed constitutional changes being debated by the legislature, but he did briefly reiterate the virtues of the existing constitution. For the moment, more pressing issues occupied Rutledge's and the legislature's attention than constitutional reform.

Rutledge recommended changes to the state's finances and criticized a recent law banning the purchase of large amounts of goods at public sales with the intent to sell them later for what was deemed an unreasonable profit. The war had led to a rapid depreciation of paper money—300 percent by the end of 1777—making it difficult for the poor to buy necessities. But Rutledge urged the legislature to combat mounting inflation by increasing supplies of vital goods rather than instituting the sorts of price controls favored by the left.

He also urged the legislature to adopt the Articles of Confederation, which the Continental Congress had sent to the states for ratification. In the midst of the war, Rutledge thought it vital that the United States establish a functioning central government.

Finally, Rutledge told the legislature that in the event of a British invasion, the president would be forced to make emergency decisions without consulting the rest of the government. At the same time, he thought it dangerous to leave it to the executive to decide "under sanction of necessity only." Any "extraordinary powers" that he was allowed to assume needed to be clarified in advance.[24] Far from being power hungry, Rutledge was concerned with the due process of law even during the exigencies of war.

The constitutional issue simmered for another year, but in January 1778 the General Assembly finally finished drafting the new constitution. Immediately the state divided in two over the proposed changes. "The lines of difference," writes the historian Raymond Starr, "pitted the Charleston-Lowcountry conservative aristocracy, desirous of maintaining control over the government and preventing internal changes of a democratic nature, against the philosophical radicals, like Gadsden and Drayton, and the Backcountry, which wanted more equitable representation, separation of church and state, and better local government."[25]

On the whole, the new document was far more democratic than the 1776 constitution, and it implicitly struck at the Rutledge family's hold on power. The legislature's upper house, led by Hugh Rutledge, attacked the new constitution but was soon forced to back down on almost every objection. Since their offices depended on the General Assembly, they had little room to maneuver. Once the two houses had worked out their differences, they sent the new constitution to John Rutledge for his signature on March 5, 1778, along with several other routine bills.

At a joint session Rutledge dutifully read and signed the bills as they were presented to him, until at last he came to the new constitution. He then "laid it before him and took a paper out of his pocket which was a speech."[26] What Rutledge did next shocked everyone. He vetoed the constitution.

Reading from his prepared text, Rutledge addressed all the problems he saw in the new constitution. He told the assembled legislators that his oath to support the earlier constitution prevented his signing the new one. More important, he did not believe they had the authority to revoke the constitution, especially as it "annihilate[d] one branch of the legislature" and changed the way the upper house was elected. "The legislative authority being fixed and limited, it cannot change or destroy itself without subverting the constitution." Doing so would threaten liberty itself.

"The more I reflect on the matter," Rutledge wrote in a letter to Laurens, "the more I am convinced that a legislature has no lawful power to establish a different one, but that such power is only in the people, on a dissolution of government, or subversion of the constitution."[27] This notion that the power ultimately resides in the people paralleled the ideas Wilson was developing simultaneously in Pennsylvania.

Furthermore, Rutledge continued, independence did not necessitate a change in government. "Admitting our form of government to be temporary, it is to continue until that accommodation shall take place, until peace between Great Britain and America shall be concluded."[28] Rutledge was not saying he wanted to renounce independence. Rather, he thought no new constitution was needed until a peace accord had been reached.

Rutledge pointed out that the people at large were happy with the existing constitution and were not calling for a new one. Allowing the general population to elect the Senate was a mistake, he believed. Letting the General Assembly elect the upper house made it "more likely that persons of the greatest integrity, learning, and ability would be chosen by and from amongst the representatives when assembled."

The document was far too democratic, he believed, and "the people also preferred a compound or mixed government to a simple democracy or one verging towards it, perhaps because (however unexceptionable democratic power may appear at first view) its effects have been found arbitrarily severe and destructive."[29]

Not only did the Assembly lack the legal right to change the fundamental law of the state, and not only was this move unnecessary, but the new constitution also shifted the state's entire power structure away from the Charleston gentry who had governed for so long. Democracy, or a government verging on it, represented a radical change in society that the legislature had no right to push through as though it were an ordinary legislative item. Only a special convention of the people could make such drastic changes to the structure of government.

Rutledge concluded his address by saying that he "was not so vain" as to think he could change their minds. If his veto had been unexpected, after his next words the legislators "stood amazed looking at one another."[30] Rutledge resigned on the spot.

Uncertain what to do next, the General Assembly made its way silently to its own chamber, where Rawlins Lowndes, a Charleston jurist who had drafted much of the new constitution, rose to speak. He admired Rutledge's integrity, he said, but did not agree with him. The legislators then conferred about whether they should even accept Rutledge's resignation. By a single vote, they agreed to accept it and to appoint a new president.

Two days later the legislature elected president the wealthy plantation owner Arthur Middleton. Echoing Rutledge's words, Middleton declined the position, saying "that he disapproved of the bill; that they had no right to pass such a one; that, if he approved of it, he could not pass it (having taken the oath) nor could any man who should take the oath, without being perjured."[31] A second vote was taken in which Rawlins Lowndes gained a plurality of votes, just ahead of Christopher Gadsden. A third vote confirmed Lowndes as the new president. He too was reluctant to accept the office but accepted it since someone had to. He then signed the new constitution into law, abolishing his own position as president in the process.

Gadsden, as usual, "found great fault" with Rutledge's actions, but his fellow legislators disagreed. By a vote of sixty-eight to fifteen, the legislature thanked the former president "for his vigilant and faithful discharge of his duties."

Rutledge replied that "the approbation of my countrymen" was "the greatest reward that any man can obtain." He thanked the legislature for its ability to rise above factional dispute and for recognizing that his vetoing the new constitution was not "a wanton abuse of power."

Rutledge was in many ways the epitome of southern conservatism, committed to working within the system to prevent radical change and fiercely protective of local hierarchy. Like all great conservatives, he knew when it was proper to oppose change and when it was appropriate to back down. During his two years as president he had defended the state against British invasion and internal chaos. His service to South Carolina was far from over, and he was soon elected to the General Assembly. He also began looking after his personal affairs, which he had long neglected—reopening his legal practice, trying to collect outstanding debts, and speculating in land. For now his political opponents had the upper hand. But the war was far from over, and few possessed his same courage and resolve in the face of danger. It would be only a short time before South Carolina was clamoring for Rutledge's return.

CHAPTER 13

THE TURNING POINT

American dreams of conquering the British in Canada ended in a blinding snowstorm beneath the battlements of Quebec on the last day of 1775. With fewer than a thousand hungry and near-mutinous troops threatening to leave because their enlistments were almost up, Brigadier General Richard Montgomery rushed to attack the well-fortified British defenders, who outnumbered him two to one. In the ensuing chaos, Montgomery was killed and his valorous second in command, Brigadier General Benedict Arnold, was wounded, his left leg shattered by a musket ball. Fifty Americans were killed, and hundreds were taken prisoner.

The invasion of Canada had been beset by problems from the start. When Congress ordered Major General Philip Schuyler to attack in June 1775, it badly misjudged how Canadians would react to an American army in their midst. The delegates in Philadelphia were hoping America's northern neighbor would join the rebellion against Britain as a fourteenth colony, but few French-speaking Catholics had forgotten Congress's virulent denunciation of the King's Quebec Act, granting French Canadians religious and civil liberties, only the year before.

Canada's harsh weather also made it crucial to attack before the season grew too late, but Schuyler was delayed by numerous ineluctable factors. For one thing, he needed to verify that enough Canadians would actually welcome his army. He also had to raise thousands of troops as well as mammoth quantities of provisions, weapons, and vehicles to carry all.

None of these efforts went smoothly. When Schuyler requested gun carriages to transport his cannons, the New York Provincial Congress refused to pay and suggested he build them himself. The province agreed to furnish iron, but Schuyler got entangled haggling over the specifications for the gun bores that the carriages would carry. Procuring munitions also required lengthy correspondence. Schuyler needed to buy and transport hundreds of barrels of peas, flour, and rice to feed the troops. He had to purchase clothing, wagons, animals, shovels, and axes. A fleet of ships had to be built to use on Lakes George and Champlain, as well as dozens of flat-bottomed boats to ferry troops. Threats of Indian attacks further delayed the northward advance. And Congress was delaying making critical appointments necessary for Schuyler to proceed. All the while the general was chronically low on funds and gunpowder.

Schuyler envisioned needing no fewer than four thousand troops to undertake the expedition, but by late summer he had been able to raise only twenty-five hundred men, scattered between Manhattan and Lake Champlain. Nor could he use all of them for the attack. At least a thousand soldiers had to remain behind to defend against British, Indian, and Loyalist raids in New York. Schuyler grew so desperate for troops at one point that he tried enlisting a regiment of Ethan Allen's Green Mountain Boys, who at that very moment were revolting against New Yorkers like himself who held legal title to lands in Vermont. In the end, Schuyler had to make due with twelve hundred men with which to take all of Canada.

Faced with so many logistical and supply problems, Schuyler's army did not get under way until late August. By then the general was already the subject of savage attacks for delays that were out of his control. Yet it was only because of Schuyler's indefatigable efforts that the invasion force was organized as quickly as it was. Though the Americans did not yet know it, it was too late for them to capture Canada.

Sickness dogged Schuyler's forces all along their northward march. More than six hundred, including Schuyler himself, fell gravely ill. "Reduced to skeleton with a complication of disorders, I have been under the distressing necessity of returning to [Ticonderoga], to procure, if possible, a restoration of my health, which is greatly impaired," he wrote.[1] Sending Montgomery and Arnold ahead into Canada, Schuyler stayed behind at Fort Ticonderoga, a star-shaped Gibraltar that guarded the portage point between Lakes Champlain and George and was known as the "key to the continent." Despite his enfeebled state, Schuyler continued to send massive amounts of provisions to his forces, who finally captured Montreal in December.

The disaster at Quebec, a devastating smallpox outbreak in Montreal, the failure of Congress to send American forces hard currency to buy supplies, and the massive accumulation of British reinforcements throughout the first half of 1776 spelled the end of America's adventure in the north. By July 1776 Schuyler's army was beating a full-scale retreat from Canada.

Now was Schuyler's greatest hour. As the British harried his army southward, he perfected the delaying and harassing tactics that would become the linchpin of America's ultimate victory. By shifting from the sort of offensive war favored by radicals to a more defensive kind, he staved off the obliteration of his forces. In this, Schuyler deserves as much credit as Washington. By keeping his army alive, he kept the British from winning the war.

Like all of America's founding conservatives, Philip Schuyler yearned for peace with Britain but would never, he declared, "tamely submit to an insolent and wicked ministry" or be "ruled by a military despotism."[2] Not quite six feet tall, deeply tanned, with dark piercing eyes, he looked every part the aristocrat he was. He dressed impeccably and spoke in a rasping voice, especially when issuing commands. Silas Deane called him "the soul of Albany county, and though he may have his faults, he is sincere, well bred, and resolute."[3] To his friends, Schuyler was known to be courteous and gentlemanly—and to have an arrogant streak that made him unpopular among some. To his enemies, it was clear that he found "social inferiors tolerable only if they kept their lowly distance."[4]

Schuyler ranked among the semifeudal patricians of New York. His landholdings were vast, ranging between ten and twenty thousand acres. Hundreds of tenant farmers lived on his land, and though their rents were frequently in arrears, Schuyler remained one of the richest Americans in the Revolution. His main property in Saratoga, about thirty-five miles north of Albany, included a well-built Georgian house, two sawmills, a gristmill, and a hemp and flax mill, manned by hired laborers and slaves.

Schuyler's dreams for developing America were as prodigious as his fortune. After touring England in 1761, he began envisioning filling his own nation with canals, coal mines, and manufacturing centers, such as he had seen abroad. As an investor, he did his best to make these dreams a reality. "General Schuyler informs me that an uninterrupted water carriage between New York and Quebec might be perfected at 50,000 pounds sterling,"* wrote the wealthy Maryland conservative Charles Carroll in 1776.[5]

Combined with his haughty temperament, Schuyler's capitalistic ambitions did little to endear him to American radicals. His insistence that America fight the British with a professional army rather than a people's militia was downright abhorrent to them. As his fellow New Yorker George Clinton

* About $6 million today.

wrote to James Duane, "Our friend Phil has good qualities, but he has contrived to make himself disagreeable and suspect by the Yankees."[6]

From the beginning of Schuyler's military career, New Englanders began plotting to remove him from command of the Northern Department. Their goal was to replace him with their favorite general, the British-born Horatio Gates. White-haired and droopy-eyed, he was known throughout the army as "Granny Gates," though whether this was because of his elderly appearance or because of his habitual reluctance to meet the British in battle was open to debate. All agreed he was an ambitious careerist, and it surely didn't escape Gates that playing up his democratic politics won him staunch allies in the "Eastern" states, as New England was called then. As Schuyler wrote to Gouverneur Morris, "My crime consists in not being a New England Man in principle, and unless they alter theirs I hope I never shall be. Gen. Gates is their idol because he is at their direction."[7]

In the "competition between him and Schuyler," wrote John Adams, "I always contended for Gates." Although "the rivalry occasioned great animosities among friends of the two generals," Adams said he felt no "personal prejudice" against Schuyler.[8] More than enough New Englanders did, however, to turn the fight between Gates and Schuyler into a proxy war between radicals and conservatives in Congress.

While Schuyler was desperately trying to keep his army intact, Gates arrived in Albany in late June 1776 armed with new orders from Congress. With the backing of his radical supporters, he had contrived to be promoted to major general and appointed commander of the American forces in Canada. This appointment presented some jurisdictional problems, largely because there were no more American forces in Canada. But Schuyler decided to reach out to Gates, assuming the radical general would defer to him. Not only did Schuyler have seniority, but he also remained in charge of the entire Northern Department. The army now fleeing back to New York, he believed, was thus under his ultimate command. Greeting Gates "with every friendly and affectionate wish," Schuyler invited him to his home in Albany and said he hoped they could work together to prevent any "increase of our misfortune in this unlucky quarter."[9] It didn't take Schuyler long to realize that Gates was, in fact, aiming to usurp his command.

By the end of the summer, Schuyler had learned the extent of the plot against him. In Congress radicals were accusing him of cowardice and misconduct and of being more concerned with turning a profit selling war supplies than with beating the British. As one of the largest landowners in upper New York, he was, in fact, uniquely suited to supplying the army's needs.

Schuyler was outraged by the attacks. His character, he said, had been "most infamously aspersed in every party of the country and all the misfortunes in Canada attributed to" him.[10] In September the general demanded a hearing before Congress to vindicate himself. He also offered to submit his resignation from the army. Congress refused Schuyler on both fronts. Fearful that the war between the generals was harming the war against the British, the delegates quickly issued a clarification. The New Yorker was indeed still in charge.

This setback did not discourage Gates and the radicals for long. After accompanying troops from the Northern Department to New Jersey to aid Washington, Gates conveniently claimed sickness to avoid fighting beside the commander in chief at Trenton and Princeton. Instead he took off for Baltimore, where Congress had temporarily fled, to recuperate under the ministrations of Sam Adams. "General Gates is here," Sam wrote excitedly to his cousin John. "How shall we make him head of that army?"[11]

As usual, the Adamses came up with a clever plan. Playing upon Schuyler's well-known short fuse, they devised a scheme to make the general lash out at Congress. The same day Sam Adams wrote to his cousin, the radicals orchestrated the dismissal of a well-respected doctor under Schuyler's command without first seeking the general's opinion. As the Adams cousins had predicted, Schuyler exploded when he learned the news, writing Congress a sarcastic letter whose haughty style was deemed "ill-advised" and "highly derogatory to the honor of Congress." Schuyler was admonished to write future letters "in a style more suitable to the dignity of the representative body of these free and independent states."[12]

It was the pretext radicals had been waiting for. Seizing upon the rebuke, they had Gates appointed commander of the American army at Fort Ticonderoga. Whether this meant he was now superior to Schuyler or at least independent of him was left unclear. But the insult to Schuyler was plain.

Recognizing that the general's "reputation has been deeply wounded by the malevolence of party spirit," as Edward Rutledge said to Jay, Schuyler's allies swung into action.[13] They lost little time launching a counteroffensive to have him reinstated as sole commander of the Northern Department. Led by James Duane, New York conservatives began "cultivating the friendship of the members of the Southern states." And they were not above opening their pocketbooks to convince holdouts, "for it was no time to consult parsimony," Duane wrote to Livingston.[14] With the southern bloc supporting Schuyler—Richard Henry Lee being the sole holdout—Schuyler was again confirmed commander of the Northern Department.

Now it was Gates's turn to lose his temper. Returning to Philadelphia in June 1777, he insisted on a hearing to address the "disgrace" of losing his command. After taking the floor, he launched into a venomous attack on Duane, accusing him of subverting the American army. Duane objected, but when Gates refused to blunt his tirade, he was declared out of order and directed to leave the building. He refused. Radicals now leaped to Gates's defense, and all sense of decorum was shattered. When the shouting died down, Gates left the State House in a cloud of anger. Nothing, it turned out, could have been better for his career.

At the same moment radicals and conservatives were battling in Congress, John Jay was submitting a draft of a new constitution to New York's Provincial Congress. The document was in his handwriting but had been thoroughly edited by his friends and fellow conservatives Duane, Livingston, and Gouverneur Morris. More important still, it had also been approved by the radicals serving on the drafting committee. More elitist than Pennsylvania's radical constitution and less so than Rutledge's in South Carolina, New York's constitution was the result of a conscious decision by the state's conservatives to craft a far more moderate system of government. It was the only way, they realized, they could survive.

Operating under the mounting threat of radical violence, "conservatives were frankly alarmed at the debate over political fundamentals the prospect of constitution-making had precipitated," writes the historian Alfred Young.[15] Increasingly vocal and militant working-class men were calling for democratic reforms that would all but end the elites' dominance of state politics. Some wanted to throw out all traditional government and start from scratch. "So far as private property will allow," wrote "Spartanus" in a series of essays titled *The Interest of America*, the people must "form our government . . . just as if we had never had any form of government before." Like Pennsylvania's left, he championed a unicameral assembly and annual elections with officials chosen through mass meetings of the people.[16]

Radicals also insisted that any constitution submitted to the Provincial Congress first had to be ratified by the people, who had "the right, which God has given them, in common with all men, to judge whether it be consistent with their interest to accept or reject" the new constitution. Moreover, they insisted the people had the "uncontrolled power to alter the constitution" whenever they felt it necessary. As the historian Edward Countryman writes, this amounted to an "eighteenth-century version of permanent revolution."[17]

It was at this juncture that Robert Livingston spoke of "the propriety of swimming with a stream which it is impossible to stem." Mindful of how thoroughly Pennsylvania's conservatives had been excluded from government, New York's right wing began working out a detailed strategy for staying in power. "You know," Livingston continued, "nothing but well timed delays, indefatigable industry, and the minute attention to every favorable circumstance, could have prevented our being exactly in their situation."[18]

Jay's constitution did include a number of democratic concessions. It provided for a weakened governor, voting by secret ballot for some offices, and measures to help the illiterate vote. The number of Assembly seats was boosted to seventy from thirty-one, and three seats that had been reserved for great manors were abolished. Jay even inserted a clause forbidding the continuation of slavery in the future, though he himself would later buy a slave. It also included annual elections for local offices and delegates to Congress, which some conservatives worried gave too much power to "the peasantry."[19]

But the New York constitution remained aristocratic in many other ways. In writing the document, Jay did his best to heed advice Edward Rutledge had sent him: "A pure democracy may possibly do when patriotism is the ruling passion, but when a state abounds in rascals (as is the case with too many at this day) you must suppress a little of that popular spirit, vest the executive powers of government in an individual that they may have vigor and let them be as ample as is consistent with the great outlines of freedom."[20]

Under the new constitution, the legislature would remain bicameral, there would be no annual elections for state officials, and the Senate would choose the governor, who would serve a three-year term. Furthermore, a Council of Revision, made up of the governor, the chancellor, and judges of the Supreme Court, could veto legislation. Jay came up with this idea as a bridge between conservatives and radicals, who had resisted granting the governor any veto power over the legislature. Though the lower and executive classes would likely control the Assembly, the Senate would be largely conservative, and the governor could open or suspend the Assembly at will. Furthermore, the governor and four senators were empowered to appoint county officials, a move aimed to prevent the appointment of "ignorant and inattentive clerks."[21]

One of the biggest concessions conservatives pried from radicals was the retention of high property qualifications. Voters for the Assembly had to have £20, while voters for the Senate and governor needed a minimum of £100. Jay also ensured that there was no direct link between popular calls for action and government response. Finally, when the document was ratified in April 1777, it was approved by the Provincial Congress and not submitted to the people.

Conservatives had high hopes the new constitution would address the greatest threat to their power—the continuing presence of extralegal revolutionary committees, which continued to issue rulings on everything from bread prices and taxation to military matters and the seizure of Tory property. In an attempt to delegitimize their authority, conservatives argued that these committees actually obstructed the will of the people, since they interfered with the new government authorized by the constitution.

Reaction to the new constitution was mixed. Some admired it as a brilliant compromise. Praising Jay's handiwork, Robert Troup wrote that the document "preserves the proper line between aristocracy on the one hand and democracy on the other." Jay replied that the line was very thin indeed: "Another turn of the winch would've cracked the cord."[22]

Criticisms came from both left and right. Some found the document distressingly conservative. Writing under the name "A True Patriot," one Pennsylvania radical said, "In perusing the New York constitution, it appears evident to me that the powers of government are thrown into the hands of the rich and wealthy."[23] Some conservatives, on the other hand, felt it ceded too much ground to the radicals. The Upper Manor Livingstons, unhappy about losing their hereditary seat in the legislature, thought the document "savors too much" of the "leveling principle." Even conservatives who supported the constitution warned it did not guarantee them political control. Gouverneur Morris likened it to an "unwieldy" machine that "will require much boiling, winding and the like before it works well for the state."[24]

To get that political machine working in their favor, conservatives began filling as many high offices as they could. Jay became the first chief justice of the state and a member of the Council of Revision. Robert Livingston became New York's first chancellor, the state's highest judicial post, and also a member of the Council of Revision. It went without saying that Schuyler, as befitting his position, would become governor. First, though, he had to win the election.

In late May 1777, John Jay and Robert Livingston began a letter-writing campaign for Schuyler's election as governor. Some asked Jay to run for the office, but Jay preferred the position of chief justice. "When I consider how well General Schuyler is qualified for that important office, I think he ought in justice to be preferred to your most obedient humble servant," Jay wrote a friend.[25]

Schuyler too assumed that the position would be his, noting with typical hauteur, "They may choose who they will. I will command them all."[26] So he was dismayed to discover how many other candidates had thrown their hat in the ring. Three main contenders emerged, each representing a different faction. Schuyler represented the conservatives, General John Morin Scott represented the urban radicals, and General George Clinton, whom conservatives were backing for lieutenant governor, represented the state's yeoman farmers. "Amongst us a beggar may be governor, a senator, or assemblyman," wrote one shocked conservative.[27]

Terrified that the radicals would take over the state, conservatives aimed all their firepower at Scott. "I dread the consequences which may ensue," wrote William Duer of New York. ". . . Mr. Scot, I am informed, rails at an *aristocratic faction* which he pretends has formed and organized the new government; his disappointed ambition will lead him to make use of every act however gross or wicked which he thinks will serve to make himself popular."[28]

Voting took place over several days in the middle of June, and conservatives were startled by the results. Scott had been soundly defeated. And so had Schuyler. Clinton won both the governorship and the lieutenant governorship. Though he did not hail from the upper echelons of society like the framers of the new constitution, Clinton was by no means a radical. A small-town lawyer from Ulster County and an expert surveyor, he had served in the Continental Congress and was a brigadier general in the militia. He was also a cunning politician who spoke the rhetoric of the common man. Clinton "played his cards better than was expected," Schuyler wrote to Jay shortly after the election.[29]

Conservative efforts to control the electorate had gone horribly awry. They had designed a constitution they thought would keep them in office, only to find it used to remove them from power. Far more New Yorkers, it turned out, had been able to meet the £100-minimum property qualification than conservatives had expected. And these men, prosperous middle-class farmers and soldiers who had no truck with radicalism, had voted en masse for Clinton. Antiaristocratic feelings following recent tenant uprisings might have contributed to the election results, but the vote also bespoke a more fundamental change taking place in American society. The middle classes were exercising new-found political freedoms. A uniquely American, commercially minded democracy was on the march, and until conservatives learned its cadences, they would continue to lose elections. Robert Livingston was among the first conservatives to realize the necessity of adapting to the torrent. Philip Schuyler was coming to understand this shift as well.

Writing to congratulate Clinton, Schuyler vowed to support the new governor. With a common enemy to confront, they agreed to check their disagreements at least until the end of the war. Privately, Schuyler believed that Clinton's "family and connections do not entitle him to" the governorship. Nevertheless, he told Jay, "he is virtuous and loves his country, has abilities and is brave, and I hope he will experience from every patriot what I'm resolved he shall have."[30]

During a quiet celebration of the first anniversary of independence, American soldiers guarding Ticonderoga were alarmed to see fires burning atop Sugar Loaf, a nearby peak overlooking the fortress. Over the previous two days, British engineers had secretly climbed the back side of the mountain and positioned artillery on it. The British, Americans quickly realized, could now decimate Ticonderoga at will.

After hurriedly meeting with his officers the next day, Brigadier General Arthur St. Clair gave the order to evacuate. His was one of the shorter commands in American military history. St. Clair had arrived only three weeks before to replace Gates, who remained so infuriated by his reception in Congress that he refused return to the fort if it meant serving under Schuyler.

Schuyler was livid when he learned how many provisions St. Clair had left at Ticonderoga. The evacuation, said Schuyler, had been "carried into execution with a precipitation that could not fail of erecting panic in our troops and inspiriting the enemy. I am confident that with a moderate degree of foresight and exertion, the greater part of valuable stores might have been saved."[31]

All the same, Schuyler recognized that St. Clair's position had been untenable. The British forces, led by General John Burgoyne, outnumbered the Americans at Ticonderoga three to one and would soon have cut off any escape route. The massive numbers of cannons, mortars, and howitzers Burgoyne had brought from Canada would have shredded the Americans had they tried to make a stand. Much of the blame for Ticonderoga's loss, however, lay with the radicals in Congress.

For months Schuyler had been pleading for reinforcements. Ticonderoga was undermanned and in disrepair, he told Congress, and what troops he had were largely local militia, who often deserted at the first sign of the British Army. He had only twenty-five hundred soldiers at the fort, and it would take at least ten thousand men, he estimated, to hold her. Congressional radicals, however, continued to see the Continental Army as a necessary evil and in the long run perhaps not even all that necessary. Any standing army, they believed, was an instrument of tyranny, and anyone who supported one a potential tyrant. It was a dispute that one radical likened to the division "between monarchical and republican principles."[32] Radicals viewed with suspicion Schuyler's insistence that he needed more troops if he was to hold upstate New York.

Conservatives likewise viewed radical intransigence in terms of virtue. The inability of state and national governments to properly equip the army was a sign of corruption, not the defense against tyranny radicals believed it to be. In a letter to a fellow general, Schuyler complained bitterly about how poorly Congress was provisioning the army and how stinting the states were with supplies and money:

> Very timely and repeated orders have been given for the latter, and frequent applications made for troops to the States that were to furnish them. A shameful tardiness has prevailed in making the levies. . . . Every effort of the enemy would be in vain if our exertions equaled our abilities; if our virtue was not sinking under that infamous venality which pervades throughout and threatens us with ruin. America cannot be subdued by a foreign force; but her own corruption may bring on a fatal catastrophe.[33]

Schuyler knew this was no time for finger-pointing. The British were barreling south, threatening to win the war by the end of the year. Burgoyne's plan was to seize Albany, where he was expecting to rendezvous with General Howe's forces, who controlled New York after Washington's defeat there the previous fall. Once linked up, the British would be able to cut off New England and slowly strangle the United States. In an apparent communications mix-up, Howe had already taken his forces south to capture Philadelphia, hoping that seizing the American capital would end the war. But Burgoyne remained supremely confident after taking Ticonderoga, believing Albany would be his by Christmas. "None but stupid mortals can dislike a lively camp, good weather, good claret, good music, and the enemy near," wrote one of his officers.[34]

With the American cause hanging in the balance, Schuyler rushed to slow the British advance. He destroyed everything in their path: crops, livestock, buildings, forests, anything the British could use. He outfitted a thousand men with felling axes, which they used to topple trees across roads, chop up bridges, divert streams, and send boulders into the path of the British Army. He put all gunpowder, musket balls, salt, flour, and rum out of Burgoyne's reach. As a result of these delaying tactics, Burgoyne spent the next twenty-four days trying to cover twenty-three miles.

As Schuyler was one of the first officers to realize, no foreign power could defeat America. His strategy, which was soon adopted by Washington, derived from the great Roman general Fabius Maximus Cunctator, whose delaying tactics had saved Italy from Hannibal in the Second Punic War. Unable to defeat the Carthaginian general in open battle, the Romans had laid waste to their own lands to starve Hannibal's army. Schuyler's effort following Ticonderoga's loss, writes one historian, was "one of the finest strategic actions of the Revolution."[35]

Though faced with one of the darkest periods of the war, Schuyler kept up hope. "Our affairs will soon wear a better face and take a more favorable turn," he wrote, "and in the fullest confidence that America cannot be conquered by Britain, why should we despond?"[36] He still desperately needed reinforcements—noting that militia would not remain for more than a week—but he swore he would battle Burgoyne every inch of the way. He also knew that his own estate at Saratoga stood directly in the path of the marauding British Army.

Schuyler's exertions made little impression on radicals, who seized upon the loss of Ticonderoga to get rid of him. In Congress, Pennsylvania radicals lined up with the Eastern states in a motion to remove Schuyler from command. They also ordered court-martial proceedings to be brought against St. Clair and Schuyler. John Adams went so far as to suggest Schuyler's execution. "We shall never defend a post until we shoot a general," he wrote.[37]

Schuyler's supporters did their best to encourage him. "Let not the hasty suspicions of the ignorant or the malicious insinuations of the wicked, discompose you," Jay wrote to his friend. "The best & greatest men in all ages have met with the like hate, and gloriously risen superior to calumny."[38] Some pointed out that much of the blame lay with New England. "As the Eastern states were to supply the troops for the station," wrote the North Carolina delegate Thomas Burke, "the officers . . . could not have done more than they did." He was irked that radicals were "unwilling to admit that any of our misfortune has happened through a weakness which they only share in common with the rest."[39]

It was a losing battle. By the end of July, the outcry against Schuyler had reached a high point, with his enemies leaving "no means unessayed to blast your character," as William Duer wrote. "The friends to truth find an extreme difficulty to stem the torrent of calumny."[40] James Duane accused New Englanders of orchestrating these attacks, but delegates from other states began to lose confidence in Schuyler as well. Radicals tried to rope Washington into replacing Schuyler, but when the commander in chief refused to take part in what he saw as a political maneuver, Congress acted on its own. On August 4, 1777, a large majority voted to recall Schuyler as commander of the Northern Army. He was replaced by Horatio Gates.

Schuyler was stoic but certain that an investigation, which he now demanded, would clear his name. He wrote, nonetheless, "I am far from being insensible of the indignity of being relieved of the command of the army at a time when an engagement must soon take place." He had prepared well for the upcoming battle. The area in which the British were trying to operate had been so thoroughly devastated that they became weaker the further they penetrated into American territory. Gates, Schuyler felt, was being handed an easy victory.

Schuyler's house at Saratoga was deserted when the British Army passed through in mid-September. By nightfall the soldiery had turned the estate "to a scene of distress and poverty," as one British officer described it.[41] By late September the house was in ruins, its windows knocked out and the wallpaper torn down. Schuyler was outraged when he learned that Burgoyne had taken shelter in his own house. Before leaving the property, the British general ordered everything burned. Schuyler's house, mills, barracks, and barns were all put to the torch. The property of many of his tenants was also destroyed, rendering them unable to pay rent or repay loans to Schuyler. All told, Schuyler's losses totaled roughly £20,000.

The first battle of Saratoga took place on September 19. It raged from noon to dark but ended in stalemate when Gates refused to commit enough troops despite Benedict Arnold's pleas for reinforcements. Arnold was furious with Gates, convinced that America could have won a decisive victory that day. After a violent argument, Gates removed Arnold from command of the army's left wing, which did not stop Arnold from leading it anyway in the subsequent battle. "If Arnold's advice had been pursued, the enemy would have been routed on the 20th of last month," Schuyler wrote.[42]

Gates lost a second chance to finish off the British Army on October 7, when again it seemed the American army was about to overwhelm the enemy. American forces had now swelled to fifteen thousand, two and a half times the number under Burgoyne's command, but Gates again held back at the last moment. Ironically, the same radicals who had castigated Schuyler for his slow, careful preparations now praised Gates for his cautiousness.

Schuyler did not stay idle during the battles. He coordinated with his former subordinates and offered tactical advice on how to defeat the British. He pointed out a swamp that could be used to separate Burgoyne's left wing from the rest of the British Army when it reached a small bridge south of "Old Dunham's house" near the Hudson River. He received battlefield reports, recruited Iroquois to join Gates, and organized wagons to transport the wounded.

Burgoyne continued to stall for time, praying for reinforcements, but after meeting with his officers, he decided he would surrender on the morning of October 16. His six thousand soldiers were exhausted, out of food, and nearly out of ammunition. At two a.m. that night, Richard Varick, an American officer, wrote to Schuyler with news of Burgoyne's imminent surrender. "I wish to God, I could say under your command," Varick added. Schuyler immediately wrote back, "The event that has taken place makes the heavy loss I have sustained sit quite easy on me. Britain will probably see how fruitless her attempt to enslave us will be."[43]

Saratoga was a watershed moment in the war. It was now clear that America, or at least part of it, would never again be ruled by the British. More important, the victory would soon lead France to formally ally itself with the United States. Gates was immediately lionized as America's greatest general—and some radicals began whispering about replacing Washington as commander in chief with him. But the turning point in America's fortunes was due far more to Schuyler's resilience and tactical brilliance. As the historian Donald Gerlach writes, "Schuyler's responsibility for seizing the advantage and buying time for his own army made him the leader most responsible for the ultimate American success at Saratoga."[44]

Hastening to the field where the British were to surrender, Schuyler, dressed in his ordinary clothes, rode upon his favorite white horse to review the soldiers as they stood at attention in two lines. Flags fluttered and fifes and drums played "Yankee Doodle" as the British forces entered the meadow from the north to lay down their arms. The music, the tramp of boot steps, and the whipping of flags were the only sounds to be heard as the thousands of stunned British troops filed past the silent American lines.

Schuyler was one of the first people Burgoyne met upon arriving, and the British general apologized for the destruction of his property. Masking his anger, Schuyler told Burgoyne "to think no more of it," adding "that the occasion justified it according to the principles and rules of war."[45]

Following the surrender ceremony, Schuyler invited Burgoyne and some of his officers to stay a few days at his Albany mansion, which had escaped the ravages of war. The captivity Schuyler provided was both luxurious and homey. One morning his nine-year-old son, Philip Jeremiah Schuyler, burst into Burgoyne's room laughing, "You are all my prisoners," and then slammed the door again.[46] Schuyler's army had been taken from him, his reputation was in tatters, and his estate had been destroyed, but he remained magnanimous to the last.

CHAPTER 14

THE PLAYWRIGHT AND THE MERCHANT

He was as wily as he was alluring, a commoner with the sophistication of a count, a self-made man and a jack-of-all-trades, a servant who boldly defied his master. Whether one is referring to the Barber of Seville or his harlequinesque creator makes little difference, for Pierre-Augustin Caron de Beaumarchais led a life as picaresque as his Figaro, a dramatic character so beloved that both Mozart and Rossini composed operas about him. A Parisian watchmaker by trade, Beaumarchais wasted little time mounting the rungs of French high society. He became a music teacher to royalty, married briefly and well, seduced frequently and shrewdly, acquired a noble title or two, succeeded and failed spectacularly in business, worked as a spy, a diplomat, a publisher of banned works, and an arms dealer, and in his spare time became one of the leading playwrights in Europe. He was also America's greatest advocate in the French court.

For Silas Deane, Congress's lone representative in France, Beaumarchais was a godsend. Speaking no French (though he did speak Latin, Hebrew, and ancient Greek) and ignorant of court etiquette at Versailles, the bewildered American latched on to the flamboyant Frenchman, who soon became his friend, partner, and guide. Beaumarchais spoke no English, but through a translator the two men discovered they were kindred spirits. Deane was, in fact, grateful for the chance to converse with anyone, even if indirectly. Fearing British agents, he refused to talk with most other English speakers he met in France. "He must be the most silent man in Paris," remarked Beaumarchais, "for I defy him to say six consecutive words" in French.[1]

A neatly dressed, kindly looking man with a high forehead and prominent nose, Deane was not an obvious choice to be the Secret Committee's envoy. The son of a blacksmith, he had never been out of the country before. But he had Yankee pluck. Despite his humble background, he had managed to graduate from Yale, study law while supporting himself as a schoolteacher, and after a good marriage, save up enough capital to go into business.

Deane had great expectations in France. He was eager to aid America, prove his patriotism, and make his fortune all at the same time. His ouster from Congress at the hands of radicals still rankled, and he wanted to show them up as well. "My enemies thought to triumph over me and bring me down," he wrote his wife, "yet all they did has been turned to the opening [of] a door for the greatest and most extensive usefulness."[2]

Deane's loyalty to America cannot be doubted. From the very start of the conflict with Britain, he had devoted his life and his wallet to the Patriot cause. "Liberty or death is before us, and I can conceive no alternative," he declared.[3] He proudly bore the nickname "Ticonderoga," for the extensive role he played planning and underwriting the American raid that had first captured the fort from the British in May 1775.

Deane's extreme precautions against British agents were not alarmist. Spies indeed surrounded him, and they included, unbeknownst to him, his own translator. Despite his efforts to enter France discreetly, Lord North's ministry learned of his presence almost immediately. "My arrival here, my name, my lodging, and many other particulars have been reported to the British administration," he wrote; "the city swarms with Englishmen and as money purchases everything in this country, I have had, and still have, a most difficult task to avoid their machinations. Not a coffee shop or theater or other place of public diversion but swarms with their emissaries."[4] The French, meanwhile, were following the British agents as closely as the British were tracking Deane.

Living frugally helped Deane avoid unwanted scrutiny. He maintained simple habits, declaring, "Parade and pomp have no charms in the eyes of a patriot."[5] At the same time, his circumstances were also limited by the fact that he had received nothing but silence from Congress since his arrival. Deane remained independently wealthy, using his own money to support his mission, but even his personal credit was insufficient to buy the great quantities of war supplies America needed. He was further perturbed by the fact that French banks had rejected as worthless all of the Continental dollars Congress had provided him. "I must again remind you of my situation here," he wrote to the Secret Committee in mid-August. "The bills designed for my use are protested, and expenses rising fast in consequence. . . . The quantity of stores to be shipped will amount to a large sum; the very charge of them will be great, for which I am the only responsible person."[6]

Eager to secure French aid as quickly as possible, Deane made his way to Versailles soon after his arrival. There, after navigating the palace's mirrored and gilt-covered halls, he met the Comte de Vergennes, France's minister of foreign affairs. Grave and stately, the fifty-four-year-old Vergennes had learned diplomacy at the great courts of Europe. Translating for him was his private secretary, Conrad Gérard. Vergennes's advisers were almost uniformly pro-American, but the *comte* was too cautious to risk war with Britain just yet. France could do nothing for America for the moment, he told the disappointed Deane. He added with a wink that as a private citizen, Deane was free to transact whatever business he pleased in France. He also casually mentioned that the army had just updated its arsenal and had old weapons it no longer needed. The first thing Deane might want to do, the minister suggested, was to get in touch with Beaumarchais.

Beaumarchais was a step ahead. Three days later an envelope addressed to "Mr. Deine" arrived at the American's residence. In his letter Beaumarchais stated that he "cherished the desire to aid the brave Americans to shake off the British yoke," and he proposed getting together to discuss how they might accomplish their mutual goal.[7] The two men met on a warm afternoon several days later and soon struck a deal to ship the Continental Army hundreds of cannons and enough muskets, ammunition, and clothing to equip twenty-five thousand men, a contract worth some two million French *livres,* or $15 million today. The details would be handled by Rodrigue Hortalez and Co., a firm Beaumarchais had set up just for this purpose. In return, Congress would promise to send some twelve thousand hogsheads of tobacco in payment.* Though American money was worthless, its rich southern tobacco was prized throughout Europe.

Knowing that only recently Beaumarchais had been fleeing his creditors, Deane was at first skeptical that the Frenchman could be helpful. But Deane soon divined that "everything he says, writes or does, is in reality the action of the ministry," which was still afraid to commit to the American side.[8] As the covert relationship between Vergennes and Beaumarchais became more apparent, Deane soon began referring to the playwright as "my minister."

Yet Beaumarchais deserves more credit than anyone else in France for supporting the American cause. Although he hadn't mentioned it to Deane, he had secretly borrowed millions from both the King of France and the King of Spain to finance his venture with Deane. Despite tacit backing from the French government, Beaumarchais was aiding the revolution at great personal

* A hogshead was a wooden barrel weighing close to a ton when full of tobacco.

financial risk. From the beginning, Beaumarchais made clear that the supplies he was sending were for purchase. They were not a gift, a point spelled out in the contract the two men signed. Like Deane, he expected to profit from the transaction.

Yet not all of Beaumarchais's motives were pecuniary. He was also moved by an idealistic impulse, a deep admiration for America as a land of equality and opportunity. As Beaumarchais's plays had demonstrated, he believed the common man was the aristocrat's equal, if not his superior.* He was exaggerating when he told Deane that he had nothing but "disinterested ardor for the cause of America," but he nonetheless believed deeply in the ideals of the Revolution.

From July until the end of the year, the two men would scour France for matériel—in addition to bombs, mortars, bayonets, and powder, they scrounged for boots, blankets, tents, and buckles. They had to do all of this in secret. And they had to find a way to ship these supplies out of the country without tipping off the British, whose ambassador knew almost everything anyway and was tormenting Vergennes with threats of war. Viscount Stormont, the British ambassador, went so far as to propose kidnapping Deane to thwart his efforts. But as long as the French minister could plausibly deny any knowledge of Deane and Beaumarchais's operation, he could play for time. Should their endeavors become public, however, the French government would be forced to halt them immediately.

Covering their tracks took tremendous effort. The partners had to remove Louis XVI's coat of arms from everything they bought, including the two hundred cannons they procured from the French Army. They also couldn't purchase anything in bulk lest they attract unwanted attention. With British agents and French police dogging them everywhere, they had to "slip between everyone's fingers and not cause anyone to squeal," as Beaumarchais told Deane.[9] Through hundreds upon hundreds of small covert deals, they amassed their precious cargo.

At the same time Deane was organizing this massive smuggling operation, he was also trying to fulfill his business obligations to Robert Morris. The Philadelphia merchant was eager to receive European delicacies that would fetch a high value on the American market, and Deane worked around the clock to send him all the oils, olives, capers, and claret he could find. To cover

* One reason Mozart's career languished a few years later, in fact, was because he had dared to set to music Beaumarchais's *The Marriage of Figaro,* which mocked the very aristocrats he depended upon for patronage.

his trail should British spies steal his account books, Deane deliberately mixed together his private and public transactions, resulting in an accounting gallimaufry that made his records nearly impenetrable. It was a shrewd idea in terms of espionage, but it would wreak havoc on his reputation.

One problem continued to gnaw at Deane. It was imperative that he establish a formal alliance between France and the United States, yet he struggled to explain to French authorities the failure of his own government to communicate with him.

"Extremely uneasy at your absolute silence," Deane wrote to Philadelphia in August. "For Heaven's sake," he wrote in October, "if you mean to have any connection with this Kingdom, be more assiduous in getting your letters here."[10] A month later he said, "The want of intelligence retards everything. As I have not had a word from you since the 5th of June last, I am well-nigh distracted."[11] Like all of his correspondence, these letters were penned with an invisible ink that John Jay's brother, a renowned physician, had given him. Made of cobalt chloride, glycerin, and water, the ink disappeared as soon as it dried, with no trace visible until the paper was treated with another chemical.[12]

Beaumarchais tried to remain upbeat. "There is no news from America, and no tobacco either," he told his friend. "This is depressing, but depression is a long way from discouragement."[13]

One particularly vexing source of embarrassment for Deane was his inability to learn if the Declaration of Independence had been formally passed. On August 10 a copy was published in London and made its way to Paris, but three months later official word had still not reached France. The news, he chastised Congress, "has given this court, as well as several others in Europe, reason to expect you would in form announce your independency to them and ask their friendship."[14] The King of France himself did not know what to make of the situation. Worried about the continued silence of the American government, its envoy's exploding debt (as well as his own), and continued British threats of war, Louis XVI decided to ban all arms shipments to America. Deane's mission and the fate of the American Revolution now hung in the balance.

Like so many of the Founding Fathers, when facing adversity Deane reached first for his pen. In a long memorandum to Vergennes, he composed one of the most compelling justifications of the Revolution ever written. Having a gifted writer like Beaumarchais coaching him helped as well. Deane explained that independence enjoyed broad support in America. It was not the work of a small faction aiming to seize power, as the British claimed. Americans, he said, "are not an ignorant unprincipled rabble, heated and led on to the present measures by the artful and ambitious few." They were, instead, "bred from their infancy in what they conceive to be the fundamental principles of liberty."[15]

Deane understood the central absurdity of what he was arguing: he was asking a monarchy to help the colonies of another monarchy set up a republic. But with Beaumarchais's help, he explained his position in a way that made aiding America appear vital to France's self-interest. It was, Deane wrote, "impossible that any events in the course of human affairs can be more interesting to France." In fact, he believed "divine will" had given Louis XVI the chance to take away Britain's power "ever hereafter to disturb [France's] repose on the continent or insult her on the ocean."[16] If France should refuse to come to America's rescue, he warned, the fledgling country would be forced to make peace with Britain. If that happened, George III would become more powerful than ever and capable of striking at French possessions in the Caribbean at will. A week later Vergennes persuaded Louis XVI to reverse himself. As the historian Coy Hilton James writes, "If [Deane] had been a seasoned ambassador, he could not have done better in defending the American interest."[17]

Vergennes expected something in return, however. Under pressure from the foreign minister, Deane began handing out commissions to French aristocrats and pretend-aristocrats eager to enlist in the Continental Army. The chance to flaunt one's courage in battle, especially while wearing a shiny new uniform, appealed to the Gallic spirit. Deane wrote to Congress requesting advice but received no response, so he thought it best to placate Vergennes. His rooms, which he had tried to keep discreet, now vaunted a line of uniformed men stretching out the door. Deane had no idea how to judge whether these men were qualified for command. Some were callow adventurers and would become a source of great resentment among the Continental ranks. But the nineteen-year-old Marquis de Lafayette and his mentor, the redoubtable Baron de Kalb, both commissioned by Deane, became two of the most valued officers under Washington's command.

It was Robert Morris who finally sent Deane a copy of the Declaration in mid-November, along with instructions to "make the act known to the Court of France and other powers of Europe." In July the Secret Committee had placed these documents on a ship that was never heard from again. Two months later the committee sent another copy aboard a second ship. Although this ship reached France relatively quickly, Deane did not get his package until the beginning of November. In the intervening months the ship's captain had forgotten to deliver it.

On November 20, Deane arrived at Versailles to present Vergennes with an official copy of the Declaration of Independence. Without waiting for specific instructions from Congress, Deane, acting as "a private individual," also proposed a formal alliance between the two countries. The foreign minister gracefully received the Declaration and Deane's proposal, but he was not yet ready to support America openly. Declaring independence was one thing. Being able to win a war against Britain was another. Before Vergennes would commit to what would ultimately descend into a world war, America needed to prove it stood a fighting chance.

Bobbing at the docks in Le Havre, France's main seaport on the Atlantic, three enormous frigates, the *Amphitrite,* the *Seine,* and the *Romain,* readied themselves for America. Hundreds of men under cover of night heaved tens of thousands of tons of supplies aboard the ships. The cargo had come from all over France, as the historian Joel Paul describes: sixty tons of cannonballs from Abbeville and Gravelines near the Channel; tents, grenades, and muskets from Douai, Sedan, and Mézières in the north; scores of cannons from Metz and Strasbourg in the east; and dozens of tons of gunpowder, hauled gingerly over hard and rutted roads, from every corner of the country.[18] Amid all the bristling weaponry, 15,264 handkerchiefs neatly awaited transport as well, some perhaps destined for the fastidious French officers waiting to board.

By December the *Amphitrite* was ready to set sail. While Beaumarchais, who was traveling under the name "Durand," was supervising the final loading of cargo, several last-minute problems arose. The French officers whom Deane had commissioned suddenly demanded a full year's pay up front before they would embark, forcing Beaumarchais to scramble for funds. He also had to purchase false papers claiming the *Amphitrite* was bound for the French West Indies and rid the ship of any incriminating documents should the Royal Navy board it. Finally, he encountered troubles of a more theatrical nature.

It turned out that an amateur theater company in Le Havre was putting on his *Barber of Seville,* and "Durand" could not resist attending. The performance was dreadful, forcing the playwright to weigh the need for secrecy against the dictates of his art. Art won. Revealing himself to the astonished director, Beaumarchais took command of the theater troupe and insisted on rehearsing them for the next three days before allowing them back on stage. It did not take long for people to learn who was directing the revised production, which became a smash hit. As at the Comédie-Française in Paris, Figaro had the audiences of Le Havre crying with laughter.

The only person not amused was the British ambassador, who stormed into Vergennes's offices at Versailles demanding that the French ships be barred from leaving port. Any other course of action, he threatened, meant immediate war. The cowed French minister had no choice but to issue the order, which arrived at Le Havre in time to stop the *Romain* and *Seine.* The *Amphitrite* had already put out to sea but soon had to return to France. For all the tons of supplies the ship was carrying, the captain had failed to pack adequate provisions for his crew. It too was impounded the moment it returned. With the British press and members of Parliament fulminating against Deane and Beaumarchais's venture, the French government again clamped down. Once again, Vergennes declared, no supplies would be allowed to reach America.

The capriciousness of French authorities was not the only thorn in Deane's side. In mid-August he received the unpleasant news that Arthur Lee, Richard Henry Lee's excitable younger brother, had arrived in France. After studying medicine in Scotland, Lee had returned home to Virginia, promptly grew bored of bleeding patients, and left for Europe again, this time to study law in London, where he soon fell in with English radical circles. There he met Beaumarchais, who had been sent to England several years earlier on business for the French government.

Pallid, bony, and afflicted with yellowed teeth, Lee had impressed the playwright with his patriotism and repulsed him with his smarmy boasting. The two discussed the idea of selling arms to America, but Lee dropped the ball. When the Frenchman met Deane, he decided he was a far more forthright and trustworthy business partner. An "insidious politician" was Beaumarchais's assessment of Lee.[19] He could have added "paranoiac" as well.

Arthur Lee was perhaps the most suspicious man in the American Revolution. John Adams, who usually tried to have something pleasant to say about his political allies, noted that Lee's "countenance is disgusting, his air is not pleasing, his manners are not engaging, his temper is harsh, sour and fierce, and his judgment of men and things is often wrong."[20] Lee himself admitted as much. "Unhappily," he remarked, "my fate has thrown me into public life, and the impatience of my nature makes me embark in it with an impetuosity and imprudence which increase the evils to which it is necessarily subject."[21]

Lee, for example, kept a list of disloyal Americans, which he continually updated. Numerous members of Congress were on it, and Lee began pestering Deane to write to Congress denouncing the delegates he suspected of treason. Peeved by Lee's lack of any evidence whatsoever, Deane refused, declaring he would not become "a second hand accuser of men of character."[22] This just confirmed Lee's suspicions that a massive conspiracy was afoot and that Deane was in on it. Since even paranoids sometimes get it right, Lee guessed correctly that Deane's secretary was working for the British. What he did not realize was that his own was too.

Lee was outraged when he learned that Beaumarchais had signed an exclusive deal with Deane to supply the American army. He tried repeatedly and unsuccessfully to insert himself into their relationship, and his resulting pique led him to do everything he could to sabotage their operation. Having two powerful brothers serving in Congress ensured that the damage he did was maximal. Lee began writing letters to his brothers, Richard Henry and Francis Lightfoot, alleging that Deane and Beaumarchais were involved in a massive scam. He claimed they were trying to bilk the American government for goods that were in fact gifts from the French government. Lee, of course, knew this was a blatant lie—Beaumarchais had made it clear to him in London that all French military equipment was to be purchased. Nevertheless he told congressional radicals there was no need to ship any tobacco to Beaumarchais as payment.

Lee's accusations that Deane and Robert Morris were putting their private interests ahead of the public's were belied by Deane's own statements. In January 1778 the American envoy wrote to Morris that his official duties were so pressing that he had been neglecting their business arrangement. The little private speculating in which he had engaged ended mostly in loss. Nevertheless congressional radicals began to accuse Deane of deliberately sending shoddy goods to America, even though no proof of this was ever offered. Washington, in fact, personally thanked Deane for the equipment he had sent without mentioning any problems. Stung by the accusations, Deane immediately wrote to his French agents urging them to double-check all goods before they were loaded on ships.

For radicals, Lee's allegations were all the confirmation they needed that America's merchant class was corrupt. Deane and Robert Morris symbolized exactly the sort of large-scale capitalism that men like Samuel Adams and

The Farmer: The most famous defender of American liberty in the decade before independence, John Dickinson was acclaimed from one end of the colonies to the other. The British dubbed him a radical, but after he used his considerable influence to delay independence until he felt America was better prepared, his political opponents labeled him a traitor. Dickinson fought in the Revolutionary War as both a colonel and a private, penned the Articles of Confederation, simultaneously led Delaware and Pennsylvania, and shaped the U.S. Constitution. His greatest contribution was to formulate modern American conservatism as a tradition rooted in natural law and historical precedent.

The Philosopher's Garden: The most beautiful home in all the colonies, John Dickinson's Fairhill, depicted here in a 1777 drawing, reflected the civilized tastes and incandescent mind of its famous occupant. The gilded weathercock atop the main house served as a glinting landmark for ships along the Delaware River, while the home's perfectly proportioned hip roofs and dormer windows rose high above the surrounding countryside. Flanking the main building were two dependencies housing Philadelphia's first greenhouse and its finest library, which connected to an ornate glass beehive. An oasis of luxuriant calm, Fairhill attracted pilgrims and politicians from throughout the colonies until British soldiers burned it to ashes after the Battle of Germantown.

The Democratic Conservative: Tall and muscular, with a ruddy face and a mild burr, James Wilson immigrated from Scotland with little but a sound education, but within a few years of studying law under John Dickinson he blossomed into America's greatest legal mind and one of its richest investors. His support for free-market economics and his conservative politics made him a lightning rod for radical attacks. Yet he championed popular democracy as a delegate to the Constitutional Convention. Wilson's outsized debt finally did him in. Though a justice of the U.S. Supreme Court, he spent his final days hiding from creditors in a rundown North Carolina tavern.

A Genius for Unkind Words: Though frequently considered a conservative, the irascible and eloquent John Adams was actually a radical throughout much of the Revolution. Heedless of the consequences, he helped orchestrate a radical takeover of Pennsylvania's government when it suited his plans. Rarely inclined to speak well of others, he alienated almost everyone who knew him. "He means well for his Country," wrote Benjamin Franklin, "is always an honest man, often a wise one, but sometimes, and in some things, absolutely out of his senses."

New England Radical: Prematurely gray, trembling of voice, and palsied in one hand, Sam Adams was a master of the back-room deal and the manipulation of public opinion. He did everything he could to bring about the split with Britain. "Damn that Adams," complained the royal governor of Massachusetts. "Every dip of his pen stings like a horned snake." A staunch Country Whig, Adams despised America's mercantile classes, longing to turn the nation into a "Christian Sparta." He would become an implacable enemy of the founding conservatives.

America's First Ambassador: Sent to France by Robert Morris's Secret Committee to secure foreign aid, Silas Deane was surrounded by British spies the moment he arrived in Paris in July 1776. (His own secretary reported his every move back to London.) Speaking no French, he nonetheless navigated the mirrored halls of Versailles and convinced the French to support America. Maligned by radicals for his conservative politics, he was recalled to Philadelphia, where the resulting political firestorm convulsed Congress and shook Americans' faith in their government.

Revolutionary Financiers: Unrelated but likeminded, Robert Morris, *right,* and his assistant, Gouverneur Morris, took control of America's economy in the final years of the war. Appointed America's Financier by Congress, the sturdy, pragmatic Robert financed the battle of Yorktown, pacified mutinying American soldiers by paying their back wages out of his own pocket, and used his own credit to maintain the nation's currency. The urbane and lusty Gouverneur contrived to protect American business interests while composing the language of the U.S. Constitution. Together, the two men established the nation's first bank and its first modern multinational corporation.

"A Youth Remarkably Sedate": Praised by his father for his sober bearing, the young John Jay soon found excitement in the revolutionary fervor of his day. He believed strongly that the upper classes needed to play a role in the fight for American rights, and he defended the pursuit of wealth against radical attacks. "Shall we shut the door against private enterprise?" Jay asked. Active in the Continental Congress and in New York's state government, he protected the privileges of the elite while recognizing the pragmatism of allowing the lower classes more political rights. As one of America's peace commissioners, he proved himself a shrewd and stalwart negotiator. President Washington rewarded Jay for his service by appointing him the first Chief Justice of the Supreme Court.

Banker to the Gods: America's wealthiest merchant finished his life a pauper in debtors' prison, but Robert Morris was richly rewarded for his contributions to the American Revolution when his image was enshrined on the ceiling of the Capitol's rotunda in 1865. Seated on a throne to Morris's right is Mercury, the god of profit and trade, handing Morris a bag of gold.

A Jovian Temper: The leader of South Carolina's government for much of the Revolution, John Rutledge was one of the most important—and forgotten—of the Founding Fathers. Almost single-handedly he saved his state from the British several times. A French diplomat described the London-trained lawyer as one of the most eloquent men in the American government "but also the proudest and most imperious." To his enemies and inferiors, he was known for his volcanic anger. To those he respected, he was the epitome of southern courtesy and charm.

The Most Suspicious Man in America: Pallid, bony, and afflicted with yellowed teeth, Arthur Lee did everything he could to destroy the conservative Silas Deane. After arriving in Paris during Deane's negotiations with the French, Lee secretly wrote to Congress that Deane was a British spy who was embezzling government funds. Lee's clandestine correspondence with the British government, meanwhile, nearly derailed America's treaty with France. As his political ally John Adams put it, Lee's "countenance is disgusting . . . his temper is harsh, sour and fierce, and his judgment of men and things is often wrong."

A Visit by the Death Squad: On August 7, 1781, a peaceful family dinner at General Philip Schuyler's Albany mansion was interrupted by shouts and explosions from the kitchen. A British raiding party had broken in, hoping to kill the general. America's master of espionage hurried his wife and children upstairs and began firing out his bedroom window. Hopelessly outnumbered and hearing the invaders charging up the stairs, Schuyler shouted, "Come on my lads, surround the house. The villains are in it." Believing that reinforcements had arrived, the British fled.

American Fabius: Using the sort of scorched-earth tactics the Romans had devised to defeat Hannibal, General Schuyler kept British forces from cutting America in two. Radicals in Congress contrived to replace the conservative Schuyler with General Horatio Gates, who took credit for the critical victory at Saratoga that Schuyler had engineered. On October 16, 1778, the British general John Burgoyne surrendered his sword and his army to Gates, *center*. Schuyler, *fifth from right,* looked on with mixed emotions.

Figaro's Father: A watchmaker, spy, arms dealer, and playwright, Pierre-Augustin Caron de Beaumarchais was as wily and alluring as the famous character he created for the theater. He also helped save the American Revolution, securing the arms and equipment that won the Battle of Saratoga. Congressional radicals did everything in their power to ruin him.

Rise of the "Dictator": After two previous attempts to take Charleston, the British surrounded the city in April 1780 and shelled it for nearly a month, with one thirty-two-pounder landing in Governor John Rutledge's front yard. Rutledge initially refused to flee but relented when his generals insisted that he get to safety. The fall of Charleston in May marked the lowest point in the war for the United States. A fugitive in his own state now, Rutledge granted himself dictatorial powers, rallied the resistance, and became a one-man government in exile.

French Fox: Louis XVI's shrewd and stately foreign minister, Charles Gravier, Comte de Vergennes, was reluctant to plunge his nation into war. But the fight between Britain and her colonies was too tempting to pass up. Publicly disavowing any support for the United States, Vergennes surreptitiously backed the American Revolution, supplying the weapons, equipment, and money that kept the Continental Army in the field. He made no secret of supporting American conservatives. Radicals came to hate him.

Court Whig: An unabashed monarchist and capitalist, Alexander Hamilton rose from humble origins to become George Washington's chief of staff while still in his early twenties. An advantageous marriage to Philip Schuyler's daughter propelled him into the upper ranks of America's founding conservatives, while his bravery at the Battle of Yorktown and his brilliance as America's first treasury secretary secured his everlasting fame. A scandal surrounding Hamilton's marital infidelity destroyed his political career, but Schuyler nonetheless mourned his son-in-law's death after he was shot in a duel.

"Proclaim Liberty Throughout the Land": Rising nearly 170 feet, the bell tower of Philadelphia's State House, later renamed Independence Hall, was the tallest structure in the city. The inscription on its famous cracked bell was an exhortation to all of the delegates who met beneath it—those who declared American independence in July 1776, those who served in the Continental Congress over the next eight years, and those who wrote the Constitution during the summer of 1787. Throughout the Revolution, the building was the epicenter of the pitched political battles between radicals and conservatives.

Richard Henry Lee despised, and congressional radicals were prepared to believe the worst. They made sure that none of Beaumarchais's tobacco shipments made it out of America, leaving Deane at a loss to explain why none of his partner's promised payments had arrived. Had Beaumarchais learned of the Virginian's mendacity, he likely would have immediately ended all weapons shipments to America. Lee's letters to Congress threatened the entire American cause.

In early December, Benjamin Franklin arrived in France with money and indigo worth thousands of pounds sterling. Congress had appointed him to head a new American delegation to negotiate with France. Deane was delighted by this development. He had been named a co-commissioner and now enjoyed official status. Congress had appointed Thomas Jefferson as the third delegate, but Jefferson declined the position, leading Congress, at the insistence of radicals, to appoint Arthur Lee in his place. In what was clearly an act of nepotism, Lee was named commissioner to Spain as well.

Neither Franklin nor Deane could stand Lee, but deciding to make the best of the situation, the two men began negotiating with the French on their own. Vergennes, for his part, was all too happy to exclude Lee. The Virginian lacked all tact, and his hostility to France was apparent. For all his radical fervor, Lee was an Anglophile at heart; mistrust of the French radiated off him. The fact was, Congress could not have chosen a more unsuitable candidate for such a delicate diplomatic mission. He "must be shaved or bled, or he will be mad for life," Deane wrote in shock. "It is very charitable to impute to insanity what proceeds from malignity of heart; but [Franklin] insists upon it."[23]

Lee's comportment continued to deteriorate. He became increasingly convinced that his co-commissioners were plotting against him. They "have been practicing against me," he wrote to his brother Richard Henry, "and what I do not know is how far it may extend."[24] He claimed that a nameless colleague had earned upwards of £60,000 trading in secret information and that Franklin and Deane were blocking his attempts to form an official alliance with France. He grew hysterical when he learned that Deane was having regular midnight meetings with Vergennes at Versailles without him. In truth, the French minister questioned Lee's sanity.

Unable to get along with his colleagues in Paris, Lee's next move was to enlist his confederates in Congress in a scheme to seize control of the American mission. In the fall of 1777, he wrote to Sam Adams and the new chairman of the Secret Committee, his brother Richard. He suggested posting Deane and Franklin elsewhere in Europe while he remained in charge in France. When Congress balked, he wrote to his brother once again. "There is but one way of redressing this and remedying the public evil; that is the plan I before sent to you."[25]

Sensing Lee's malaise, Deane felt it was time to clear the air. In December 1777 he asked to meet in person and offered to supply any information the Virginian felt he lacked. This, he said, would be "certainly a more honorable and just way, between equals at least, than private insinuations and threatening billets or complaining ones."[26] Lee never responded. Most likely, Deane would never have reached out if he had known that just two weeks before Richard Henry Lee had submitted a disturbing motion in Congress: "Resolved that Silas Deane be recalled from the court of France."[27]

One of the first triumphs Deane and Franklin enjoyed was in persuading the French to reverse Vergennes's export ban several weeks after it had been imposed. Beaumarchais's ships would soon be released. Deane pressed his case and negotiated for another million-*livre* loan from France. By February, Beaumarchais's three ships, now joined by a fourth, the *Mercure,* were under way. A month later three more ships departed. Yet another, laden with desperately needed supplies, soon set sail as well.

Beaumarchais's financial situation was worsening as Congress continued to withhold his reimbursement. "I have exhausted myself in money and in work," he wrote to Deane, "without being able to know by now if anyone but you appreciates it all."[28] On the brink of bankruptcy, he sent his nephew to America to investigate the cause of the holdup. His nephew wrote back that Beaumarchais should expect never to be repaid. "There is no doubt that what you have done has been presented here in a false light," he explained. "I expect to have many prejudices to destroy and many heads to set right."[29]

Despite being incredulous at what he read, Beaumarchais signed a new contract with Congress. Deane assured him the American government would come through. Robert Morris had promised him as much. "I am much concerned that we have been so unfortunate in our remittances to you," Morris wrote to Deane in one of the rare letters that made it to France. "You will think yourself unlucky in these untoward circumstances and you have really been so, but this must not dispirit us, for you may depend on it, I will persevere in making you the necessary remittances with all possible expedition."[30]

Morris, however, failed. Because of Lee's interventions, Congress refused to honor Beaumarchais's new contract too. All the same, the playwright continued to do his part. Before the war was over, he would send some forty ships to America.

In May 1777 news arrived that the *Mercure* had arrived in Portsmouth, New Hampshire. Beaumarchais's other ships outmaneuvered the British blockade too and soon began arriving in Portsmouth and Falmouth, Massachusetts. Tons of gunpowder, dozens of cannons, and tens of thousands of cannonballs, along with blankets, cloth, and uniforms for thirty thousand men, were hurriedly transported to Schuyler's beleaguered forces holding off the British surge from the north. These were the supplies that saved the American Revolution.

Over the next two months, the matériel made its way through farmland and over Vermont's thickly forested mountains to the gently rolling hills at Saratoga. While Schuyler was being replaced by Gates, word spread that America now stood a fighting chance against Burgoyne's well-accoutered troops. Volunteers streamed in, boosting the American ranks by more than ten thousand men. It was the tipping point that won the battle. When news of America's victory at Saratoga reached Paris in late 1777, Deane and Franklin rushed to tell Vergennes.

Within forty-eight hours, Vergennes's secretary was discussing with them the possibility of a formal alliance between their two countries. Franklin and Deane submitted two treaties, a commercial and a military one, based on drafts Deane had previously proposed to the French. When the French continued to hesitate, Deane and Franklin hatched an ingenious plan.

With Franklin's approval, Deane began secretly meeting with a British agent negotiating on behalf of the British government. Stunned by the loss of Burgoyne's army at Saratoga, Britain was now prepared to end the war and guarantee American rights if Congress would renounce independence. Aware that nothing in Paris remained a secret, Deane surmised that Vergennes would immediately learn of his rendezvouses with the British agent. It was all the spur the French needed. The last thing Vergennes wanted was for Britain to regain her colonies. France quickly signed the treaties, with the stipulation that America never make a separate peace with Britain.

Franklin, Deane, and Lee were invited to present their credentials to King Louis at Versailles on March 20, 1778. A military band struck up a tune as their coach approached the outer courtyard. The French flag was lowered in official salute, and an honor guard presented arms. Upon entering the grand building, a major of the Swiss Guard presented them to the court as "*les ambassadeurs des treize provinces unies*." The court, with the exception of the

King, then rose and saluted. Perhaps the greatest mark of honor granted the Americans was that Louis XVI himself spoke directly with Franklin.

Deane's great accomplishments during twenty-two months in France were marred by the appearance of a letter from the Secret Committee one day in early 1778. Congress, Deane was stunned to learn, was recalling him. John Adams had been selected by the radicals to take his place. "I wish to know what has been the complaint against me," Deane wrote, "for I have not received one word on the subject from Congress or my particular friends."[31]

Beaumarchais immediately blamed Lee, who had made Deane "an object of suspicion to Congress."[32] In a letter of support, the playwright wrote to Congress, "I certify that if my zeal, my money advances and shipments of munitions and merchandise have been agreeable to the noble Congress, their gratitude is due to the indefatigable exertions of Mr. Deane throughout this commercial affair."[33] After having shown remarkable restraint in the past, Franklin too blew up at Lee. "I saw your jealous, suspicious, malignant, and quarrelsome temper, which was daily manifesting itself against Mr. Deane and almost every other person you had any concern with," he wrote.

Vergennes saw larger forces at work in the recall. Partly, he blamed radicals who opposed the alliance with France. "We are informed," he wrote the King, "that there is a numerous party . . . which is endeavoring to fix as a basis of the political system of the new States that no engagement be contracted with the European powers."[34]

And partly, the foreign minister saw the hand of the British government, which had been pilfering Deane's papers. "If we compare dates," one French official wrote to Vergennes, "we find the recall of Mr. Deane coincides with the period when Lord North was able to intrigue in Congress, guided by what he had read in the dispatches he had caused to be stolen. Mr. Deane's head was a good one for him to strike."[35] Scholars speculate that the British set into motion an elaborate plan to get Deane recalled by having its agents fill Lee's head with suspicions about his fellow commissioner, not that he needed help being suspicious. Franklin didn't worry the British half as much as Deane. In a report marked "confidential," Stormont, the British ambassador, wrote to London, "Whatever [Franklin's] talents . . . I am persuaded that he is a less dangerous instrument than Deane."[36]

Vergennes was sorry to see the American go. Deane had convinced him that their two countries' interests were indeed linked, and Deane's enemies, he felt, were now his own. Vergennes furnished the departing envoy with letters of commendation from all of France's top ministers and arranged for Louis XVI to present Deane a diamond-encrusted golden snuffbox with the King's portrait. "You will not, I presume, Sir, refuse to carry to your country the image of its most zealous friend," Vergennes said.[37] Accompanying him to Philadelphia would be Vergennes's secretary, Conrad Gérard, as France's newly appointed minister plenipotentiary to the thirteen *provinces unies,* aboard the flagship of a squadron of France's most powerful warships. American radicals didn't know it yet, but they were about to face the fight of their lives.

Chapter 15

THE SEED TIME OF GLORY

Bloody smears streaked the snows of Valley Forge, traces of the cracked and blackened soles of men without shoes.[1] The scene at Washington's encampment during the winter of 1777–78 was one of unparalleled suffering. After their defeat outside Philadelphia, the whipped remnants of the Continental Army retreated some twenty miles to a wooded area nestled between the twin peaks of Mount Misery and Mount Joy along the Schuylkill River.

Without adequate food, clothing, or shelter, American soldiers began to die. Of the twelve thousand men who had followed Washington to Valley Forge, twenty-five hundred were killed by disease and another third were declared too sick to be fit for duty. Half of the survivors went barefoot through ice and rain with no respite from the perpetual wet. His troops, Washington said, were "oftentimes starved; always in rags, without pay, and experiencing, at times, every species of distress which human nature is capable of undergoing."[2]

The encampment was littered with the bloated carcasses of animals and filled with the stench of putrefaction and latrines. To stave off hunger, the men chanted the same songs over and over, leading visitors to question their sanity. "There comes a bowl of beef soup," said a doctor in the Connecticut line, describing a typical meal "full of burnt leaves and dirt, sickish enough to make a Hector spew."[3] By the springtime, three mutinies had broken out over the lack of food.

To maintain order, Washington imposed harsh discipline. Soldiers caught deserting or falling asleep on watch were hanged. Even small transgressions could earn the offender a hundred lashes across his bare back. With the help of the young Lafayette, who was recovering from a wound received at the Battle of Brandywine, and several other formidable officers, Washington managed to keep his army alive during that brutal winter. This feat alone constituted a victory as great as any triumph on the battlefield. He was "our great Fabius Maximus," as his quartermaster general, Nathanael Greene, affectionately called him.[4]

But even Washington was starting to despair. He wrote to Henry Laurens, the rich Charleston merchant who had become president of Congress, "I am now convinced beyond a doubt that unless some great and capital change suddenly takes place in that line, this Army must inevitably be reduced to one or other of these three things. Starve—dissolve—or disperse."[5] As the condition of his army worsened, Washington sent repeated appeals to Congress for aid—to little avail. Hamstrung by radicals' mistrust of power, the American government was powerless in many respects. It lacked the power to levy taxes or institute a draft. And the states, on whom Congress depended for money and manpower, were reluctant to supply either.

In January 1778 Congress, exiled to York during the British occupation of Philadelphia, appointed a delegation to visit the camp and report back on how the army was faring. Included in the group was Gouverneur Morris, now twenty-six years old, who was selected to go to Valley Forge on his first day in Congress. Recently elected from New York, Morris quickly began making enemies. One radical mocked him as "the tall boy," highlighting both his youth—he was among the youngest delegates in Congress—and his extreme height.[6]

Though he remained skeptical of mass democracy, Morris was eager to serve his country. When his mother, a Tory, wrote to him in frustration that British soldiers were stealing her books and chopping down trees on her estate, Morris replied that he wished he could "solace and comfort" her in person. "The duty I owe to a tender parent," however, was outweighed by the needs of the nation. "Whenever the present storm subsides, I shall rush with eagerness into the bosom of private life," he said. But "while my country calls . . . I hold it my indispensable duty to give myself to her."[7] The sacrifices he was making were even more severe than he let on to his mother. To Robert Livingston he confided, "There are no fine women here at York."[8]

On his way to Valley Forge, Morris stopped for the night at an inn in Lancaster, Pennsylvania. There he encountered a group of British officers with safe conduct passes from Washington to bring clothing and medicine to British prisoners of war. A quarrel broke out after the officers bought some food. The British wanted to pay with gold and silver coins, for which the innkeeper was offering a steep discount. But a Pennsylvania official accompanying the British objected. State law, he insisted, required them to pay a vastly inflated amount in paper money.

Morris immediately intervened, not because he supported the British, but because this episode had the potential to threaten the preeminence of Congress over the states. Since Washington had given the British safe passage, he argued, they were protected "by the law of nations," which covered military matters. They "were not subject to the municipal laws of the separate states as long as they [conducted] themselves consistently with the terms" of their agreement with Washington.[9] As a member of Congress, Morris claimed the right to overrule the Pennsylvania officer. Radicals were livid when they heard what had happened, and the fight quickly escalated into a power struggle between Pennsylvania's government and Congress. Like most of the founding conservatives, Morris favored a strong national government, which he saw as an essential check on radical power and the key to winning the war. His subsequent decision to rebuke the Pennsylvania Assembly in a letter did little to smooth things over.

During the three months he spent at Valley Forge, Morris was stunned by both the misery and the patriotism he witnessed. "Our troops, *Heu miserors*!" he wrote to Jay. "The skeleton of an army presents itself to our eyes in a naked, starving condition, out of health, out of spirits."[10] At the same time, he felt confident that America would triumph if Washington could hold the army together. "This is the seed time of glory as of freedom," he wrote to Robert Livingston in one of his most ringing phrases.[11]

Morris loved the army, and he was determined to do whatever he could to help it. His sense of devotion, he told Washington, sprang "from acquaintance of some individuals and for the sufferings which as a body they had bravely and patiently endured."[12] He was especially moved by a performance of Addison's *Cato,* which Washington had ordered performed for them. The soldiers enjoyed the show, but with so many of them perishing from disease and exposure, the choice between liberty and death was one they had little say in.

Washington was blunt about the army's prospects. His numbers were dwindling and many who went home on furlough failed to return, preferring, Washington noted, to establish "themselves in more lucrative employments."[13] One of the worst problems Washington faced was recruiting and retaining seasoned officers, but he had an idea for solving it. It was traditional for British officers to receive half-pay pensions for life at the end of their service. The American commander in chief now wanted Congress to institute half-pay pensions for his officers too.

Morris championed Washington's proposal with zeal. Financially, it made sense, he told Congress; it was cheaper to pay lifetime pensions to officers who were thinking of leaving the army than to recruit and train new ones to take their place. "We wish to see the military placed on such a footing as to make a commission a desirable object to the officer and his rank preserved from degradation and contempt," Morris's committee wrote to Congress in recommending the half-pay pensions.

Radicals immediately opposed the idea. Pensions for officers, they feared, would lead to a permanent military establishment in the United States, a standing army that could be used to threaten the republic in peacetime. "A standing army, however necessary it may be at some times, is always dangerous to the liberties of the people," Samuel Adams explained.

> Soldiers are apt to consider themselves a body distinct from the rest of the citizens. They have their arms always in their hands. Their rules and their discipline is severe. They soon become attached to their officers and disposed to yield implicit obedience to their commands. Such a power should be watched with a jealous eye.[14]

Fear of a professional military was so deep-seated among the American left that it was embedded in the very text of the Declaration of Independence. In listing the various abuses perpetrated by George III, Jefferson deliberately included "He has kept among us . . . standing armies" and "He has affected to render the military independent of and superior to the civil power." For radical Whigs, these were grievous charges.

Radicals furthermore refused to believe that the pensions were necessary. American officers should serve out of a sense of selfless patriotism, they believed. And the very notion that they might be motivated by baser interests was a sign of corruption that would, in the words of one Massachusetts radical, "debase human kind and lay waste the natural and moral world."[15] James Lovell, one of Silas Deane's chief antagonists, wrote to Sam Adams that the pensions were a "mode of introducing into society a set of haughty idle imperious scandalizers."[16] President Laurens objected as well. Virtue and patriotism should motivate American officers, he argued, not lucre: "There are many thousands whose hearts are warm with the reasonings which induced the original compact and who have not bowed the knee to luxury nor to Mammon."[17]

Washington, along with the conservatives, found such objections naïve. He was under no illusion as to what motivated his men: self-interest. "To expect such people, as comprise the bulk of an army, that they are influenced by any other principles than those of interest," he said, "is to look for what never did, and I fear never will happen."[18] He entreated Congress to pass the measure, arguing, "I do most religiously believe the salvation of the cause depends on it, and, without it, your officers will molder to nothing, or be composed of low and illiterate men, void of capacity for this or any other business."[19]

Conservatives recognized that creating a professional army led by professional officers was the only way to win the war. Militias were simply too unreliable. "They come in you cannot tell how, go, you cannot tell when; and act, you cannot tell where," Washington complained. They "consume your provisions, exhaust your stores, and leave you at last in a critical moment."[20] When radicals argued that "from a well regulated militia we have nothing to fear," Washington must have suspected that the British were all too likely to agree—just not in the sense that radicals meant it.[21] As both conservatives and many in the army saw it, the military and the nation were inextricably linked. "It is a favorite toast in the army," Major General Henry Knox wrote to Gouverneur Morris, " 'A hoop to the barrel,' or 'Cement to the union.' "[22]

Since the earliest days of the war, many on the right had concluded that only a powerful government could provide the necessary muscle to defeat the British. The states, like the militias, were simply too undependable. Conservatives thus became ardent nationalists during the American Revolution. And nowhere was this philosophy better exemplified than in Dickinson's draft of the Articles of Confederation, which had yet to be approved.

Dickinson's vision of a strong national government conflicted on a fundamental level with radical antagonism to centralized power. His draft made the central government the supreme authority of the United States, as he had dubbed the new nation, and he went so far as to refer to the states as "colonies" within a federal system. In the twenty articles he laid out, he barred states from forming their own armies and granted the central government sole power over war and peace. States were forbidden to form separate treaties with foreign powers and to impose duties and tariffs that might hinder trade. He gave the government control over the money supply and exclusive jurisdiction over western lands, a provision that pleased investors in western land companies greatly. Congress was to be given the "sole and exclusive right and power" for settling disputes between the states. Dickinson even proposed creating an executive body called the Council of States, which would run a national bureaucracy empowered to control the military and spending when Congress was not in session.

Yet Dickinson also insisted that the states had an important role to play within the context of a strong central government, a position Gouverneur

Morris and other economic conservatives were less fond of. All states were to have equal representation in Congress rather than proportional representation based on population. Article III of his draft, moreover, reserved for each state, "as much of its present laws, rights and customs as it may think fit, and reserves to itself the sole and exclusive regulation and government of its internal police, in all matters that shall not interfere with the Articles of this Confederation."[23]

It was a remarkable achievement, especially given the speed with which Dickinson wrote it. Like almost every other proposal before Congress, however, it attracted its fair share of criticism from both left and right. Edward Rutledge, who had served on the drafting committee with Dickinson, found the draft's reasoning too subtle. It had, he wrote to Jay, "the vice of all [Dickinson's] productions to a considerable degree; I mean the vice of refining too much."[24] He was also worried about creating too powerful a central government, fretting that New Englanders, whose "leveling principles" he feared, might control it.

Dickinson's ambiguous language, however, was no accident. It was, he believed, the only proper way to carefully and incrementally augment the federal government's power. A document that allowed wide room for interpretation inevitably enhanced the power of those who did the interpreting.

With debate over Dickinson's draft crescendoing in the summer of 1777, Congress split along numerous fault lines. Large states quarreled with small states. States with western land vied with ones without such claims. Slave states contended with free ones. An ideological split between left and right, however, was harder to discern. "Both radicals and conservatives disagreed among themselves on so many issues," writes H. James Henderson, "that it is difficult to reduce the struggle over the Articles to differences in political philosophy."[25]

The greatest opponent of Dickinson's draft was an Irish immigrant to North Carolina, Thomas Burke, who had arrived in Philadelphia to represent his state in February 1777. Everywhere he looked, Burke saw conspiracies to overthrow American liberties. With Dickinson now absent from Congress, and persona non grata in much of the state, it fell largely to James Wilson to defend the idea of a strong national government. The Scotsman deplored Burke's argument that sovereign power resided ultimately in the states. If this was the case, Wilson said, the federal government would have the power neither to win the war nor build a great nation.

The antipathy between Wilson and Burke exploded when they were assigned to the same committee to write an address to the American people on the progress of the Articles of Confederation. They disagreed over everything from political ideology to points of grammar. Never one to avoid attacking despotism or eloquent writing, Burke inserted querulous comments at every turn. When Wilson wrote that the British had "turned a deaf ear" to the colonists' complaints, Burke pounced. "Is not this a vulgarism?" he insisted. "Amend it thus, 'refuse even to hear.'"

Wilson concluded the address with a reaffirmation of conservative principles. Borrowing from Dickinson's favorite biblical passage, he envisioned an America where all men would sit "under your own vine, and under your own fig tree. . . . All political power," he wrote, "will be derived from you; and will be exercised only by such persons, during such terms in such manner and for such purposes as you shall appoint."[26] The states, Wilson was coming to believe, were not the ultimate repository of all sovereign power. Rather, governmental authority derived from the American people themselves. It was an idea Wilson would develop with increasing sophistication over the next decade.

Despite Wilson's eloquence, Burke's blistering criticisms caused Congress to shelve the address and never reconsider it. His dogged opposition to any form of powerful central government, moreover, led the delegates to strip the Articles of Confederation of much of their potency. Dickinson's twenty articles were cut to sixteen, and over Wilson's objections, Burke persuaded his fellow legislators to abolish the executive body. They cut Dickinson's provision making Congress the arbiter of all disputes between the states and replaced it with a clause that made Congress "the last resort on appeal." The national government, in other words, was no longer obliged to settle differences between the states. Nor were the states obliged to let Congress resolve them.

Burke blasted Dickinson's Article VI, which prohibited states from making separate peace treaties with other nations, as "very unnecessary restraints."[27] Although the Articles intentionally avoided granting Congress any taxing power, Burke claimed they allowed the national government "an unlimited power over all property . . . a power to tax at pleasure."[28] He saved his most blistering attacks for Dickinson's Article III, which prevented the states from interfering with any police action by central government. This clause, Burke insisted, "resigned every other power" to Congress. If it were not changed, it would leave it "in the power of the future Congress or General Council to explain away every right belonging to the States and to make their own power as unlimited as they pleased."[29]

Congress did reject some of Burke's proposals, including his motion granting the states the option to remain neutral in time of war. But the underlying thrust of his arguments carried the day. Ultimate authority would reside in the states. When it was finally completed in November 1777, the new draft of the Articles of Confederation turned the United States into little more than a loose accord between thirteen sovereign states. The completion of this draft, however, did not end the disagreements among the states. With the issues of representation and western land still unresolved, Congress let the Articles languish for another four years.

By the spring of 1778, conservatives realized they had to find other means for strengthening the central government. The key, they realized, lay in controlling the purse. Right around the time Gouverneur Morris returned to York in April, he proposed a series of sweeping reforms to improve the nation's finances. In a report to Congress on the nation's money problems, he urged the establishment of a single national currency and a ban on state-issued scrip. He wanted the government to publish its debts to boost transparency and attract investors and advocated ending all restrictions on interstate trade and abolishing price controls.

Reorganizing the way the government ran the economy would also be necessary. Throughout the war, America had been governed by congressional committees. But mixing legislative and executive functions had been a disaster, and Dickinson's proposed Council of State had been rejected. Morris now called for appointing a treasurer, a comptroller, and an auditor. "Every gentleman acquainted with our public affairs," he said, must know "that a body such as the Congress is inadequate to the purposes of execution." What was needed was "either a committee of three or a single officer such as [a] Chief of the States who should superintend the executive business" of America.[30] His conservative allies agreed. In his *Causes of Depreciation of the Continental Currency,* Philip Schuyler lamented that there were so few members "of Congress adequate to the important business of finance."[31]

The nation's poor credit was also devastating the war effort. To boost confidence in the government's ability to repay its debt, Morris devised a bold new plan, one that was just as controversial in 1778 as it would be today. He urged the imposition of more taxes and tariffs. This was an act of political courage, and perhaps of political suicide as well, since the very issue of taxation had helped trigger the revolution. It was also an indication of just how much conservative positions can change over time.

"For Heaven's sake, my dear friend, exert yourself strenuously in the great leading business of taxation," Morris told Jay.[32] To Governor Clinton of New

York, he wrote, "The blinkered policy of delaying taxation is so evident that the people ought to take exemplary vengeance upon those, whoever they may be, who are causes of such delay."[33]

To be clear, Morris was particular about the kind of taxes he wanted to see imposed. He proposed a nationwide tax of one dollar per person, postal fees, and a national tariff. What he did not want was a tax on wealth, which he argued would drive money out of the economy. "Money is of too subtle and spiritual a nature to be caught by the rude hand of the law," he wrote. Taxing the rich for having money would be more than unproductive. It would also encourage cheating. "It must be admitted, that some men would by perjury elude the law, and this being admitted, it follows that the law would be a tax upon honesty and not upon money."[34]

But worse than all taxation was the steady depreciation of the currency, which robbed money of its value. As long as the government kept running its printing presses without establishing a matching source of income, Continental currency would continue to lose value. Washington was reminded daily of this problem. Pennsylvania farmers eagerly sold their goods to the British forces occupying Philadelphia for hard currency. The American army, dying en masse at Valley Forge, found few willing to accept Congress's paper notes.

Only a steady stream of revenue, Morris argued, would stabilize the nation's finances. Revenue would help stop the decline in currency. It would also help attract desperately needed international loans, something conservatives advocated frequently and which radicals opposed.

Congress had another potential source of wealth it could use to secure investors—western lands. In yet another controversial proposal, Morris suggested that the states hand their titles to land west of the Appalachians to the central government. In exchange, the states would receive a reduction in their debt burden. This land could then be used as collateral when borrowing from abroad. In a sign of just how seriously he took Washington's concerns for veterans, Morris further suggested using a portion of this land to establish a new state to give to soldiers at the end of the war.

Morris had once asserted that the "natural indolence of my disposition" prevented him from achieving much, but the truth was that he accomplished a staggering amount in his first few months in Congress.[35] His own letters belie his claims of idleness. "Let me paint my situation," he wrote to Robert Morris halfway through his first year as a delegate. "I am on a committee to arrange the treasury and finances. I am on the medical committee and have to prepare the arrangements of that department. I have the same thing to go through with relative to the Commissary's Quarter master and Clothier General's departments. I am to prepare a manifesto on the cruelties of the British. I have drawn and expect to draw almost if not all the publications of Congress of any importance."[36]

Morris was so involved in American foreign policy that one historian has called him "in many respects, Congress's foreign secretary."[37] By the end of his first year, he had served on sixty-five committees and had chaired all the most important ones. In other words, he did most of the work. As chairman, he said, he "received and answered all letters and other applications, took every step which [I] deemed essential, prepared reports, gave orders, and the like, and merely took the members of a committee into a chamber and for form's sake made the needful communications, and received their approbation which was given in due course." And that was not all. "I was moreover obliged to labor occasionally in my own profession as my wages were insufficient for my support," he added.[38]

In the end, radicals blocked every one of Morris's proposals for revamping American finances. For the moment, nothing could be done about his ideas, but his fellow conservatives took careful note and waited.

The issue of half-pay pensions for officers was tabled for several months, but in May 1778, at the urging of Washington and Morris, the matter resurfaced. Conservatives and radicals now mobilized for and against it respectively, leading to weeks of heated debate. It was, said Washington, "the most painful and disagreeable question that hath ever been agitated in Congress."[39] To defeat the measure, radicals came up with a cunning plan. They brought a motion to refer the matter to the states for consideration. There, amid the thirteen feckless and squabbling state legislatures, it was sure to die.

Counting heads, Gouverneur Morris realized that Pennsylvania's delegation would cast the deciding vote. He pleaded with Robert Morris, who was out of town, to return as fast as he could. "Massachusetts is against us," he said. "Think one moment and come here the next."[40] The older Morris arrived just in time, providing the swing vote that defeated the measure six states to five.

Two days later a compromise was hashed out. Although radicals refused to bend on the issue of lifetime pensions, they finally agreed to enact half-pay pensions for seven years. In return, they insisted that enlisted men be considered as well. Nonofficers would now receive eighty dollars and land if they served out the rest of the war. The vote was nearly unanimous, with two Massachusetts delegates maintaining their dogged opposition to any sort of pension. Ultimately, two victors emerged from the half-pay fight: the Continental

Army and Gouverneur Morris, who had emerged as one of the most formidable conservative statesmen on the national scene.

Washington's sympathies for conservative policy did not go unremarked by radicals, who increasingly attacked the general's handling of the war. After the Battle of Saratoga, for example, John Adams told his wife how pleased he was that Gates was getting all the glory and that the victory was "not immediately due to the commander in chief." He feared Washington might have grown too powerful otherwise. "If it had been, idolatry and adulation would have been unbounded; so excessive as to endanger our liberties." The New Englander liked Washington—he had nominated him for commander in chief—but he did not think the general "a deity or a savior."[41]

Others were more spiteful in their criticism. "Good God!" James Lovell wrote to Gates. "What a situation we are in!" Mocking Washington's strategy of delay and caution, he said, "If it was not for the defeat of Burgoyne, and the strong appearances of an European war, our affairs are Fabiused into a very disagreeable posture."[42] John Adams too questioned the general's strategy, stating he was "sick of Fabian systems in all quarters."[43] Conservatives, on the other hand, backed the general's strategy implicitly. Gouverneur Morris, who had witnessed the effectiveness of Schuyler's slash-and-burn campaign in upstate New York, commented, "I will venture to say that if we lay it down as a maxim never to contend for ground but in the last necessity, and to leave nothing but a wilderness to the enemy, their progress must be impeded by obstacles, which it is not in human nature to surmount."[44]

Impatience for victories, however, soon led a core group of radicals to begin questioning whether Washington was fit for command at all. As one New England congressman told Lovell, "Two battles he has lost for us by two such blunders as might have disgraced a soldier of three months standing."[45] Sam Adams couldn't have agreed more, telling Richard Henry Lee that the Continental Army was being led by a "miserable set of general officers."[46] Even Benjamin Rush wished to replace Washington, longing for "a Gates" to take command of the army and whip it into shape.

These rumblings might have amounted to little had Gates not become so infatuated with the laurels heaped at his feet after Saratoga. He began scheming to oust Washington. After all, his radical allies had already taken down one general for him. Why not another? Henry Laurens began writing to his son John, a lieutenant colonel and an aide to Washington at Valley Forge, about nebulous intrigues in Congress. One unidentified man, he said, for whom Washington had "the most favorable sentiments," had to be especially watched.[47] The general, who undoubtedly learned of these shadowy plottings through his aide, grew apprehensive.

Washington was not without his ardent supporters. Lafayette, who had become like a son to the childless general, swore to stand by him. Running into battle with an unsheathed sword and without regard for his personal safety, the Frenchman had quickly won Washington's admiration. "I am now fixed to *your* fate," Lafayette declared, "and shall follow it and sustain it as well by my sword." He called the general's enemies "stupid men who without knowing a single word about war undertake to judge you, to make ridiculous comparisons; they are infatuated with Gates without thinking of the different circumstances."[48]

Edward Rutledge was especially concerned when he heard rumors of a plot to replace the commander in chief. Anyone hoping to replace him was bound to be among "the factious and the ambitious," he wrote. They would, in other words, be completely unlike Washington. "The fate of America," he concluded, "will then be like the fate of most of the republics of antiquity, where the designing have supplanted the virtuous, and the worthy have been sacrificed to the views of the wicked."[49]

The scheme against Washington might have gone further had a copy of a letter not fallen into the general's possession in November 1777. In it General Thomas Conway, an Irishman who had served in the Prussian army under Frederick the Great before coming to America, made disparaging comments about the commander in chief. With muzzled fury, Washington wrote to Conway the next day:

> Sir: A letter which I received last night contained the following paragraph. In a letter from Genl. Conway to Genl. Gates he says: "Heaven has been determined to save your country; or a weak general and bad counselors would have ruined it." I am Sir Yr. Hble. Servt.[50]

Conway was chagrined. He immediately wrote back to protest his innocence and offered to resign. Washington made no objection. The Irishman had long irritated him with his perpetual speculations about what Frederick the Great would have done had he been leading American troops. Citing his contretemps with Washington, Conway submitted his resignation to Congress.

The radicals, however, refused to accept it. Instead, they saw that Conway was promoted to major general over twenty-three other more senior officers and also appointed inspector general of the Continental Army. They then went one step further. They had Gates appointed president of the new Board of War. Washington's subordinate was now technically in a position to give him orders.

Washington's advocates were incensed. Lieutenant Colonel Laurens wrote to his father asking "whether General Washington is to be sacrificed for General Conway. . . . I hope that some virtuous and patriotic men will form a countermine to blow up the pernicious junto spoken of above."[51] When Conway appeared at Valley Forge, there was talk that the commander in chief would challenge him to a duel. One of his officers beat him to it and shot the new inspector general in the jaw. Conway survived but returned afterward to Europe.

Washington reserved his greatest ire for Gates. Over the next few months, the generals sent each other a series of increasingly scathing letters, forcing Congress to mediate between the two. "I am wearied to death with the wrangles between military officers high and low," wrote John Adams. "They quarrel like cats and dogs. They worry one another like mastiffs. Scrambling for rank and pay like apes for nuts."[52] In the end the controversy died down after Gates disavowed any intrigue with Conway and then lied about having previously corresponded with him. Washington, for his part, was ready to let the matter rest.

Historians have long questioned whether the "Conway Cabal," as the episode has been called, ever amounted to a serious threat to Washington or represented at most a fevered whispering campaign by malcontents. The truth is lost to history, but Washington's advocates were convinced that only the general's unexpected discovery of Conway's letter prevented a radical coup within the army. In his memoirs, Lafayette openly accused Gates and the Adams-Lee faction of forming such a cabal. For the rest of his life, Washington remained convinced that "a malignant faction had been for some time forming to my prejudice."[53]

CHAPTER 16

THE RUIN OF MR. DEANE

Vice-Admiral Charles Hector, Comte d'Estaing, commanded the most magnificent and deadly warship of his day. Mounting ninety guns and measuring 184 feet long, the *Languedoc* was larger and more powerful than anything in the British navy. As it sailed across the Atlantic in the late spring of 1778, d'Estaing's flagship was escorted by a fleet of twelve ships of the line, each with more than fifty cannons. Accompanying these were five swift and lightly armed frigates along with four thousand fighting men, approximately half the number in the entire Continental Army.

After learning of the approaching French fleet, British forces abandoned Philadelphia in mid-June. The news that France had entered the war had an instant impact on imperial war strategy. Many of the thousands of troops stationed in America would have to be immediately transported to the Caribbean to safeguard British possessions there.

Americans found their capital devastated as they slowly trickled back into the city. Trees and fences had been torn down for firewood. Churches and public buildings were filled with litter and heaps of human waste. Private houses had been pillaged, their windows and doors ripped out, their gardens and orchards cut down. On July 2, Congress returned to Philadelphia, where it found the State House, which had been used as a British military hospital during the occupation, stacked with corpses. It would take weeks to cleanse the building thoroughly.

At the same moment the delegates were covering their noses and looking for another place to meet, Silas Deane was entering Delaware Bay at the head of the mightiest armada Americans had ever seen. His homecoming was not without bitterness. His wife had died while he had been abroad, and he had just missed seeing his thirteen-year-old son, Jesse. John Adams, who had been sent to France to replace him, brought the boy along in the hope of re-uniting him with his father, but Deane left before learning of Adams's arrival. Franklin took Jesse in until his father could return.

From the *Languedoc,* Deane sent word to Congress that the new French ambassador, Conrad Alexandre Gérard, was accompanying him. One week later the fleet dropped anchor at Chester, ten miles below Philadelphia. On July 12, a bright, scorching day, a congressional delegation headed by John Hancock rode down river to meet them. A dozen soldiers dressed in special red and silver uniforms rowed their barge, but no display of American resplendence could match the naval might of France floating in the water before them. The delegates bobbed in awe.

Deane's grand return had been scripted to perfection by Beaumarchais, who wanted his friend to make as theatrical an entrance as possible. If the radicals were impressed by the display of power and influence, however, they didn't show it. Deane had expected to confront his enemies, whom he assumed were the Lees and a few others, clear his name, and immediately return to France. What he hadn't counted on was a completely polarized Congress. As President Laurens commented, almost all the delegates had already "absolutely taken sides."[1] Convincing Congress of his innocence would take far more time.

While awaiting the pleasure of Congress, Deane found lodging with Benedict Arnold, whom he had last seen several years earlier when they had planned the American assault on Ticonderoga. Washington had appointed Arnold, partially disabled by his war injuries, as Philadelphia's new military governor. The city's radicals instantly despised him for his love of luxury and his flirtation with the daughter of a prominent Loyalist, whom he later married. Radicals eventually pressured Congress to court-martial him on trumped-up charges relating to some of his business investments, igniting the general's disaffection for the American Revolution. Deane's association with Arnold did little to help his cause.

It was a month before Congress granted Deane an audience. The day before his hearing, Gouverneur Morris wrote to Jay, "Your friend Deane, who hath rendered the most essential services, stands as one accused. The storm increases and I think some one of the tall trees must be shorn up by the roots."[2]

Deane had just begun presenting his letters of commendation, when he was interrupted and asked to leave the hall. A furious debate erupted over whether he should present his statement in writing instead of in person. After two roll-call votes, Deane was asked to return two days later. Deane waited and returned, just to be interrupted again and be asked to return two more days later. Then there was yet another delay. Finally, on August 21, 1778, Deane managed to get through his opening statement. After two days of testimony, during which he was barred from answering the delegates' questions, he was given "leave to withdraw."

Deane was infuriated. Without any clear charges against him, he had nothing concrete to fight against. The only thing he did hear were complaints about his having commissioned too many French officers. "He sent us over majors, colonels, brigadiers and majors general in abundance," groused Sam Adams, "and more than we knew what to do with, of his own creating."[3] None of his enemies, however, mentioned the truly exceptional officers he had commissioned as well.

Deane felt unprepared for the sheer animosity he was encountering in Congress. He had hurriedly departed France so the French fleet could sail without alerting the British. As a result, he had not had time to collect all of his records from the agents and vendors whom he had employed throughout France. He had deliberately left behind many of his account books in Paris to safeguard them from the British.

For their part, the Adams-Lee faction was in no hurry to confront Deane. The longer the affair dragged out, they felt, the more it would help them in their ultimate goal, which was to harass conservatives in general. The radicals had three main motivations for persecuting Silas Deane. To begin with, they simply despised him and everything he represented. His success would have validated the notion that self-interest could play a role in the republic. "What Mr. D's political principles were if he had any I never could learn," said Sam Adams. "His views always appeared to me commercial and interested."[4]

To radicals, it was clear that American conservatives were either in league with the British or wished to preserve so much of Britain's traditional system of government and finance that they might as well have been. Sam Adams denounced Deane's allies as "artful Tories, who would cordially receive such a character [Deane] into the bosom of their councils." Arthur Lee agreed, telling Adams, "we have the battle to fight all over again against the Tories."[5] In this internal replay of the struggle against Britain, it was the radicals, Adams declared, who were "honest and zealous Whigs."[6]

Another reason for the campaign against Deane was his support for France. Radicals feared the French monarchy, they loathed Catholicism, and they fretted over the hedonistic ways of the French. A nervous Sam Adams railed against the "inundation of levity, vanity, luxury, dissipation and indeed vice of every kind which I am informed threatens that country which has heretofore stood with unexampled firmness in the cause of liberty and virtue."[7]

This is not to say that conservatives especially trusted the French either. Rather, they recognized the practical benefits of allying with England's hereditary enemy. As H. James Henderson writes, "Ideologically, the contest was a struggle between the imperatives of revolutionary purity and the dictates of pragmatism."[8]

Finally, the Deane-Lee fracas represented a brazen attempt to grab power. If radicals could discredit Deane, and by extension his patrons Robert Morris and Benjamin Franklin, they could at a stroke seize control of American foreign and financial policy. "The wickedness of Deane and his party exceeds all belief," Richard Henry Lee wrote to his brother Arthur, "and must in the end fail them notwithstanding the art with which they clothe themselves."[9]

As radicals readied a plan to finish off Deane, Robert Morris remained unworried. "I think our friend D has much public merit," he told Jay. Deane "has been ill used but will rise superior to his enemies."[10]

At the end of September, Richard Henry Lee began his prosecution in earnest, calling a surprise witness before Congress. William Carmichael was a young Maryland merchant who had briefly worked as a secretary for Deane and Franklin in Paris. Carmichael would show, said Lee, that "Deane had misapplied the public money." Further, he said, Carmichael would testify that Deane had deliberately excluded his brother Arthur from negotiations with the French, leading to "an open rupture" among the commissioners.[11] Radicals were giddy with anticipation.

When Carmichael took his seat before Congress, however, his testimony proved so vague and inconclusive that it was hard to say whether it did more harm or good to Lee's case. In response to Lee's leading questions, the confused young man repeatedly answered, "I do not recollect," and "I did not pay sufficient attention to answer with precision." The best evidence he could muster was that Deane had used some government money to help Beaumarchais outfit a privateering mission against British shipping. If anything, Deane should have been applauded for this. "Mr. Carmichael seems rather to perplex than clear our views," James Lovell admitted.[12]

Carmichael's testimony proved to be only a slight setback for the Adams-Lee junto. It kept its case against Deane alive by introducing Arthur Lee's letters, a steady stream of invective that continued to arrive from France. At the same time, the radicals refused to let Deane respond to them. "I beg leave to lay before Congress a few observations on the extracts of Mr. Arthur Lee's letter, dated Paris, June 1, 1778, read in Congress the 3rd instant," Deane pleaded with Henry Laurens in a lengthy letter. After all, he pointed out, "Arthur Lee . . . by his own account, is my irreconcilable enemy."[13]

Deane wrote again the next month, "I am still so unhappy as to be without the honor of any reply to the several letters I have written . . . to Congress, praying that honorable body to favor me with an audience."[14] Three weeks later he wrote, "Nothing would give me greater satisfaction than to learn by what part of my public conduct I have merited the neglect which my letters and most respectful solicitations, four months past, to be heard from Congress, have been treated?"[15] Yet even to this letter Congress gave no response. The delegates, it seemed, preferred to keep their bickering over his fate secret.

Deane was perhaps most frustrated by Congress's refusal to permit him to return to France. One Virginia delegate commented, "We are plagued to death with quarrels and recriminations relative to our commissioners abroad. It is absolutely necessary that Deane should be sent over to Europe . . . but some gentlemen are determined to ruin an innocent character."[16]

After four months in limbo and dozens of unanswered appeals to Congress for a fair hearing, Deane had had enough. He now had a plan to blow the lid off the affair. Writing to his brother, he said, "I have heretofore delayed it, hoping I should not be put to the disagreeable necessity, and knowing the effects it must have on public affairs, but the law of self-defense being the first of all I shall no longer be silent."[17]

In the December 5 *Pennsylvania Packet,* the American public was shocked to see a three-thousand-word exposé of the Deane-Lee feud. "To the free and virtuous citizens of America," Deane began. "I was content even while sacrificed to the aggrandizement of others; but I will not see an individual, or family, raised upon the ruins of the general weal." Deane's account dripped with venom for the Adams-Lee faction. He detailed how close Arthur Lee had come to ruining America's diplomatic mission to France and how he "gave rise to universal disgust to the nation whose assistance we solicited." He also revealed that Lee had colluded with British agents. Right after the American commissioners had signed the treaty with France, Lee had in fact revealed its contents to a member of Lord North's cabinet, violating an agreement to keep the accord secret for the time being. Lee's only motivation had been to destabilize the alliance. Deane said he wanted to share his evidence with Congress, but "their ears have been shut against me" by the Lee clan.[18]

Deane's revelation hit Philadelphia like a bombshell, and the reverberations were felt across the nation. For the first time, the American public saw just how rent with strife their government had become. Congress's facade of public decorum had been cracked, and Deane's testament became one of the most transformative events in American revolutionary politics. No other battle between radicals and conservatives would attain such heights of ferocity or have as great an impact on the Continental Congress. It brought every partisan dispute to the surface, from foreign policy to price controls. It threatened the newly formed French alliance and adversely affected the war against the British.

Word of Deane's essay spread around the globe. Reading it in Paris, John Adams called it "one of the most wicked and abominable productions that ever sprang from a human heart." He feared it would "endanger a civil war in America." Only two outcomes were now possible, Adams declared: "There appeared to me no alternative but the ruin of Mr. Deane or the ruin of his country." He knew which course of action he would take. He thought Deane should be "hunted down for the benefit of mankind."[19]

Now that all of the acrimony was in open view, both sides took off their lace gloves. Henry Laurens demanded that Deane be publicly censured. When Congress procrastinated, the president declared that "the honor and dignity of this house, the great representative of an infant empire, upon whose conduct the eyes of Europe are fixed," had been traduced. He then quit the presidency of Congress, much to the shock of radicals and the delight of conservatives. Seizing the initiative, conservatives successfully replaced him with John Jay, newly reelected from New York.

Washington, for his part, was horrified by the political warfare in Congress. "Party disputes and personal quarrels are the great business of the day," he said, "whilst the momentous concerns of an empire, a great and accumulated debt; ruined finances, depreciated money and want of credit . . . are but secondary considerations and postponed from day to day, week to week, as if our affairs wore the most promising aspect."[20]

But the frenzy surrounding Deane continued to expand. The Lees and their supporters now launched an all-out pamphlet war against Deane, enlisting Thomas Paine as their deadliest pen for hire. As the secretary for the Committee on Foreign Affairs, Paine was able to start using secret government documents, including Arthur Lee's letters from France, to craft his attacks on Deane. Signing as "Common Sense," Paine railed against the merchant's "barbarous, unmanly and unsupported attack" on the Lees. He reiterated Arthur Lee's contention that the military supplies that had secured the victory at Saratoga had been "a present" and that there was no need to repay Deane or Beaumarchais. He accused Deane of "embezzlement" and demanded a nationwide investigation into "what mercantile connections" existed between Deane and members of Congress.[21]

Paine next zeroed in on the radicals' true target. In an open attack on Robert Morris, he charged the merchant with causing the rapid depreciation of

American money and with stealing public funds as head of the Secret Committee. Morris, who had kept silent in public until now, waded into the fray. He had had, he revealed, commercial dealings with Deane—three to be exact. Two had ended in failure and one in success. All had been attempts to supply arms to the American army. And according to his accounts, the government still owed Willing & Morris some £2,200 for the deal.

Protesting Paine's more insidious accusations, he wrote, "I do not conceive that the state I live in has any right or inclination to inquire into what mercantile connection I have had or now have with Mr. Deane, or with any other person. As I did not, by becoming a delegate for the State of Pennsylvania, relinquish my right of forming mercantile connections, I was unquestionably at liberty to form such with Mr. Deane." He reiterated that Deane was "a man of honor and integrity."[22]

Paine responded by calling Morris unfit for office. "To what degree of corruption must we sink, if our delegates and ambassadors are to be admitted to carry on a private partnership in trade?" he asked. "Only let this doctrine of Mr. Morris' take place, and the consequences will be fatal to both public interest and public honor."[23]

Gouverneur Morris now entered the fray, attacking Paine as "a mere adventurer from England, without fortune, without family or connections," and worst of all, "ignorant even of grammar."[24] In referencing government documents in his attacks, Paine had violated his oath of secrecy to the Committee on Foreign Affairs, and Morris insisted he be fired. The delegates split over the motion, but Paine spared them the trouble by resigning. Knowing that he was out of a job, Gérard and the new Spanish ambassador to the United States, Juan de Miralles, offered Paine a thousand dollars a year to stop attacking Deane and to praise America's new allies. Paine refused, preferring to continue his attacks on Deane.

After Henry Laurens lashed out at both Morrises, the gyre of vituperation widened even more. More and more delegates and their proxies entered the donnybrook until inevitably it turned violent. Laurens fought a duel with another delegate, and Paine, who happened to cross paths with a furious American officer in Philadelphia, was beaten and knocked into the gutter. His vivid prose no longer aroused the same reverence it had in 1776.

Congress's reputation suffered as well. A writer in the *Baltimore Advertiser* wrote that an organized faction in Congress had taken control, one he referred to as the "Junto." He traced its origins back to the First Continental

Congress and described it as composed of delegates from the North and South who were vying against delegates from New York and the middle states. He argued that something had to be done or the Junto would continue to control Congress. The article was soon republished in the *Virginia Gazette* and the *New York Packet*.

For all the uproar it was causing, Deane's screed had done the trick. On December 23, 1778, he finally received his hearing, with his friend Jay now presiding over Congress. Washington, another of Deane's friends, was also in attendance. With the temperature dropping outside, more logs were fed into the fire warming the Assembly Room. Over the next three days, Deane read into the official record his account of everything he had done since leaving Philadelphia more than three years before. Though lacking his account books and records, he tried to detail all his expenses.

"The settlement of the public accounts, which I am exceedingly anxious for, will show, whether, during that time, I have applied one shilling of the public moneys for my own use," he stated. "It is well known that my private fortune in America, which at the time I left my country was moderate, has not been augmented, but the contrary, by my absence." Except for one hundred guineas or Louis d'ors and a few silks left with his brother, Deane assured Congress, "I brought nothing with me from France excepting my clothes."[25]

While most were impressed with Deane's controlled and eloquent defense, radicals were livid. "Although Deane had two colleagues," fumed Francis Lightfoot Lee, "the word *We* is never used in his narrative, *I* did everything. I procured supplies, brought about the alliance, procured D'Estaing's fleet, conducted them to America, discovered the designs of the enemy and baffled them, in short I have established the liberty and independence of America."[26] Paine reiterated the charge that Beaumarchais's arms deliveries had been gifts and not purchases.

But these arguments had less traction now that Conrad Gérard was pressuring Congress to set the record straight. He also made it clear that the French government refused to have any more dealings with Arthur Lee. His influence and Jay's presidency gave conservatives the upper hand for the first time in the controversy. In January the delegates unanimously agreed that the suggestion that "the supplies shipped in the *Amphitrite, Seine,* and *Mercury* were a present from France is untrue," that the publication of such accusations was intended to "mislead and deceive the public," and that Thomas Paine's attempt "to authenticate the said false insinuations . . . is an abuse of office."[27] It was the first official confirmation that Deane had been telling the truth.

* * *

Over the next few months, Congress debated recalling Arthur Lee from France. He survived by only a single vote, but it was a sign that the clout of the Adams-Lee faction was ebbing. On the other hand, the feud strengthened the position of Pennsylvania radicals. Elections in late 1779 gave the radicals complete control over the state Assembly, which did not reappoint any conservatives to Congress. As Pennsylvania's chief justice, Thomas McKean, commented, "It seems the General Assemblies resent the treatment of Doctor Arthur Lee by Congress."[28]

Robert Morris was unbowed by the episode. "We have been passing a most jolly merry winter here in spite of all the enemies external and internal could do to disturb us," he wrote.[29]

Deane was less sanguine. His financial situation was worsening, and he wrote to Congress, "my own family and private affairs, as well as those of one intrusted [*sic*] to my care, have long suffered by my absence; they must suffer to the last degree, if longer delayed."[30] He grieved over his deceased wife and had not seen his teenage son in years. "My situation, which for eight months past has been peculiarly distressing, is now become such as to oblige me to leave this city without further delay," Deane said.[31] But as long as radicals held one mite of influence, they saw to it that he was not granted permission to leave Philadelphia. Henry Laurens, who had originated the motion blocking Deane from leaving the country, commented that if Deane did leave without permission, he would be "pleading guilty."[32]

In August 1779, more than a year after Deane had returned to the United States, Congress finally ordered its European commissioners and commercial agents to send all of their accounts and vouchers in triplicate to the Board of Treasury for a thorough examination. It also resolved "that the board of treasury be directed to report for Mr. Deane a reasonable allowance for his time and expenses for the expiration of three months after the notice of his recall to the present time."[33] He was finally free to go.

Deane thanked Congress but pointed out that before he could return to France, he needed to be paid all he was owed for his service abroad. He faced total ruin otherwise. He begged for haste and suggested having his accounts examined in Europe before they were sent to the United States. He also asked for payment in advance.

Over the protests of Henry Laurens, Congress granted Deane $10,500, but he promptly refused the paltry sum. With the Continental dollar rapidly depreciating, the money Congress was offering him would soon be worthless. It was also nowhere near what Congress owed him. Deane tabulated that he was due some 300,000 *livres,* or $2.3 million today.[34]

In the end, Deane decided to return to Europe without his money, determined to clear his name and rebuild his fortune abroad. "You will think I write with a gloomy, desponding turn in mind," he wrote his brother. "I do not, but I am not gay."[35]

Robert Morris told Franklin of Deane's upcoming departure and commented, "I consider Mr. Deane as a martyr in the cause of America. After rendering the most signal and important services, he has been reviled and traduced in the most shameful manner. But I have not a doubt the day will come when his merit shall be universally acknowledged, and the authors of those calumnies held in the detestation they deserve."[36]

After a forty-one-day crossing, during which his ship narrowly evaded the British blockade, Deane returned to France. It was early August 1780, and he was heartened to be reunited with the son he had not seen in so many years. But in many ways he was a broken and embittered man. He wrote to James Wilson, with whom he had partnered in a deal to ship American masts to Europe, "For myself, almost everything I depended upon when I left America has failed."[37] He got by on loans from Vergennes. Beaumarchais too tried to help, but the playwright's own finances were in shambles because of America's broken promises.

As the bloom on the French-American alliance began to fade, the French began what would become one of their favorite pastimes, criticizing the United States. Deane found himself in the uncomfortable position of so many Americans visiting Paris, having to defend unpopular actions at home that they themselves did not necessarily condone. As his mood continued to darken, Deane stopped justifying the American Revolution. Next he began to disparage it himself. "I know the weakness of Congress to say no worse of it and the malignity of A. Lee and associates," he wrote to Jay, "but the state of America wrings my very soul."[38] Jay wrote back urging Deane to be circumspect in what he wrote.

Deane did no such thing. He began questioning whether a "democratical government" was capable of governing properly. "We ought to inquire if any country ever was, for any time, even for one century, at peace, free, and happy, under a democracy," he wrote in an unfinished letter to his brother Simeon. In the end he lost all of his earlier optimism for the American cause. All that had been good about the old order had been lost, he feared. "Noisy and designing individuals had risen from the lowest order," he said, "and displaced the best and most respectable members of society."[39] He feared Britain might still win the war, he urged peace talks, and he speculated about reconciling with George III.

Deane's private musings about American society had been meant only for close friends and family. But while he was away on business in Ghent, British agents in Paris broke into his quarters and stole a month's worth of his unsent letters. It was a propaganda gold mine for the British secret service, and it was only a matter of time before James Rivington, a New York Tory, began printing Deane's correspondence in New York City. Soon Deane's heretical opinions were published throughout the United States.

Over the centuries scholars have speculated about whether Deane had deliberately leaked these letters and had in fact been a British spy all along. That, at least, was the position the Adamses and Lees took, and they made sure to spread their perspective as widely as possible. "Deane actually was a traitor as well as a speculator," writes one prominent historian.[40] But other historians disagree, and the facts support Deane's innocence, starting with George III's own correspondence.

Soon after Deane's return to Europe, for example, the King contemplated bribing him $500,000 in today's currency. He was well aware of Deane's misery and thought he could be turned by such a generous sum. Deane's deepening poverty, however, indicates he refused the bribe if indeed it had ever been offered. And he himself pointed out that he had nothing to gain by America's defeat. If Congress were dissolved, he would lose all hope of recovering the money owed to him. And if he had taken British bribes, why was he living hand to mouth? "I am at this moment indebted to Dr. Franklin and others at Paris for sums borrowed for my support, and, being unable to pay, am obliged their kindness even for my personal liberty."[41]

Deane also told his brother that many of his letters had been doctored by the British. He had indeed been critical of America after his treatment, but the British had made his comments sound far more caustic. A month after Deane's first series of letters was published in New York, George III told his prime minister to authorize the printing of another "intercepted letter from Mr. Deane." If Deane had been working for the British, clearly his letters would not have been "intercepted."[42]

Nevertheless the letters were so inflammatory that many of Deane's old allies turned their backs on him. Robert Morris refused to answer his letters, as did Washington and Jay. He continued to write them, growing ever more frenzied. "Our former friend Mr. Deane has lost himself entirely. He and his letters are universally condemned," Franklin wrote to Morris. "He continues however to sit croaking at Ghent, chagrined, discontented, and dispirited."[43]

Unable to make ends meet on the Continent, Deane moved to England in the early 1780s, where he lived off the charity of friends.

Deane's fortunes never improved, and by the late 1780s his health had deteriorated. Reviewing his complaints, medical historians have concluded that he was suffering from "chronic, debilitating" tuberculosis.[44] After Washington's election as president, Deane wrote to congratulate him and to ask him to review his long-ignored claims for compensation. Now that enough time had elapsed since the scandal involving his letters, Deane's friends in America decided it was safe to help him again. In late 1789 Washington and Jay discreetly arranged for Deane to return to America. His exile was about to end.

On September 23, 1789, at the age of fifty-one, Deane felt well enough to board a ship. He left London aboard the *Boston Packet,* grateful to be returning home and full of ideas for moneymaking ventures. He envisioned expanding access to the American interior with canals and land development schemes. Suddenly, just as the ship was about to leave the Thames, Deane collapsed in the captain's arms. A few hours later he was dead. The *Boston Packet* returned to shore, where Deane was buried in an unmarked grave. Some historians have speculated that a British spy killed Deane with a fatal dose of curare, but no conclusive proof has ever been found. Whatever the truth, the bitter partisan battles he had fought against congressional radicals were clearly what poisoned him in the end.

On July 27, 1841, after decades of petitioning, Congress finally paid Deane's heirs $37,000, or $971,000 today. Perhaps more important to Deane's memory was a congressional report that found that "Mr. Deane performed highly important and valuable services for this country." A previous audit performed by Arthur Lee, Congress added, had been "*ex parte* erroneous and a gross injustice to Silas Deane."[45]

Beaumarchais's heirs were not so fortunate. During the French Revolution, the playwright was exiled to England, where he was thrown in debtors' prison and narrowly escaped the death sentence. He returned to France several years later and died in poverty while fruitlessly trying to recover the money Congress owed him. In 1789 Alexander Hamilton told Congress that the United States still owed Beaumarchais 2.28 million *livres,* or $18 million today. The creator of Figaro was never repaid.

CHAPTER 17

FORT WILSON

By the fall of 1778, James Wilson had become the most hated man in Philadelphia, no small feat in a city rent with discord. Recent elections had given conservatives enough seats to renew their campaign to replace the radical constitution, and Wilson used the occasion to call for a referendum to get a "sense of the people." Radicals were livid, once again seeing a threat to their authority. The Assembly approved the measure and ordered that at the end of March, voters would be able to cast two ballots in two different boxes. In the first, they would write whether or not a new constitutional convention should be held. In the second, they would put the name of a delegate they wished to nominate. If a majority voted yea to a new convention, the top six names from each city and county would be chosen to attend.

Not since 1776 had the radicals' political power been so threatened, and they immediately swung into action. Across the state they circulated petitions calling for the referendum to be scrapped. Whipping up popular hysteria, they claimed Wilson's anticonstitutionalist Republican party was in the pay of the British. They were part of a Tory conspiracy, bent on establishing a House of Lords in America.

Wilson tried to assure votes that these accusations were "the greatest absurdity" and that he was a devoted Patriot. "Are we all desirous of becoming lords?" he asked. It was true that he wanted to establish a second house in the legislature, but only because the radical unicameral government had itself become tyrannical. It had destroyed the rule of law, and judges were but leaves in the wind, "tossed about by every veering gale of politics."[1]

Wilson's reasoned arguments did little to counter the wave of radical propaganda. Within weeks thousands of petitions demanding a halt to the referendum flooded the Assembly. On February 27, 1779, the Assembly voted to rescind its previous decision to allow a plebiscite on a new constitution. The conservatives had been defeated again.

When Wilson's relentless efforts at constitutional reform cost him his seat in Congress, he returned to the practice of law. Financially he was successful, but his choice of causes and clients made radicals despise him even more. He fought radical attempts to take over the College of Philadelphia, a bastion of conservatism. He defended the supremacy of the national government when he represented Gideon Olmsted, a young American privateer who had seized the British sloop *Active* only to have his prize taken from him by the government of Pennsylvania. More than anything else, his defense of Quakers accused of aiding the British sealed his reputation as "an aristocrat."

Abraham Carlisle was a prominent Quaker carpenter who stood accused of standing guard for the British Army during Howe's occupation. Bound by their belief in pacifism, Quakers publicly refused to take sides in the war, although many privately sympathized with the British. Perhaps even more galling to radicals was their refusal to swear a loyalty oath to the Pennsylvania constitution. When Carlisle's trial began on September 24, 1778, in the court of oyer and terminer of Philadelphia County, the prosecutors came seeking blood.

Wilson admitted his client had stood guard for the British, but he argued that the carpenter had never carried arms for them. Working as a civilian for the British, though odious to most Patriots, did not in itself constitute treason. Wilson then produced a dozen witnesses who testified to Carlisle's many acts of kindness while standing guard. Relying on the formidable legal training he had received under Dickinson, he cited a 1351 law, enacted during the reign of Edward III, establishing that accusations of treason had to be backed by proof. The law had been a watershed in English jurisprudence, transforming a way of punishing those who had lost the king's favor into a strict legal doctrine controlled by Parliament. Proving treason required at least two witnesses, but the prosecutors had produced only a single unreliable one. If Carlisle were convicted, Wilson argued, a sound principle of law four centuries old would be rejected and a dangerous new precedent established.

After deliberating twenty-four hours, the jury voted to convict Carlisle. At the same time, Wilson's defense had moved them, and they petitioned Pennsylvania's Executive Council to show mercy. The jury's plea was bolstered by a petition signed by 386 prominent citizens. Fearful of becoming the targets of mob violence, however, the council refused to show leniency, and Carlisle was hanged on November 4. Wilson subsequently defended four other Quakers accused of treason. Three were acquitted and another was hanged, even though Wilson had cast this man's guilt into serious doubt as well.

These trials had a powerful impact on both Wilson and the radicals. The execution of his clients would rankle Wilson for the rest of his life. Nor would radicals soon forget his aid to men they considered the enemy. As inflation ran rampant in the spring of 1779, Wilson's staunch opposition to price controls placed him at the center of a bull's-eye.

On the night of May 22, 1779, pamphlets appeared on almost every street corner of Philadelphia calling on the militia to take arms against the rich. Under the headline "For our Country's Good," the broadside declared, "In the midst of money we are in poverty and exposed to want in a land of plenty. You that have money, and you that have none, down with your prices, or down with yourselves. . . . We have turned out against the enemy and we will not be eaten up by the monopolizers and forestallers."*[2]

By 1779 the depreciation of American currency had reached catastrophic levels. Shortages were endemic and the economy lay in tatters. More than $200 million was now circulating in what had until then been a barter economy; all the while, Congress's printing presses continued to pump out an additional $10 million every month to pay for the war. Most states were also printing money, leading to an ever-widening spiral of inflation. The price of beef had increased by 400 percent during the year, and a soldier's monthly salary was now barely sufficient to buy a single bottle of second-rate rum. "People are now so afraid of the money," complained one officer, "that it is almost impossible to purchase grain at any rate."[3]

Rather than blaming the laws of economics, however, radicals pointed their fingers at merchants, whom they accused of "monopolizing" and "engrossing."† A Philadelphia writer calling himself "Come on Warmly" excoriated "overbearing merchants, a swarm of monopolizers and speculators, an infernal gang of Tories."[4] It was not unusual for crowds to descend on shops stocking such essential goods as salt, tea, or flour and demand them at a "just price." Merchants who refused such offers ran the risk of being tarred and feathered. By May 1779 the consequences were worsening.

On the morning of May 23, club-wielding militiamen began inspecting stores throughout Philadelphia, judging on the spot whether prices were too

* Forestalling is the act of cornering a market in order to charge higher prices.

† Engrossing is keeping goods off the market while waiting for prices to rise.

high. Merchants found guilty were summarily hauled from their shops and marched through town. Many were beaten and several thrown in prison. Warehouses and homes were invaded, ships seized, and private property impounded. The attacks continued the next day, and that afternoon radicals held a large meeting in the State House yard.

In his booming voice, the radical merchant Daniel Roberdeau told the angry crowd that merchants were "getting rich by sucking the blood of this country." A vast conspiracy, he said, was surely afoot. "I have no doubt but combinations have been formed for raising the prices of goods and provisions, and there the community, in their own defense, have a natural right to counteract such combinations, and to set limits to evils."[5]

The best way to combat rising costs, radicals believed, was through price controls. Soon after the outbreak of war with Britain, price control committees had sprouted up throughout the country. In late 1776 the New England states had sent delegates to a special convention in Providence to discuss establishing price controls. When Congress debated adopting the convention's proposals, conservatives, led by James Wilson, vigorously opposed any such action. First, they felt the meeting had undermined Congress's authority. Second, they rejected the underlying economics.

In an essay they wrote on behalf of their fellow merchants, Robert Morris and Pelatiah Webster of Philadelphia said trying to cap prices by decree was folly. "The most effectual way to turn scarcity into plenty is to raise the price for the article wanted," they said. "Like him who owned the goose which laid golden eggs, you will cut off the source of all future supplies, and like him too, when you repent, you will repent in vain."[6] Events soon bore out these arguments. After a Philadelphia merchant named Levi Hollingsworth was caught selling flour to an agent from Maryland, he was kidnapped, jailed, and run out of town. Several weeks later radical leaders begged him to send supplies to the city, which was now running desperately low.

What was new in 1779 about the price control debate was that these extralegal committees were increasingly backed by the threat of popularly condoned violence.[7] Crowds now carried semilegal authority, and they stood ready to enforce "the radical politics of equality" at the point of a gun, as one historian puts it.[8] In New York State, for example, one merchant who refused to lower his prices was visited by a mob soon afterward, which "had orders from the committee to search his house."[9] Accompanied by armed Continental soldiers, the angry crowd could not be stopped.

New York conservatives like John Jay, Robert Livingston, and Egbert Benson (one of the leaders of the New York Assembly) fought vigorously to contain the power of extralegal committees, which threatened the "subversion of the constitution," as Benson put it. In the face of a sudden resurgence of such committees in 1779, he told Jay he hoped the "limitation [of prices] may be limited to the city of Albany."[10] Radicals decried any effort to restrict the power of committees. "As soon as the authority of your committees ended," wrote one New York radical, "knavery showed its head, villains of every class came forth and practiced with impunity."[11]

Nowhere was the fervor for price controls greater and more controversial than in Pennsylvania. In Philadelphia the Committee of Inspection and Observation grew rapidly from about forty people to one hundred, and its power increased proportionately. Not only did it regulate the price of scarce commodities and shut down the stores of merchants who violated its edicts, but it also began hunting down people it felt had uttered treasonous opinions. One ironmonger who wrote a pamphlet defending Robert Morris was attacked in the middle of the night. He drove off his assailants with a brace of pistols, but his sister was "dangerously wounded . . . in the head."[12]

Morris was, in fact, a frequent target of radical committees. At a mass meeting in May 1779, a committee was elected to investigate his business dealings. The *Victorious,* a French ship carrying one of his cargoes, had been docked at Philadelphia's waterfront for more than a month while prices continued to rise. Radicals were certain that Morris was deliberately holding on to his cargo in order to make a higher profit. The committee, led by Thomas Paine, confronted Morris only to discover that the cargo was actually under the control of a French agent in Baltimore. Paine's committee reluctantly had to back off.

Radicals again took aim at Morris when a citizens' committee seized 182 barrels of flour being held in Wilmington under his name. Again, radicals were forced to withdraw their complaints after Conrad Gérard complained to Congress. The flour, it turned out, belonged to the French military and Morris was simply storing it for the French fleet currently protecting American shores. Henry Laurens, chagrined that he had been forced to side with Morris, nevertheless used the occasion to attack "that bane of patriotism, commerce."

Tensions mounted throughout the summer of 1779. At a mass meeting in the State House yard on July 27, 1779, a committee of 120 men was appointed to regulate prices. In order to control the proceedings, radicals announced they would allow only those who had taken their oath of allegiance into the yard.

Next to the speaking platform they stationed a hundred men with clubs and fife and drums to drown out dissenters.

Conservatives braved these threats and showed up anyway. When General John Cadwalader tried to speak out against price controls and the illegal seizure of property, he was drowned out by loud jeers. James Wilson and Benjamin Rush managed to say a few words, but others who tried to oppose radical measures were silenced when the armed men began marching in front of the stage beating the drums and blowing the fife. When it was clear the interference could not be stopped, the conservatives moved to the college yard to hold their own meeting. There Robert Morris urged the adoption of several resolutions to counter price controls, and all denounced the threats and rumpus that had prevented their speaking. The rampant anarchy they had warned of in the buildup to independence seemed to be upon them. Social stability was disintegrating, and government was being subverted. As one conservative put it, "every man who takes a club in his hand to town meetings (which by-the-by, have been very frequent of late) undertakes to be governor."[13]

But the violence was just beginning. "We have arms in our hands and know the use of them," declared the city's artillery militia. "Nor will we lay them down till this is accomplished." If the committees could not bring down prices, they warned, "our drums shall beat to arms."[14] Radicals began laying plans to seize the wives and children of men they deemed to be Tories and pack them onto a ship bound for British-held New York.

By the end of July, tempers were flaring. After Whitehead Humphreys, the owner of a steel furnace, anonymously attacked Thomas Paine in the *Evening Post,* a mob seized the newspaper's printer and forced him to reveal the author's name. The crowd then moved on to Humphreys's house. He was not home, but Edward Langworthy, a congressional delegate from Georgia, was lodging at his residence and assumed the mob was coming for him. A scuffle broke out, and Langworthy helped Humphreys's family bar the door. When Humphreys returned home and armed himself, the mob enlisted a column of Continental soldiers to support them. Eventually the crowd retreated, but Langworthy was furious that radicals had pulled in the Continental guard. Complaining to Congress, he said that the mob next planned to attack Gouverneur Morris and Silas Deane. Over the protests of radicals, Congress ordered an investigation, but nothing much came of it.

By September Wilson had become the object of frequent violent attacks in the press. Anonymous critics decried his legal defense of the Quakers and his well-known "Tory toleration." It was claimed that he held secret dinners at his house with a cabal that was planning to overthrow the state. Wilson responded that although he disliked the state constitution, he had always attempted to reform it through peaceful means. In fact, he had been so busy of late that he had not undertaken any action against it. "No endeavors have been lately made to change the Constitution," he said. "Nothing of the kind, that I know, is now intended."[15]

The tension in Philadelphia finally snapped on Monday, October 4. Throughout the city a leaflet began to circulate urging members of the militia to "drive off from the city all disaffected persons and those who supported them."[16] At nine in the morning, militiamen began assembling in the commons across from Paddy Burns's Tavern. All were armed and preparing to strike. Charles Willson Peale, a militia captain who had led the attack on Humphreys's house, was asked to take command, but he and other radical leaders were growing frightened of the roiling fury that was rapidly enveloping the city.

Making his way to the commons, Peale, who would later have better luck as a painter than as a military leader, desperately began trying to calm down the militia he and other radicals had spent years working up. He called for the mob to draw up a series of resolves outlining their grievances. But the militia wanted blood, not pen and paper. Peale left in frustration. "To reason with a multitude of devoted Patriots assembled on such an occasion was in vain," he said, and he ran for the house of Joseph Reed, the president of Pennsylvania, who was sick in bed.[17] Though they were political rivals with the conservatives, Peale and Reed had no desire for a revolution within the Revolution, especially one they doubted they could contain.

Conservatives were well aware of the brewing trouble that morning, and thirty of them gathered at the City Tavern to discuss how they might defend themselves. They were Philadelphia's conservative upper crust, men "distinguished for their wealth, virtue, learning, and liberality of manners," as Benjamin Rush put it.[18] Along with Robert Morris and James Wilson, there were a number of men with military experience, including Colonel Stephen Chambers of the militia, and Captain Robert Campbell, Major David Franks, and General Thomas Mifflin of the Continental Army. Weapons were handed out, and General Mifflin began instructing the uninitiated on how to load and fire a musket. They also sent word to the City Light Horse, a group of militia composed entirely of Philadelphia's elite and mocked by radicals as the "Silk Stocking Brigade." Commanded by General Cadwalader, the cavalry company agreed to stand ready.

By noon, however, no trouble had erupted, and the members of City Light

Horse left its stables to go home for dinner. It was then that the mob struck. Marching to the Friends Meeting House on Fourth Street, the militiamen seized Jonathan Drinker, a wealthy Quaker. They then marched to the homes of three more merchants, Buckridge Sims, Thomas Story, and Mathew Johns, all supposed Tories, and dragged them from their homes. Surrounded by the raucous and heavily armed mob, the four prisoners were marched and taunted through the streets.

Pleased with its accomplishments, the mob returned to Burns's Tavern, where flowing alcohol fueled its indignation and its courage. The increasingly drunk mob began murmuring about killing the city's profiteers and monopolists, people it referred to as "un-American elements." When two militia officers asked the crowd what they wanted to do next, the mob didn't hesitate in its response.

Two words rang out: "Get Wilson."

With the sobering effect of a sense of purpose, the militia grabbed their weaponry and marched out of the tavern to the beat of an unsteady drum tapping out "The Rogue's March."

As the militiamen began making their way down Arch Street, their four captives in tow, General Mifflin ran to confront them. He ordered them to disband. In reply, he was hit from behind with the butt of a musket. Benedict Arnold, the city's military governor, also tried to intervene and was chased off by a hail of rocks and curses.

Told that the mob was approaching, Wilson called on the Assembly to send protection. The Assembly suggested he refer the matter to President Reed. Wilson and his companions decided they could rely only upon themselves. As the din of shouts and drumbeats grew louder, they ran to Wilson's house, which was only a block away on the corner of Third and Walnut. Wilson's children and his wife Rachel, who was about to give birth to their fourth child, were hurried off to Morris's house for safety.

Wilson had a predilection for beautiful homes and expensive furnishings. His wife had a pianoforte in the drawing room, and in his living room he had a brilliant red Turkish carpet, Venetian blinds, and enormous brass andirons guarding the fireplace. But it was no time to start worrying about collateral damage. The military men began analyzing how best to fortify the brick house, which was three stories tall in the middle with two single-story wings on either side.

Dubbing the home "Fort Wilson," the defenders began reinforcing the windows and doors and stuffing pistols into their silk pockets. General Mifflin, who had recovered from the musket blow, returned to take command. With Wilson as his lieutenant, he had the thirty defenders marching up and down Walnut Street for some hasty drilling. As the militia grew nearer, the men of Fort Wilson retreated into the house and barred the doors and windows. Gun barrels emerged from the second-floor windows, glistening in the afternoon sun.

The mob was now swollen with supporters and gawkers. The drumbeat grew louder and braver. Just as they rounded Second Street and flooded onto Walnut, they were confronted by two Continental officers, Colonel Grayson and Captain Allen McLane, standing in their path. The Continental officers ordered the militia to turn back. The sheer bravado of their command seemed to work, for the marchers stumbled to a halt. Then two militia officers charged up to the front brandishing their muskets. One jabbed at Captain McLane with his bayonet, threatening to skewer him unless he moved. With McLane distracted, a group of militia burst forward and surrounded the officers. Others surged down the street until they reached the front of Fort Wilson.

Eyewitness accounts differ over what transpired next. Some say Captain Campbell fired into the street from inside the house. Others say he simply shouted an order for the militia to keep moving. All agreed on what happened next. A bullet from the crowd killed him instantly. In response, a deafening thunder of musket fire roared from the house. Smoke fogged the air, and the stench of gunpowder burned in everyone's noses. As the mob dived for cover, five fallen bodies were revealed, bleeding onto the cobblestones. McLane and Grayson dashed for the house, where General Mifflin opened the door for them.

As the conservatives reloaded, the militia regrouped. One detachment ran for crowbars and sledgehammers. Another went to secure a cannon. The sound of random shots echoing off the cobblestones mixed with the taunts of militiamen, who knew they would soon have the advantage. When General Mifflin again called out for the militia to disperse, a bullet shattered the window next to him, raining shards of glass and wood. Mifflin unloaded two pistols at the street below.

A team of militiamen stripped to the waist arrived with hammers and crowbars. Covered by supporting fire, they made for the rear door and, after a few swings, smashed it down. Several men rushed inside, only to be mowed down by fire from Colonel Chambers, who was lying in wait on the stairs. But too many men were pouring in for Chambers to handle alone, and while reloading, he was bayoneted. The invaders didn't press their attack and ran from the house shooting wildly. After tending to Chambers, the defenders heaped tables and chairs against the broken back door. Their chances were not looking good. Militiamen were now swiveling two field pieces around the corner and readying to blow up the house.

It was at that moment that the cavalry arrived. A sickly President Reed rode in with the City Light Horse, a pistol held in one hand and his reins gripped in the other. Reed had roused himself from bed so quickly that his boots remained unlaced and his knee buttons were unfastened. Dragoons with unsheathed swords rode behind him. "Charge all armed men," Reed called. The sight of the mounted reinforcements and their slashing swords was enough to disperse most of the rioters. Twenty-seven who remained behind were arrested and thrown into prison. In the end four militiamen lay dead along with a young black boy who had been watching the battle; another fourteen radicals lay wounded. Even the city's capture by the British had been less violent.

Fort Wilson's defenders came through relatively unscathed. Only Captain Campbell had been killed. Several others had minor injuries, including General Mifflin's brother, John, who had been shot through the hand. Colonel Chambers recovered from his bayonet wound.

Benedict Arnold came as soon as he could, his distrust of the militia confirmed. The general was also disgusted with Reed, whom he had never liked. "Your president has raised a mob, and now he cannot quell it," he told the defenders. The fact that Reed had saved the day meant little to him. As Arnold toured the damaged house, he peered out one of the second-floor windows and drew his pistols, as if searching for some remaining militiamen he might be able shoot.

Euphoric at their survival, the conservatives marched up Second Street and across Market, but no cheering crowds came out to greet them. That evening bricks and stones rained down upon the City Light Horse as it tried patrolling the city. Guards had to be posted outside the city jail after a mob tried to break in and free the captive militiamen.

Despite Wilson's victory, it was clear that Philadelphia was far from safe for him. Morris told his friend that his life was at risk as long as he stayed, and he pleaded with him to go into hiding. Wilson balked, but with Morris now in hiding himself and communicating through his slave James, he relented. Morris promised Wilson that his wife and children would be taken care of, and he arranged for his friend to be taken to his country estate, The Hills, where Wilson hid in the attic. Morris told him to avail himself of the tea in the house and the wines in the cellar. There was an old mattress and some blankets he could use. James, he promised, would bring food as soon as he could.

The radicals' defeat had done little to calm their tempers. The next morning a group of militia officers appeared at the Court House demanding that the prisoners be released. At the same time, word came that the Germantown militia was readying to march on the city. Reed hurried off to Germantown, leaving Timothy Matlack to handle the angry officers. Bowing to their threats, Matlack released the prisoners, who lined up outside the prison and cheered in defiance. Reed succeeded in getting the Germantown militia to disband, but the threat of renewed violence was growing.

President Reed tried downplaying the battle as best he could, calling it "the casual overflowings of liberty."[19] Few shared his appraisal. Alarm spread quickly throughout the state and then the country. "God help us—Terrible times," wrote Samuel Patterson, a mill owner and colonel of a Delaware battalion. "The poor starving here and rise for redress. Many flying the city for fear of vengeance."[20] Renewed violence threatened to break out at any moment.

Two days after the attack, Morris reported that it was still too dangerous for Wilson to return to the city. "The ferment is particularly high against you," he said. "The poor unfortunates who lost their lives yesterday have been buried this evening with the honors of war—a circumstance not calculated to allay the passions of men in a ferment."[21]

That afternoon, for example, a mob attacked Benedict Arnold in the street. Armed with his pistols, the general managed to scare off his assailants, but he had been shaken and demanded that Congress supply him with a bodyguard of twenty men. Clearly, he argued, state officials were powerless to protect him. The incident did much to confirm Arnold's growing conviction that the American Revolution had spun out of control. Though his eventual defection to the British stemmed mostly from vanity and cupidity, his rage over the way radicals treated him played no small role in his decision.

To placate the angry crowds, Reed demanded that Fort Wilson's defenders post bail and appear before him. Wilson was infuriated when he learned the news. He told Morris that he was tired of being cooped up in his attic and that he wanted to return as soon as possible to clear his name. Trying to make as little noise as possible while writing, Wilson drew up a list of witnesses who could attest to the fact that the militia had fired first, not the conservatives. And he described to Morris a plan to organize an armed posse that could put down future uprisings and "give some stability to our defense of the first rights of man."

But Morris counseled restraint. "Retreat until the ferment is over," he advised, "you may then be heard patiently and have justice done you. In the present state of things, the passions of men might do you injustice."[22]

Conservatives were aghast when the radicals won full control of the Assembly in an election one week later. Their success in repelling the attack on Fort Wilson had been turned against them, and now they had lost essentially all political power. "Poor Pennsylvania has become the most miserable spot upon the surface of the globe," Benjamin Rush lamented. "They call it a democracy—a mobocracy in my opinion would be more proper."[23]

Yet the electoral rout and the battle of Fort Wilson served as a wake-up call to the state's anticonstitutionalist Republican party. Many conservatives began questioning whether unremitting opposition to popular positions was a prudent strategy. To a great extent, their refusal to make concessions had led to the radical constitution in the first place. They had only to look at neighboring Maryland for an example of a state where elites had embraced "the wisdom of sacrifice," in the words of Charles Carroll of Carrollton, perhaps the richest man in America and one of the few Catholics. When Carroll's father wrote to him complaining that radical economic policies exceeded "in iniquity all the acts of the British Parliament against America," the son countered that "great revolutions" did not "happen without much partial injustice and suffering."[24]

Even men who had hitherto sided with the radicals were having second thoughts about embracing the popular unrest, realizing that it might not be possible to stoke the mob without igniting an explosion. "We are at this moment on a precipice," Henry Laurens wrote to John Adams, "and what I have long dreaded and often intimated to my friends, seems to be breaking forth—a convulsion among the people."[25] A number of radical leaders even began to concede the uselessness of their economic policies. "We regulated the price of flour (farina) until there was none in the market," Thomas Paine commented.[26]

Memories of the Fort Wilson Riot did not fade quickly. Five years afterward it was still remembered in Philadelphia as "the most alarming insurrection it had ever felt."[27] In many respects, America was fortunate it was still fighting the British and that the war was going badly. "Had there been no Revolution," writes the historian Charles Page Smith, ". . . the incident might have grown into a minor civil war."[28]

More than two weeks after the attack, on October 19, Wilson finally returned to Philadelphia and posted a bail of £10,000. For the sake of peace, other defenders of Fort Wilson did the same. Morris's advice had been sound, and the willingness of conservatives to shoulder some of the blame for driving up prices had a remarkable soothing effect on the city. In March the Executive Council issued "an act of free and general pardon," and everyone was pleased to see the matter end. Both sides had won something, and both had lost. Conservatives had lost all power in the Assembly. At the same time, calls for price controls and support for radical committees quickly died away as well. There was a war going on, and both radicals and conservatives were coming to understand that they had to cooperate if America was to win.

CHAPTER 18

AMERICAN DICTATORS

Seventeen-eighty was the year America began to lose the war. It was the year Congress ran out of money. It was the year Benedict Arnold defected to the enemy and began leading Redcoats on devastating raids along the coast. It was the year the British captured a second major city and wiped out two American armies. It was the year Americans began hating the Continental Army as Washington's seizure of private property increased. Finally, it was the year European powers began to discuss imposing a peace settlement, leaving Britain in possession of a sizable part of America. Something had to be done before it was too late.

After France's entry into the war, the British shifted their focus to the American South, where they believed a large Loyalist population would rally to their side. They were not disappointed by the early results. At the very end of 1778, the British took Savannah, Georgia. The next year they seized Augusta, Georgia, and repulsed a combined American-French assault on the city. With Georgia now largely under British control, General Henry Clinton was able to turn his attention to Charleston and begin strategizing about how to capture the city that had defeated his forces four years earlier.

As South Carolina's alarmed leaders watched British might surge at their southern border, they also had to contend with political division at home. Charleston had largely avoided the social turmoil that plagued Philadelphia, but mob power played an influential role in the city's politics. When President Rawlins Lowndes and Vice President Christopher Gadsden dared to keep pardoning Loyalists who had missed an official deadline to take a loyalty oath to the United States, crowds erupted in anger. Many called for John Rutledge to return to power. "Had Mr. R been president, nothing of this sort would have happened" became a popular refrain.[1]

The Rutledges too criticized Lowndes's and Gadsden's actions, but they were not about to let the mob tear down the government over it. At a public meeting on June 10, 1778, Edward Rutledge argued against calls to impeach Lowndes and Gadsden and urged the crowd to issue a resolution reaffirming stiff penalties for Tories who had not taken the loyalty oath. His "popularity and earnest advice" carried the day.[2] Support for the Rutledges mushroomed in the following months, with one Charleston printer noting that the people "now declare [John Rutledge] the best President they can get, and I make no doubt but he will be re-elected next winter."[3]

On February 5, 1779, "amidst the acclamations of numerous spectators" and the firing of artillery throughout the city, John Rutledge was elected South Carolina's first governor under the state's new constitution.[4] His first concern, as it had been during his previous presidency, was to bolster the state's defenses. Three days earlier two hundred British soldiers landed on Port Royal Island near Beaufort, South Carolina. General Moultrie and Edward Rutledge, now captain of a state artillery company, immediately moved south to drive them away. After a heated battle, the Redcoats returned to their ships, which was fortunate for Rutledge's forces. They had just about run out of ammunition.

Never before had South Carolina faced such peril. Benjamin Lincoln, the general in charge of the state's Continental forces, had fewer than thirteen hundred men fit for duty. Arguing that the state militia was not adequately prepared, he asked Rutledge to petition the legislature for him. The general wanted militiamen to be subjected to stricter discipline and permitted to serve outside the state. Rutledge agreed, and in making the case, he asked the legislature to grant him greater powers to wage war in general.

At first the legislature seemed inclined to grant the governor's request, but unexpectedly, amid old arguments between authority and liberty, the Senate voted against him. Rutledge was incredulous, unable to understand how the state's legislators could quibble over constitutional niceties with so much at stake. "Suspicions and jealousies . . . of the power of the executive almost . . . kill[ed] us," he remarked. And it seemed to him that some politicians were far more willing to "trust their freedom" to the British than to Patriots like himself. Personally, he was ready to do whatever it took to win the war. If his actions were deemed illegal, then he would "trust to the mercy of his country for pardon after he shall have saved her from ruin."[5]

Only after General Moultrie explained how dire the situation was did the Senate reverse itself, passing a new law "for the Better Defense and Security of this State during the recess of the General Assembly." Rutledge was relieved to have the backing of his legislature, but something even more serious was now bothering him—the lack of reinforcements from the Continental Army. After beseeching Congress for help, he was instructed to ask Virginia and North Carolina for the extra troops. But Rutledge's northern neighbors were also reluctant to help. "It is scarcely credible that neither the Confederacy of the States, or their Allies can furnish a ship, a man, or a musket," Rutledge said.[6] He was not alone in his growing sense of disillusion with Congress. Increasingly, South Carolina's leaders felt abandoned in their hour of need. Some even questioned whether their state's neglect had severed its ties to the Union.

Tired of waiting for the British to strike, General Lincoln decided to take the fight to them. In April he started for Georgia, just at the moment when the British began marching toward Charleston along a different route. With Lincoln gone, there was now nothing standing between the British and Charleston. The city was completely vulnerable. Rutledge sent word urging Lincoln to return as fast as possible. In the meantime, he declared martial law and ordered a scorched-earth campaign around the city. Anything that could aid the British, from livestock to bridges, was to be destroyed ahead of their advance.

Over three days, on May 9, 10, and 11, British troops led by General Augustine Prévost began arriving outside Charleston. Believing their forces to be vastly outnumbered, the city's residents were "frightened out of their wits," Moultrie noted.[7] Rutledge began stalking the American lines, berating any militiamen he found "inattentive to their duty." One soldier's lack of discipline enraged him so much that "he struck [him] with his rattan or twig whip."[8] Rutledge returned the next day to apologize, but his loss of composure was understandable. His chief engineer had just told him to expect massive numbers of civilian casualties when the British attack came.

At a three a.m. meeting with Moultrie, Rutledge discussed their dwindling options. Both men agreed the city would not be able to withstand an assault. The question was whether they could hold out long enough for Lincoln to return. Moultrie said he would abide by Rutledge's decision, and early that morning they asked Prévost what his surrender terms would be. Rutledge was indeed prepared to surrender if he had to, but he also recognized the tactical importance of opening negotiations. As long as they could keep the British talking, it "would retard their movements" and buy Charleston's defenders precious time.

When the British commander sent back word that he would not negotiate with civil authorities, Rutledge and Moultrie knew they had no choice but to fight. All day they steeled themselves for the opening fusillade; strangely, none came. Looking out past their barricades the next morning, they discovered that the British had hastily decamped during the night. Prévost had intercepted a message from Lincoln announcing he was on his way back. Not wanting to risk getting trapped between the city and the approaching Continental forces, the British had fled.

Yet there was little time for rejoicing. The British retreat, Rutledge knew, was only a reprieve, not a victory. They would be back, and throughout the summer and fall of 1779, he wrangled with the legislature over augmenting his wartime powers. In October he was shaken by the news that a joint French-American expedition had failed to retake Savannah and had suffered heavy losses. He was positively alarmed when he learned in January 1780 that General Henry Clinton had set sail from New York with eight thousand Redcoats bound for Charleston. By the middle of February, Clinton was only thirty miles from Charleston.

Despite this ominous news, the legislature continued to deny Rutledge permission to draft militiamen. It did, however, begin granting him some additional authority. "In times of danger and invasion," the legislature acknowledged, "it has always been the policy of republics to concenter the powers of government in the hands of the supreme magistracy for a limited time."[9]

Strict limits were nonetheless imposed on him. He was barred from imposing the harsh discipline of the Continental Army on the militia. He was forbidden from taking any citizen's life without a trial. And he was prohibited from calling out more than one third of the militia at a time, except when enemy forces were within an eighty-mile radius of their position. He was, in other words, now prevented from using the state's full strength to fight the British.

Rutledge threw himself into a frenzy of activity trying to raise recruits for the defense of Charleston. But turnout was meager. Even after he threatened to seize the property of any militiaman who failed to report for duty, many refused the turnout. With the governor's powers restricted, they knew it was unlikely they would ever be punished. Yet every day Clinton's forces got closer. At the end of March, the British began digging deep trenches across from Charleston's defenses. On April 7, after sealing the harbor, they began shelling the city, with one thirty-two-pounder falling right in Rutledge's yard.

Never before had Charleston's situation looked so bleak. Conceding that he could not hold out much longer, Lincoln advised Rutledge to flee the city with his Privy Council. He told the governor he would be able to do more good on the outside, where he could continue to raise money, soldiers, and supplies. Rutledge refused. Only after Lincoln presented him with a letter signed by all his generals imploring him to leave did he relent. On April 13, accompanied by three members of his Privy Council, Rutledge successfully evaded British patrols and crossed the Cooper River. Had he waited another day, it is doubtful he would have gotten out.

Lincoln's army was now trapped in the city, and when British reinforcements led by Lord Charles Cornwallis arrived soon afterward, the American general realized all hope was gone. On May 12, Charleston capitulated. If that news wasn't hard enough to bear, Rutledge also learned that his brother Edward had just been captured trying to smuggle a report out of the city to him. The fall of South Carolina's capital, however, represented more than just a personal loss for Rutledge. It was also the greatest military disaster of the Revolution, the largest single loss of American soldiers in the entire war, and a standard of British might driven deep into southern soil.

Rutledge was flabbergasted when many of his closest advisers voluntarily returned to British protection, including two of the three privy councilors who had sneaked out of the city with him. In June hundreds of Charleston's citizens signed a congratulatory letter to General Clinton. Those who refused to submit to the Crown were punished harshly. Patriots were barred from practicing their trades or professions and denied access to the courts. Their homes were burned to the ground and their wives and children sent into the woods without provisions. Rutledge's own estates were pillaged and hundreds of his slaves sold off. His brother Edward was transported to a penal colony in Florida. "The enemy seems determined to break every man's spirit," he said, "and if they can't, to ruin him."[10]

Rutledge was now a fugitive in his own state. Almost all his top officials had been captured, and he had no money or military forces at his command. All by himself, one historian concludes, he was "virtually the government of South Carolina during the most critical months of British occupation."[11] In this, his darkest hour, Rutledge resolved to sacrifice what little he had left, including his life, to save South Carolina.

On July 3, 1780, Rutledge arrived in Philadelphia, where he was pleased to learn that Horatio Gates had been appointed to lead the American counterattack in South Carolina. The governor went to offer Gates his support, "for the civil authority may be of service in aid of the military," he told the general.[12] He was also relieved to find that Washington and Congress were committed to helping him as much as they possibly could. South Carolina would not be abandoned. Maryland advanced him $14,000, and Congress authorized him to draw on the Continental Treasury. It had taken the loss of Charleston to rouse the delegates from their torpor.

Rutledge raised weapons and soldiers for the state, as well as food for American prisoners of war in Charleston. Sitting with his state's delegates, he persuaded Congress to send as many troops as Washington could spare and to raise $100,000 in hard currency for the sale from a bill of exchange Benjamin Franklin had negotiated in France. Feeling hopeful for the first time in months, the governor left Philadelphia in August eager to join Gates, who had already departed for South Carolina with his army.

But before he could reach the Continental forces, he received devastating news. On August 16, Gates's troops suffered one of the bloodiest defeats of the entire war, in Camden, South Carolina. Gates had recklessly sent his unseasoned, outnumbered men headlong into Cornwallis's strongest position. One thousand soldiers had been killed or wounded and all their artillery and equipment lost. General Johann de Kalb, who had sailed with Lafayette, had lost his life as well. One person did manage to make it out unscathed. Escaping on the fastest horse he could find, Gates had ridden almost 180 miles over the next three days before finally pausing for breath, and one assumes a new horse, in North Carolina. It was the second American army to be lost within three months.

"At present, our prospect is truly gloomy," Rutledge wrote to South Carolina's congressional delegates. "We must not, however, despair, though at present I do not see how we are to retrieve our affairs."[13]

Arriving in South Carolina shortly after Gates's catastrophe, the governor rallied the state to keep fighting. The fact that he refused to bow down to the British when so many of his compatriots had was an inspiration to many. He was, said some, "the best recruiting sergeant South Carolina ever had."[14] Riding into towns alone, he would stand on a bench in a public square urging his fellow citizens to join the militia. With Tory gangs often hot on his trail, he would usually speak for no more than an hour, but by the time he was finished, many men were ready to enlist.

He worked tirelessly organizing guerrilla raids on British outposts and wagon trains, personally taking part in at least fifty skirmishes against the British. Upon appointing Thomas Sumter brigadier general in charge of the state's militia, he ordered him to harry enemy positions relentlessly, "in short, that they be harassed and attacked in every quarter of So. Carolina and Georgia."[15]

To combat inflation, he suspended laws making paper money legal and ordered the prosecution of looters. He appointed magistrates and other vestiges of civil authority, and he requisitioned any food he could find for the army. He commandeered indigo, which he sent to Philadelphia at two dollars a pound to raise money. Announcing that anyone accepting British "protection" was guilty of treason, Rutledge offered to pardon those who renounced allegiance to the Crown within thirty days. Though the British still controlled much of the state, hundreds returned to the American side as a result of his order.

Throughout South Carolina, Patriots began calling their governor "Dictator John." It was usually said with affection. In the eighteenth century, the term *dictator* lacked the totalitarian overtones it has today. Derived from the same root as *dictate,* it originally meant "first speaker." Steeped in the classics, the founding conservatives hearkened back to ancient Rome, where generals were given dictatorial powers for limited periods during emergencies. The Roman Senate granted these powers for a maximum of six months, but they were often relinquished sooner.

Rutledge's dictatorial powers did give rise to critics, who pointed out that in ancient Rome there had also been dictators who had never given up their authority. Writing as "Cassius," Aedanus Burke, a radical Charleston jurist, said that even in time of war the governor had no right to overthrow the state constitution. Burke also attacked Rutledge for trying to disenfranchise the poor and middle classes and placing power in the hands of a few elite families.

Criticism came from the reactionary right as well. Writing as "Agricola," the Tory John Wells condemned Rutledge for executing men without a trial, a charge that was never proven. Another Loyalist complained that South Carolina had "vested more power in the breast of one man than is possessed by the most despotic power in Europe."[16]

Even those who fully supported Rutledge grew wary when he approached. "One day last week," a young farmer named Nameby Caton wrote to his brother in late 1780, "Ma saw Dictator John coming up the road, an' hustled me an' Josiah to cover the corncrib. He set with us for supper . . . an' then he sayed how the army needs corn terrible. So I showed him the corncrib, and he tuk most the corn, too, an' made me an' Josiah tote it to town next day. Ma blessed us out terrible."[17]

Scholars are almost unanimous in their praise for Rutledge's actions. As the historian Edward McCrady writes, "Without the partisan leaders of South Carolina and their followers, the independence of America would never have been achieved."[18] But for all that South Carolina's one-man government was doing to battle the British, he knew that the best he could do was pester them. In order to expel them from his state, he would need a large Continental force commanded by competent officers. At the end of 1780, Rutledge got his wish.

Congress appointed two of the most capable generals in the entire American army to lead a new force into South Carolina. Daniel Morgan was promoted to brigadier general, and Nathanael Greene, Washington's most trusted officer, was given command of the entire Southern Department, replacing Gates.

Time was running out. Word soon reached America that an Austro-Russian peace settlement might be in the works that would guarantee *uti possidetis,* a legal doctrine that allowed each side in a conflict to retain whatever land it possessed when peace was established. If overseas powers were to impose a peace settlement on America, in other words, Europe might consider New York City and everything south of North Carolina to be Britain's. America would be dismembered.

Traveling the state together, Greene and Rutledge worked on a strategy they hoped would bring them swift victory. Rutledge advocated brutal, unrelenting guerrilla warfare until the British abandoned Charleston. Greene knew it would not be easy. Such a long campaign would have to be backed by adequate supplies and superior logistics, but Rutledge was determined to persevere. "This country must be recovered, (if ever it is regained)," he wrote, "inch by inch."[19]

Conservatives favored establishing dictatorial powers at the national as well as the state level, and the chief proponent of this idea was Philip Schuyler, who had returned to Congress in November 1779. Schuyler had been alarmed by the news of Gates's defeat at Camden, but not surprised. It was an unmitigated disaster that could potentially cause America to lose all of the Deep South. Yet Schuyler could not help seeing a silver lining, because the event would at least "be attended with one good." Gates's disgrace would end, once and for all, radical attempts to replace Washington. "The adherents in Congress to the gallant commander," he commented sarcastically, "will not have it any longer in their power to play him off against the General."[20]

Gates's actions after his ignominious flight to safety following the defeat at Camden could not have stood in sharper contrast to Schuyler's conduct after the loss of Ticonderoga. Gates refused any suggestions that he face a court-martial and did everything he could to avoid one. Schuyler, on the other hand, embraced his. Five days after Arthur St. Clair was acquitted for having abandoned Ticonderoga in September 1778, Schuyler's court-martial began. After presenting the orders he had issued in minute detail and calling several witnesses, Schuyler rested his case. The judges, most of whom were officers who had served under Schuyler, quickly acquitted him with "the highest honor."

Washington soon offered him his old position as head of the Northern Department, but Schuyler had had enough of congressional politics for the moment. He resigned his commission as major general and the following year turned down the opportunity to become president of Congress. He wanted to return, he told Duane, to "the luxury of private life which becomes every day more inviting."[21]

But prompted partly by a plea from Washington and partly by his own growing sense of alarm, Schuyler accepted a seat in Congress. The American cause was in trouble, and the government, he believed, needed all the help it could get. The winter of 1779–80 was proving to be even more brutal than the previous one. Three blizzards had blanketed every state north of Virginia in four feet of snow, and the harbors of New York, Philadelphia, and Baltimore were closed. Starvation now posed an even greater danger than the British. Temperatures fell as low as twenty degrees below zero throughout the North. At Morristown, New Jersey, where Washington had established his winter headquarters, skeletal soldiers huddled around fires, colder and hungrier than they had been at Valley Forge the year before.

After visiting Washington's encampment, Schuyler returned to Philadelphia in early March with two goals firmly in mind: to reform the nation's financial chaos and to aid the army. One of the main problems was that America was fighting a war without an official government. The Articles of Confederation, which Dickinson had composed four years earlier, had still not been ratified. And as the document had been edited to take into account different states' objections, it had been successively watered down. While Dickinson's draft envisioned a mildly powerful central government, the current, unratified version would leave Congress substantially weakened.

Yet Congress's lack of power was precisely the problem. If "no adequate means are pursued for the future subsistence and pay of the army," Schuyler feared, "our cause is lost, unless another system of government is adopted." The army's desperate condition, he believed, should have demonstrated to the states "the necessity of parting with so much of their sovereignty, respectively, as would enable the governing power to draw forth the strength and resources of the county."[22]

Schuyler was not alone in recognizing the need for a stronger government. Nathanael Greene, who had served as Washington's quartermaster general before heading to South Carolina, advocated "a new plan of civil constitution."[23] Washington too argued that "an entire new plan" was needed, one that would give Congress power "adequate to all the purposes of the War." Otherwise, he was convinced, "our Independence fails and each Assembly under its present Constitution will be annihilated, and we must once more return to the Government of Great Britain."[24]

One of the main reasons conservatives began advocating a stronger government was that the states were incapable of fulfilling their promises. Congress had requisitioned $60 million from each of the states to finance the war but had received only $3 million in total. And still the states tried to avoid their obligations. On his first day back in Congress, Schuyler voted to block Massachusetts's request to withhold $6 million of its tax quota. "One state will comply with a requisition of Congress," Washington wrote in May 1780, "another neglects to do it. A third executes it by halves, and all differ either in the manner, the matter, or so much in point of time, that we are always working up hill, and ever shall be."[25]

Serving in Congress confirmed something Schuyler had long suspected but had not known for certain: America's government was completely dysfunctional. The Treasury was broke, and yet no one had any plan for fixing the nation's finances. Gouverneur Morris had started to address the issue the year before, but he had not been reelected. Now the situation was far worse. America's European allies grew increasingly reluctant to supply money, warned James Wilson. Congress's inability to deal with the nation's financial crisis had "shaken all faith in the integrity and character of America. It is interpreted to mean that the United States are bankrupt."[26]

Two days after Schuyler arrived in Philadelphia, Congress accepted his proposal to form a committee to address the nation's disastrous finances, placing him in charge. He chose Robert Livingston and as many like-minded delegates as he could to join him on his committee. Nine days later the committee submitted its first report, which was largely Schuyler's work. In order to get the money supply under control, Congress would devalue existing paper money and replace it with new, interest-bearing notes that would be redeemed at a fixed ratio of forty-to-one.

Congress voted to adopt Schuyler's proposal almost immediately and with little modification. "New issues," it was announced, "were to bear interest at five per cent, that interest likewise to be paid in specie upon the redemption of the bills, or (at the option of the holder) annually in sterling bills of exchange drawn by the United States on their commissioners in Europe."[27] Essentially, Congress had just repudiated $200 million in debt. The move was highly unpopular with the public, but it was a first step toward eradicating paper money, getting the inflation under control, and shoring up the nation's finances. It did not, however, get to the root of the problem of anemic government.

* * *

On April 28, 1780, Schuyler and a new committee he had formed to help the army arrived at Washington's headquarters in Morristown. The situation at Washington's camp was dire, Schuyler told Congress. Meat was about to run out in two days and all supplies by May 12. The army also had no means of transportation, and state law barred officers from making purchases, a statute Schuyler urged Congress to petition New Jersey to change. If immediate help was not sent, Schuyler's committee wrote, "we will not pretend to say what may be the event!"[28]

What irked Schuyler was that he knew the United States possessed the resources—the money, manpower, and supplies—to properly provision the Continental Army. What was lacking was political will. And he blamed excessively democratic politics. "Popular bodies," Schuyler wrote to James Duane, were "unequal to that celerity so requisite to the effectual prosecution of military operations." Congress, he recommended, "should resume, or even take new powers. The present occasion will justify it."

Schuyler then proposed to "lodge dictatorial powers either in the Commander in Chief, or in him, conjointly with a small committee of Congress."[29] He had in mind himself, Duane, Livingston, and a number of other conservative allies in Congress. Like Rutledge, Schuyler believed that men such as himself could be safely entrusted with enormous power. Viewing themselves as latter-day Romans, the founding conservatives argued they could be trusted to relinquish dictatorial authority at the appropriate time. In a letter to Alexander Hamilton, Washington's brilliant twenty-five-year-old chief of staff whom he had grown fond of while visiting Morristown, Schuyler proposed creating a national "dictator" for the rest of the war, with "vice-dictators" in charge of the states.

Hamilton had risen from obscure origins in the Caribbean (John Adams referred to him as that "Creole Bastard") and joined the Patriot cause while still a student at King's College in New York. After demonstrating extraordinary bravery on the battlefield as a militia captain, he was appointed a lieutenant colonel in the Continental Army. He was soon handling most of Washington's correspondence and as his deputy quickly became comfortable operating in the highest echelons of the military, government, and society.

The suffering he witnessed at Valley Forge and Morristown and his frustration with the lack of support for the army led him to conclude, "The fundamental defect is a want of power in Congress."[30] In a seven-thousand-word letter to Duane, he advocated giving Congress "complete sovereignty" and devised a plan for replacing congressional boards "with great officers of state—A secretary for foreign affairs—A President of War—A President of Marine—A Financier."[31] It was a bold idea that conservatives immediately rallied around.

Washington himself fully supported the idea of granting Schuyler's committee extraordinary powers. He could think of "no man who can be more useful as a member of the committee than General Schuyler. His perfect knowledge of the resources of the country, the activities of his temper, his fruitfulness of expedients and his sound military sense make me wish above all things he may be appointed."[32] The two generals shared similar political outlooks, and scholars believe that a good number of Schuyler's proposals originated with the commander in chief.

For radicals, such proposals were as repugnant as continued British rule. They represented nothing more than an aristocratic power grab. Even moderates were unsettled by Schuyler's suggestions. John Witherspoon, a Presbyterian minister who had come to America to become president of the College of New Jersey (now Princeton) and had been elected to Congress in 1776, was a great admirer of Washington and a supporter of greater centralized power, yet he feared granting Congress the authority to coerce "those states which refuse to comply with reasonable requisitions."[33] "That resolution," he wrote to the governor of New Jersey, "is of such a nature that I should never give my voice for it unless you or my constituents should specifically direct it, perhaps *even not then*."[34] Conservatives were well aware that they faced an uphill battle. "To a republican form of government," Duane told Schuyler, "jealousy in conferring authority is natural."[35]

Congress did agree to increase some of the powers of Schuyler's committee, but not to any significant extent. It instructed Schuyler to "expedite the drawing forth of supplies" and to request that the states help them more. At the same time, it called on the states to contribute an extra $10 million each. But Schuyler's proposal to establish dictatorial powers was passed over in silence. Schuyler remained frustrated. Without any means of coercing the states, Congress's pleas for money would continue to be ignored.

Pressed by Washington to seek more power, Schuyler's committee decided to appeal directly to the states, making "bold to thrust its admonitions into the very face of Congress itself."[36] On May 25, 1780, the committee issued a public declaration outlining the military's many problems: the fact that pay was five months in arrears, that there was no meat left and no more than a week's worth of other provisions left, and that it lacked equipment, horses, carriages, and medical supplies. Schuyler implored the states to deliver what they had promised for the good of the army and the sake of the nation.

Morale was so low, Schuyler's committee informed Congress three days later, that previous warnings of mutiny were coming to pass. Two Connecticut regiments had marched through camp fully armed and were now threatening to desert because of lack of food. Only increased authority could solve the problems of the army, Schuyler told Congress: "The meaning of this admonition . . . is sufficiently clear: Do not wait for the states to grant you powers; take them."[37]

When no answer was forthcoming, Schuyler decided to follow his own advice. He began making requisitions directly from the states, asking for specific quantities of meat, flour, and rum. He realized that he could get better deals if he hired private drivers who used their own horses and oxen to pull wagons. Drivers of publicly owned wagons had little incentive to take care of their equipment and animals. He insisted that contracts be paid for in specie rather than paper money. And he chastised President Reed of Pennsylvania for not corresponding with his committee. It was, he said, an insult to his committee and to the dignity of Congress. No detail was too small for his attention, because he knew just how high the stakes were, especially after the British victory at Charleston. Should troop levels fall any further, he wrote to the states, "the consequences must in all human probability be fatal."[38]

Schuyler's vehemence eventually started to irk Congress, and at the beginning of August he received word from Philadelphia saying his committee was interfering with matters that were not its concern. He was also rebuked for criticizing President Reed. On August 11, by a vote of eleven to two, Congress ordered Schuyler's committee disbanded. New York and South Carolina were the two states that had voted nay. Schuyler was particularly insulted when he learned that Congress had ordered his committee to return to Philadelphia to make a full report of its undertakings. The implication was that he and his committee members had performed their work improperly. Schuyler had had enough. He had no wish to be scapegoated again and decided to return home instead. From now on he would focus on New York politics. Washington wrote to Congress to express his gratitude for the committee's efforts. But the commander in chief knew that by rebuffing Schuyler, Congress had destroyed all hope of ending the war in 1780.

In September the discovery that Benedict Arnold had been planning to hand West Point over to the British further demoralized the army and shook the nation. If even a decorated hero like Arnold could switch sides, many began to wonder what chance America stood of winning the war. Schuyler was outraged when Hamilton informed him of Arnold's treachery. Arnold had been his friend, and he had personally helped secure the traitor's appointment as commander of West Point. Now Schuyler said he wished that the musket ball that had shattered Arnold's leg at Saratoga had instead struck his heart. He was even more disgusted when he learned that Arnold was now leading British troops as a brigadier general. "I cannot believe," said Schuyler, "that men of honor can so far sacrifice their feelings as to serve under such a character, which is debased beyond description."[39]

The dismal year ended with one bright note for Schuyler. While visiting her father at Morristown, Schuyler's daughter Elizabeth had attracted the attentions of Washington's young adjutant. Almost the instant he met "Betsey," Hamilton was smitten with the dark-eyed "charmer," whom he found "most unmercifully handsome."[40] The interest was mutual. With his slim, graceful figure, chestnut hair, and azure eyes, the young lieutenant colonel had always been a favorite among the ladies. Schuyler was wary. His eldest daughter, Angelica, had already eloped with a smooth-talking ne'er-do-well from the West Indies, and he wanted to make sure Hamilton was respectable enough before allowing the romance to continue. But when Elizabeth announced that she too was prepared to elope if her father refused his blessing, Schuyler and his wife relented. Hamilton's accomplishments, intelligence, and political leanings, they decided, made him a more-than-acceptable match for the daughter of New York's aristocracy. On December 14, 1780, the couple was wed at Schuyler's mansion in Albany. It was, to say the least, an advantageous marriage for Hamilton. Through his father-in-law, he would soon be introduced to the nation's leading conservatives.

CHAPTER 19

POWER, CONSEQUENCE, AND GRANDEUR

On New Year's Day 1781, ten regiments of the Pennsylvania line left their barracks near Morristown, New Jersey, and began marching on Philadelphia. For almost a year, they had received no pay and little food, and they had decided that only a show of force would make Congress do something about it. More than a hundred officers tried to block their path, but there was little they could do to stem the swollen river of angry mutineers, who numbered in the thousands. One captain was killed and several other officers wounded in the attempt. Washington declined to pursue the soldiers, lest more mutinies break out while he was away from his own encampment near West Point.

At Princeton, Joseph Reed, the president of Pennsylvania, met the mutineers at the head of Philadelphia's First City Troop. Reed was eager to avoid violence. For the next ten days, he listened to the mutineers' complaints, and his promise that he would secure their back pay finally persuaded them to turn around. The crisis, a small one in the grand scheme of things, had been defused, but it had been enough to shock Congress out of lethargy. For the first time, a majority of the delegates now supported conservative calls for vigorous action.

After five long years of war, this was the moment the conservatives had been waiting for. Their plans for strengthening the powers of Congress were about to be realized. On January 10, 1781, acting on Hamilton's suggestions, James Duane persuaded Congress to replace its ineffectual Committee for Foreign Affairs with a secretary of foreign affairs. On February 3 a plan to impose a five percent impost, or import duty, which would create a permanent source of revenue for Congress, was proposed and seconded. Four days after that Duane persuaded the delegates to establish the posts of secretary of war, secretary of marine, and superintendent of finance. Individuals with executive power would at last be running America's government.

They would have to work fast if they hoped to avoid disaster. France, America's greatest ally, was beginning to waver in its support. With the French treasury running low, Louis XVI was having second thoughts about continuing to fund America's war with Britain. Two major American cities were under British control, and Cornwallis, who continued to rampage through the South, seemed unstoppable. Moreover, the Austro-Russian-mediated peace talks currently taking place in Vienna boded ill for the young republic. Unless America could secure a major military victory soon, the French would be forced to abandon America.

France's foreign minister, the Comte de Vergennes, had no doubt about what that would mean—America's fight for independence would instantly be ended "by means of a long time truce *uti possidetis* between the Colonies and mother country."[1] It was a possibility that France needed to be ready for. In a secret letter to his ambassador to the United States, the Chevalier de la Luzerne, Vergennes sent instructions designed "to prepare the Americans to be led, if necessary in the last extremity, to the abattoir at Vienna."[2]

Still, Vergennes prayed for American victory. Knowing he had perhaps one last chance to help Congress, he offered the American government a new subsidy of six million *livres.* Privately, he also urged Luzerne to support congressional conservatives as much as possible. It wasn't long before Luzerne was intervening subtly but powerfully in Congress's choice of its new executives. The clear favoritism the French showed for the founding conservatives aroused enormous resentment, and old political divisions began to go by new names. Congressional conservatives started to be called the Gallican party, while the remnants of the Adams-Lee faction were now referred to as the anti-Gallicans.

The fight over who would handle America's foreign affairs concerned Luzerne greatly. Anti-Gallicans were hoping to elect Arthur Lee, who had returned from France in the summer of 1780, as secretary of foreign affairs. Luzerne had other ideas and implored Chancellor Robert R. Livingston to return to Philadelphia to run for the position. "*Je vous ai invité à venir dans le Congrès mon cher Chancellier, et je presse plus que jamais d'y venir,*" his secretary wrote to the Chancellor.*

After months of behind-the-scenes jockeying, voting began in August 1781. On the first tally, Lee won Massachusetts, Connecticut, New Jersey, Delaware, and Virginia, but he was two votes shy of victory. Alarmed that

* "I invited you to come to Congress, my dear Chancellor, and I urge you more than ever to come."

Lee might succeed, Luzerne immediately began deploying his influence and his purse full of gold and silver *livres*. The next day "Virginia was prevailed on to throw away its vote," a furious Lee told Sam Adams. New Jersey then changed sides, and the following day Livingston was elected, eight states to four. Pleased with himself, Luzerne wrote to Vergennes that the chancellor's election was entirely his doing. It was an exaggeration—Livingston was genuinely admired by most of the delegates—but Luzerne's help certainly had not hurt.

Lee would never forgive the French intervention, warning America's minister in Russia not to trust any instructions he received from the new secretary of foreign affairs. "Whatever you receive from [Livingston] you may consider as dictated by the French Minister," Lee wrote. "He made him what he is."[3] But the Virginian had little luck fomenting any revolt against the French or against Livingston. With the American cause hanging by a thread, the delegates were far less interested in reviving the sort of partisan rancor that had paralyzed the government three years before. "Arthur Lee has, I believe, been much disappointed on and since his arrival in Philadelphia," James Wilson wrote. "No éclat, no proceedings against those whom he dislikes."[4]

With Livingston's election, conservatives were poised to control almost all positions of power within Congress, with Duane its foremost power broker. "Whose friends fill all the high offices? Mr. Duane's," fumed one radical journalist. "Who are at the treasury board? Mr. Duane's friends. Who are at the admiralty board? Mr. Duane's friends. . . . In short, who puts up and puts down at his pleasure? Mr. Duane."[5]

Conservatives were amazed by the extent of their influence. It was the first time since the First Continental Congress, some said, that "party intrigue" and "old prejudices" had been defeated by "mild spirits" and "sensible men."[6] Conservatives were able to help Washington institute needed military reforms, doing away with short-term enlistments and replacing them with enlistments of three years or for the duration of the war. They also set about building a stronger national government, which, Gouverneur Morris predicted, would help win the war and have the added benefit of helping "restrain the democratic spirit."[7]

One of the most important victories conservatives won early in the year was the ratification of the Articles of Confederation. After the British invasion of the South the year before, a coalition of southern and middle states began to overcome resistance to a formal national government. Even Thomas Burke, now governor of North Carolina, abandoned his former hostility to stronger central power once he saw his state overrun by enemy forces.

By 1781 the last remaining impediment to adoption of the Articles was the issue of western territories. In particular, small landless states like Maryland and Connecticut refused to sign the document until large states like Virginia and New York renounced their extravagant claims to western land. Virginia, for example, maintained that its borders extended all the way to the Pacific Ocean, then called the South Sea. Since all thirteen states had to ratify the Articles for it to go into effect, the small states' dissent was preventing the United States from establishing an official government.

Conservatives were on the whole sympathetic to the plight of the landless states, despite their eagerness to ratify the Articles. According to James Wilson, British officials never intended to give Virginia so much territory when they had originally approved its charter. "They thought the South Sea within one hundred miles of the Atlantic Ocean," he said. "It was not conceived that [the land] extended three thousand miles."[8] Seconding Maryland's objections, Wilson argued that Pennsylvania would never support Virginia's claims. Partly, he was defending his own self-interests. As a speculator in western land, Wilson had much to lose if Virginia's claims stood, since the state was selling the exact same tracts to other investors. But his stance also reflected the conservative belief that the United States would never become a great nation if states like Virginia were permitted to sprawl across the continent.

Two men eventually broke the impasse. Recognizing the importance of ceding some of his state's land claims for the good of the nation, Philip Schuyler began negotiating with representatives of Maryland and Connecticut. After asking just how far New York might claim land, he wrote, "I was then carried to the map, and Mr. [Roger] Sherman [of Connecticut] explained himself." New York, they agreed, would be bounded by the St. Lawrence River to the north and Lake Ontario to the west. In a feat of legislative virtuosity, Schuyler then convinced New York's government that such territorial concessions were the only way to save the Confederation. It was a sacrifice, Virginia's Joseph Jones noted to Thomas Jefferson, that was "worthy of imitation."[9]

The final push for compromise came from Luzerne, who told Congress that America would never achieve respect abroad without an official national government. On February 2, 1781, under unrelenting pressure from the French, Virginia agreed to renounce its western land claims with the proviso that the land be reserved for new states and not given for land speculators. Maryland, the last holdout, then voted to permit its delegates to approve the

Confederation, and on March 1, 1781, America officially established a national government.

While ratification of the Articles of Confederation was a remarkable achievement, the most important conservative accomplishment of 1781 was the creation of a superintendent of finance. Hamilton was the first to propose Robert Morris for the position, and most agreed that no one else would do.

Morris was reluctant to accept the position, knowing how much political mudslinging he would face. He also knew just how difficult a job lay ahead of him: "The derangement of our money affairs. The enormity of our public expenditures. The confusion in all our departments. The languor of our general system. The complexity and consequent inefficacy of our operations."[10] Moreover, the position involved more than just running America's finances. Like Britain's prime ministers, who were originally chancellors of the Exchequer, the American financier would be responsible for running almost all aspects of the government. He would become America's first chief executive, a position historians have compared to the presidency.

Morris's supporters would not let him back out. "You may render America and the world no less a service than the establishment of American independence!" Hamilton wrote to Morris. "'Tis by introducing order into our finances—by restoring public credit—not by gaining battles, that we are finally to gain our object."[11] General Greene had argued as much three years before. "It appears to me more and more probable," he said, "that this dispute will terminate in a war of funds."[12] And only Morris, Congress knew, had the ability to win such a financial war. On February 20, 1781, it voted unanimously to appoint Morris to the position of financier, with only Sam Adams and another Massachusetts delegate abstaining.

In March, Morris agreed to accept the post, but with two important caveats. First, he demanded that he be allowed to continue his private commercial activities. Radicals were aghast at this stipulation. Leading the opposition, Sam Adams insisted on taking a roll-call vote and initially succeeded in blocking Morris's request. James Duane, however, persuaded Congress to reverse itself and pass a motion allowing Morris to conduct private business while in office.

Morris's second stipulation was equally controversial. He insisted that he be given "absolute power" to fire anyone working for him as well as anyone else in the government who dealt with public property, a group that comprised almost everyone in public service. Adams again blocked Morris's request, arguing that it placed too much authority in the hands of one man. But again with Duane's help, the radicals' victory was reversed a month later. As Joseph Reed commented, "Mr. Morris was inexorable, Congress at [his] mercy."[13] Having gotten everything he wanted, Morris finally accepted the position on May 14. He was especially pleased when Gouverneur Morris was named assistant financier.

Robert Morris now possessed more authority than anyone else in Congress. As an expert in shipping, he was quickly named secretary of marine as well. He was given broad diplomatic authority and was put in charge of handling income from foreign loans, supplying the entire Continental Army, and importing and exporting all goods on behalf of the United States. He created a sizable and remarkably effective bureaucracy to help him carry out his plans, including a large staff of tax receivers throughout the states. Morris amassed so much power so quickly that, according to the historian E. James Ferguson, he "soon possessed the greatest influence of any man in the country except, perhaps, George Washington."[14] As one military commander commented after the Financier had been in office only a few months: "The most trifling thing can not be done in any department but through Mr. Morris."[15]

Morris immediately put his new powers to use, for he had bold plans for America. He would devote himself to "the *necessity, the absolute necessity,* of a change in our monied system to work salvation."[16] In the process, he envisioned transforming the country from an agricultural land into a modern nation state that would "rise into power, consequence, and grandeur." Only such a shift, Morris argued, would "open to us the prospect of American glory."[17] For conservatives like Morris, the Revolution was a means for remaking America.

Gouverneur Morris supported his boss's plans wholeheartedly, advocating "vigor, organization, and promptitude to render this a considerable empire."[18] Only then would America become as powerful as Great Britain, whose financial and military might both Morrises hoped to recreate across the Atlantic. The key was to unleash the explosive forces of unrestricted capitalism in America. And this meant allowing total economic freedom, even if it flew in the face of traditional republican beliefs in economic equality. "It is inconsistent with the principles of liberty," Robert Morris declared, "to prevent a man from the free disposal of his property on such terms as he may think fit."[19]

This attitude was far from common in America at the time, but as a devotee of Adam Smith, whose *Inquiry into the Wealth of Nations* had been published in 1776, Morris was an ardent supporter of free-market, laissez-faire economics. The Financier found Smith's thought so persuasive, in fact, that he gave out copies to members of Congress. It is likely that both Gouverneur Morris and James Wilson had also read Smith, whose understanding of the role of self-interest and commerce was often at odds with classical Whig thought. American conservatives differed with Smith over one important point, however. While the Scottish thinker opposed government support for business, Wilson and the two Morrises believed government could serve as a positive influence, aiding the development of the new nation by working with investors.

Like Britain's Court Whigs, American conservatives believed the nation could achieve freedom and independence only through economic strength.[20] And like Prime Minister Walpole's allies at the start of the eighteenth century, they understood that capitalism, more than courage, won wars. No one grasped this principle better than America's commander in chief. "In modern wars the longest purse must chiefly determine the event," Washington observed, and no one wielded a mightier purse than Britain's. "Their system of credit is capable of greatest exertion than that of any other nation."[21] To radicals, this sort of veneration for Britain's government and banking system was anathema. To conservatives, it was simple pragmatism.

One of the most important lessons Morris took from Britain's Court Whigs was the necessity of creating a national bank. On June 8 the year before, Morris, James Wilson, and Thomas Willing, Morris's old business partner, had met with other "men of property" at Philadelphia's Coffee House to discuss creating a pool of funds to help the army. In just over a week, they raised £400 in gold and silver coin and another £1,364 in depreciated Continental paper. The fund would then be used to raise supplies, money, and munitions for the army. In return, the investors would receive interest-bearing bonds paying six percent.

"A bank is established in this city for the purpose of facilitating provisions and rum for the army," Morris wrote to Deane, "and I need not tell you the real satisfaction I feel in being essentially useful in forming, promoting and supporting these measures."[22] Though it was not a commercial bank in the modern sense, Morris, Wilson, and Willing called the fund the Bank of Pennsylvania.

The day the bank opened, Morris sent five hundred barrels of flour to Washington. Money was now pouring into the fund, and three days later he raised another £270,000 in hard currency, which he used to procure beef, pork, coffee, sugar, and salt, and five hundred hogsheads of rum. It was enough food to feed forty thousand soldiers for seventy-five days. By the end of June, Morris was promising to send the army boxes of "segars" from Havana as well.[23] The shipments had come in the nick of time, saving the Continental Army just as it was about to disintegrate. "Our greatest hopes," wrote James Madison, a young Virginian delegate to Congress, "are founded on a patriotic scheme of the opulent merchants of this city."[24]

By September relentless attacks by radicals, who harbored the old Country Whig animosity toward banking, as well as a drying up of funds, put the Bank of Pennsylvania out of business. But the bank's founders were not daunted. Now, they decided, was the time to establish a true commercial bank, one that was national in scale and that would help stabilize the American economy. Calling for the creation of a bank along the lines of the Bank of England, Wilson argued that such an institution would become "a great engine of the state." Unlike the defunct Bank of Pennsylvania, it would "not so much depend upon the extent of their original capital, as upon the regulations they observe in granting credit."[25] Wilson understood that while having money was important, it could always run out. What was more important was having good credit, which permitted an indefinite stream of money. A bank would help establish just that.

No further action was taken until Morris took office, but three days after he assumed the duties, the Financier formally asked Congress for permission to create America's first modern, commercial bank. Reflecting their continental ambitions, Morris and Wilson named it the Bank of North America. On November 1 a group of shareholders, many of whom were survivors of Fort Wilson, met at the City Tavern to elect the bank's officers. Wilson was chosen one of the twelve directors, and Willing became the bank's president, much to the horror of local radicals. To place such a well-known merchant in charge of the bank, it was claimed, was "a discouragement to the Whigs, is a wound to the cause of patriotism, and is trampling on the blood of those heroes and martyrs, who have fallen in the defense of our liberty." For the perpetually disgruntled Arthur Lee, the creation of the bank was proof that Philadelphia had become "torified."

Congress finally chartered the Bank of North America at the end of 1781. One week later, on January 7, 1782, it opened its doors. The plan was to capitalize the bank at a relatively modest $400,000 by selling one thousand shares at $400 each. Dividends were to run at six percent. The problem was that only two hundred shares were sold. The Bank of North America remained severely undercapitalized.

Since few Americans had ever before seen a commercial bank, many remained skeptical. To reassure investors, Morris made a great show of taking silver out of the bank for loans and then secretly redepositing it so it could be ostentatiously "loaned" again. He also helped devise a special pulley that ran in an endless loop inside the bank, hoisting silver out of the bank's vaults and spreading it on the counters. The money was then discreetly smuggled back down into the vaults, where it could be carried up again. These tactics helped raise more money over the next few weeks. Morris was not above using his position within the government to finance his bank. He had the government loan the bank $100,000. When a French frigate arrived carrying $470,000 in hard currency for Congress, Morris used the money to purchase more bank shares. And as secretary of marine, he sent American navy ships to Havana to import more specie.

The government's initial investment turned out to be well worth it. Over the next three years, the Bank of North America loaned the government more than $1.2 million. It loaned money to American merchants who bought goods to supply the army. For the first time since the outbreak of bloodshed, American soldiers were getting properly equipped and fed. The bank also provided a significant boost to Philadelphia's economy. Morris later said he could not have done his job as Financier without the bank. By the time he left office in 1784, the United States was no longer broke; in fact, it had a surplus of $22,000. Without a doubt, the bank played a decisive role in the fight against Britain.

Yet the bank was more than just a means for winning the war. It was also a way to restore confidence in the government and finances of the United States. "If I can regain for the United States the Confidence of Individuals so as they will trust their property and exertions in the hands of government," Morris wrote, "our independence and success are certain but without that confidence we are nothing."[26] In order to build trust in the government, Morris knew he had to reduce that nation's debt, which had, he said, "swelled beyond all reasonable bounds."[27]

It was not that Morris opposed all debt. Like the Court Whigs, the Financier understood that a national debt, funded by a national bank, was one of the most powerful tools for uniting a nation. By inducing private individuals to invest their money in government debt, Morris hoped to make their private interests coincide with the government's. "I mean to render this [bank] a principal pillar of American credit," Morris wrote to Franklin, "so as to obtain the money of individuals for the benefit of the Union and thereby bind those individuals more strongly to the general cause by ties of private interest."[28] He was, in other words, scaling his conservative philosophy of enlightened self-interest to encompass the entire nation.

Since only the participation of the rich and powerful could save the nation's finances, Morris argued, it was vital to link their interests to America's. As he saw it, the relationship would be a virtuous circle. Because the federal government would owe money to the upper-class bondholders, their loyalty to the Union would be cemented. In return, the interest payments they received would cause money to flow "into those hands which could render it most productive." Investments would multiply in America, leading to more economic growth. The money flowing in and out of the central bank would "convert those debts into a real medium of exchange," establishing a stable currency, further boosting growth.[29] It was a farsighted, complex vision that would reshape American society in such a way, he told Jay, as "to unite the several states more closely together in one general money connection, and indissolubly to attach many powerful individuals to the cause of our country, by the strong principle of self love, and the immediate sense of private interest."[30]

In order to get the entire system to work, however, Morris needed to make bondholders dependent on the national government and not on the states. A public debt, he argued, could be paid off only through federal taxes. Using every mite of influence he possessed, he got Congress to start consolidating its debts and assuming responsibility for money owed to and by the army. At the same time, he blocked the states from paying off the central government's obligations, a practice he saw as dangerous. "There is in it a principle of disunion implied which is ruinous," he warned.[31]

Morris's greatest hope for paying off the national debt lay in establishing a permanent source of federal revenue. Livingston had already raised the possibility of adopting a five percent duty, but although Congress favored the plan, the recently approved Articles of Confederation reserved the right to tax to the states. To implement such a measure, the states would need to endorse it unanimously. Morris immediately started campaigning for a federal impost, arguing that if passed, "it is possible the public credit might be restored." If, however, the states failed to pass the measure, "our enemies will draw from thence strong arguments in favor of what they have so often asserted: that we are unworthy of confidence, that our Union is a rope of sand, that the people are weary of Congress and that the respective states are determined to reject its authority."[32]

Morris's efforts to reengineer the American economy were put on hold by desperate news from the army. On May 8, Washington wrote that he had again run out of flour. If Morris did not help him immediately, the commander in chief said, it would soon be "next to impossible to keep the Army together."[33] Since the U.S. Treasury had no money left, Morris realized it was up to him to save the Continental Army. Pledging his own money and credit, he wrote to Schuyler and another merchant asking them to secure a thousand barrels of flour and send them immediately to Washington's forces. This would be barely enough to keep the army alive, so he also contacted other flour merchants he knew directly. To allay fears they would not be repaid, Morris said, "Lest you like some others believe more in private than in public credit I hereby pledge myself to pay you the cost and charges of this flour in hard money."[34]

Over the next few months, Morris wrote a series of circular letters to the governors of the states imploring them to meet their requisition quotas and explaining his economic plans for the United States. He kept in close contact with Washington to discuss ways to keep the army supplied and to cut its expenses, since it was the government's primary expense. In August Morris and Wilson traveled to Washington's camp at Dobbs Ferry, New York, along the banks of the Hudson, to discuss the state of the army.

Early on the morning of Wednesday, August 14, Morris was awakened by the beat of reveille and was asked to come immediately to Washington's headquarters. A courier had arrived with momentous news. A French fleet composed of twenty-nine ships and carrying three thousand soldiers would arrive in the Chesapeake in the middle of October under the command of Admiral de Grasse. Washington, Morris, and Wilson knew immediately what this signified. It was the tipping point that would change the course of the war. Washington and Schuyler had had their heart set on retaking New York, but with the French arriving well to the south, only one course could be taken. The Continental Army would have to rendezvous with de Grasse's forces to attack Cornwallis, who was fortifying his position on the Virginia coast.

Transporting most of his army 450 miles south would be far from easy. Even though a sizable part of the army would be left behind to mislead the British into thinking an attack on New York City was imminent, the mass movement of troops and matériel would still be the largest of the entire war. Fortunately, Washington had America's greatest expert in logistics by his side. On Saturday, Morris bade Washington adieu and, escorted by a company of twenty-six light horse, returned to Philadelphia to begin planning for the upcoming campaign. He didn't have much time. By the time he reached Congress, six thousand American soldiers had already begun marching south.

Raising provisions and equipment for the troops proved trickier than ever. The nation's coffers were empty, and Pennsylvania's currency, which Morris controlled, had depreciated too much to buy much of anything. Since the Bank of North America had not yet begun operations, the bank would be unable to help. Only one option remained: Morris would finance the attack on Cornwallis himself. Backed by his own personal credit, the Financier began circulating his own currency, hiring a local engraver to carve copper plates with which to print it. The notes ranged in value from $20 to $100, were signed by Morris, and bore the watermark "United States."

"Morris Notes," as the new money came to be called, were quickly recognized as the only trustworthy currency in America. Immediately redeemable notes were dubbed "short Bobs"; those of longer duration became known as "long Bobs." Throughout Philadelphia, merchants instantly began accepting the currency. "My personal credit, which thank heaven I have preserved through all the tempests of the war, has been substituted for that which the country has lost," Morris wrote. "I am now striving to transfer that credit to the public."[35] Even after the Bank of North America opened and began circulating its own currency (which in a sense was also issued by Morris), Morris Notes continued to circulate freely throughout the country, losing little of their printed value.

As Washington's forces approached Philadelphia, stretched out in a column two miles long and accompanied by fife and drum, the threat of mutiny arose once again. The soldiers were now refusing to march any further unless they received a month's pay. Out of funds himself, Morris decided to apply to the French, who agreed to loan the Americans another $20,000 in hard currency, which had arrived in barrels aboard de Grasse's fleet. Standing before the ranks of tattered and surly American soldiers, Morris smashed open the barrels, releasing torrents of silver dollars that collected in clinking, metallic puddles around the astonished troops' feet. Never before had the Continental Army been paid in hard currency. Washington himself was awed by the spectacle. "It will soon be a matter of wonder," he remarked, "how Mr. Morris had done so much with so small means."[36]

Even now that he had exhausted his own reserves, Morris was still pressed for more money. That same day intelligence arrived that the British were contemplating another attack on Philadelphia. State officials begged Morris to find funds to call up three thousand militiamen. Again the Financier rose to the task, personally bankrolling the Pennsylvania forces. "The late movements of the army have so entirely drained me of money," he wrote, "that I have been obliged to pledge my personal credit very deeply, in a variety of instances, besides borrowing money from my friends; and advancing, to promote the public service, every shilling of my own."[37]

By October 1, thanks in large part to Morris's planning and organization, the allied armies were able to field twenty thousand men, half French and half American, along the banks of the York River in Virginia. Although Cornwallis had only half that number, he held the high ground and was well entrenched. His position, however, remained precarious. With de Grasse's fleet anchored just off the coast, no British ships could resupply or evacuate him.

Five days later Washington began his bombardment, steadily pulverizing British batteries over the next week. By October 14, Cornwallis had only two redoubts left. These, however, were heavily fortified, and French and American engineers determined that only a ground assault would be able to take them out. The French were tasked with taking out one of the gun emplacements. After pleading with Washington, Hamilton was given command of the American charge against the other one.

Hoping to surprise the enemy, Hamilton led his 320 men through the dead of night. Fearing an accidental musket discharge would give them away, he ordered his troops to unload their weapons and advance with bayonets. The assault team made it to the very edge of the British position before they were spotted. A maelstrom of musket fire flared in the darkness. Ignoring the musket balls zipping past him, Hamilton jumped onto the British fortifications, calling on his men to follow. They quickly took the parapet with minimal casualties, and the French forces were equally successful in taking theirs.

Two days later Cornwallis realized the noose around him had closed. On the morning of the seventeenth, he sent a drummer boy and an officer waving a white kerchief to signal his surrender, the news of which flashed up and down the continent as fast as riders could carry it. In every state, rejoicing Americans lit bonfires to celebrate if not the end of the war, then at least the beginning of the end. Washington was lionized as America's savior, and Morris was likewise feted, for he too, writes the historian E. Wayne Carp, "deserved a large portion of credit for the victory at Yorktown."[38]

The aftershocks of Yorktown soon rippled around the world as well. In Vienna, talk of imposing peace *uti possidetis* quickly dwindled. In London, support for Lord North's ministry began foundering and George III began contemplating the distasteful possibility of having to replace it with Edmund Burke's peace party. And in Paris, Louis XVI ceased all discussion of abandoning America.

Wishing to properly congratulate their American allies, the French decided to throw a party. All that was needed was a suitable occasion, and in early 1782 the Chevalier de la Luzerne found one. Several months earlier a dauphin, Louis Joseph Xavier François, the second child and first son of Louis XVI and Marie-Antoinette, had been born at Versailles. To the great relief of the French court, a male heir to the French Crown had finally been produced. Luzerne would invite the upper echelons of American society to celebrate his birth.

The event would require months of planning, but it would be the social event of the decade, indeed of all American history up to that point. Eleven hundred guests from across America made their way to Philadelphia for the July 15 party, which for weeks was the only talk of the city.

The French spared no expense. A special dance room forty by sixty feet was built just for the occasion with large painted pillars. The ceiling was covered with paintings and designs. Next to the dance hall, gardens had been pruned and shaped into beautiful walks through artificial groves that smelled of cedar and pine. Thirty cooks were borrowed from the French Army. And throughout the city tailors and hairdressers, milliners and the makers of mantuas, the long formal dresses favored by eighteenth-century women, saw businesses boom so much that they were, according to one witness, often seen panting for breath and covered in sweat. Ladies who waited too long to make a hair appointment could find slots available only between four and six a.m.

The evening of the party ten thousand people turned out to watch the arrival of the guests, who pulled up at the French embassy in one clattering carriage after another. Not wanting to deprive the onlookers of the pleasure of gawking, Luzerne ordered a fence torn down, but he was dissuaded from offering Madeira and money to the crowd for fear it would spark a riot.

Once inside, partygoers were stunned by the variety of dresses, the lights, the music, and the sheer splendor of the room. It was pure "enchantment," gushed Benjamin Rush, who attended with his family.[39] A friend of Rush's remarked upon entering that "her mind was carried beyond and out of itself."

All ranks, factions, and professions had been invited, Whigs and former Tories, soldiers and politicians, radicals and conservatives. "Here were ladies and gentlemen of the most ancient as well as modern families," said Rush. "Here were lawyers, doctors, ministers of the gospel. Here were the learned faculty of the college, and among them many who knew not whether Cicero plead in Latin or in Greek; or whether Horace was a Roman or a Scotsman. Here were painters and musicians, poets and philosophers, and men who were never moved by beauty or harmony, or by rhyme or reason. Here were merchants and gentlemen of independent fortunes, as well as many respectable and opulent tradesmen."[40]

Conversation swirled about the greatness of the American Revolution, the battles that had taken place, and the generosity of the French. Washington and Dickinson conversed together several times. When his gout made standing too painful, Dickinson rested against a pillar with Robert Morris. Gouverneur Morris, whose left leg now ended in a peg after he had lost the lower part of it in a carriage accident two years before, looked especially rakish to the young ladies that night. Thomas Paine, wandering alone, seemed lost in the brilliance of his own ideas, Rush noted sarcastically. John Rutledge of South Carolina chatted with James Duane of New York. Indian chiefs in full regalia conversed with French counts bedecked in military splendor.

At eight thirty the dancing began. The ladies were all provided with partners, but the summer heat led half of them to sit out. Those who felt fatigued were offered cool drinks and cakes and perfectly ripened fruit by servants who darted in and out of side rooms. Quaker ladies, whose dresses prevented them from dancing, were provided with a private room below the orchestra where they could observe the proceedings from behind a gauze curtain.

At nine p.m. a fireworks display such as had never before been seen in Philadelphia was set off. Rockets shot skyward from a vacant lot in front of the ambassador's house to the cheers and applause of thousands. Then the orchestra struck up again and dancing resumed until midnight, when supper was set out under three large tents erected to form a single enveloping canopy. Gentlemen helped ladies to their seats at seven large tables for a simple and elegant cold meal, followed by more cakes and seasonal fruit. "With all the splendor of the minister and all the politeness of a gentleman," the Chevalier de la Luzerne made his way to each table to address each seated lady.[41]

Of all the sensations that greeted the guests, it was the exquisiteness of French cuisine that stunned the American diners, used as they were to plainer, heartier fare. So awed were they with the tastes they were experiencing that an immense silence dropped over the eleven hundred guests as soon as their forks passed their lips. Not a word was spoken, not a laugh heard. An ode written in honor of the Dauphin went unread. They "looked and behaved more as if they were worshipping than eating," several gentlemen agreed. The mood instantly, irrevocably turned sober as the weight of a decade of strife and devastation drained from these men and women who had led the Revolution. The evening's sublimity could only remind them of all the gaiety that had been missing from their lives for so long, and the memory of the dead was suddenly too much to bear.

By one in the morning, the party quietly began to disperse. By three, all the candles had been blown out and the minister's house and grounds lay still in the darkness. The night would be fondly remembered for years. But that evening no one in attendance had the slightest inkling that seven years later the young boy they were celebrating would be dead of tuberculosis. His unborn younger brother, named King of France following his parents' guillotining, would be dead by age ten, locked in solitary confinement in a French prison at the height of another revolution.

CHAPTER 20

THE PAUSE THAT SAVED THE REVOLUTION

Philip Schuyler and his family were seated around the supper table of his Albany mansion when a loud crash and violent yelling erupted outside the kitchen. The general rushed everyone upstairs to his bedroom, where he kept his firearms, and hunkered down. With him were his wife, five daughters—including the two married ones, both pregnant—three sons, and three infant grandchildren. The children screamed as Schuyler started firing his pistols out the window at dark shapes creeping toward the house. Schuyler did not expect to hit anybody, but he did hope the noise would alert the town. The British assassination squad he had long been expecting had finally shown up.

Although Schuyler no longer commanded an army, he continued to serve a vital role in the war as a master of espionage. He interrogated captured spies and disloyal Americans, intercepted British correspondence, and through secret sources actively collected information on enemy troop movements. His greatest coup had been to convince the British that American forces were about to launch all-out assaults on Quebec and New York City, just as Washington was covertly marching his troops south toward Yorktown. He did so by making sure a letter "calculated to mislead the enemy with respect to Gen. Washington's intentions" accidentally found its way into the hands of a British general.[1] As confused as the British were about the Continental Army's plans, they were certain of one thing. They had to get rid of Philip Schuyler.

Running a spy ring soon proved more dangerous to Schuyler than leading an army. "It is now a notorious fact," he told Washington, "that three parties have been expressly sent from Canada to take or put me to death."[2]

As word reached Schuyler that two assassination squads were skulking in the woods outside Albany in the summer of 1781, a guard from the Second New York Regiment was sent to supplement his retinue of servants and slaves.

It was not enough to prevent the attack. At eight p.m. on the evening of August 7, twenty heavily armed men led by Captain John Waltermeyer of Roger's Rangers broke through Schuyler's back gate and forced their way into his kitchen. Other assailants began to surround the house. Four servants flew to their weapons to try to hold off the invaders, but they were soon overpowered. As Waltermeyer noted in his report afterward, "The attack and defense of the house was bloody and obstinate, on both sides; when the doors were forced, the servants fought till they were all wounded or disarmed."[3]

Schuyler's own firing had indeed alerted the town, but any help would arrive too slowly to save him. With the invaders now charging up the creaking stairs to his bedroom redoubt, Schuyler realized he had to think quickly. An old trick saved him. As loudly as he could, he shouted, "Come on my lads, surround the house. The villains are in it." As he wrote the next day, "This I did to make them believe that succor was at hand and it had the desired effect."[4] Miraculously, the invaders retreated down the stairs as fast they could. It was only a matter of minutes before the militia actually did show up, but they were too late to catch Waltermeyer and his attackers, who carried off two of Schuyler's servants, along with some of his good silver. (It would take Schuyler far longer to secure the release of his silver than his servants, much to his annoyance.)

Eliminating Schuyler remained a top priority for the British. After Waltermeyer reported that only a much larger force would be able to take Schuyler, the British sent a raiding party of ninety Tories and three hundred Indians, who were stopped in Ulster County only by a large contingent of New York militia. Another Tory death squad was discovered lying in wait along the road to Schuyler's estate in Saratoga. Fearful for his friend's safety, Washington ordered a detachment of thirteen soldiers to stand guard outside his house. Well after Yorktown, the threat to Schuyler remained high. Rumors swirled that the British now planned to burn down all of Albany, a heavy-handed tactic, but one that certainly would have boosted their chances of killing the general.

As was becoming all too clear to war-weary Americans, the victory at Yorktown had not ended the conflict. Rather, it led to a lull in hostilities that forced the British to change strategies once again. Certain that Britain could bankrupt France and America into submission, George III was determined to keep fighting. The Royal Navy continued blockading most of the coast, shutting down American commerce and sending the economy into yet another tailspin. Merchants were hit especially hard. It was the sort of economic warfare Morris feared more than any military assault. Meanwhile the threat of a renewed attack kept him vigilant.

The British position remained strong. They held New York and Charleston and continually threatened to sweep down from Canada. Across the northern United States, they strengthened fortifications at strategic locations, including at Ticonderoga. And in February 1782 they began holding what Governor Clinton of New York called "treasonable and dangerous" peace talks with Ethan Allen and his brother Ira, who were frustrated that Vermont had still not been allowed to enter the American Confederation. Should Vermont become a separate country allied with the British, it would threaten all of New England.

The King's determination to keep fighting was not unopposed, however. The parliamentary struggle over America came down to a battle of wills between George III and Edmund Burke, and Burke was slowly winning.[5] After the loss of Cornwallis's army, support for Burke and Rockingham's opposition Whig party began to surge. And on March 20, 1782, about to lose a no-confidence vote, Lord North tendered his resignation. The King was so aghast he considered abdicating, but he was talked out of it and finally realized he had no choice but to appoint Rockingham as prime minister.

Almost immediately the new Whig government opened peace negotiations with America's representatives in Paris—Jay, Franklin, and John Adams. Although King George continued to fear that the loss of his American colonies would destroy British commerce, Burke and Rockingham took a more enlightened approach. Embracing the laissez-faire economics of Adam Smith, they held that free trade was more important than sovereignty. Rather than threatening British commercial interests, a prosperous United States would be a boon to British trade and manufacturing. That didn't mean, however, that they would concede anything they didn't have to.

The peace negotiations were complicated by the fact that America's war for independence was part of a wider global conflict. They were also complicated by America's treaty with France, which required the French to be a party to any negotiations. Moreover, the French were themselves bound by treaty obligations to Spain, which was also at war with Britain, making any settlement difficult to achieve. Inevitably, French and American interests began to diverge. As much as Vergennes admired the American Revolution, he was not about to place the concerns of his New World allies above his own, a fact the British were all too happy to share with the American representatives in Paris.

Secretly corresponding with the British, Jay learned that Vergennes was attempting to block two major American peace objectives, one securing the right to fish off Newfoundland and the other the right to settle land as far as the Mississippi River, which was controlled by Spain. The French would have preferred to keep America cooped up between the Appalachians and the Atlantic. Jay recognized how much America owed France, but he was not about to sacrifice his own country's interests. "Let us be honest and grateful to France," he wrote to his old friend Robert Livingston, America's secretary of foreign affairs, "but let us think for ourselves."[6]

Jay embarked on a bold plan that he knew would provoke an uproar if discovered back home. As soon as he had verified that Adams and Franklin were on board, the three American negotiators began meeting secretly with the British—a direct violation of their treaty obligations to the French. Knowing how much influence Luzerne exercised in Philadelphia, the commissioners were careful not to divulge much in their reports to Congress. Soon they stopped reporting back altogether. "Why we have nothing from our own ministers," Washington wrote to Livingston, "is, as you observe, truly unaccountable."[7] But the negotiations with the British government bore fruit. On October 26, 1782, Jay, Adams, and Franklin completed preliminary articles of peace, making sure to include Newfoundland fishing rights and a western boundary at the Mississippi. A month later they signed a preliminary treaty, agreeing that no final treaty would be signed until France and Britain concluded their own war.

Hints that a settlement might be in the offing began filtering back across the Atlantic as ships docking in American ports unloaded vague rumors and shards of news along with their cargoes. Peace would certainly be welcomed by all Americans, but it also raised concerns among conservatives. Their plans to strengthen the central government and transform the American economy depended in large part on continued British hostility. Without this external threat, Gouverneur Morris noted, they would be deprived of "that great friend of sovereign authority, a foreign war."[8]

With little time left, conservatives began devising ways to pressure Congress and the states into adopting their most prized policy goal: a permanent source of revenue for the federal government, including but not limited to an impost on foreign goods. Conservatives were aided in their efforts by the return of John Rutledge, who had been elected to Congress after stepping down as governor, and James Wilson, back after a four-year hiatus. They also welcomed Alexander Hamilton, newly elected from New York and in a hurry to make his mark. Soon after resigning his commission after Yorktown, Hamilton had earned a law degree in about six months rather than the typical three years. With help from his father-in-law, he got special dispensation from the legislature to skip an apprenticeship and then holed himself up in James Duane's private law library to study for the bar. Supporting the conservatives in their nationalist agenda was a brilliant valetudinarian from Virginia, the young James Madison.

Conservative efforts to pass the impost were largely successful. By the summer of 1782, every state had approved the measure except Rhode Island, and by the fall it seemed likely the tiny state would vote for it as well. But recent elections were about to derail their plans. After a Country Whig party came to power, Rhode Island abruptly replaced its old delegates with new ones led by David Howell, a linguist and mathematician who taught at Rhode Island College (later Brown University). In a series of essays under the pseudonym "A Farmer," Howell compared the new tax to "that fatal day when the Stamp Act was hatched by an infernal junto of British Ministers."[9] He advised his state's legislature to resist Morris and warned that the national government would grow to monstrous proportions if the impost were approved. Then "the bond of union, to use the phrase of the advocates of these measures, would be complete," Howell warned. "And we will add the yoke of tyranny fixed on all the states, and the chains riveted."[10]

Despite intensive lobbying by conservatives, in early November 1782 the Rhode Island legislature unanimously rejected the impost, a vote that would have seismic repercussions. Following a motion by Hamilton, Congress sent a group of representatives to Rhode Island to plead with the legislature to change its mind, but before they reached their destination, word came of another political setback. Virginia had just voted to rescind its previous approval of the impost. Conservatives were stupefied. At the start of December, Arthur Lee had slipped through the motion, doing it so quickly and quietly that it took the state's governor, Benjamin Harrison, another three weeks to learn that the House of Burgesses had revoked its support for the impost.

"The fatal repeal is wrapt up in more than common mystery," the state's attorney general wrote to a shocked James Madison. "An opportunity was presented to the Lees of piquing Morris."[11]

Morris quickly conferred with Hamilton, Gouverneur Morris, and Schuyler about what to do next, discussing the possibility of harnessing the army's discontent to push through the impost. The perfect opportunity presented itself a few days later. On December 29, 1782, a delegation led by General Alexander McDougall arrived in Philadelphia with a petition from the army. With the war about to end, officers and enlisted men were growing increasingly fearful that they would never receive the pensions Congress had promised them or their back pay. Already two New England states, Connecticut and Rhode Island, had barred their delegates from approving the pensions, and Massachusetts clearly did not favor them either.

Before presenting the petition to Congress, McDougall asked for a meeting with Morris and showed it to him. "We have borne all that men can bear," the petition read. "Our property is expended, our private resources are at an end, and our friends are wearied out and disgusted with our incessant applications." While the overall tone was respectful, the menacing subtext was clear. If Congress failed to act, "fatal effects" might result. McDougall confirmed to the two Morrises that a mutiny against the national government was a serious possibility. Should the central government fall, he feared, it would be only a matter of time before civil war broke out among the states.

Gouverneur Morris immediately saw how the army's grievances could assist the conservatives' larger political goals. "The Army have swords in their hands," he wrote to Jay the next day. "I think it probable that much convulsion will ensue." Such an outcome did not trouble him. On the contrary, "I am glad to see things in their present train," he wrote. "It must terminate in giving the government that power without which government is just a name."[12]

The Financier and his assistant told McDougall's delegation that there was nothing they could do to help unless Congress first addressed its funding issues, but they did suggest that the army ally itself with other government creditors in order to force the issue. The frustrated officers then presented their petition to Congress, which appointed Hamilton, Madison, and Rutledge to consult with Morris about the issue and write a report. Congress had sent the issue right back to where McDougall had started.

The next day word came that the British had finally abandoned Charleston. While Morris welcomed the news, he knew it would further complicate his job. Without an enemy to fight, soldiers stationed in the Southern Department would soon be released from service and clamor to be paid. Events were rapidly coming to a head. Yet by the end of January, Congress had still not acted. Infuriated by the political gridlock, Morris decided it was time to play his trump card. On January 24, 1783, he issued Congress an ultimatum. Unless significant progress was made on debt and taxation, he would resign his office at the end of May. In a private letter to Congress, the Financier explained that without support for his policies, he would never be able to stabilize public credit. "To increase our debts while the prospect of paying them diminishes, does not consist with my ideas of integrity," he wrote. "I should be unworthy of the confidence reposed in me by my fellow citizens if I did not explicitly declare that I will never be the minister of injustice."[13]

Terrified at the prospect that Morris's letter would throw the nation into turmoil if it leaked out, Congress decided to keep it secret. In the meantime, it scrambled for a way to address the Financier's concerns. As conservatives saw it, now was the moment to push through their funding proposals.

Standing before Congress on January 27, Wilson argued with typical eloquence that throughout the Revolution the United States had "displayed both an unexampled activity in resisting the enemy, and an unexampled patience under the losses and calamities occasioned by the war." In one area, however, the nation remained woefully deficient: "a cheerful payment of taxes." He understood that taxation lay at the root of America's dispute with Britain, but, Wilson argued, taxes should be repugnant only in tyrannies. In a free nation, this antipathy made no sense; citizens were "the sovereign as well as the subject; and as receiving with one hand what they paid with the other." America's honor and national security could not be defended, he declared, "but by the establishment of general funds to be collected by Congress."[14]

When antinationalists tried to rebut Wilson's arguments the next day, they were forced to change tactics. His arguments had been too persuasive to ignore. Now they argued not against establishing any source of federal revenue but against how that money was collected. The states, they said, rather than the national government, should collect the taxes.

Wilson immediately ridiculed the proposal. Relying on the states was what had caused the nation's debt crisis in the first place, he said.

Arthur Lee countered that giving Congress the power to tax would be "subversive of the fundamental principles of liberty."

Not so, replied Wilson. Congress needed this power to help bind the states together. "The funding of a common debt in the manner proposed," he said, would "produce a salutary invigoration and cement to the Union."

Hamilton stood to second Wilson's arguments but in doing so made a tactical error. While Wilson had carefully emphasized how the new taxes would unite the states, Hamilton pointed out that the measure would also strengthen "the power of Congress." And he pointed out that the demands of the army could be linked to those of the government's creditors.

Madison cringed when he heard this, noting, "This remark was imprudent and injurious to the cause which it was meant to serve."

It was a costly slip. Arthur Lee and another colleague from Virginia began whispering that "Mr. Hamilton had let out the secret."[15] It seemed to confirm what Lee had long suspected, that conservatives were behind a conspiracy to subjugate the states and establish a tyranny.

Sensing a shift in mood among the delegates, Wilson told Congress that he had no hidden agenda. Rather, he was motivated only by "the deplorable and dishonorable situation of public affairs." And he was willing to agree to any reasonable scheme for improving the situation. He then presented the details of what was the first comprehensive revenue plan for the United States. What he wanted was to create "a system as would place the finances of the U.S. on an honorable and prosperous footing."

There was no getting around the tremendous sums of money the federal government owed. Wilson estimated foreign and internal debt to be about $37 million, "which in round numbers and probably without exceeding reality can be called $40 million." At six percent, the interest alone on this amount came to $2.4 million, but with hostilities with Britain a distinct possibility, "it will be prudent to add 600,000, which if the war continues will be needed, and in case of peace may be applied to a nay." In order to pay its debts and for the military, he calculated, Congress needed to raise about $3 million a year. Backed by Madison, Wilson again urged Congress to reconsider a five percent impost. After months of debate, Congress was back at square one.

The difficulty of securing an agreement began to fracture old alliances. Breaking with other conservatives, John Rutledge now proposed establishing an impost only to pay the army. Other public creditors, he said, would be left to petition the states. After calculating that Wilson's and Madison's latest motion had little chance of success, Rutledge probably thought it wise to offer a more appealing alternative to the delegates. But his change of opinion also reflected something deeper, an underlying southern distrust of a powerful national government.

Unlike northern conservatives, who had no doubt they would be the ones running the central government, southern conservatives feared what would happen if they established a strong central government and then lost control of it. Numerically weaker than the North and fettered to slavery, they had far more to lose should a powerful federal government decide to intervene in southern affairs. Most other southerners shared Rutledge's sentiments, and Arthur Lee immediately seconded his motion.

Wilson, Madison, Hamilton, and the two Morrises remained adamant in their stance. To further add pressure, Robert Morris inveigled Philadelphia's creditors to lobby Congress heavily. Wilson and Hamilton then pushed through a motion to open the debate to the public. Wilson said he simply wanted their constituents to "see the prospect themselves and to witness the conduct of their delegates."[16] Conservatives then packed the galleries with angry creditors, who dunned the delegates with shouts and threats.

Adding to the growing sense of crisis was that on March 1 Congress allowed Morris to make his resignation letter public. Morris promptly informed Washington and Dickinson, who had recently been elected president of Pennsylvania. The news traveled the country as fast as a lit fuse, and his letter was widely reprinted.

Morris's allies outside Congress were stunned. "Your office is neither an easy nor a pleasant one to execute," Jay wrote to his friend, "but it is elevated and important." He urged Morris to remember "that triumphs do not precede victory, and victory is seldom found in the smooth paths of peace and tranquility. Your enemies would be happy to drive you to resign, and in my opinion both your interest and that of your country oppose your gratifying them."[17]

Morris's many enemies were confused about how to respond. Eventually, they decided to attack him for quitting the very position they wished to see him leave. Assailing Morris's character before Congress, Arthur Lee argued that "the man who had published to all the world such a picture of our national character and finances was unfit to be a minister." Hamilton and Wilson countered Lee by delivering "a copious defense and panegyric of Mr. Morris."[18]

The news hit Washington's encampment at Newburgh, New York, like a spark to a powder keg. Enlisted men and officers alike were now certain they would never be paid a cent of what they were owed. In coming to this conclusion, they had been guided by certain conservatives hoping to exploit the army's grievances. Gouverneur Morris, for one, had repeatedly written to officers at Newburgh warning them not to trust the states to repay the army.

"During the war they find you useful," he told General Knox, who had signed McDougall's petition, "and after a peace they will wish to get rid of you, and then they will see you starve rather than pay a six-penny tax." The only solution, Morris said, was "for the army to connect themselves with the public creditors of every kind both foreign and domestic and unremittingly to urge the grant of general permanent funds."[19]

Word soon reached Philadelphia that a massive military revolt was brewing. "The opinion seems to be well founded," said Madison, "that the arms which have secured the liberties of the country will not be laid down until justice is secured."[20]

Arthur Lee, whose conspiracy theories turned out to be right for once, told Sam Adams, "Every engine is at work here to obtain permanent taxes. . . . The terror of a mutinying army is played off with considerable efficacy."[21]

Robert Morris made no secret about backing the army. When asked how the mutinying soldiers would get food if they refused to disband, he replied, "I will feed them."[22] Whether he supported an armed insurrection, though, remained unclear.

On March 10 two anonymous circulars traveled through Washington's camp at Newburgh, which consisted of some 550 officers and more than nine thousand enlisted men. One of the pamphlets called for an unauthorized meeting of the officers, a clear challenge to Washington's authority. The other exhorted the officers to "change the milk-and-water style" of their supplications and "assume a bolder tone—decent, but lively, spirited and determined, and suspect the man who would advise to more moderation and longer forbearance," a probable reference to Washington. The address urged the army not to disband and to rise up against civil government if necessary. "If this be your treatment while the swords you wear are necessary for the defense of America, what have you to expect from peace?"[23]

The broadsides had been penned by Major John Armstrong, Jr., General Gates's able young aide, an indication that Gates had a hand in fomenting the unrest. Historians disagree fiercely about the extent of his role, but it seems more than likely that the general wanted to take advantage of the unrest to replace Washington.[24] Many young officers, impatient with Washington's moderate approach, began gravitating toward the old radical general, who seemed prepared to fight for their rights. While most officers continued to revere the commander in chief, enough had defected to Gates to make the threat of a coup d'état a dangerous possibility.

The meeting to discuss the insurrection had been set for the eleventh, but Washington intervened and ordered it moved five days later in order to give hot tempers time to cool off. On the morning of Saturday the fifteenth, officers from regiments all around Newburgh gathered at the "New Building," a log and board meetinghouse that the commander in chief had ordered built to encourage "sociability." Gates was presiding.

Just as the meeting was about to start, Washington unexpectedly appeared. He had misled the conspirators into thinking he would not attend. The commander in chief asked if he could speak. Feeling no little shame, the stunned officers could only agree.

Washington walked slowly to the podium on the stage at the front of the meetinghouse, the low ceiling just inches from the top of his head. He began bluntly. He had nothing but contempt for Armstrong's anonymous pamphlets, which were "unmilitary" and "subversive of all order and discipline."

Then he turned to Armstrong's second broadside. No one, he said, could doubt his loyalty. "I have been a faithful friend of the army," he declared, "the constant companion and witness of your distresses." Despite his undying support for the army, he could never countenance what the circular was proposing.

"My God! What can this writer have in view?" Washington asked. "Can he be a friend to the army? Can he be a friend to this country? Rather is he not an insidious foe?"

As slow as Congress had been to respond to the army, the general pointed out, it was working tirelessly to establish the funds necessary to pay the army. The delegates, he assured his officers, "will not cease till they have succeeded, I have no doubt." In the meantime, the army must shun any attempt to "overturn the liberties of our country" and "deluge our rising empire in blood."

From his pocket, Washington pulled out a letter from the Virginia congressman Joseph Jones, which he said would confirm Congress's good faith efforts. Washington then stopped a moment to search his other pockets. It was the pause that saved the Revolution.

Pulling out his spectacles, Washington peered over his strong aquiline nose at the assembled soldiers. "Gentlemen, you will permit me," he said. "I have not only grown grey but almost blind in the service of my country."[25]

Had Washington trained for the stage, he could not have been more affecting. His gravity, sincerity, and charisma caused the entire assembly to break down in tears.[26] By the simple gesture of putting on his reading glasses, Washington had turned Gates's plans to dust. No one in that room would ever raise a hand against Congress.

"Never through all the war," said Schuyler, who arrived toward the end of the meeting, had Washington achieved "a greater victory than on this occasion—a victory over jealousy, just discontent and great opportunities." He added that he had "no doubt that posterity will repeat the closing words of his Excellency's address—'Had this day been wanting, the world had never seen the last stage of perfection to which human nature is capable of attaining.' "[27]

In the days following the aborted coup, Washington tried to find out who in Philadelphia had been behind it. "The Financier is suspect to be at the bottom of this scheme," he wrote to Hamilton, but he later said his suspicions centered on Gouverneur rather than Robert Morris.[28] Replying to Washington, Hamilton defended conservative attempts to link the army and the nation's creditors. "The men against whom the suspicions you mention must be directed," he said, "are in general the most sensible, the most liberal, the most independent and the most respectable characters in our body." They were without a doubt, "the most unequivocal friends of the army, in a word they are the men who think continentally."[29]

Hamilton had certainly played a large part in inciting unrest in the army—he had admitted as much in front of Congress. But whether he intended to foment a coup is a matter of considerable debate among scholars. In all likelihood, conservatives had wanted only to stir up enough trouble to incite Congress to act. It was Gates and his acolytes who wished to take advantage of the unrest and turn it into a full-fledged revolt.

It is also difficult to imagine that conservatives, who universally despised Gates, would have selected him to lead their putsch. Hamilton, as Philip Schuyler's son-in-law, certainly had no love for the darling of the radicals. Horrified that things were spiraling out of control at Newburgh, Hamilton had written to Washington a week before, urging him to keep "a complaining and suffering army within the bounds of moderation."[30] Only Washington, he believed, had the necessary authority to soothe the roiling waters.

"It is of moment to the public tranquility that your Excellency should preserve the confidence of the army without losing that of the people," Hamilton said. "This will enable you in case of extremity to guide the torrent and bring order perhaps even good, out of confusion."[31]

Washington himself was sympathetic to conservative policy and had no objection to linking the demands of his soldiers with those of the nation's creditors. "It is clearly my opinion," he told Hamilton, "unless Congress have powers competent to all general purposes, the distresses we have encountered, the expenses we have incurred, and the blood we have spilt in the course of an eight year war, will avail us nothing."[32] But he drew the line at reducing the army to a pawn of congressional politics. "The army was a dangerous engine to work with," he said, "as it might be made to cut both ways."[33]

The conservatives had learned their lesson. Never again would they threaten the nation with armed revolt in order achieve their aims. If anything, they would try to stamp out unrest whenever it flared up. Washington, through sheer strength of character, had shown them the wisdom of moderation, his own behavior remaining the standard to which all others aspired. "I shall," he told Hamilton, "pursue the same steady line of conduct which has governed me hitherto."[34]

CHAPTER 21

OUR AMERICAN TUMULTS

In the years following the destruction of Fairhill, John Dickinson began spending much of his time at Poplar Hall, his boyhood home near a bend in the Jones River in Delaware. The estate encompassed thirteen thousand acres of rich, loamy soil far more suited to active farming than to contemplative perambulations. Half a dozen slaves and numerous tenant farmers worked the land, tending crops through miasmic, mosquito-filled summers and harvesting in the fall. While Dickinson's wife, Mary, and twelve-year-old daughter, Sally, preferred staying at the family's Philadelphia townhouse, which he visited as often as he could, the Farmer enjoyed plantation life.

He wrote frequently to Mary, wishing she were by his side:

> Our place affords a luxuriant prospect of plenty, the clover lawn as green as a favorable season can make it—About twenty head of cattle grazing and gamboling over the verdure—The trees bending down to the grass with red and reddening apples—peaches and damascenes without number. Two mills promising by their flow sounds like fine cider and spirits, prodigious fields of corn—a beautiful sheet of buckwheat flowering—the winter grain is all peeping out of the ground—and around the house as many turkeys and chickens of various broods as you or our precious one would wish to see—What blessings.[1]

Dickinson's political career had largely stalled after he left Congress in 1776, freeing him to tend his farmlands. Managing the plantation was lonely and time-consuming work; he kept meticulous records of the number of hides tanned, the amount of yarn bought, and how much flax his spinning wheels produced.[2] But the work was also restorative after all the invective he had endured following the fight over independence. His spirits revived as old allies began trying to make amends. Benjamin Rush wrote several times trying to rekindle their friendship. A few years later, as a token of esteem, Rush and James Wilson would name the new college they were founding in Carlisle, Pennsylvania, after Dickinson. Many wished to see him return to public service. Hoping to enlist his political talents to fight the radicals, Rush wrote in 1778, "I have no doubt but what that large and respectable body of men who have been driven into retirement by the violence of the times will at some future day step forth and form a party that will shake the influence and temper the violence of the present rulers of Pennsylvania."[3]

Dickinson remained reluctant to reenter the bloody scrum of Pennsylvania politics (the "dung cart," was how Benjamin Rush referred to it), but in 1779 he agreed to serve as one of Delaware's delegates to Congress.[4] He worked closely with James Duane that year, trying to resolve America's deepening currency crisis and voting to recall Arthur Lee from France during the Silas Deane controversy. He was especially eager to forge a peace settlement that recognized America's independence from Britain.

The following year Dickinson returned to his plantation. In August a Tory raiding party ransacked the estate. He was fortunate to be visiting his family in Philadelphia at the time. Although Pennsylvania radicals continued to revile Dickinson, Delaware Tories considered him one of the chief instigators of the Revolution and were keen to kidnap him or do worse. The fifteen marauders made do with carrying off all Dickinson's sheets and china, all his liquor save one small keg of cherry rum, and most of his furniture. As they were leaving, they also volunteered to take all his slaves to freedom. One slave named Isaac took them up on the offer. Dickinson's property losses came to about £1,500, but it was Isaac's departure that weighed on him most heavily. Increasingly disquieted by slavery and inspired by Mary's abolitionism, Dickinson decided to manumit all of his slaves in September 1781.

Just over a month later, another dramatic event took place. Over his protestations, Dickinson was elected president of Delaware. Knowing Mary had no desire to leave Philadelphia, he wrote somewhat apologetically that the position had been thrust upon him, "notwithstanding the most positive and solemn declarations by me that I could not accept the office. . . . How to avoid [it] I know not."[5]

Once inaugurated, on his forty-ninth birthday, Dickinson threw himself into the job, which required his full attention. Delaware had been devastated by the war. The British Army had marched through the state, and Loyalist raiders continued to plague the coast. Corruption had become endemic, and throughout the state virtue seemed to be declining. One of Dickinson's first acts was to issue a Proclamation against Vice and Immorality, which banned "Drunkenness, blasphemy, profane swearing, profanation of the Lord's Day," as well as "Gaming Houses, and other lewd and disorderly houses." The order proved popular, and Philadelphia newspapers began reporting favorably on the activities of Delaware's new president.

Dickinson also began trying to heed Congress's request for funds, something his predecessor had neglected. In November he met with John Rutledge in Philadelphia to discuss how to address the nation's financial morass, understanding how vital it was to help the Confederation in whatever way he could. Dickinson was especially eager to carry out Washington's request that a military hospital be built in Wilmington to care for wounded soldiers returning from the southern theater. Since Delaware's treasury was broke, Dickinson loaned the state his own money to help furnish the hospital. And he used his personal credit to secure yet more funds for the state.

The Farmer's return to politics and his successes in Delaware were closely watched by friends in Philadelphia. In the fall of 1782, anticonstitutionalists began gaining ground against supporters of the radical constitution, and in the October election they won a majority in the Assembly. Welcoming Dickinson back to Pennsylvania, they first elected him to the state's Supreme Executive Council, formerly a bastion of radical power, and on November 7 they named the president of Delaware president of Pennsylvania as well. Officially, Dickinson's full title was "Captain General and Commander-in-Chief in and over the Commonwealth of Pennsylvania." Conservatives now wielded more power than they had since the creation of the 1776 constitution. It was a happy time for him. The day before, his wife had given birth to another healthy daughter, Maria, a blessing to a couple that had lost three other children in the previous few years.

Dickinson was pleased to be elected in a state where his wife wanted to live, but he was all too aware how vicious his opponents were going to be. Still, he made a plea for unity. After marching down Market Street accompanied by "Constables and their staves, Sub-Sheriffs with the wands, [the] High Sheriff with his wand, Coroner with his wand, Judges of the Supreme Court," along with the "Provost and Faculty of the University, General and field officers of the militia, [and] Citizens," Dickinson took the oath of office at Philadelphia's Court House. He exhorted his fellow Pennsylvanians: "Let every individual constantly remember, that he is a citizen as well as a man—Let him love his country, that is his fellow citizens and be anxious for their combined glory and happiness as for his own."[6]

Radicals were livid at their loss of power and genuinely feared what conservatives might do. They warned that the anticonstitutionalists would restore the Penn family's lands and return Pennsylvania to the British Crown. Reed and other radicals made speeches hinting at the use of armed force to preserve radical test oaths and the constitution, and members of the militia swore to do their part. Conservatives in turn accused the radicals of trying to foment a civil war. Their prime objective, they said, was to put the state's finances in order, and they fully backed Morris's nationalist agenda. To help Morris strengthen the central government and pay back public creditors, Dickinson saw to it that Wilson and other conservatives were elected to Congress.

As Dickinson had suspected, radicals targeted him almost immediately. One writer named "Valerius" penned a series of malicious articles in the *Freeman's Journal* calling the new president's reluctance to embrace independence a sign of moral depravity. After Dickinson replied with overlong rebuttals, Valerius turned on James Wilson, calling him a slave to party interests. Anticonstitutionalists responded by calling radicals an association of skunks, and these were some of the kinder remarks they made. The mutual attacks grew so obscene that when American newspapers reached France, Benjamin Franklin became afraid to lend them to foreigners until he had read them through and removed any parts that would "disgrace" his nation.[7]

One of Dickinson's most pressing concerns was dealing with the ongoing warfare with Connecticut over the Wyoming Valley in northeastern Pennsylvania. New England settlers had moved into a large area of the state and claimed it for their own. While this was one of the few issues Pennsylvania anticonstitutionalists and radicals could find common ground on, conservatives were especially eager to protect the area, since many of them were land speculators. Violence between settlers had already erupted several times in the region, and Dickinson sent in a garrison of Pennsylvania troops under the guise of providing protection against Indians. The real motive, however, was clearly to protect the state's interests and forcibly remove the Connecticut settlers if necessary.

Fearing for their safety, the New Englanders petitioned Congress to establish a court to decide the issue, citing Article IX of the Articles of Confederation, which stated that the national government would be "the last resort on appeal in all disputes and differences now subsisting or that may hereafter arise between two or more states concerning boundary, jurisdiction, or any other cause whatever."

Congress appointed commissioners from different states to resolve the case, and a hearing was set for November 18, 1782, in Trenton, New Jersey. Dickinson made sure to send Pennsylvania's best legal minds to represent the state, selecting Wilson and several other well-known conservative jurists. From the outset, Connecticut tried to delay the proceedings, claiming special documents were on the way from England, but the hearing began as scheduled.

As the Connecticut side began its opening arguments, all sides, including the judges, found the proceedings "very dull," a feeling that was exacerbated by one Connecticut representative who "speaks twenty times a day, and scarcely ever finishes one sentence completely."[8] All sides sat up, however, when Wilson opened the arguments for Pennsylvania.

"We have the pleasure," he began, "to meet your Honors upon a very important contest. You are now to decide a territorial controversy, which with other nations would have been decided by the sword. This being a court of the first impression in any part of the globe—and the subject of litigation being of considerable value—I hope the honorable court will pardon the tedious discussion I am now to make."[9]

It was a dazzling beginning. In his short opening statements, Wilson had made the commissioners aware of the importance of their role. Though the case ostensibly concerned only Pennsylvania and Connecticut, Wilson demonstrated that it had national and international significance. It marked the first time, he explained, that the central government of the United States was deciding a dispute between the states. Though he didn't say so at the time, the case also showed Wilson just how lacking the Articles of Confederation were. The United States, he realized, needed an organized federal judicial system to hear such cases in the future. Going through Article IX every time there was a dispute was simply too cumbersome.

Wilson spoke for three days, and by all accounts his arguments were learned and persuasive. Even Joseph Reed, his sworn political enemy, praised his delivery. Although the other representatives were staying in Trenton during the trial, Wilson found lodging across the Delaware River in Morrisville, Pennsylvania, on land belonging to Robert Morris. As an increasingly active investor, he needed to be able to oversee his affairs in Philadelphia and check on the nearby iron foundry he had invested in with his brother-in-law. The location, however, was not ideal. When a winter storm caused the Delaware to flood dangerously, all ferry service to Trenton was canceled, and the court had to wait three days for Wilson to reappear.

When he returned, he made sure to move in for the kill, out-arguing and out-documenting his opponents. For the two Indian land deeds that Connecticut produced, both suspect, Wilson submitted thirty-nine for Pennsylvania, as well as numerous treaty ratifications, all the while citing legal precedent and history to buttress his facts. He proved that Pennsylvania settlers had lived in the valley twenty years before the first Connecticut families appeared. And he forced Connecticut lawyers to throw out their Indian deeds as invalid. Joseph Reed closed for Pennsylvania, but it was clear that Wilson had made the greatest contribution to the case. On December 30 the commissioners found unanimously for Pennsylvania.

The Trenton decision was supposed to be final, but the following year Connecticut tried to overturn it, telling Congress the court had decided only who had jurisdiction over the disputed territory, not who had the right to live there. Arthur Lee immediately backed Connecticut and called for a new court to determine who had the right to own property in the Wyoming Valley. Alarmed, Dickinson dispatched Wilson to Congress once again, telling Pennsylvania's other delegates to remain vigilant. "We wish you by all means to prevent any step being taken by Congress, that may in the smallest degree lead toward a revision of the cause determined by the Court at Trenton," President Dickinson wrote. Wilson's "professional knowledge and laborious preparation for the late trial," he said, would be invaluable to the Pennsylvania cause.[10]

Dickinson predicted his state would once again win at trial, but in the end none took place. Congress's habitual indolence prevented any further progress on the question. The dispute was finally resolved in February 1786, when Connecticut renounced its claims in exchange for Pennsylvania's promise to support the claims of western land speculators from Connecticut. For Wilson and Dickinson, this outcome was a double victory. The Wyoming Valley now belonged incontrovertibly to Pennsylvania, and Connecticut agreed to support conservative calls for a stronger government.

On March 12, 1783, copies of the provisional peace agreement with Britain arrived in Philadelphia aboard the *Washington Packet.* Twelve days later confirmation of a general peace arrived aboard a ship that had just sailed in from Cádiz, Spain. Robert Morris was at home in Philadelphia dining with friends that Sunday afternoon when he found out. One guest ran out to share the information with other friends and colleagues, but as soon as he could he "returned to Morris' to get drunk."[11]

It was glorious news and at the same time a devastating blow to conservative plans. Although the final treaty was not signed until September 3, momentum for the nationalist agenda evaporated almost immediately. "Peace has, so to speak, so abruptly pounced on us," Morris commented, "that we find ourselves thrown into a state of disorder."[12]

One of the biggest questions on everyone's mind was what to do about the money owed to the army. Washington had just thwarted one of the greatest threats to civil government in the nation's history, but tensions remained high. Sending soldiers home without pay, he warned Congress, would likely result in "civic commotions and end in blood."[13] This time he doubted he could do much to stop a revolt. Riots among the troops were already breaking out, and Washington was forced to whip troublemakers into obedience.

The Newburgh incident had already "oppressed the minds of Congress with an anxiety and distress which had been scarcely felt in any period of the revolution," Madison noted.[14] And in doing so it aided conservative goals in the short term. Rhode Island and Connecticut both reversed their opposition to granting officers a pension, and on March 22 Congress voted to commute half-pay pensions for life into full-pay ones for five years. On April 18 conservatives scored another victory. Congress voted to pass a temporary impost, but with state-appointed rather than federal tax collectors. Hamilton was so disgusted by the watered-down compromise that he wound up voting against the impost he had championed for so long. In the long term, the failure to create a permanent federal revenue represented a significant setback for nationalists. It was soon clear that under the Articles of Confederation the central government would never be able to pay its debts in full.

When Congress told Washington it wanted to keep the army together until peace with Britain had been finalized, Morris reported that there was simply no money to do so: "Unless they are disbanded immediately the means of paying them even in paper will be gone." In response, Congress instructed Morris to grant the army three months' back pay as a parting gift. Knowing the army would object to being discharged without its full pay, Congress employed a clever legal fiction. On May 26 it ordered Washington to furlough his soldiers. In theory, the army could still be called back to duty. In reality, the army slowly melted away over the next few weeks, as soldiers, tired of waiting for their pay, simply tied up their few belongings and tramped back home "without a shilling to assist themselves . . . many having several hundred miles to go in this very distressed situation."[15]

Technically, since Congress had still not tackled the nation's debt issues to his satisfaction, Morris's last day in office was supposed to be at the end of May. But after an appeal by Hamilton and Wilson, the Financier chose to ignore his ultimatum and stayed to help the army. He estimated it would cost between $600,000 and $750,000 to pay the soldiers. With no money left in the treasury, he had no choice but to print more Morris Notes, issuing them in $100,000 batches. By the time the money reached Washington's camp in mid-June, most of the soldiers had already trudged away.

Not all American soldiers accepted the terms of their furloughs with such resignation. In Philadelphia, soldiers of the Pennsylvania Line informed Congress that they would not disband until they were paid. In Lancaster, Pennsylvania, soldiers were even angrier. Tired of waiting for their money, they set off for Philadelphia to see if they could get it themselves.

On June 19, Dickinson received word that three hundred soldiers were approaching the city, led by their sergeants and fully armed. Two captains, Henry Carberry and John Sullivan, had covertly been egging on the troops, hoping to take charge once the soldiers reached Philadelphia. Dickinson immediately consulted with Robert Morris when intelligence came that the Bank of North America was to be a target. Morris advised Dickinson to call out the militia as soon as possible to block the soldiers' advance, but the president demurred. Fearing a reprise of the Fort Wilson Riot, Morris fled the city with his family, returning only after he had deposited them safely at a friend's house.

The soldiers arrived the next morning to cheering crowds, who applauded as the mutineers paraded through the streets to fife and drum. Soldiers stationed in Philadelphia welcomed the Lancaster men into their own barracks. The mutiny was now spreading. That night Hamilton and Gouverneur Morris visited the barracks promising a month's salary if the soldiers immediately departed. Their proposal was rejected outright.

The next day, Saturday, June 21, while their officers were at lunch, the soldiers lined up and marched toward the State House to confront the Pennsylvania Executive Council. When they arrived, they surrounded the building and posted guards at all the exits. Sending a message inside to the council with their demands, the soldiers said, "You have only twenty minutes to deliberate on this important matter." If they didn't, "we shall let in those injured soldiers upon you."[16] The council refused to be threatened and rejected the soldiers' demands. Not knowing what else to do, the protesting soldiery lingered outside while local taverns served them spirits. Though the group as a whole was orderly, some occasionally pressed their muskets against the State House windows or shouted obscene comments.

Hearing of the commotion, Congress quickly called an emergency session at the State House to discuss what to do if the Bank of North America were attacked. A quorum could not be attained, but the delegates who did show up decided their best course of action was to ignore the angry horde knocking at the windows with loaded weapons. The soldiers, unsure what to do next, kept close watch. They hadn't counted on simply being ignored. At three o'clock Congress adjourned, and with great solemnity the delegates exited the building, pushing past the soldiers with feigned indifference. The renegades, Hamilton commented, were nothing but "an armed banditti." Another delegate dubbed them "the offscourings and filth of the earth."[17] That night Robert Morris again met with Dickinson, urging him again to use force.

On Sunday morning at nine a.m., the council and members of Congress met at Dickinson's house to try to resolve the problem. Dickinson urged Congress to grant them more time. Infuriated that the militia had still not been called out, the congressmen warned the Pennsylvania government that they would depart for Princeton unless he calmed the situation. The authority of the United States government, they said, had been "grossly insulted by the disorderly and menacing appearance of a body of armed soldiers." Congress also sent word to Washington, asking for reinforcements to suppress the revolt.

It was Dickinson's cool head that prevented a greater conflagration. "Without some outrages on persons or property," he told Congress, "the militia could not be relied on." Calling them out would just add to the numbers of soldiers surrounding the State House. He too feared a repeat of Fort Wilson.

Congress's demands put him in a bind. He had no desire to see Congress leave Philadelphia. At the same time, he and the Executive Council doubted the militia would take arms against their fellow soldiers. Truth be told, Dickinson also felt that the mutineers' requests for pay were justified. Most important, the soldiers had not actually been violent. As usual, Dickinson advocated moderation when he felt the situation warranted it. It was a stance that drove Hamilton into a fury, but Dickinson refused to be bullied by anyone, neither by Congress nor by the mutineers.

On Tuesday, Dickinson did meet with senior militia officers to evaluate the situation. Everything he already believed was confirmed. "It would be imprudent to call upon the militia now," said one officer, "as we are convinced it would be ineffective."[18] Only if the situation deteriorated did they propose resorting to violence.

Congress had had enough. On Tuesday morning it announced that, having received no "satisfactory assurances for expecting adequate and prompt exertion of this state for supporting the dignity of the federal government," it was adjourning to Princeton forthwith.[19] Hamilton, who had initiated the call to leave, vented his fury at Dickinson, calling "the conduct of the executive of this state . . . weak and disgusting."[20] But in pushing for the government's exit, the young congressman helped plant the seeds of his own party's destruction.

Congress's announcement, along with word that Washington was sending fifteen hundred troops to quell the rebellion, had an immediate impact on the insubordinate soldiers. On Wednesday they sent a written apology to Dickinson and the Executive Council. The apology was ignored. In order to be forgiven, the soldiers first had to submit to their officers and "make a full and satisfactory submission to Congress." In case the soldiers balked, Dickinson now called up five hundred militiamen and officers to defend "the state from disturbance and the city from injury."[21] Having demonstrated both patience and fairness, Dickinson had secured the militia's obedience.

Fully beaten, the rebelling Philadelphia troops showed up at Dickinson's house that evening and formally submitted to their officers' authority. The Pennsylvania president came out accompanied by a servant holding a candle. Standing on a table that had been set up for him, he lectured the troops on their "unprecedented and heinous fault."[22] It was just the right touch. The troops quickly asked for forgiveness. Because the Lancaster troops had remained at the barracks, however, Dickinson said he would forgive them only if they joined the militia the next day in confronting the soldiers who continued to defy civil authority. By the following evening, the remaining soldiers were marching back to Lancaster. Dickinson had defused a major revolt through a combination of steely resolve and late-night scolding.

Reaction to the Pennsylvania revolt split over party lines. Pennsylvania's conservative press defended Dickinson, saying the soldiers' actions had been no cause for alarm. "Our American tumults (if they may be called tumults) are the most orderly, quiet, harmless and peaceable of any in the world," said one writer in the *Pennsylvania Packet*.[23] Another anticonstitutionalist journalist placed the blame with Congress and its failure to pass Morris's impost. "Had it been laid, agreeable to the Financier's plans," he wrote, "the duties . . . would have produced a handsome fund for a speedy diminuation [*sic*] of army debts; and the soldier's distress might have been greatly alleviated by a generous payment."[24] Several conservatives mocked Congress for its timorous flight to Princeton.

The radical press, on the other hand, pilloried Dickinson for his mild approach to the uprising, all the while suggesting that Robert Morris and his conservative cabal had somehow been behind it. These criticisms reflected the opportunistic illogic of the ideologically rigid. Nothing, in fact, pleased the radicals more than Congress's departure. They were overjoyed when Congress indicated it had no intention of returning anytime soon, despite repeated petitions by Morris and the Pennsylvania government. Conservatives' "poisonous influence" over the national government had finally been ended, commented one radical.[25] Radicals saw, quite correctly, that with Congress away from America's financial center, conservatives would have a far harder time pushing through their policies.

For Country Whigs like Samuel Osgood, Philadelphia had become the ground zero of tyranny. "Plans for absolute government," he wrote to John Adams, "for deceiving the lower classes of people, for introducing undue influence, for any kind of government, in which democracy has the least possible share, originate, are cherished and disseminated from thence." Congress's move, he believed, had come in the nick of time, ending "systems which would finally have ended in absolute aristocracy."[26]

Pennsylvania's partisan battles only intensified after the insurrection. Both sides were now focusing on the upcoming gathering of the Council of Censors, which met every seven years to consider constitutional changes. By law, only the Council of Censors could amend the document, and now that conservatives were in power, they planned to do anything they could to break the source of radical power once and for all. When the council began meeting in the winter of 1783–84, anticonstitutionalists controlled a majority of the appointees, but they did not have the two-thirds majority needed to call a new convention.

Conservatives nevertheless began proposing substantial changes to Pennsylvania's form of government, including a bicameral legislature, a one-man governor, and the end of term limits. The Council of Censors would itself be abolished. They then presented their plan to the public, hoping to pressure radicals into acceding to a new constitutional convention. Another press war erupted, with constitutionalists accusing the anticonstitutionalists of trying to "introduce among the citizens new and aristocratic ranks" and creating a governor who sat in a "throne of royalty."[27]

With opposition mounting to their plans, conservatives backed off and decided to reconvene the council in June after further appeals to the public, which was now barraged by six more months of political vitriol. Anticonstitutionalists labeled the radicals enemies of commerce and shirkers of their military duty: "Their patriotism has scarcely extended beyond brawling in a coffeehouse or tavern."[28] But as the pamphlet war escalated, the conservatives overreached. Their proposed changes to the constitution went too far, the public began to feel, and their partisan attacks had grown too extreme.

Through a series of resignations and new elections, anticonstitutionalists lost their majority on the Council of Censors, dashing their hopes for another convention. It would be another seven years before they could try again. Then they suffered a worse setback. In the election of October 1784, anticonstitutionalists were trounced, with radicals capturing all but two counties in Pennsylvania.

Part of the problem was that the heavy-handed tactics that conservatives had used to try to influence the Council of Censors had backfired. But their defeat can also be attributed to the fact that they made almost no effort to get elected. Gentlemen did not electioneer. The way they ran for office was to ignore the election completely and expect their merits to speak for themselves. The lower classes, on the other hand, had no such qualms. "Our party do not possess half the activity and address which prevail amongst the factious leaders of the opposition," commented one anticonstitutionalist.[29] As a result, conservatives lost the Assembly. Although Dickinson was reelected president of the Supreme Executive Council, he no longer had any legislative support. A month later the new Assembly replaced its entire congressional delegation with a slate of radicals.

After Congress's removal from Philadelphia, Robert Morris traveled several times to Princeton, but he found few delegates there and a markedly more hostile atmosphere. Remaining in Princeton served no purpose, he decided, with his base of operations in Philadelphia. Explaining his departure, he told the president of Congress that "the public service may be materially injured unless I should speedily return to Philadelphia."[30]

Arthur Lee was positively gleeful when he heard the news: "Robert Morris' undue and wicked influence . . . has manifestly diminished since the removal from Philadelphia, and the fixing of Congress in any other place will I hope restrain it within due bounds."[31]

Though technically he remained America's superintendent of finance, Morris's influence and his nationalist political goals lay in ruins. He spent less and less time at Congress, which began tottering vaguely northward, leaving Princeton to convene at Annapolis, Trenton, and finally New York after the British evacuated in November 1783. With radical power in ascendance, Arthur Lee began hounding the Financier any way he could, hoping to drive him from office. Lee's brother William called Morris the most dangerous man in America, and Arthur had no doubt that Morris would try to sabotage American finances before quitting, since "he and his immoral assistant have malignity enough to endeavor to ruin where they can no longer plunder."[32]

Launching a series of public investigations into Morris's affairs, radicals revived the old Silas Deane controversy and questioned Morris's actions as head of the Secret Committee. They opened another inquiry into a lost clothing shipment from Europe that Morris had overseen and still another into whether Morris was speculating in his own Morris Notes. Morris responded as best he could, but he drew the line at opening up his private records. "The Superintendent of Finance," he informed Lee coldly, "has no official knowledge of the private concerns of Mr. Robert Morris."[33] If anything, Morris had neglected his own business concerns substantially while in office.

Morris spent his remaining time in office winding down his affairs and slowly redeeming Morris Notes. "Nothing material this day," he wrote in his diary on July 10, 1784. "Some applications this day of little consequence" read an entry for an entire day in August.[34] Hamilton had already given up trying to reform America's finances and had quit Congress the year before. And Robert Livingston had stepped down as secretary of foreign affairs a year before that. On November 1, 1784, Morris finally resigned as Financier, replaced by a new board of treasury led by Arthur Lee. If conservatives could not hold power under the existing state constitutions or within the Confederation, they would set their sights elsewhere.

CHAPTER 22

CAPITALIST INDUCEMENTS

Feeling unwell on St. Patrick's Day 1784, John Rutledge decided to send word that he would not be attending the Sons of St. Patrick's annual dinner, which was to be held at William Thompson's City Tavern in Charleston. He dispatched a slave of his named Beck to Thompson's house, but what happened when she reached her destination sparked a controversy so bitter that it inflamed class tensions throughout South Carolina. The contretemps began when Beck reported back to Rutledge that Thompson had refused to accept her message. The former governor then sent over his son to demand that Thompson appear at once and explain himself.

The innkeeper fumed while he walked the two and a half blocks up Broad Street to Rutledge's house. He had served as a captain during the war and had become far more accustomed to giving orders than receiving them. Once at Rutledge's house, he denied that Beck had tried giving him a message. In fact, he said, the slave woman had refused to identify her owner, asking only to watch an artillery display celebrating the ratification of America's peace treaty from Thompson's second-story window. Shocked by her "impertinence," the innkeeper had demanded she leave.

When Rutledge called for Beck, however, she repeated her side of the story. Believing his slave over the innkeeper, Rutledge called Thompson insolent and threatened to teach him a lesson. The former captain, for his part, was outraged that Rutledge would take a slave's word over his own. The next day he sent the statesman a letter calling his behavior "unsufferable except between a haughty lordling and his wretched vassal" and challenged him to a duel.[1] Rutledge demanded an apology. Thompson refused.

At the State House the following day, Rutledge, who had returned from Philadelphia to serve the South Carolina legislature, reported the incident to his fellow delegates. His brother Hugh, the speaker of the House, referred the matter to the Committee on Privileges and Elections, which ordered Thompson arrested for committing "a gross insult on . . . an honorable member of this House, and a flagrant violation and breach of the privileges thereof."[2]

Thompson was kept imprisoned as long as he refused to apologize, but his captivity did nothing to silence him. "The great John Rutledge was individually offended by a plebeian," he jeered. Attacking Charleston's "nabob tribe" of patricians in general, he asked why those "who detest republicanism" were permitted to continue running the state. After another gentleman testified that he had seen Thompson showing disrespect toward other members of the upper class, the innkeeper accused him of lying and swore that "if he offers this to my face, by the Eternal God I will kick his a_ _."[3]

Thompson soon became a cause célèbre for South Carolina's lower and middle classes, who were chafing at the strict social hierarchies that the elites hoped to reimpose now that the war was over. Thompson had, moreover, been a member of the recently formed Marine Anti-Britannic Society, an organization devoted to limiting trade with Britain, beating up Tories, and harassing South Carolina aristocrats, whom they suspected of colluding with the Tories. The society issued a proclamation thanking Thompson "for his spirited, manly, and patriotic conduct, by the defense of his fellow citizens' rights and privileges, violated in his own person, when aristocratical principles endeavored to subvert and destroy every genuine idea of real republicanism."[4]

Thompson was finally released at the end of the legislative session in April. Shunned by the elites, the City Tavern soon fell on hard times, and Thompson decided to return to his native Pennsylvania. But the storm he had provoked continued to grow. Newspapers debated the incident for another half year, with agitation for political reform reaching a climax during the summer, when a volunteer cavalry detachment broke up peaceful demonstrations following July Fourth celebrations.

By the end of the Revolution, Americans were toppling old patterns of deference as relentlessly as gilded statues of King George.[5] A new world of greater social mobility and political participation was rapidly coming into being. And while hostility to the rich continued to exist, the changes taking place in American society were far more democratic than radical. It wasn't that the lower classes wanted to limit wealth. It was that they too now demanded the right to earn it. One of the greatest shifts was that the common man was now able to settle and own western land, which new laws required be sold openly rather than secretly to the upper classes. In an age when owning land meant independence, this development had profound effects on American culture. Finally, widespread enlistment in the military led ordinary Americans to expect new rights and responsibilities in return for their service. Conservatives were none too pleased by these changes. Now that the war was over, many "found it very difficult to fall back in the ranks," Edward Rutledge observed. As a result, he believed, South Carolina was being overrun by "too many commanders in chief."[6]

As this populist revolution gathered speed in the mid-1780s, New York conservatives grew especially worried. The state had instituted the harshest anti-Tory legislation in the country, and many feared it was only a matter of time before the Patriot elite faced similar persecution. Laws were passed expelling Tories, seizing their estates, and barring them from suing debtors. One problem was that these statutes violated the peace treaty with Britain. On a more fundamental level, they also threatened the sanctity of private property. For John Jay, the mass expulsion of Tory merchants could only be counterproductive, depriving the nation of prosperous, hardworking citizens. "I would rather see the sweat of their brows fertilize our fields than those of our neighbors," Jay wrote from Europe.[7]

These laws also undermined confidence in American business at home and abroad. In a letter to Hamilton, Robert Livingston lamented "the violent spirit of persecution" among the general populace and feared "its consequences upon the wealth, commerce, and future tranquility of the state."[8] Hamilton, in turn, warned Livingston that the populists seemed to be "evidently directed to the confusion of all property and principle." Now was the moment "for those who are concerned for the security of property . . . to endeavor to put men in the legislature whose principles are not of the leveling kind."[9] Almost a century and a half after the English Civil War, the threat of leveling still sent shudders through the upper classes.

As the elections of 1785 drew near, conservatives realized they needed to develop new tactics to deal with the rapid changes in American society. Over the previous few years, they had lost power at all levels of government precisely because they had failed to understand these developments. "This country never had such a hard trial since the Revolution between democracy and aristocracy as it will have this election," commented one of Livingston's many cousins. "All the parties are alive. Letters and lists contending . . . and every subterfuge invented by both parties."[10]

For the first time, conservatives had to accustom themselves to the idea of campaigning for political office. They also had to put aside internal disagreements and "stick close to each other," as another Livingston cousin wrote to

Hamilton. Victory could be secured only by "uniting the interests of the Rensselaer, Schuyler and our family, with other gentlemen of property in the county in our interest."[11] New electoral strategies, however, could take conservatives only so far.

At the start of the Revolution, the American right had survived by coming to terms with the inevitability of change. Once again they needed to transform what they stood for if they were to have any relevance in the new republic. Expecting the masses to vote unquestioningly for their social superiors was no longer a viable electoral strategy. But promising prosperity through economic growth was. While conservatives continued to shun the idea of sharing power with the lower classes, they began forging a new political ideology that even nonelites could support—the belief in a strong United States and a rising standard of living. Market capitalism would replace gentlemanly elitism as their way of appealing to the common man.

Most of the founding conservatives embraced the new economic order wholeheartedly. Large-scale capitalism, they held, would be the engine that drove America to greatness, while the nation's boundless resources would be the fuel that allowed it not only to rival European powers but surpass them one day. It was a profound insight, since the connection between capitalism and conservatism was far from self-evident.

While in Britain industrial development clashed frequently with conservatism, the American right found a novel way to balance its customary resistance to change with modern capitalism, one of the most powerfully transformative forces ever unleashed in the world. It did so by incorporating traditional Whig beliefs about virtue in a uniquely American way. No longer would virtue be measured solely by martial feats or service to the state; it would be measured by financial success as well. Commerce, which only a century before had been the most feminizing of forces, was now developing into a measure of manliness. It was a natural fit for the American people, said Gouverneur Morris, since they were "highly commercial, being as it were the first born children of extended commerce in modern times."[12]

Conservatism in the United States was thus far more dynamic than was its counterpart in Britain. For American conservatives, radical change would be held in check by the opposition of competing self-interests, not by the frozen hierarchy of inherited social orders, as in Europe. They still believed the few would govern the many, but only because some men would always be more talented than others, creating natural distinctions and inequalities. A natural aristocracy, they held, would always rise to the top as industrial society divided into workers and owners. Inevitably, Gouverneur Morris said, "the time is not distant when this country will abound with mechanics and manufacturers who will receive their bread from the employers."[13]

Concentrations of money and power were not only inescapable, Morris believed; they were desirable as well. In a series of essays in the *Pennsylvania Packet,* which he signed simply as "An American," Morris denied that monopolizers had dishonorable motives. They were, wrote the editor of Morris's papers, driven only by the "same motives of all other dealers, namely, to make money by selling at a higher price than the one at which they bought." Taking a position shockingly at odds with orthodox republicanism, Morris argued that rather than harming America, monopolies were "productive of advantages to the community, which could have arisen no other way."[14] They boosted commerce and created low, steady prices.

Conservatives began embarking on numerous large-scale investment projects that required enormous infusions of capital. In South Carolina, John Rutledge chaired a committee on the construction of canals between the state's largest waterways. Using his clout in the legislature, he secured laws authorizing clearance of the Wateree, Pee Dee, and Edisto Rivers. With other investors, he became an organizer and vice president of the Company for Inland Navigation, which connected the Santee and Cooper Rivers. Since Rutledge owned part of the land that the canal eventually would run through, he stood to make money from tolls that boats would pay along the way. Edward Rutledge invested in canal projects as well, obtaining a charter from the North Carolina legislature to open up the Catawba River, leading a "great part of the trade of North Carolina to flow into that channel" and then down past Charleston.[15]

In New York, Philip Schuyler made detailed surveys of the state's waterways and estimated "that an uninterrupted water carriage between New York and Quebec might be perfected at 50,000 pounds sterling."* In 1783 he gained Washington's approval to connect the Mohawk River and Wood Creek. Appointed a commissioner to oversee canal construction, he toured upstate New York and envisioned a system of waterways extending all the way to Lake Ontario. After he reported to the legislature that "such an establishment would tend greatly to facilitate and advance the internal commerce of this state, and promote the convenience and prosperity of the people thereof," a canal law was passed authorizing the incorporation of the Lock Navigation Co. and the Northern Inland Lock Navigation Co. Schuyler made lucrative investments in both.[16]

* About $6 million today.

In the middle states, James Wilson invested in iron furnaces and forges and with his brother-in-law bought the Delaware Works, which they were determined to turn into the largest nail factory in the country. Despite the high value and favorable prospects of these ventures, money was a constant concern. Writing to "certain Dutch capitalists" about his need for more funding, Wilson described his recent investment in "a very extensive system of works, consisting of rolling and slitting mills, grist mills, saw mills, and a forge on the River Delaware." To make a return, he said, "it will be absolutely necessary for us to be in possession of still larger sums." But he assured the Europeans that no one could ever lose money investing in American real estate. "From the progressive rise of the price of real estates in this country (which in many instances is very rapid) they will, without any money being expended on them, become more valuable every year."[17]

Robert Morris busied himself in all manner of investments both before and after he stepped down as Financier. Signing a deal with the French Farmers-General, a "tax farm" that controlled tobacco sales in France, Morris secured a monopoly on tobacco shipments to France in 1785. After the French advanced him one million *livres,* he was effectively able to corner America's tobacco market and make a sizable profit. Outraged farmers in Maryland and Virginia organized protests, calling for boycotts of French wine and spirits. Morris nevertheless was able to secure a monopoly on all tobacco sales to France for another two years.

Morris's tobacco venture turned out to be one of his most profitable investments, but his most audacious was organizing America's first commercial expedition to China. It took more than a year to secure financing; Morris put up the seed money, and Gouverneur Morris and others soon joined the enterprise. The idea was to sail around South America, up the coast of California, and then across to Asia, opening up the Pacific to American trade. "I take the lead of the greatest commercial enterprise ever embarked on in this country," exclaimed Morris's partner, John Ledyard, a visionary adventurer who had sailed with Captain Cook and spearheaded the idea of trading with the Far East.[18] As the prospects of a substantial return on investment beckoned, five more trips were planned. Morris, as secretary of marine for the U.S. government, easily obtained ships for the venture. On February 22, 1784, the *Empress of China,* a three-masted, copper-bottomed former privateer, broke through the ice in New York's East River. After firing a thirteen-gun salute as it passed the Battery, it began its fifteen-month voyage, heading for Canton with $20,000 in silver and 250 barrels of ginseng.

To assist in such ventures, conservatives helped set up banks, trade organizations, and manufacturing societies. They lobbied for protective tariffs, supported the growth of factories, and offered prizes for new inventions. In New York, Alexander Hamilton set up the Bank of New York. In New Jersey, the Camden Agricultural, Horticultural, and Industrial Society was established, with similar organizations opening in Boston, New York, and Baltimore. The Rumsean Society of Philadelphia aided in the construction of steamships, while the Pennsylvania Society for the Encouragement of Manufactures and the Useful Arts built a factory for spinning cotton using carding and spinning machinery. In 1788 the factory produced eleven thousand pounds of woven cotton and linen. The following year the Assembly invested £1,000 to help boost production.[19] Although most manufacturing in the United States continued to be handled by small-time artisans and mechanics who worked from home, conservatives had no doubt that large-scale manufacturing would one day be the rule rather than the exception.

The idea that America might become an industrial powerhouse was utterly alien to most Americans at the time, especially those who viewed the world entirely through the prism of classical Whig thought. John Adams, who had begun shedding his former radical politics after becoming enamored of European pomp and alarmed by reports of licentious behavior back home, failed completely to understand the economic thinking of men like Wilson, the Morrises, and Hamilton. "I say," he wrote to Franklin, "that America will not make manufactures enough for her own consumption these thousand years."[20] Even as Adams drifted ever rightward, the founding conservatives remained skeptical of his politics.

For the far left, the rise of corporations and monopolies represented nothing less than a betrayal of the Revolution. "What was it [that] drove our forefathers to this country?" asked an incredulous representative from Georgia. "Was it not the ecclesiastical corporations and perpetual monopolies of England and Scotland? Shall we suffer the same evils to exist in this country?"[21]

Thomas Jefferson, who had replaced Franklin in Paris in 1785, was horrified by the industrial revolution, whose genesis he witnessed in Europe. Americans, he vowed, would never experience the conditions of workers "of the great cities in the old countries . . . with whom the want of food and clothing . . . [had] begotten a depravity of morals, a dependence and corruption."[22] A devout democratic agrarian, Jefferson was convinced that importing large-scale capitalism from Europe would corrupt American society irrevocably. "Our enemy has indeed the consolation of Satan on removing our first parents from paradise," he warned; "from a peaceable and agricultural nation, he makes us a military and manufacturing one."[23]

Jefferson and his allies would do everything in their power to keep Europe's "sad catastrophe at a distance."[24] At all costs, America had to be kept safe from a "funding system, aided by a British influence, and directed by another Walpole," a reference to Britain's famous prime minister that Americans still comprehended decades after the Court Whigs had left office.[25] The American left was fully in favor of commerce and trade, supporting the use of machinery and small-scale handicraft industries. But it insisted that such innovations take place within and for the benefit of an agrarian society. For populists, the endless acreage of America's frontier provided the path to salvation. As long as almost every man could own some small property, American virtue would be safeguarded and the dark forces of industrialization kept at bay. It was "not too soon," said Jefferson, "to provide by every possible means that as few as possible shall be without a little portion of land."[26]

Conservative plans for developing the frontier could not have been more different. Instead of the helter-skelter settling of the West by individual farmers as advocated by the left, they envisioned a more orderly, corporate process. Along the way, great windfalls stood to be made as well. In South Carolina, the Rutledges began speculating heavily in the western part of the state, along the North Carolina frontier, and even beyond the Appalachians, borrowing heavily in the process. In New York, the great landowners—Philip Schuyler, James Duane, the Livingstons, and the Rensselaers—ceased running their vast landholdings like feudal estates and started treating them more like investments, selling out to their former tenants whenever it became profitable. They then reinvested the money in land farther west. "The promise of large returns in land speculation schemes," writes the historian Charles Page Smith, "attracted aggregations of capital and schooled a new class of capitalists in techniques of large-scale capital finance."[27]

At the start of the Revolution, Duane alone owned thirty thousand acres west of Schenectady. By its end, he had added thousands more. Duane's goal was to turn isolated tracts of forest into bustling towns. He hired surveyors, built roads, and advertised for settlers. After founding the town of Duanesburgh in the rolling hills of upstate New York, he laid out hundred-acre farms and a four-hundred-acre plot for the town where merchants and mechanics would live and work. As settlers began buying parcels for £70, paid either up front or over the course of a decade at seven percent interest, Duane set up sawmills and gristmills and became the town's banker, loaning tools, money, and livestock in return for services.

No one had grander schemes for colonizing the West than James Wilson. Riding the circuit as a country lawyer, he had become enchanted by the pristine beauty of America's frontier lands. In his native Scotland, almost every square inch was owned by the Crown or the aristocracy. In America, however, an ordinary man could rival a baron. Beginning with thousands of acres along Pennsylvania's frontier, Wilson began purchasing westward in ever larger parcels. His holdings became some of the most valuable in all of America, remaining the object of intense speculation well into the late nineteenth century.[28] He created the Canaan Company to buy land in southwestern New York. He bought 56,000 acres in Virginia and with partners another 321,000 acres south of the Ohio River, near land owned by Washington.

It was an age of epic dreams. With Silas Deane, Robert Morris, and several French investors, Wilson became a major backer of the Illinois-Wabash Company, which laid claim to one of the largest tracts of land in all of North America. Formed out of two earlier land companies chartered under royal authority, Illinois-Wabash claimed title to more than sixty million acres divided into eighty-four shares of 800,000 acres each. In recognition for his legal work for the company, Wilson was elected president and granted half a share. He borrowed more money and bought another share on his own, giving him 1.2 million acres of frontier land. As the legal representative of several other investors, he eventually had effective control of close to three million acres of Illinois-Wabash land alone.

Like Duane, Wilson foresaw the need for large numbers of settlers to populate America's vast open spaces. As Silas Deane had written to him, the quickest way to make money in America was by "adventuring in lands and procuring inhabitants from England and Germany to settle them."[29] When it came to the settlement of the West, conservatives argued, virtue and commerce dovetailed especially well. Wilson and Duane believed they were performing a vital service both for potential settlers and for the United States. They were the middlemen of national development. And it was only fair if they took a cut along the way.

In his essay "On the Improvement and Settlement of Lands in the United States," Wilson outlined an ambitious plan for settling the American interior along the lines of the old English joint-stock companies that had colonized the original thirteen colonies. While the United States was rich in land, he said, it was poor in capital and population. Europe had the opposite problem. It was therefore obvious, he said, that "a plan, by which the surplus labor and stock and capital of Europe would be employed on the unimproved lands in the United States, must be eminently advantageous to both."[30]

Wilson then set about describing how to transfer settlers and capital between the Old and New Worlds most efficiently. He anticipated which European ports ships would need to sail from and expatiated on which lands would be most suitable for settlement. He detailed the logistics involved in moving thousands of people thousands of miles over sea and land. Upon disembarking from their ships, immigrants would be given accommodation until they felt ready for the next stage of their voyage over land.

Once arriving at their plot of land in the West, settlers would find "a house already built, a garden already made, an orchard already planted, a portion of land already cleared, and grain already growing or reaped." Good surveyors would need to be hired and land offices established, and new settlers would be expected to pay for these conveniences through their labor and their crops. Undertaking such an extensive operation would require vast sums of capital at the outset, but the potential rewards for those who invested early were beyond imagination. "To capitalists inducements should be offered, sufficient to determine them to take such a share in the business," Wilson wrote.[31]

As an investor in many of these lands, Wilson was certain that a sizable portion of the proceeds would be his as well, and he continued to buy land whenever and wherever he could. His debts ballooned, but he remained idealistic about America's prospects and correct in his analysis of its long-term prosperity. He was also hopelessly naïve in his estimation of how long it would take to see a return on his investments.

Nowhere was the rise of commercial capitalism more apparent than in the operations of the Bank of North America. It was America's first modern corporation, with full legal standing, an official seal, and a government charter that allowed it to exist "for ever after." It enjoyed many of the same rights as individuals, including the power "to have, purchase, receive, possess, enjoy and retain lands, rents, tenements, hereditaments, goods, chattles and effects."[32] In contrast to America's typical small-scale, owner-operated enterprises that had strong ties to the community and a relaxed way of doing business, the bank followed only the impersonal logic of the market, separated ownership from management, and enforced punctuality "with too much violence," as one Philadelphia lawyer put it.[33] Americans had never before seen anything like it.

The Bank of North of America grew so powerful so quickly that it dominated all business in Philadelphia. It amassed more money than even the largest mercantile firms, and merchants across the city had to do business with it or risk going bankrupt. Without a line of credit from the bank, they risked being overwhelmed by competitors who did have one. Moreover, as the historian George David Rappaport points out, the bank transformed the way American business was transacted. It boosted the amount of money in the economy and the speed with which it circulated, promoting new types of consumerism and market-oriented behavior.[34]

All of which was why radicals began targeting the bank as soon as they returned to power in the fall of 1784. "I cannot behold this dreadful engine working such horrid mischiefs without raising my voice aloud, and crying out to you," said one radical, "exterminate the bank!" On February 23, 1785, newspapers across Philadelphia began publishing petitions to revoke the bank's charter. The ostensible reason was that the institution had refused to accept the paper currency that the Assembly had ordered printed over President Dickinson's objections. At the heart of the attack, however, lay deep-rooted fears about the impersonal nature of commercial capitalism and the tremendous power it generated in the hands of the few. The bank was a new form of aristocracy, radicals claimed, its unlimited charter the equivalent of a hereditary title.

In response, the Assembly created a committee to investigate the complaints. Its conclusions were harsh:

> The accumulation of enormous wealth in the hands of a society, who claim perpetual duration, will necessarily produce a degree of influence and power, which cannot be entrusted in the hands of any set of men, whatsoever, without endangering the public safety. . . . If this growing evil continues, we fear the time is not very distant, when the bank will be able to dictate to the legislature, what laws to pass and what to forbear.[35]

Not grasping the severity of the threat, conservatives were slow to respond. Since the bank was protected by a congressional charter, Thomas Willing, its president, refused to believe Pennsylvania had any authority to revoke its state charter. But when the committee voted in favor of repealing the bank's charter, conservatives knew there would be trouble. In August, Wilson, who was simultaneously one of the bank's chief investors and one of its main debtors, appeared before the Assembly to defend the bank. He described how essential the institution had been in funding the army and how helpful it was to the economy. At the core of his argument was a fundamental constitutional question: "Had the United States in congress assembled a legal and constitutional power to institute and organize the Bank of North America, by charter of incorporation?" Once again the authority of the national government was being pitted against that of the states.

Like any shrewd lawyer, Wilson began by investigating his opponents' main arguments. Nowhere in the Articles of Confederation, he conceded, did it say that Congress had the power to establish a bank. Moreover, the Articles maintained that the states retained every power not "expressly delegated to the United States in congress assembled," seeming to imply that the Congress could not incorporate a bank. The problem with this argument, Wilson pointed out, was that no state could incorporate a bank on behalf of all the states either. This left open a huge hole in legal theory, one that Wilson said Congress must fill: "Whenever an object occurs to the direction of which no particular state is competent, the management of it must, of necessity, belong to the United States in Congress assembled."

In order for Congress to manage the "general interests of the United States," as the Articles charged it with doing, the national government had powers that resulted not from all the particular states separately but from "the union of the whole."[36] It was the birth of the doctrine of implied powers, an issue that would remain contentious for decades to come.

Finally, Wilson addressed the issue of private contracts in a nuanced way. "It may be asked," he said, "has not the state power over her own laws?—May she not alter, amend, extend, restrain, and repeal them at her pleasure?" He allowed that it did, but with one crucial caveat. The state did have the right to alter laws that affected the citizens in general, but not those that interfered with private parties. Contracts that involved individuals or groups could not be simply abrogated by the legislature even in the name of social good. If they could "be repealed without notice, without accusation, without hearing, without proof, without forfeiture," he asked, "where is the stamp of their stability?" Society itself would become unstable were government given such coercive powers, and private property would be left without protection.

Wilson rested his case after a day and a half, but his eloquence and insight had been in vain. With radicals controlling a majority of the Assembly, the bank's destruction had been foreordained. A week after Wilson's appeal, the legislature repealed its charter. Only twelve conservatives remained in power to vote against the decision, and they issued a scathing statement afterward saying that the Assembly had dishonored the national government. Radicals could not have cared less. "We are not bound by any terms made by Congress," said one radical assemblyman. "Congress are our creatures!"[37]

The effects of the decision were immediate. Cash in the bank's coffers shrank from almost $60 million to $37,000. As Wilson had predicted, news of the repeal had a devastating impact on American interests abroad. One "American gentleman" living in The Hague wrote that the repeal had "done more mischief to our country than you can conceive. Hundreds of people . . . in England were preparing to embark for America; others . . . were about to invest their cash in our lands; and a few more were about to lodge money in your bank, when the tidings of the attack upon it reached London. They have all changed their minds, and now consider nothing as secure in the new states."[38]

With the help of Dickinson, who had bought twenty shares of its stock, the bank obtained a new charter in Delaware, but being able to operate freely in Pennsylvania was vital if the institution were to survive. A campaign to overturn the Assembly's decision was launched. Debate raged for the next half year, as pamphlets arguing for and against the bank flooded the state. In April 1786 the Assembly again took up the issue, its galleries packed to the bursting point for four straight days. The controversy was the talk of the state. Anticonstitutionalists again lost the vote, but by campaigning vigorously, they finally persuaded a majority of the public to accept the merits of their side.

In elections in the fall of 1786, conservatives won a one-vote majority in the legislature. Pressing their case, they brokered a deal to restore the bank's charter. To address fears about the bank's power, they agreed that its capital would be limited to $2 million and its charter to thirteen years. Robert Morris was far from pleased with the compromise, but Wilson felt the issue was moot: "The modification of the bank charter as to limitation of time or capital will not affect the Congress charter."[39] Conservatives might have won, but they would never overcome a deep-seated populist mistrust of banking in America.

The battle over the Bank of North America convinced many on the right that now more than ever a powerful union was necessary. Only a strong central government would be able to defend commercial capitalism and provide sufficient aid to help it grow. Only robust federal authority would be able to maintain civil order, which Americans of all political persuasions felt was rapidly deteriorating.

The sense of malaise was especially pronounced in New England. In Connecticut, farmers were being evicted for failing to pay taxes raised to pay for government bonds owned by these same farmers. In Massachusetts, the outbreak of Shays's Rebellion, during which angry militiamen shut down courts and seized armories to protest tax and debt collection in the fall of 1786, seemed to confirm everyone's worst fears about the perilous state of the republic. Even radicals like Sam Adams moved to suspend habeas corpus and execute rebel leaders to crush the unrest. In the end, a show of overwhelming force by the Massachusetts government, along with last-minute tax reforms, prevented the conflagration from spreading.

Congress too had voted to raise troops to put down the rebellion, but its powers had grown so atrophied that it was unable to send any actual assistance. Over the previous two years, fewer and fewer delegates had been showing up. In December 1785 it had taken days to form the quorum necessary to call for an adjournment. A year later Congress barely functioned at all, and what little it was able to get done was due largely to the efforts of John Jay, who had taken over as secretary for foreign affairs. For lack of a quorum, the final treaty guaranteeing independence from Britain had not been ratified on time. Moreover, so little money remained in the treasury that the French actually paid a British sea captain to carry the document back with him to Europe. The United States was dying.

Or so it seemed. Scholars point out that throughout America's "critical period," as this time of tumults is called, the economy continued to expand at a steady clip. Crops were good, and ordinary Americans had never before known such prosperity. And yet the growing fear that the Confederation was disintegrating reflected a very real political crisis even if an economic one did not materialize. Without an effective central government, centrifugal forces were pulling the nation apart.

States were imposing punitive taxes on one another's imports. Trade wars were erupting between New York and Connecticut, Maryland and Virginia, and Pennsylvania and New Jersey. And the threat that actual warfare might break out between Pennsylvania and Connecticut and between New York and Vermont alarmed many. Worst of all was the open talk of secession. After New England proposed establishing a separate confederacy, newspapers began advancing the idea of creating three separate nations, with a Middle Confederacy and a Southern Confederacy joining the one in New England.

"These confederacies, they say, will be united by nature, by interest, and by manners," wrote Benjamin Rush, "and consequently they will be safe, agreeable and durable."[40] But he was far from convinced that this would be the case. What was needed, he argued, was constitutional revision to address the glaring weaknesses of the Confederation. Only then would property be protected and domestic tranquillity ensured. "A bramble will exercise dominion over us, if we neglect any longer to choose a vine or a fig-tree for that purpose," Rush warned.[41] All conservatives, in fact, were horrified by the idea that the Confederation might break up. It would leave the nation vulnerable to predation by European powers, raise the threat of civil war, and end all hope of establishing market capitalism in America.

In September 1786 representatives from five states met in Annapolis, Maryland, for a special convention to discuss the nation's trade problems. Chaired by Dickinson, the convention debated for three days and concluded that none of America's problems could be addressed without completely revamping the Articles of Confederation. The delegates issued a series of resolutions, written largely by Dickinson, calling for a "Grand Convention of the States" the following May that would revise the Articles and "render the constitution of the federal government adequate to the exigencies of the Union."[42] They then forwarded their findings to Congress.

Time was running out. "Without some alteration in our political creed," Washington wrote to Madison that fall, "the superstructure we have been seven years raising at the expense of so much blood and treasure, must fall. We are fast verging to anarchy and confusion."[43]

CHAPTER 23

EXPERIENCE MUST BE OUR GUIDE

After four days in the saddle on the dusty, treacherous roads between Mount Vernon and Philadelphia, George Washington arrived in the nation's former capital on Sunday, May 13, 1787. Only reluctantly had he agreed to attend the constitutional convention that was to start meeting the following day. A dozen years in his nation's service had left the former commander in chief yearning for time to look after his affairs and a few moments of repose to enjoy his bucolic estate. Close friends had exhorted him to attend, however, leading Washington to wonder "whether my non-attendance in this convention will not be considered as a dereliction to republicanism."[1] The convention also offered the old general the chance to achieve what every eighteenth-century statesman dreamed of—to be called "the glorious republican epithet," Henry Knox told him, "The Father of Your Country."[2]

Just outside the city, Washington was pleasantly surprised to be greeted by the Philadelphia Light Horse, which escorted him through the streets. Cheering throngs, pealing church bells, and the boom of cannonades accompanied the procession, which brought the great war hero to the door of Mrs. Mary House's upscale boarding house on Fifth and Market, where his fellow Virginian James Madison was already staying.

No sooner had Washington settled in than Robert Morris arrived, insisting his old friend lodge at his elegant home two blocks away. Washington could hardly say no to the comforts of Morris's liveried staff, French butler, and excellent collection of claret. The weather was gloomy as he rode to Morris's townhouse, as it had been all month, causing him to ruminate about America's prospects. Despite the difficulties the nation faced, Washington's hopes remained high. "No morn ever dawned more favorably than ours did," he wrote; "and no day was ever more clouded than the present."[3]

A lack of quorum prevented the convention from meeting as scheduled on

Monday, much to Washington's annoyance. "These delays," he fumed, "serve to sour the temper of the punctual members, who do not like to idle away their time."[4] At last on Friday, May 25, enough delegates had arrived for the proceedings at Philadelphia's State House to begin. Nine states were now present.

The first order of business was to select a presiding officer, and it came as no surprise when Washington was elected. Following the vote, Robert Morris and John Rutledge led him to his seat upon the raised dais, where he would spend the next four months overseeing the convention. Washington would remain silent for most of the debates that were to determine the basic shape of America's government, influencing the proceedings more through his stately bearing than through any learned arguments.

While fifty-five men eventually attended the convention, fewer than thirty sat for most of the debates, many spending days or weeks at a time away from Philadelphia. Almost all the participants were political veterans. Forty-four had served in Congress, and for a number of men, it was their first time in three years back in the luminous, high-ceilinged room after Congress's flight during the Pennsylvania insurrection. Many had served in state legislatures. Thirty-nine were lawyers and judges. Two were college presidents, and three were or had been professors. Almost half had served in the Continental Army or the militia. They were, commented Jefferson from Paris, "an assembly of demigods."[5] For those who actually attended the debates, the truth was more prosaic. The convention, said Gouverneur Morris, was composed merely of "plain honest men."[6]

American conservatives were well represented at the convention. As individuals, each delegate contributed greatly to the constitution. Collectively, they exerted a defining influence on the document's final shape. John Dickinson came to the convention representing Delaware rather than Pennsylvania. Though a champion of federal power, he was nonetheless committed to protect the rights of small states. Meeting him at the convention, the Georgia delegate Major William Pierce was awed to come face to face with the man "famed through all America for his Farmers Letters." At the same time, Pierce found the fifty-five-year-old Dickinson distracted and his speech "irregular." The truth was, the old Farmer was debilitated for much of the convention by a painful flare-up of gout. Sitting through each session was a daily torture, but the importance of the undertaking and the caliber of the other delegates helped revive him to some extent. "The convention is very busy, of excellent temper," Dickinson told his wife, "and for abilities, [it] exceeds I believe any assembly that ever met upon this continent, except the first Congress."[7]

The lone conservative on New York's divided delegation, Alexander Hamilton, felt frustrated for much of the convention. His two left-leaning colleagues were so opposed to augmenting the power of the central government that they left Philadelphia in disgust after six weeks. Without a delegation, Hamilton could do little but listen, but his brief contributions made a powerful impression on the other participants. In his epistolary portraits of the other delegates, Major Pierce noted that "Colonel Hamilton is deservedly celebrated for his talents. . . . To a clear and strong judgment he unites the ornaments of fancy."[8]

Heading the South Carolina delegation was the forty-eight-year-old John Rutledge, whose "reputation," said Pierce, "gave him a distinguished rank among the American worthies." Determined to defend his state's economic interests, which included slavery, he opposed granting the central government as much power as others sought to give it. Yet he remained committed to shoring up its weaknesses. Sharing his brother Edward's belief that Shays's Rebellion had threatened "a general distribution of property," he feared that if nothing were done to correct the faults of the national government, similar uprisings might sweep down the continent "and precipitate a general civil war between debtor and creditor."[9]

Pennsylvania conservatives included the fifty-three-year-old Robert Morris, the thirty-three-year-old Gouverneur Morris, and the forty-five-year-old James Wilson. Though celebrated as "a merchant of great eminence and wealth . . . and a worthy patriot," as Pierce put it, the elder Morris participated little in the debates. Most of his contributions were behind the scenes, often at the lavish dinners he threw for the other delegates at his home. His former assistant, on the other hand, spoke more than any other delegate, delivering 173 speeches. The younger Morris was, said Pierce, "one of the geniuses in whom every species of talents combine to render him conspicuous and flourishing in public debates."[10] He was so prolific in his ideas that many of them inevitably would be shot down. Yet he displayed grace at every setback. "The brilliancy of his genius," Madison commented, was "a readiness in making the best of measures in which he had been overruled."[11]

More than any other delegate, with the possible exception of the soft-spoken, stammering Madison, James Wilson was the most preeminent nationalist of the convention. He certainly ranked, wrote Pierce, "among the foremost in legal and political knowledge." The combined contributions of Madison and Wilson outweighed those of nearly all the other delegates put together. While Madison has frequently been called the father of the constitution, Wilson deserves as much credit in drafting the fundamental laws of the United States. In many regards, his vision of American government was the more insightful and enduring. He took part in every important debate and, after Gouverneur Morris, spoke more than all the other delegates, a total of 168 times. He would become one of only six delegates to sign both the Declaration of Independence and the Constitution.

For all the unity conservatives had displayed during the war—their agreement on such issues as declaring independence, supporting the bank, creating a professional army, and forming a more powerful central government—they hardly marched in lockstep at the convention. Sectional differences, disparities in state size, disputes over western land, and arguments for and against slavery all began taking on more importance than the ideological divide between left and right. While Dickinson, Hamilton, Rutledge, the two Morrises, and Wilson continued to espouse similar political creeds, each one was conservative in his own way, reflecting the richness and complexity of conservative thought at the birth of the nation.

On the second day of the convention, Monday, May 28, the delegates voted to keep the proceedings completely secret. They had good reason. Congress had charged them with revising the Articles of Confederation, but the delegates quickly realized that no amount of tinkering would solve the government's problems. What was needed was an entirely new political framework, one that superseded the Articles. In many respects, what the delegates were undertaking amounted to a coup d'état. Until they had a finished document in hand, it was better, they decided, that the rest of the nation not know how their business had evolved.

Sweeping changes to America's system of government were proposed almost immediately. Rising before the convention on the next day, Virginia's governor, the tall, eloquent Edmund Randolph, introduced a series of resolves that came to be called the Virginia Plan. Crafted largely by Madison while the convention had been awaiting a quorum, the resolutions vastly expanded the powers of the central government and denied the states any role in it. Following classical constitutional thinking, Randolph outlined a government divided into three branches: an executive, a legislature, and a judiciary. Among other things, the plan called for a bicameral legislature, with the lower house elected directly by the people and the upper house elected by the lower. In the process, the plan gave far more clout to the large states than the small ones.

The delegates quickly agreed to create an upper and lower house, but the question of how they should be elected sparked immediate controversy. Ironically, it was New England, the bastion of radical democracy, that objected most strenuously to the direct election of representatives by the people. "The people," objected Roger Sherman of Connecticut in his nasal voice, "should have as little to do as may be about government." They are, continued the former shoemaker, "constantly liable to be misled." Elbridge Gerry of Massachusetts seconded Sherman, stating, "The evils we experience flow from the excess of democracy." While he counted himself "still however republican," he "had been taught by experience the danger of the leveling spirit."[12] The shock of Shays's Rebellion had turned many against the vagaries of popular power.

Southern aristocrats like John Rutledge agreed wholeheartedly. State legislatures, he argued, should elect the lower house of the federal government. They would be more "refined" and send "fitter men" to office than would the general public.[13] He also opposed giving a salary to legislators. As propertied gentlemen, they should have enough means at their disposal so as not to need money. Only then would the legislature be truly independent.

The most controversial part of the Virginia Plan, however, was the proposal to base representation on population. It meant that states with larger populations would dominate the national government, a prospect the smaller states found unacceptable. Large states like Pennsylvania and Virginia thought it was only proper that they have more influence in the national government. One of the main problems with the Confederation, in fact, was that all states had an equal vote. A majority, Wilson pointed out, could be achieved even though it represented only one-third of the nation's population. And he would never consent to a system that let one-third of the people impose their will on the remaining two-thirds.

Although the large states had the votes to push through proportional representation, delegates from the small states made it clear they would never consent to such a scheme. On May 30, George Read of Delaware reminded the convention that his delegation had been barred from agreeing to any change in the way the national legislature was elected. He insisted that the constitution maintain the principle of equal representation by the states. If the large states continued to push for their plan, he warned, it would become Delaware's "duty to retire from the convention."[14] It was no small threat. Delaware, and presumably the other small states, would refuse to remain part of the United States.

No one was more outraged than Wilson. "Can we forget," he asked, "for whom we are forming a government? Is it for men, or for the imaginary beings called states? Will our honest constituents be satisfied with metaphysical distinctions?"[15] Though a near-fatal victim of mob violence himself (he had the bullet holes in his house to prove it, one historian quipped), Wilson nevertheless believed passionately in the fundamental principle of government by the people.[16] It was a point he made repeatedly throughout the convention and for years afterward. "The absolute and uncontrollable authority remains with the people," he declared.[17]

Wilson was the most democratic of the founding conservatives in this sense. It was not that he believed in direct democracy. In fact, one of the main reasons he championed a powerful central government was to maintain order amid the excesses of democracy. Yet he insisted that all sovereignty ultimately resided in the people, relying on Christian natural law theory to buttress his arguments.[18] In what was one of his favorite metaphors, he advocated "raising the federal pyramid to a considerable altitude" and giving "it as broad a basis as possible." It was the only way to ensure political and social stability in a republican system, he believed, since "no government could long subsist without this confidence of the people."[19]

Wilson recognized the unusual nature of his argument. In Britain, after all, an ideal "mixed" government implied combining aspects of monarchy, aristocracy, and democracy. But America was different, he said, and mixing these three principles was not appropriate in the New World. Democracy, "the best and purest" of these systems of government, was all that was necessary. "We have found that in order to arrive . . . at a point of perfection hitherto unattained," he wrote, "it is not necessary to intermix the different species of government."[20]

It was a stunningly modern conception of politics. While many of the founders, most notably John Adams, argued that the one, the few, and the many had to be represented in government, Wilson maintained that each branch of government should be based upon the people as a whole, not on different social classes. Wilson's conservative genius was to recognize that while sovereignty had to be based in the people, government itself need not be overly democratic if properly structured. The constitution, he explained, "in its principle, is purely democratical; but its parts are calculated in such a manner as to obtain those advantages also, which are peculiar to the other forms of government in other countries."[21]

What this implied was that the lower house did not have to represent the lower classes and the upper house did not have to be the bailiwick of the rich. Yet a balanced government could be achieved all the same. In response to fears that two houses would not check each other, Wilson argued for "double representation" of the people. The benefits of bicameralism could be attained even if both branches were elected directly by the people. Natural differences would arise between the two houses as they developed their own norms and spirits. They would become increasingly distinct, keeping each other in check.

The principle of democratic sovereignty led Wilson to become the only important founder to advocate the modern concept of one man, one vote. Unlike his fellow conservatives, who wished to preserve the prerogative of the upper classes, Wilson opposed property qualifications for voting. Even agrarians like Madison supported rudimentary property qualifications in the hope of protecting yeoman farmers from the unpropertied urban masses. Classical republicanism, as everyone knew, held that voters could not be independent without possessing land.

Wilson, on the other hand, argued that capitalism was evolving to the point that citizens could be independent without needing landed property. In contrast to Edmund Burke, he believed that while "security of property is one of the great objects of government," it was not "the sole or primary object of government and society."[22] Rather, the fundamental object of government was the happiness of the governed and "the cultivation and improvement of the human mind."[23] Property was but the means to an end and thus could not be used to exclude voters.

"It would be very bad and disagreeable for the same persons at the same time," Wilson pointed out to the convention, "to vote for representatives in the state legislature and to be excluded from a vote for those in the national legislature."[24] The fight over property qualifications was finally overcome when Wilson worked out a compromise with Gouverneur Morris. Federal election rules, the delegates decided, would follow state regulations in determining who had the right to vote.

Wilson's arguments about democracy solved all manner of theoretical problems. The delegates were baffled, for example, over whether the federal government or the states were superior, because it did not seem possible that both could be superior at the same time. It was the same problem, in fact, that Britain had faced at the start of the Revolution. One of the reasons Parliament had objected so strenuously to American demands for self-representation was because of its belief in *imperium in imperio,* the roman legal doctrine that "sovereignty within sovereignty" was impossible. In the years before the Revolution, Dickinson had argued that the issue of dual sovereignty did not pose a problem between Britain and America. Now his former student applied this same argument to the relationship between the national government and the states, arguing that there was no contradiction in the idea of overlapping governments. As long as ultimate sovereignty derived from the people, both the federal government and the states would be supreme in their own spheres. It was a brilliant solution to the objections some delegates were making. And it would define the legal relationship between the United States government and the states for centuries to come.

Wilson's novel arguments notwithstanding, tensions between the small and large states continued to mount. Neither side would bend, while those states that remained undecided became increasingly worried. South Carolina's delegation did not oppose the Virginia Plan outright, but Rutledge commented that he "could not well decide to vote until they should see an exact enumeration of the powers" to be granted to the central government. His South Carolina colleague Pierce Butler repeated his "fears that we [are] running into an extreme of taking away the powers of the states."[25]

Now it was Dickinson's turn to leave his mark. The question of equal versus proportional representation, he said, was "so important that no man ought to be silent or reserved." On June 2, rising to address the issue despite the excruciating pain in his feet, he reviewed the history of classical republics. The main problem with earlier republics, he said, was that they tended to "flourish for a moment only and then vanish forever." This did not mean that all republics inevitably failed, just that previous republics "were badly constituted." America, he believed, could avoid these mistakes because of "the accidental lucky division of this country into distinct states." Glancing at representatives of large states, he added, "a division which some [seem] desirous to abolish altogether."

The key was to model the American constitution upon the British one, which all had to agree was a model of stability. While Dickinson personally believed that a limited monarchy was "one of the best governments in the world," he nevertheless recognized that "a limited monarchy was out of the question" in America. "The spirit of the times—the state of our affairs, forbade the experiment if it were desirable." America could not reproduce the British constitution exactly, but it was possible to reproduce the best parts within a republican setting. The secret to Britain's stability, Dickinson argued, was its House of Lords. "A House of Nobles was essential to such a government," he declared. "Could these be created by a breath, or by a stroke of the pen? No. They were the growth of ages, and could only arise under a complication of circumstances none of which existed in this country."[26]

Yet Dickinson believed America had the functional equivalent of a House of Lords—the states. He agreed with the Virginia Plan that the lower house should represent the people. But the upper house, he declared, should represent neither the people nor the upper classes. It should represent the states, which, like Britain's hereditary baronies, were permanent institutions of great power. Refining his arguments a few days later, Dickinson said it was "essential" that one branch of the legislature be drawn from the people, and the other from the state legislatures. "The combination of the state governments with the national government," he told the convention, "[is] as politic as it [is] unavoidable." Choosing the Senate "through such a refining process" would "assimilate it as near as may be to the House of Lords in England."[27]

It was a dazzlingly good idea, combining Dickinson's reverence for tradition with the realities of the American political scene. It also neatly addressed the impasse between the large and small states. It was just the sort of middle-of-the-road compromise at which the Farmer had always excelled.

The next day, June 7, Rutledge moved to reconsider the question of direct election. Most of the delegates now agreed that the lower house should be elected directly by the people, and Dickinson formally moved that the "second branch of the national legislature be chosen by the legislatures of the individual states."[28] Though he did not state so explicitly, his motion implied that the states would have equal or near equal representation in the Senate.

Wilson immediately rose to object. Thin and weak with gout, Dickinson now addressed his former student. Invoking once more Britain's House of Lords and House of Commons, he declared that basing the House and the Senate on different sources would provide "mutual checks on each other, and will thus promote the real happiness and security of the country." He compared the government to the solar system, with the states revolving in their orbits around a central federal government. Or, he said, invoking another metaphor, "like the union of several small streams, [it] would at last form a respectable river, gently flowing to the sea."[29] In either case, the "gentleman from Pennsylvania," he said, pointing to Wilson, "wished to extinguish those planets."[30]

Wilson respectfully countered that he was not "for extinguishing these planets as was supposed by Mr. Dickinson—neither did he on the other hand, believe that they would warm or enlighten the sun. Within their proper orbits they must still be suffered to act for subordinate purposes." He saw no danger of the states being devoured by the federal government. What he wanted to ensure, rather, was that the states did not consume the federal government. Moreover, he denied that America should follow Britain's example. "The British government cannot be our model," he explained to Dickinson. "We have no materials for a similar one."[31]

Wilson's old teacher could not have disagreed more. While both men sided with the right in much of their thinking, Dickinson's position was the more traditionally conservative, "in some deep Burkean sense," as the historians Forrest McDonald and Ellen Shapiro McDonald have put it.[32] (It should be noted that Dickinson's constitutional arguments were made in 1787, while Burke's famous attack on the French Revolution would not be written for another two years.) But whether Dickinson's thought was deeply Burkean, or Burke's thought deeply Dickinsonian, both Dickinson and Burke established the principle of traditionalism in modern political thought. Dickinson just did it first.

No statement of Dickinson's captured his essential conservatism better than the speech he delivered in the middle of August. "Experience must be our only guide," he told the convention. "Reason may mislead us." He did not just mean personal experience, but historical too. History provided enduring models that had stood the test of time. And there was no better model for America to follow than Britain's ancient constitution. It was a stance at odds with the tenets of liberalism, whose founder, John Locke, had argued a century earlier, "Reason must be our best judge and guide in all things."[33] Moreover, it directly contradicted the work of the French philosophes, who were at that very moment extolling reason as a means for tearing down old political structures and erecting new ones in Europe.

For Dickinson, statesmen who rejected tradition in favor of abstract principles did so at their peril. "It was not reason that discovered the singular and admirable mechanism of the English constitution," he said. "It was not reason that discovered or even could have discovered the odd and in the eyes of those who are governed by reason, the absurd mode of trial by jury. Accidents probably produced these discoveries and experience has give[n] a sanction to them. This then is our guide."[34]

As the long hot summer wore on, the deadlock over the Virginia Plan intensified. The large states clearly had the votes to push through proportional representation, but nothing they did could compel the small states to agree to their plan. "I will never consent to the present system," declared William Paterson of New Jersey on June 9. "Myself or my state will never submit to tyranny or despotism."[35]

On Friday, June 15, Paterson dropped another bombshell on the convention. He presented the delegates with a new plan of government, one that directly opposed Randolph's resolutions from a fortnight before. The New Jersey Plan, as it became known, called for only minor revisions to the Articles of Confederation, not outright rejection. It did grant Congress greater powers to regulate trade and raise taxes—something conservatives had championed for years—but it also called for a unicameral house, just like the Continental Congress and Pennsylvania's own dysfunctional government.

The proposal immediately threw the convention into turmoil. "The eagerness displayed by the members opposed to a national government," reported Madison, "began now to produce serious anxiety for the result of the Convention."[36]

In promoting his plan, Paterson took specific aim at Wilson's assertion that "all power is derived from the people." While he agreed that this view "is right in principle," he said it was "wrong in the application to the question now in debate."[37]

Standing to defend himself, Wilson raised one of the main concerns of modern conservatism: the prospect that tyranny can arise not only from the executive but other branches of government as well. "Despotism comes on mankind in different shapes," he told Paterson; "sometimes in an executive, sometimes in a military one. Is there no danger of a legislative despotism?" As Wilson knew too well from Pennsylvania politics, the masses, as democratic as they might be, could easily tyrannize society if they gained control of the government. He and other conservatives certainly disagreed with John Adams's assertion that "a democratical despotism is a contradiction in terms."[38] The single house Paterson was proposing was a recipe for disaster. "If the legislative authority be not restrained," Wilson warned, "there can be neither liberty or stability; and it can only be restrained by dividing it within itself, into distinct and independent branches. In a single house there is no check, but the inadequate one, of the virtue and good sense of those who compose it."[39]

Even Dickinson was aghast. He no more wanted a unicameral legislature with equal representation to be established than he wished to see the Virginia Plan succeed. "You see the consequences of pushing things too far," he told Madison furiously. The Virginian would do well, Dickinson said, to remember that he and those who thought like him were "friends to a good National government." Their ideas for federal union coincided in many ways. Dickinson agreed that the government should have an executive and a judicial branch. He agreed to creating a bicameral legislature with sufficient power to deal with issues that the states were unable to handle. What he objected to was permitting the central government to obtain a coercive power over the states. He especially disliked the idea of replacing the role of the states in the federal government with a system of proportional voting based on population.

Seeing that neither side was willing to compromise, Dickinson did as he was wont to do in such situations. He went off by himself for the rest of the weekend to work out a common ground. On Monday, he submitted to the convention a proposal that combined the best of both positions.

Before the delegates could take up Dickinson's ideas, Alexander Hamilton, who had been largely silent until now, took the floor. Speaking for nearly six hours, he delivered the longest single speech of the convention. It was also the most notorious. While other conservatives couched their language in the rhetoric of classical republicanism, whether out of political shrewdness or sincere belief, Hamilton bluntly expressed his admiration for hierarchy, capitalism, and monarchy. Dickinson hoped merely to take the best of the English constitution. Hamilton wanted to copy it wholesale. He was, in many ways, the only pure Court Whig among the founding conservatives and would have been far more at home in Walpole's Britain of the 1720s than in the United States of the 1780s.

America, Hamilton began, was simply too large to be able to support a republican form of government. To the shock of the other delegates, he openly called for the establishment of monarchy. "The British government was the best in the world," he said, and he "doubted much whether any thing short of it would do in America." To his mind, Americans should forget democracy, since the chaos it brought, he predicted, would soon cure them of their love for it. He then proceeded to detail his own plan for a monarchical, capitalistic, industrial society.

Hamilton's peroration made his political allies cringe. For three weeks, Wilson and Madison had been trying with utmost care to avoid igniting the left's smoldering fears that the nationalists wanted to establish an aristocracy. Yet here was Hamilton confirming everything the opponents of strong government had been whispering, about a plot to establish tyranny. Hamilton, to be fair, may have had another purpose in mind. By stating opinions so far to the extreme right, he made the Virginia Plan seem as almost tame in comparison. The immediate effect of Hamilton's speech was unclear, but it might have been more helpful than Wilson and Madison credited.

Finally on Tuesday the nineteenth, Dickinson moved for compromise, suggesting the delegates contrast the two plans, "one with the other, and consolidate such parts of them as the committee approve."[40] Madison and Wilson immediately attacked the idea, but the Farmer's good sense and moderation began to win converts, most notably Roger Sherman of Connecticut, who reversed his earlier opposition to Dickinson's proposal that the Senate be elected by the state legislatures. But it was not enough.

By the end of the month, the convention was ready to break up. On June 30,

Gunning Bedford of Delaware declared that if the large states refused to agree to their demands, "the small states will find some foreign ally of more honor and good faith, who will take them by the hand and do them justice."[41] Suddenly the fracturing of America seemed a real possibility, and conservatives and nationalists had no doubt that foreign powers would rush in to divide up the pieces. That night Dickinson composed an ardent plea for moderation, but before he could deliver it, he was struck violently ill. Too weak to stand, he was forced to retire from the convention for almost a month.

Fortunately, other delegates began to recognize the urgency of reaching a compromise. On Monday, July 2, over the objections of Madison and Wilson, the delegations voted unanimously to appoint a committee, chaired by John Rutledge, to work out a settlement. After a day of patriotic festivities on the Fourth, the committee read its report the next day. The compromise they suggested was clear: the lower house would be based on proportional representation and the upper house on equal representation by the states.

Yet another week of bitter debate ensued, with Wilson announcing that he would not bend. It was the most delicate moment in the entire convention. Tempers were strained, and a single false statement from either side would have ended the convention at that moment. The delegates waited another week for tempers to cool, and on Monday, July 16, they decided to hazard a formal vote on the committee's recommendation. Roger Sherman of Connecticut had helped broker a backroom deal, and the convention now voted five to four to give each state an equal vote in the Senate and to distribute seats in the House proportional to population, with one seat being granted for every forty thousand people. Every large state, with the exception of a deadlocked Massachusetts, voted against the measure.

When a frustrated Randolph proposed adjourning, Paterson declared that if the large states were unable to accept defeat and wanted to adjourn indefinitely, he "would second it with all his heart."[42] Randolph apologized for seeming to suggest he wanted to walk out of the convention. He wanted merely an adjournment until the next day. As the delegates filed out of the State House, John Rutledge admitted that no further compromise was possible. Either the large states had to accept the will of the small states, he said, or the Confederation would crumble.

For all the roiling acrimony within the State House, the delegates did manage to keep up a facade of harmony on the outside. They maintained such total secrecy that no one else in Philadelphia had a clue just how close the convention was to breaking up. "So great was the unanimity . . . that prevails in the convention upon the great federal subject," reported the *Pennsylvania*

Packet on July 20, "that it has been proposed to call the room in which they assemble—Unanimity Hall."[43]

Finally on July 23, the large states agreed to what came to be called the Great Compromise, which established the basic architecture of America's two legislative houses. Occasionally referred to as the Connecticut Compromise, for Roger Sherman's part in brokering the deal, the agreement did not, in fact, originate with the Connecticut delegation. It had been Dickinson's position from the very beginning, and it slowly won supporters as other delegates recognized the merits of his arguments.[44] When he returned from his sickbed two days later, Dickinson could not have been more pleased.

On July 26, the convention adjourned for a much-needed two-week break. During the interval, a five-member Committee of Detail, chaired by Rutledge, would hammer out the basic contours of what had been agreed to so far. Many of the delegates immediately repaired to some of Philadelphia's fine taverns, the Man Full of Trouble, the Indian Queen, and the City Tavern. Others longed for some quiet in the countryside.

Washington and Morris departed for Valley Forge that same day to go trout fishing. Their quarters would be far more luxurious since the last time they had stayed there. Robert Morris was putting them up in his nearby country estate. With their bellies full and the air full of the fragrant bloom of summer, the two comrades made their way by horse to the Schuylkill, which ran alongside the old army camp. As Morris set up his tackle, Washington suddenly found himself too agitated to while away the hours by the riverbank. He spent the remainder of the trip mounted in his saddle, tracking back and forth over the "ruins" of his old earthworks, remembering with no little emotion the winter of death and privation he had spent there almost a decade before.[45]

CHAPTER 24

WE THE PEOPLE

On a warm day in late summer, the delegates of the Constitutional Convention sat by the banks of the Delaware River to witness America's future. They had yet to resolve some of the most contentious political questions facing them—the judiciary, the presidency, and slavery—but the fresh air and festive occasion were a welcome respite from the tense, sweltering atmosphere inside the State House. As they picnicked on meat pies and watermelon slices, the delegates beheld a rumbling twelve-oared machine bobbing in the water before them. It was a steamship, one of America's first technological innovations, and John Fitch, a war veteran, frontiersman, and silversmith, had come to Philadelphia to demonstrate his invention. The former lieutenant hoped to persuade the delegates to include some form of intellectual property protection in the Constitution. He also wanted to raise capital.

Crowds of onlookers erupted in cheers as Fitch shoved off from the Front Street Wharf and began chuffing against the current. His paddles, modeled after the Indian war canoes that had ambushed him in the Ohio River Valley, rose and fell at each turn of the axletree, propelling his forty-five-foot skiff at nearly three miles an hour. Black smoke belched from the boat's chimney, the first industrial pollution the city had ever seen.

It has never been established exactly how many of the delegates attended the demonstration, but likely it was a majority. "There was very few of the convention, but called to see it," Fitch noted in his diary.[1] Several reportedly took turns riding the rattletrap vessel, and James Wilson surely took special interest in this show of technological ingenuity. He was a part owner of Fitch's company and one of three delegates who had begun investing in industrial manufacturing.

The delegates were impressed by the power of Fitch's device. America was a land of swift, expansive rivers and would soon have need of such devices to conquer the interior of the continent. The day after Fitch's demonstration, the Connecticut delegate William Samuel Johnson wrote to present "his compliments to Mr. Fitch." Assuring "him that the exhibit yesterday gave the gentlemen much satisfaction," Johnson promised that he "and no doubt other gentlemen will always be happy to give him every countenance and encouragement in their power which his industry and ingenuity entitles him to."[2] Fitch's timing could not have been better. Only four days before his demonstration, the convention had begun discussing the intellectual property clause. How much Fitch influenced the wording of the Constitution is uncertain, but there is no doubt many of the delegates had already begun debating the rapid advance of technology and manufacturing.[3] Fitch's invention was a vivid reminder that the document they were fashioning had to address America's changing economic landscape as well as its governmental framework.

Nobody articulated the importance of these changes better than Tench Coxe, a thirty-one-year-old Philadelphia merchant who had served as secretary to the Annapolis convention the year before. One of the most astute men of the founding generation, Coxe was a self-educated economist. For years he had collected and combed economic data, teasing out trends that pointed ineluctably toward the growth of machine technology. Only by balancing agriculture with industrialization, Coxe argued, would the nation's economy grow and a "more exalted state of civil society" be attained.[4] He was convinced that only Congress could help American manufacturing flourish, especially in the face of European competition. Fearing disunion and economic collapse in the spring of 1787, Coxe saw the convention as the "salvation of the country." It was up to the delegates, he declared, to create a system that nurtured this sort of "balanced economy" in the United States.[5]

Though not a delegate himself, Coxe was determined to influence the framing of the Constitution. On May 11, as the representatives were trickling into Philadelphia, he addressed the Society for Political Enquiries at Benjamin Franklin's home. The society's fifty-odd members listened enthusiastically to his speech, "An enquiry into the principles, on which a commercial system for the United States of America should be founded . . . [and] some political observations connected with the subject." Afterward Coxe had it published and "inscribed to the members of the convention."[6]

Interest in Coxe's thoughts ballooned over the summer. On August 9, with the convention in full swing, he delivered the inaugural address to the Pennsylvania Society for the Encouragement of Manufactures and the Useful Arts at the request of its president, Benjamin Rush. The United States, he declared, needed to study other advanced countries in order to obtain "methods of encouraging manufactories, and pursue such of them as apply to our own situation." Addressing the convention specifically, he stated that the government needed to offer "premiums for useful inventions and improvements" and "assist the efforts of industry, and hold out the noble incentive of honorable distinction to merit and genius." Land, he believed, was one of the best inducements the government could use to encourage talented men to create "useful invention."[7]

One of Coxe's gifts was his ability to appeal to both sides of the political spectrum. His positions on industrialization were fundamentally conservative, but by couching his thoughts in the rhetoric of republicanism, even agrarians like Jefferson and Madison gravitated toward his ideas. Rather than fostering dependence, Coxe said, manufacturing would aid "the independent proprietors of the soil." He carefully avoided praising Europe's grim factories, where underfed women and children labored through the night, as Hamilton enthusiastically did. Instead Coxe emphasized how machinery could liberate farmers, minimizing manual labor and encouraging small-scale handicraft production.* Side by side, agriculture and industry would make America strong. "On the one side we should see our manufactures encouraging the tillers of the earth," he said. "Commerce, on the other hand . . . would come forward with offers to range through foreign climates in search of . . . supplies . . . which nature has not given us at home."[8]

If the United States were ever to become independent of Europe, Coxe argued, it was vital to develop machines that "by wind and water" created "pig and bar iron, nail rods, tire, sheet-iron, sheet-copper, sheet-brass, anchors, metal of all kinds," and not least, "gunpowder." New innovations needed to be encouraged. "Steam mills have not yet been adopted in America, but we shall probably see them after a short time." Where it would all lead nobody could predict, but the results would redound to the nation's glory. "Combinations of machines with fire and water," he proclaimed, "have already accomplished much more than was formerly expected from them by the most visionary enthusiast."[9]

Although such views were held by only the tiniest percentage of the population, some Americans were already inventing powerful new technologies. At the same moment Coxe was addressing Philadelphia's leading citizens, Oliver Evans, a self-taught Delaware farmer, was building the world's first automatic

* Coxe would later serve as Hamilton's assistant in the Treasury Department and help him write his famous *Report on the Subject of Manufactures* of 1791.

production line at his water mill. Like Coxe, Evans was a "visionary enthusiastic," imagining within his lifetime steamships plying the nation's waterways and overland steam engines carrying passengers between Philadelphia and Boston in a single day.

Among those most caught up in Coxe's mesmerizing vision was James Madison. In August he and Charles Pinckney of South Carolina rose before the convention to propose turning Coxe's ideas into law. Under the constitution, Congress would be empowered to issue patents, reward technological advancements, and promote "commerce, trades, and manufactures."[10]

Conservatives fully supported such measures and lobbied for more. As they saw it, the Constitution would not only ensure social stability but also nurture and safeguard American business interests, a crucial first step for turning the nation into the financial and industrial powerhouse they had long envisioned. For American conservatives, business and politics were often intertwined. There was no guarantee their plans would succeed, however. With debate turning back to more controversial political issues, the convention now threatened to splinter apart. Should that happen, they knew, the United States likely would too.

Rutledge's Committee of Detail had been hard at work during the two-week break in the middle of the convention. As the delegates retook their seats on August 6, the committee presented them with a rough draft of the Constitution. Wilson seems to have performed the lion's share of the work, but Rutledge edited the draft heavily. As much as Wilson was eager to expand the power of the central government, Rutledge made sure to insert language that protected the interests of the states in general and South Carolina in particular. In several cases, the former governor ignored agreements hammered out earlier in the debates and added provisions that had not been discussed by the other delegates. It was a fine balancing act that shaped and smoothed the language of the document.

One of the most important issues the committee had to decide was how specifically the powers of the national government should be defined. An earlier agreement to grant Congress almost unlimited authority was scrapped. To compensate for this reduction of federal power, Wilson, scholars believe, gave Congress the right "to make all laws that shall be necessary and proper for carrying into execution the foregoing powers." The vagueness of the language allowed it to sail through the convention but also made the clause a flashpoint of controversy for decades to come.

Wilson also used his position on the committee to enshrine a principle of law close to his heart. Horrified at the flimsy evidence that had been used to hang his Quaker clients for treason after the British occupation of Philadelphia, he was adamant that such a travesty would not happen again. Rutledge's notes gave Congress only the right "to declare it to be treason to levy war against or adhere to the enemies of the US." It was presumably Wilson who insisted on adding, "No person shall be convicted of treason, unless on the testimony of two witnesses." The new clause, he said, was "a great improvement," since it was "not only a legal but a constitutional security against the imputation of treason."[11]

Finally, Wilson likely inserted what would become the Supremacy Clause into the committee's draft. Over the previous two months, the nationalists had tried repeatedly to give the federal government power to veto state laws, only to be outvoted each time. After persuading Madison of the need for compromise, Wilson integrated his ideas about dual sovereignty into the Committee of Detail's draft. In its own sphere, he wrote, federal law would be "the supreme law of the land," while state law remained supreme in its separate sphere. Where there was conflict between the two, a Supreme Court, he envisioned, would decide the matter.

For Wilson, the creation of a vigorous, independent federal judiciary was crucial. He was seconded by Dickinson, who was particularly disturbed by a proposal to grant the executive judicial powers. The executive's role, Dickinson argued, was to execute the law. The judicial branch's was to interpret it. If there were a national legislature, he said, there ought to be a national judiciary as well. It was an argument that swayed many of the delegates and led to the founding of the third branch of government.[12]

Wilson went further than Dickinson, though, in his advocacy for a strong federal judiciary. Explaining the concept of judicial review to the convention, he proposed using the courts to keep Congress in check. As the branch of government closest to the democratic masses, the legislature was also the most dangerous. So it was crucial to create a Supreme Court that had the power to strike down not only unconstitutional laws passed by Congress, Wilson said, but also laws that ran counter to God's natural law.[13] "In the United States the legislative authority is subjected to another control, besides that which is arising from natural or revealed law," he wrote; "it is subjected to the control arising from the constitution."[14] It was a controversial subject from the beginning. Radicals despised the idea that a judge could reverse the will of a democratically elected legislature. Even those who mistrusted legislative power felt reluctant to give judges the right to decide the constitutionality of federal laws.

"The judges in England have no such additional provision for their defense," Nathaniel Gorham of Massachusetts objected, "yet their jurisdiction is not invaded."[15]

Rising to defend Wilson, Madison argued that a judicial check was essential, since the legislature had "a powerful tendency . . . to absorb all power into its vortex. This was the real source of danger to the American constitutions."[16]

Gouverneur Morris too backed Wilson, pointing out that since some check is "necessary on the legislature, the question is in what hands it should be lodged."[17] In Britain, the king had the authority to block dangerous legislation, he said, but in America the executive was bound to be far weaker.

Knowing the opposition he faced, Wilson was careful not to push too hard for an active judiciary. A judge had to remain "prudent and cautious." Above all, he had to "remember, that his duty and his business is, not to make the law, but to interpret and apply it."[18] It was even possible, Wilson added, that "laws may be unjust, may be unwise, may be dangerous, may be destructive; and yet not be so unconstitutional as to justify the judges in refusing to give them effect."[19]

On July 23, after a heated debate, Wilson's motion to incorporate judicial review into the constitution lost by a single vote. It would be for the Supreme Court, to which Wilson would be appointed two years later, to establish the principle as an integral part of its constitutional role.

The debate over what sort of executive America would have was perhaps the most acrimonious of the convention. The subject was raised at the start of June and would not be settled until September. "This subject has greatly divided the House," Wilson commented, "and will also divide the people out of doors. It is in truth the most difficult of all on which we have had to decide."[20]

It should hardly be surprising that the issue sowed such discord. The United States was founded by men who feared tyranny. How they feared it, though, was largely what differentiated them politically. While conservatives tended to fear it more in the legislature, for the left nothing was more terrifying than the prospect of an executive tyranny in America. A war, after all, had been fought to end the authority of the Crown. Could a president now be entrusted with great power, no matter how circumscribed? The question proved so divisive that many on the right felt conflicted about it as well.

The controversy began on Friday, June 1, when Wilson moved that "the executive consist of a single person." Charles Pinckney of South Carolina seconded the motion. Then "a considerable pause" followed, so shocked were the delegates by the proposal. Finally the elderly Franklin spoke, asking to hear the opinions of others before the motion was voted on.

Rutledge rose to oblige him. He said he was in favor of "vesting the executive power in a single person," but he opposed "giving him the power of war and peace. A single man would feel the greatest responsibility and administer the public affairs best." But war powers, he believed, remained the prerogative of the legislature.

Edmund Randolph, who had first proposed Madison's Virginia Plan, vehemently opposed the idea. A "unity in the executive," he declared, was "the fetus of monarchy." Though he believed in an executive that possessed "vigor, dispatch, and responsibility," he did not see why such powers could not be entrusted to a three-person committee, rather than a single man. To him, Wilson's proposal reminded him too closely of the government of Great Britain.

On the contrary, countered Wilson, a single man would be "the best safeguard against tyranny."[21] Again he insisted he had no desire to copy the British system of government. In response to William Paterson's calls for a plural executive, Wilson delivered one of the most pithy comments of the convention: "In order to control the legislative authority you must divide it. In order to control the executive, you must unite it."[22] Otherwise, he believed, no single person would be held accountable for the actions of government.

Before tensions grew too strained, the delegates agreed to postpone any vote on the question. Debate continued through the next day, and at last they came to a consensus on one point. The United States would have some form of executive, the delegates agreed. Under the Articles of Confederation, there was none. But progress remained slow. Dickinson too initially opposed a single executive, and many continued to respect his opinion. As the former president of Pennsylvania's Executive Council, he believed a plural executive could function admirably if properly structured. Wilson soon convinced him, though, that a single executive would not be a threat to liberty.

The next day, Sunday, was warm and sunny, and the delegates looked forward to their day of rest. Most attended church in the morning and in the afternoon enjoyed a hearty dinner. Wilson could not help feeling anxious about the debate he knew he would lead the next day. That evening he retired to his library to consult the works of the great political philosophers, taking notes and jotting down quotations from Locke, Montesquieu, and the thinkers of the Scottish Enlightenment to sprinkle into his arguments.

The weather remained fair and fresh on Monday morning as the delegates made their way to the Assembly room, many stopping to chat or smoke before resuming their deliberations. Wilson was the first man to speak. And he was eloquent. Recalling the fear of monarchy that resonated from the earliest days of the Revolution, Wilson argued that there was still more danger from a weak executive. What's more, the American people understood the difference between a king and a "single magistrate." Almost all the states, in fact, had created constitutions with single executives. Finally he expressed his fears that members of a plural executive would fight among themselves, leading to "uncontrolled, continued, and violent animosities." As they vied for power, they "would not only interrupt the public administration, but diffuse their poison through the other branches of government, through the states, and at length through the people at large."[23] He recalled how in ancient Rome Caesar had outmaneuvered his two other triumviri.

Over George Mason's objections that the convention was establishing "a more dangerous monarchy, an elective one," the delegates now took a vote.[24] Wilson's arguments had proven persuasive, and the convention made its first substantial decision. By a vote of seven to three, the executive of the United States would be a single person. The dispute over the executive, however, was just beginning.

The question of whether to give the executive a veto again threw the convention into an uproar. When Wilson proposed giving the president an absolute check against Congress, Roger Sherman immediately opposed the idea. "No man," he said, "could be found so far above all the rest in wisdom."[25] Many still recalled how colonial governors had abused their veto powers, but Gouverneur Morris ridiculed this opposition. "We form a strong man to protect us," he said, "and at the same time wish to tie his hands behind him."[26] In the end the delegates compromised, allowing a presidential veto but giving a two-thirds majority of Congress the ability to override it.

Finally the question of how to elect the president proved to be the most contentious of all. Many representatives of the small states wanted Congress to appoint the executive. If he were not "absolutely dependent" on the legislature, Sherman feared, the executive would become "the very essence of tyranny."[27] Dickinson, on the other hand, was adamant that the executive should be independent. Wilson agreed, and on June 1 he proposed what was one of the most revolutionary motions of the entire convention. The president, he said, should be elected directly by the people. If the legislature derived its authority from the people, he believed, the executive should too.

It was a curious situation. Those on the left were arguing against greater democracy, while many on the right wanted to see increased political participation. Again, the explanation for this seeming contradiction came down to a fundamental disagreement over whether Congress or the president represented the greater threat to liberty. A vigorous executive, Gouverneur Morris told the convention, would "be the guardian of the people, even of the lower classes, against legislative tyranny."[28] Wilson held that the president must be "a man of the people."[29]

But with many delegates dead set against popular elections, conservatives immediately saw that compromise was the only way around the impasse. On June 2, Wilson proposed an unusual mechanism: an extra electoral layer inserted between the president and the people. First the states would be divided into districts. Then qualified voters would select special electors, who would then choose the executive. It was the first draft of what would become the Electoral College. Although Maryland and Pennsylvania supported the idea immediately, the motion failed without much debate.

But no one else had a better idea. Discussion of the issue subsided for a while; then in mid-July Gouverneur Morris raised it again. He could see "no alternative," he said, "for making the executive independent of the legislature, but either to give him his office for life, or make him eligible by the people."[30] And no delegate wanted the president to serve for life—except Alexander Hamilton, who had proposed the idea.

Dickinson now rose to give an impassioned speech against legislative appointment of the president. Suddenly Wilson's proposal for an Electoral College seemed inspired, and the convention began to reexamine the idea. A compromise seemed to be within reach when the delegates agreed that the state legislatures, not the people, would choose the presidential electors, but it was not until September 6 that the details were finally worked out.

The last major area of controversy, and in the long run the most malignant, was slavery, the fatal wedge that split the founding conservatives. They had stuck together through war and economic chaos. They had maintained solidarity in the face of radical intrigue, mob violence, and British depredation. But the divide between North and South proved too great to overcome.

More than 600,000 slaves lived in the United States, over half a million of them in the South. Northern states had slaves as well; New York had 23,000,

New Jersey 11,000, and Pennsylvania 8,000. New England states as well kept blacks in chains. Opposition to slavery, however, was slowly growing, and it was northern conservatives who took the lead.

Despite owning slaves himself, John Jay, along with Gouverneur Morris, had already founded one of the first abolition societies in America and as early as 1777 had drafted legislation in New York to abolish slavery. Wilson too was an outspoken opponent of slavery, despite being a slave owner as well. Not only was slavery "unauthorized by the common law," he wrote, "it is repugnant to the principles of natural law, that such a state should subsist in any social system."[31]

By the time of the convention, Dickinson had already freed all his slaves and was urging the delegates to discourage slavery in any form. Gouverneur Morris too had manumitted his slaves. Of all the delegates, he was perhaps the most outspoken critic of the slave trade, which, "in defiance of the most sacred laws of humanity," he said at the start of August, "tears away his fellow creatures from their dearest connections and damns them to the most cruel bondages."[32] Not only was slavery morally repugnant to Morris, it perpetuated the agrarian economic system that he wished to replace with an industrial one.

The problem for northern abolitionists was that representatives from the Deep South had made it clear at the outset that they would march out of the convention and out of the United States should any constitutional prohibitions against slavery be passed. Rutledge insisted on looking at slavery from a purely economic perspective. "Religion and humanity had nothing to do with this question," he told the delegates. "Interest alone is the governing principle with nations."[33]

Morris was ready to see the South go. If "the southern gentlemen" persisted in these threats, he said, "let us at once take a friendly leave of each other."[34] Dickinson was more practical. He thought the southerners were bluffing, but recognizing the need for compromise, he moved that Congress should be barred from prohibiting the importation of slaves for another twenty years. The measure passed, leaving Wilson feeling ambivalent. Although the Constitution did not outlaw the slave trade, as he had hoped, it did allow Congress the power to do so after 1808. The clause, he said, laid "the foundation for the banishing of slavery out of this country."[35]

Dickinson for his part was appalled that the word *slave* never actually appeared in the Constitution. He thought the verbal contortions used to avoid it were hypocritical and made a motion to substitute the actual words *the slave trade* and avoid what he saw as ugly euphemisms. "The omitting of this word will be regarded as an endeavor to conceal a principle of which we are ashamed," he said.[36] His motion was unanimously rejected.

As a slave owner himself, Madison was torn between his allegiance to the South and his belief in a strong federal government. Recognizing that the North outnumbered the South in terms of both population and number of states, he feared the federal government might be used to harm southern interests. "The real difference of interests lay, not between the large and small but between the Northern and Southern states," he said in the middle of July. "The institution of slavery and its consequences formed the line of discrimination."[37]

To compensate for their disadvantage, Madison suggested having one house elected only by free people and the other be granted representation "according to the whole number counting the slaves as if free." Rutledge, for his part, was adamant that property be counted in apportioning representation, arguing that slaves should be counted as wealth. His beliefs were not without precedent. The South Carolina constitution already factored in wealth when distributing political power. And "property," Rutledge insisted, "was certainly the principal object of society."[38]

Gouverneur Morris would have none of it. Why should slaveholders be shown special treatment? he asked. If one special interest were given preference in the Constitution, all should be. "Why then is no other property included?" he asked. "The houses in [Philadelphia] are worth more than all the wretched slaves which cover the rice swamps of South Carolina."[39]

Wilson's solution was to propose counting three-fifths of a state's slave population for the purposes of assessing representation. It was the same formula the Articles of Confederation had used, and the South Carolina delegates at last were satisfied. Morris's objections notwithstanding, the measure passed. With the three-fifths compromise, he said in disgust, he was "reduced to the dilemma of doing justice to the Southern States or to human nature."[40]

At last by September 8, the delegates had ironed out their major disagreements. It was time to put the Constitution into its final form, and for that purpose a five-man committee was appointed to "revise the style" and "arrange the articles." Although Madison and Hamilton were also assigned to the committee, responsibility for the actual phrasing of the document fell to Gouverneur Morris, who had been elected chairman largely for his well-known dexterity with words. It was he who "wrote" the Constitution.

It took him four days to complete the task, but it was not just the speed with which he worked that left the other delegates speechless. Morris had cleaned up the grammar, reduced wordiness, condensed the number of articles from twenty-three to seven, and composed the Constitution in a graceful style that was almost modern in its simplicity and force. It also had flair. Perhaps his most important literary contribution was that he made the Constitution sound as though lawyers hadn't written it. "Having rejected redundant and equivocal terms," Morris later said, "I believed it to be as clear as our language would permit."[41]

For the most part, Morris stayed within the parameters set by the convention, but he took enough liberties with the document to leave his own indelible stamp on it. Most significant, he subtly altered the language of the Constitution to advance the cause of conservatism and promote the interests of American business. "Conflicting opinions had been maintained with so much professional astuteness," Morris wrote, "that it became necessary to select phrases, which expressing my own notions would not alarm others."[42]

In Article VI, for example, Morris changed the basis of the federal government's power. It went from being "the supreme law of the several states" to "the supreme law of the land," emphasizing the authority of the central government over the states. He made it clear that the federal government was responsible for all government debts incurred before the Constitution was written as well as after, ensuring the new government's financial credibility abroad. He streamlined the "full faith and credit" clause in Article IV, obliging the states to respect one another's laws. And in Article II he left the language governing the judiciary deliberately vague, allowing Congress to set up the Supreme Court through the Judiciary Act of 1789 and leaving later courts free to establish the principle of judicial review.

Some of Morris's changes were caught, as when he tried adjusting punctuation to suit his political views in Article I, Section 8. When given to the Committee of Style, this section had read, "The legislature shall have power to lay and collect taxes, duties, imposts and excises, to pay the debts and provide for the common defense and general welfare of the United States."[43] In order to enlarge the powers of Congress, Morris changed the comma after "excises" to a semicolon.

In the original draft, everything after the comma simply modified "excises." In Morris's version, everything after the semicolon now became a new "distinct power of Congress," as Albert Gallatin, Jefferson's future secretary of the treasury, commented.[44] The "trick," as it was called, was spotted by Roger Sherman, who insisted the semicolon revert to a comma.

Morris's most audacious alteration, one that Wilson helped him compose, slipped through. In Article I, Section 10, Morris inserted a short clause with far-reaching consequences. It stated that no state could pass a law "impairing the obligation of contracts."[45] Morris had in mind the travails of the Bank of North America when he added this line, but its inclusion in the Constitution would have profound effect on all American commerce. The term *contract* did not, in fact, come from British common law, which preferred the term *conveyance*. In England, however, the word *conveyance* did not carry the same binding sense as the American word *contract*. In many ways, the Contract Clause, as it came to be called, was a uniquely American invention, and a conservative one at that. At a time when most of America remained precapitalistic, the Contract Clause paved the way for the sort of market-based economy that Morris and the other founding conservatives wished to establish.

The most beautiful part of the Constitution was undoubtedly Morris's preamble, fifty-two words of political poetry. The draft he received from the convention began with a repetitious list: "We the people of the States of New Hampshire, Massachusetts, Rhode Island . . . Connecticut," and so on all the way south to Georgia, "do ordain, declare, and establish the following Constitution for the government of ourselves and our posterity."[46]

Morris changed this to something far more mellifluous and meaningful, a miniature essay on the basic intent and noble aspirations of American government. He used internal rhymes and felicitous alliteration to make his words ring. Most significant was his opening phrase, which reaffirmed federal authority. The people as a whole and not the separate states, Morris was saying, constituted the United States of America:

> We the people of the United States in order to form a more perfect union, to establish justice, insure domestic tranquility, provide for the common defense, promote the general welfare, and secure the blessings of liberty to ourselves and our posterity, do ordain and establish this Constitution for the United States of America.

Not all the delegates were pleased with the document they had labored four months to complete. George Mason refused to sign the Constitution, certain it would "end either in monarchy, or a tyrannical aristocracy."[47] So too did Governor Randolph of Virginia. Connecticut's Elbridge Gerry, who also declined to sign, went so far as to propose incorporating plans for a second convention to address the shortcomings of the first. He was unanimously voted down. The nation, the other delegates felt, would be so disappointed if this convention failed that they doubted a second one would do any better. There would be no second chances.

Fearing that many of the delegates had mixed feelings, Morris wrote a short speech for Franklin to read, urging them to support the new Constitution, whatever their misgivings. He knew that many mistrusted him, but all looked up to the eighty-one-year-old Dr. Franklin. Morris also shrewdly ended the document with the words, "Done in convention by the unanimous consent of the states present." It was a rhetorical sleight of hand, designed to allow all of the delegates to sign the new constitution. Even those who objected to the finished document could still concede that their state's delegation had approved it.

On Monday, September 17, the delegates assembled for the final time. With feelings of exhaustion, trepidation, and satisfaction, they scratched their signatures onto the animal-skin parchment before them. Dickinson, who had refused to endorse the Declaration of Independence, again missed his chance to sign his name. Plagued by ill health, he had left two days earlier for Wilmington to recuperate. His name did appear, however. Before leaving, he had asked George Read to sign for him.

To toast their triumph, the delegates repaired to the City Tavern, where musicians serenaded them and mugs overflowed with Madeira, claret, porter, beer, and punch. After dining together, the delegates "took cordial leave of each other," Washington reported.

The old general then returned to Robert Morris's home to review papers and "meditate on the momentous work which had been executed."[48] At one p.m. the following day, Morris served a small final dinner to Washington and Gouverneur Morris. After their meal, the three friends rode together to Gray's Ferry on the Schuylkill River, where they bade each other farewell. The younger Morris turned his horse northward to return to New York. Washington steered south toward Mount Vernon. After watching his old comrades depart, Robert Morris returned home. A new nation awaited him.

EPILOGUE

With the death of John Jay in May 1829, the last of the founding conservatives finally passed away, but the America of their birth had long since disappeared. What had started as thirteen British colonies huddling on the edge of the Atlantic seaboard had blossomed into twenty-four bustling states expanding ever westward. Commerce was booming as steamships, canals, and railroads penetrated deep into the continent. The Missouri Compromise, which split the nation into slave and free states, was already almost a decade old, and South Carolina was provoking a constitutional crisis by claiming the right to nullify federal law. Andrew Jackson, a hero to the common man and "King Mob" to early nineteenth-century conservatives, had been elected president the year before, and two new political parties, the Democratic Party and the National Republican Party, were vying for power. It was a nation many of the founding conservatives would have found alien, exciting, and lucrative. The United States was becoming the flourishing "empire" they had long before envisioned. One thing hadn't changed, though. The debate over inequality was still every bit as divisive as it had been during the Revolution.

Economic disparity was among the issues foremost on James Madison's mind that year when he made one of the most astonishing predictions in recorded history. At a convention to amend Virginia's state constitution in December 1829, he estimated that within "a century or a little more" America would face unprecedented economic and social upheaval.[1] The seventy-eight-year-old former president could scarcely have pictured American society on the eve of the Great Depression, but he had long been certain that rising inequality would lead to "a dependence of an increasing number on the wealth of a few." Extrapolating from population trends, he calculated that in roughly a hundred years the nation's supply of free land would run out, leading the majority of Americans to be "without landed or other equivalent property and without the means or hope of acquiring it." At this point, he said, the country would be split into "wealthy capitalists" and "indigent laborers" who worked for them.[2]

Madison shuddered to think what this development would mean for America. He had no doubt it would spell the end of virtue, and for someone raised on classical political theory, that portended the death of the republic.[3] Though 1929 may have seemed distant to men in frock coats and breeches, Madison insisted the date was not "too remote to claim attention."[4] It was a problem that had concerned him as far back as 1792, when he proposed laws that would "reduce extreme wealth towards a state of mediocrity" and help prevent "unnecessary opportunities" for the "accumulation of riches."[5] At the time, however, there had been little he could do to put such statutes into effect. Conservatives had seen to that.

For more than a decade after the ratification of the Constitution, conservatives were ascendant. During the presidencies of George Washington and John Adams, many of them joined the new Federalist Party, which viewed the Constitution as "a splendid opportunity to attempt traditional Court politics on a continental scale," as the historian John M. Murrin has written.[6] Continuing the policies of Robert Morris from the previous decade, Washington's young treasury secretary, Alexander Hamilton, established the Bank of the United States, a funded federal debt, and a powerful central government. Above all, Federalists supported the creation of large concentrations of capital.

Washington had, in fact, hoped Robert Morris would serve as his new treasury secretary, but Morris turned his old friend down. He had no desire to be a lightning rod for political controversy anymore. "I can recommend a far cleverer fellow than I am for your minister of finance," he told Washington, "in the person of your former aide-de-camp, Colonel Hamilton." Washington expressed surprise that Hamilton "had any knowledge of finance," but Morris assured the president-elect of the young man's abilities.[7]

Opposing the Federalist Party was America's first national opposition party, the Democratic-Republicans. Founded by Jefferson and Madison, the Democratic-Republicans epitomized Country Whig politics, championing an agrarian economy dominated by small yeoman farmers. Like the radicals during the Revolution, the Democratic-Republicans fully supported American trade and commerce. What they feared was the sort of centralized power and monopolistic capitalism advocated by the Federalists.

Over the past few decades, historians have noted the "quite startling extent" to which the conflict between Federalists and Democratic-Republicans was "a replay of the debates of the Court and Country as much as a hundred years before."[8] Yet as much as scholars express their astonishment at these similarities, Americans at this time were well aware of them: Democratic-Republican writers attacked Hamilton's economic program as "a funding system aided by a British influence and directed by another Walpole [Britain's Court Whig prime minister]."[9] The fact is, however, that this conflict between Country and Court ideas did not begin in the 1790s. It was a direct continuation of the battles between radicals and conservatives during the Revolution.[10]

While the politics of the early nineteenth century lie beyond the scope of this book, the fate of the Federalist Party is worth keeping in mind, since it is instructive for conservatives in any age. During Washington's administration, the party's hold on power had seemed unassailable, but by the time John Adams came into office in 1797, the popular tide was turning against it. The Federalists lost the presidency after Adams's single term and never regained it. Then they lost control of Congress. And though they controlled the judicial branch under Chief Justice John Marshall, by 1815 the party had essentially disintegrated. Its demise stemmed largely from its slowness in abandoning elitist politics and accepting America's increasingly democratic ethos.[11] It had, in other words, forgotten one of the key lessons conservatives had gleaned during the Revolution: adapt to change or risk irrelevance.

The fortunes of many of the founding conservatives paralleled those of the Federalist Party. After an initial period of glory, their long decline began. Alexander Hamilton, for example, followed this trajectory all too closely. He played a significant role in the battle to ratify the Constitution, his greatest contribution being the *Federalist Papers,* a series of essays defending America's new system of government. Enlisting John Jay and James Madison to help him with the project, Hamilton wrote fifty-one of the eighty-five essays, which helped turn public opinion in favor of the Constitution and became one of the most eloquent explanations of America's system of government ever penned. Persuaded by Hamilton's writings, as well as by his behind-the-scenes maneuvering, New York became the eleventh state to ratify the Constitution, by a vote of thirty to twenty-seven in July 1788.

Hamilton served as Washington's secretary of the treasury until 1795, when he was forced to resign in scandal. It was revealed not only that he had been cheating on his wife, Eliza Schuyler, but also that his lover and her husband had been blackmailing him to keep the affair secret. Publicly disgraced, Hamilton returned to the private practice of law. He remained active in national politics nonetheless, doing everything he could to sabotage John Adams's election as president, even though both men belonged to the same political party. The former treasury secretary had never liked Adams, believing him to be "out of his senses," as Franklin had put it, and he mistrusted the New Englander's former radicalism.[12] He failed to stop Adams in 1796, but in 1800 he sowed so much discord among Federalists that Jefferson was able to snag the presidency in a heavily contested election.

Hamilton's political machinations caused him increasing trouble. In 1804 his public feud with Aaron Burr, Jefferson's vice president, grew so heated that the two men agreed to a duel in Weehawken, New Jersey, on the same spot where Hamilton's oldest son, Philip, had been killed in another duel three years earlier. Hamilton reportedly missed Burr deliberately, but his opponent was less gracious. Hamilton was mortally wounded and ferried back to New York City. Hearing the news, Gouverneur Morris rushed to his friend's side, staying with him until he died the next day. It was, Morris wrote, "a most melancholy scene—his wife almost frantic with grief, his children in tears, every person present deeply afflicted, the whole city agitated."[13] Morris delivered the eulogy at the funeral and arranged for wealthy friends to pay off Hamilton's sizable debts, which totaled nearly $100,000.

Despite turning down Washington's offer of the Treasury Department, Robert Morris did agree to serve in the United States Senate from 1789 to 1795, helping advance the Federalist economic platform. At the same time, Morris continued to invest heavily in land, borrowing and spending freely. He began building himself the most sumptuous house in Philadelphia, a marble palace designed by the French architect Pierre L'Enfant, who designed Washington, D.C. The project, which Morris never finished, put him so heavily in debt that it was soon dubbed "Morris's folly." Washington urged Morris to rein in his spending, but the merchant replied, "My dear general, I can never do things in the small; I must be either a man or a mouse."[14] Unfortunately for Morris, war in Europe sparked a cascade of business failures across America. Morris's ventures, heavily financed by debt, were among those worst hit. His former business associate, Carter Braxton of Virginia, sued him for tens of thousands of pounds but died penniless in 1797 when he was unable to recoup any money. Braxton's claim, however, was the least of Morris's troubles. His debts now reached into the millions of dollars, and by the late 1790s the former Financier was hounded by lawsuits.

Yet ever hopeful of a turnaround, Morris continued to speculate in western land, buying tens of thousands of acres in Ohio and Virginia. Morris's lawyer, John Marshall, tried desperately to protect his client, but at last the sheer volume of lawsuits overwhelmed him. Morris, who finally realized that his arrest was imminent, took to hiding out in his country estate, The Hills. "My money is gone; my furniture is to be sold; I am going to go to prison and my family to starve," he wrote to a business partner. "Good night."[15] When angry creditors finally besieged him there, Morris barred his front door, communicating only through a bucket he lowered from his second-floor window. In 1798 he finally left The Hills when Philadelphia's sheriff came to escort him to debtors' prison. The collapse of Morris's financial empire caused a minor economic meltdown in the city, as dozens of creditors were wiped out along with him.

Morris tried to keep up his spirits while imprisoned, but slowly his health deteriorated. Washington visited his friend once, dining with him in his cell. Gouverneur Morris, to whom he owed $24,000, visited his old patron as well, forgiving the debt and raising a small annuity for Morris's wife, which allowed her to rent a small house in Philadelphia. In August 1801, after three and a half years in prison, Morris was released a broken man. "I now find myself a free citizen of the United States," he wrote, "without one cent that I can call my own."[16] He tried unsuccessfully to rebuild his reputation and attempted to reenter government service, traveling to Washington, D.C., to dine with Jefferson and Madison, who were, he reported, "very polite, very attentive, but that is all."[17]

When Morris passed away in May 1806, his will expressed his "regret at having lost a very large fortune acquired by honest industry." But, he acknowledged stoically, "Fate has determined otherwise and we must submit to the decree, which I have done with patience and fortitude."[18] Morris's services to the nation have been largely forgotten today, but his presence can still be felt in the heart of American government. In 1865 his image was enshrined on the ceiling of the Capitol's rotunda in Washington, D.C. Seated on a throne to Morris's right is Mercury, the god of profit and trade, handing him a bag of gold.

After the rigors of the Constitutional Convention, Gouverneur Morris decided to take a break from politics. He turned down Hamilton's plea to contribute to the *Federalist Papers* and headed south to represent Robert Morris's tobacco interests. The following year the elder Morris sent him on business to France, where he fell in love with the country's wine and cuisine. France held other allures as well. Soon after his arrival, he began an affair with Adèle de Flahaut, the twenty-eight-year-old wife of a royal official, not minding that she also happened to be mistress to Charles Maurice de Talleyrand, one of France's most powerful statesmen.

Morris's cozy relationship with the French aristocracy and his naturally elitist disposition led him to regard the onset of the French Revolution with horror. He began advising Louis XVI, composing speeches for him, and writing a new constitution for France modeled after America's but substituting a king for a president. In early 1792, Washington appointed Morris the U.S. minister to France, over the loud objections of Democratic-Republicans. In Congress, James Monroe called Morris a "monarchy man."[19] He was not incorrect. In addition to his diplomatic duties, Morris did everything he could to assist the French King, safeguarding one million *livres* for him and organizing an escape plan for the royal family that involved bribing French soldiers. Morris's efforts, however, could not prevent Louis's beheading on January 21, 1793. After being arrested several times himself and witnessing far too many guillotinings, Morris decided it was time for him to leave France. He took an extended tour of the Continent and England, finally returning to New York at the end of 1798.

During the presidential election of 1800, Morris's old friend Robert Livingston was convinced that Morris could have won had he run; Jefferson, after all, only narrowly eked out a victory. Instead, Morris was content to join the U.S. Senate, where he did his best to promote the moribund Federalist cause. Though he supported Jefferson's Louisiana Purchase in 1803, he was increasingly irritated by Democratic-Republican policies. By the outbreak of the War of 1812 during Madison's presidency, Morris had become so frustrated that he supported New England Federalists in their attempt to secede. The Union he had helped create in 1787 now seemed to be entirely lacking. Morris nonetheless continued to believe in America's greatness and became one of the main backers of the Erie Canal, which he saw as a powerful means for boosting American commerce.

In the last years of his life, Morris finally renounced his long-cherished bachelorhood and married his housekeeper, Anne (Nancy) Cary Randolph, a cousin of Thomas Jefferson's who had fled Virginia surrounded by scandal. Morris became a father at the age of sixty-one and lived another three years. Though his debts were sizable, he managed to leave his widow Morrisania, his grand estate in the South Bronx, and an annuity of $2,600 per year. His will stipulated that should she find a new husband, her bequest would be increased to $3,200. Anne never remarried.

* * *

John Jay became one of the most lauded and vilified of the founding conservatives. He contributed several essays to the *Federalist Papers* and at the same time continued to run the remnants of America's old government until the members of the first Congress of the United States took their seats in 1789. Jay declined the position of secretary of state but did allow Washington to appoint him chief justice of the Supreme Court. In 1795 he resigned from the Court, when Washington sent him to England as chief negotiator for a new treaty between the United States and Great Britain. After a decade of peace, the two countries were edging back toward war, as Americans grew more outraged by the British practice of capturing American ships and "impressing" their sailors into the Royal Navy against their will. Jay's main goals, which were backed by Hamilton and Washington, were to get British forces to abandon fortresses they continued to occupy on American territory, end impressment, and secure compensation for roughly three thousand slaves who had been carried away during the War of Independence.

The British proved tough negotiators, and Jay was forced to make several major concessions. Although Britain agreed to pull its forces from American soil the following year and to compensate the United States for the ships it had seized, it did not agree to stop impressing American sailors and refused to pay for any slaves Redcoats had led to freedom. Federalists were generally pleased with the terms of Jay's Treaty, which opened British ports to American shipping and secured valuable trade agreements. The Democratic-Republicans were horrified, viewing it as a sell-out to mercantile interests. Southerners were especially incensed by Jay's willingness to drop the issue of slavery.

Jay returned to New York City on May 28, 1795, greeted by cheering throngs, pealing church bells, and ceremonial cannonades. He also discovered that in his absence he had been nominated and elected to the governorship of New York. But when details of his treaty leaked out a month later, the praise quickly turned to obloquy. Throughout the United States, his effigy was burned, guillotined, and blown up. He was depicted holding a pair of scales with a bag of gold on one side and his treaty on the other. From his mouth came the words "Come up to my price, and I will sell you my country." One sign in Massachusetts proclaimed, "Damn John Jay! Damn every one that won't damn John Jay!! Damn every one that won't put lights in his windows and sit up all night damning John Jay!!!"[20] Newspaper editors called for him to be murdered in gruesome ways, and Hamilton was stoned trying to defend the treaty in public. Over Madison's bitter objections in Congress, Washington nevertheless managed to push through the treaty, but the controversy continued to fester for years.

Jay's governorship proved relatively placid. He turned down John Adams's offer to return him to the Supreme Court and in 1801 retired from politics to his eight-hundred-acre estate in Bedford, New York. "Party feuds give me concern," Jay wrote in 1808, "but they seldom obtrude upon me."[21] He lived for another twenty-one years, watching American society alter beyond recognition and tending quietly to his farm.

Like his son-in-law Alexander Hamilton, Philip Schuyler was a devoted Federalist, active in both national and New York State politics throughout the 1790s. He served in the U.S. Senate from 1789 until 1791, when he lost his seat to his arch political enemy Aaron Burr, but he was elected to the New York State Senate the following year. Schuyler's tireless efforts to elect Jay governor of the state paid off in 1795, but by 1797 age and exhaustion led him to long for retirement. In addition to holding public office, Schuyler was president of two lock and navigation companies in upstate New York. With Gouverneur Morris, he had long championed the creation of canals, and his management of these companies proved deft and profitable. In March 1797, despite his growing fatigue, Schuyler accepted reappointment to the U.S. Senate—the chance to throw Burr out of office, apparently, was too good to pass up. But illness dogged the old general, and he resigned his seat the following year.

Out of office now, Schuyler did his best to stay active in the political scene, through letter writing and advice giving, but the steady erosion of Federalist power left him increasingly despondent. Deaths in his family were also a source of great disconsolation: only eight of his fifteen children had survived to adulthood. He grieved when his grandson Philip Hamilton was shot to death in 1801. He grew despondent when his wife passed away two years later, and when Burr took Alexander Hamilton's life in 1804, his sadness was all but unbearable.

In a letter to his daughter Eliza Hamilton after her husband's death, Schuyler begged God to remove "every thorn" that might block her family's "future path" and offered to help her in any way he could. "My dearly beloved child," he said, "how greatly do your affections, and those of my other children, sooth[e] and comfort me, and how sincerely do I reciprocate those affections." Schuyler died a few months later in November 1804. In a eulogy published a week later, the *Albany Gazette* noted that for all of Schuyler's many accomplishments, it remained difficult to draw "a full and complete portrait of this eminent man." It was likely, in fact, that the full measure of his greatness would never be known to posterity. "Even in history, something will be lost or defective," the paper wrote, "because genius . . . often pervades a system unseen . . . communicates in an influence that cannot be traced."[22]

After spearheading the ratification of the Constitution at South Carolina's ratifying convention in 1788, John and Edward Rutledge became loyal Federalists. The following year Washington appointed John to the Supreme Court. Many thought the president should have made him chief justice and told him so, but Washington had already decided to offer the position to John Jay. Asked his opinion on the matter, John Adams had told Washington: "if ability is to decide, take Rutledge—if politics, Jay."[23] Rutledge had been looking forward to "ease and retirement," but he accepted the post.[24] He had never let comfort stand in the way of duty. Riding the circuit proved hard on Rutledge's health, and in 1791 he was forced to step down. At the same time, he was gratified to be appointed chief justice of South Carolina. When Jay sailed for England four years later, Washington finally named Rutledge acting chief justice of the U.S. Supreme Court.

These plans were interrupted when news of Jay's Treaty reached South Carolina. Though the Rutledge brothers supported Federalist economic policies, they found themselves siding with the Democratic-Republicans in their condemnation of the treaty. As southerners, they deplored Jay's decision not to press for compensation for lost slaves. And like many of Jefferson's supporters, they too mistrusted growing federal power, especially when that power appeared to be used to advance northern interests. Though they remained suspicious of the democratic ideals espoused by the Democratic-Republican Party, they remained on good terms personally with Jefferson. Thus when Charleston exploded in fury when the treaty's terms became known, the Rutledges found themselves swept along in the outrage. Mobs roamed the streets, burning copies of the treaty and dragging charred remnants of the Union Jack in front of the British consul's residence. Jay and other northern Federalists were massacred in effigy.

At a public meeting on July 16, 1795, John Rutledge delivered a tirade against the treaty, calling Jay a "knave or fool."[25] Though he made an appeal for "a calm, firm and decisive line of conduct, and the most deliberate and cool discussion," he nonetheless declared that he had "rather the President should die, dearly as he loves him, than he should sign that treaty."[26] When word of Rutledge's nomination to the Supreme Court first came out, the Federalist press had hailed the southerner as a "true patriot." Then copies of his fiery speech arrived, and the praise turned into venomous attacks. Angry Jay supporters spread rumors that Rutledge was "deranged in his mind."[27]

In August, Rutledge arrived in Philadelphia, once again America's capital, and immediately took his seat on the Court. As acting chief justice, he was able to begin hearing cases, but he still had to be confirmed by the Senate. Rutledge ruled on two cases that summer, largely concurring with his fellow associates in his decisions. Then he traveled back south to preside over the Southern Circuit. In the meantime, the campaign against his confirmation grew. "C[hief] Justices must not go to illegal meetings and become popular orators in favor of sedition," declared John Adams, "nor inflame the popular discontents which are ill founded."[28] Federalist newspapers labeled Rutledge a drunkard, a deadbeat, and a madman. Although Democratic-Republican papers rushed to defend him, in truth a series of failed investments had caused his finances to crumble. His emotional health had begun suffering as a result. Yet Rutledge's judicial decisions during this period continued to be lucid and insightful, a reflection of his legal expertise and powerful intellect.

On December 15, by a four-vote margin, the U.S. Senate voted to reject Rutledge's nomination to the Supreme Court, viewing him as a "popular demagogue and disorganizer."[29] Rutledge would not know of the Senate's decision for several more weeks. But he was well aware that his nomination was likely to fail. Even Washington had ceased supporting him. Depressed over his mounting debt, the recent deaths of his wife and mother, and the assaults upon his honor—that most precious of commodities to a southern gentleman—Rutledge began to talk of taking his own life. His family kept close watch on him, but early one morning in late December he stole out of his house and walked into the Ashley River fully clothed.

Startled to see a man disappear under water, a young slave girl cried for help; a group of slaves on a nearby boat rushed to save him. "The fellows had the presence of mind to run with a boat hook and catch hold of his arm," reported one account. "He made violent opposition to them but they dragged him out and detained him by force, they calling for assistance, while he cursed and abused them."[30] Several days after the suicide attempt, Rutledge wrote a letter to Washington resigning as acting chief justice, saying he found himself "totally unequal to the discharge of the duties of the office." He still didn't know whether the Senate had rejected his nomination. Rutledge's mood improved for a while, but with his assets dwindling and creditors harassing him with lawsuits, he grew increasingly reclusive.

Edward Rutledge aided his brother as best he could, assuming some of his debts and harming his own solvency in the process. He remained active in politics, helping John's son win election to the U.S. House of Representatives and serving as governor of South Carolina in the late 1790s. Though Edward sided largely with Federalist policies, he remained independent enough to win the support of Democratic-Republicans as well. In January 1800 he suffered a severe stroke and died two weeks later. John was plunged into "the deepest melancholy" by the loss of his brother; his health deteriorated and he passed away on July 23.[31] He was sixty-one. South Carolina had lost its two leading conservatives, but conservatism itself did not disappear from the state. Incensed over John Rutledge's treatment by northern Federalists and increasingly suspicious of their economic policies, the southern right began adopting elements of Democratic-Republican thought, forging in the process a new type of southern conservative ideology that would leave a lasting imprint on American politics.[32]

Few men had played as great a role in the ratification of the Constitution as James Wilson. In the acrimonious aftermath of the convention, Wilson led Pennsylvania Federalists in a struggle so fierce that it dwarfed the earlier bank war and Silas Deane affair. Pamphlets, newspaper articles, and speeches for and against the Constitution barraged the citizens of the Keystone State. Throughout the state, fights and riots broke out after dark. Even getting the Assembly to call for a ratifying convention was fraught with trouble. In the end, Federalist mobs resorted to kidnapping radical assemblymen, who had been in hiding, and forcibly marching them to the State House in order to form a quorum.

At the ratifying convention, Wilson was the only delegate who had also attended the convention that had drawn up the Constitution, and he regaled his colleagues with his theory that ultimate political power resided in the people. In doing so, he laid out his vision of the thriving, capitalistic society that the new federal government would bring to America. On December 12, 1787, by a vote of 46 to 23, Pennsylvania became the second state to ratify the Constitution.

In 1790 Wilson turned his attention to the last bastion of radical power in Pennsylvania, the old state constitution of 1776. Along with other conservatives, he drummed up support for a new state constitutional convention, enlisting Pennsylvania's most talented writers to submit articles defending the idea. Thousands of handbills flooded the state. Tench Coxe, the economic visionary, composed four influential articles that circulated throughout the middle states, and Robert Morris declared that only a new constitution would be "capable of protecting life and property and of establishing a due execution of justice."[33] By the time the Assembly called for a new state convention, it had received ten thousand signatures supporting the idea. Opposition, however, remained fierce.

In November 1790, as the convention opened on the second floor of the State House, Wilson submitted his own draft for a new constitution. Though many of the delegates were radicals, Wilson had devised a shrewd plan to secure victory. He secretly met with the radical leader William Findley, who admitted he had never actually liked the old constitution. Wilson accepted several of Findley's suggestions. In return, the radical leader agreed to accept most of Wilson's draft. Over the next few weeks, the two put on a lively show for the other delegates, arguing points of law and the ends of government, but the result of the convention was now a foregone conclusion. A number of modifications were made to Wilson's draft, but when the convention adjourned on September 2, Pennsylvania now had an executive, a bicameral legislature, a clear separation of powers, and the protections for property and free markets Wilson had championed over the previous sixteen years.

Wilson remained active in national politics as well. He had written to Washington at the start of his presidency asking to be named chief justice of the Supreme Court. The President, aware of Wilson's towering debts and of the animosity he had aroused in Pennsylvania over the years, felt Wilson would be too controversial a choice. Instead he named Wilson an associate justice.

Wilson had remained unmarried after his wife Rachel died in 1782, but in the spring of 1793, riding the judicial circuit, he met a beautiful eighteen-year-old, Hannah Gray, in the pew next to his at the Brattle Street Church in Boston. Wilson was nearly thirty years older and already had six children, but he was smitten on the spot. The two married at the end of the summer and wintered in New York, where Wilson received bad news. Creditors were threatening to foreclose on his landholdings. The newlyweds raced back to Philadelphia in a blinding snowstorm to deal with the matter. But Wilson's financial empire was beginning to crash down around him, just as Hannah became pregnant.

Wilson owed the Bank of North America more than $70,000, and this was the least of his debts. Yet he continued to borrow money to invest. He built a series of water mills designed to power industrial looms that would weave hemp and flax into sails and other types of cloth. If successful, the investment would soon be netting over $100,000 a year. He built sawmills and continued to invest in land. By 1795, Wilsonville, the town he built, had grown to twenty-one houses and shops. His cloth mill, four stories tall, was already in operation, and one sawmill was producing 2,200 feet of board a day. And still Wilson kept borrowing, desperately trying to keep his creditors at bay.

When the financial crash of 1797 hit the nation, Wilson knew he was ruined. Most of his landholdings were seized, and he went into hiding at the Morris Tavern in Bethlehem. Fearing arrest, he pleaded unsuccessfully for his fellow justices to take over the Southern Circuit for him. Back in Philadelphia, his rent was unpaid and his children and young wife were going hungry. Venturing out one day, Wilson was caught by a creditor and thrown in prison. His eldest son managed to raise $600 to release him, but another creditor to whom Wilson owed close to $200,000 had him imprisoned again. Eventually Wilson got free and sped to North Carolina, where Hannah found him holed up at the seedy Horniblow Tavern in Edenton.

Once one of the most prosperous men in America, Wilson now looked gaunt and haunted. His clothes were stained and threadbare, and he spent long moments staring silently out the window, afraid to leave his room. In July he contracted malaria, and in the blistering heat, Hannah did her best to wipe away the sweat continually beading on her husband's brow. Wilson improved briefly, but then suffered a stroke. He began babbling incoherently about arrest, debt, and bankruptcy. Eating and sleeping little, Hannah sat by his side as he died over the next three days.

Hearing the news, Wilson's friend, Supreme Court Justice James Iredell, came and led Hannah away. Even in death, Wilson made enemies. His demise caused a string of bankruptcies among his business partners, even after most of his possessions were auctioned off. His remaining land went for £200,000, his judicial robes for $17, and his desk for $8. Someone paid $253.75 for his law library. The extensive collection included twelve copies of the Pennsylvania Constitution of 1790, Wilson's masterpiece.

That so many of the founding conservatives were torn apart by the very forces of capitalism they helped unleash should not have surprised them. At some level, all of them understood that the vagaries of the market were unpredictable. Yet even in the midst of losing their fortunes, none of them lost their confidence in America's endless capacity for economic growth. And that, in the end, was what the founding conservatives were truly investing in. Their expectations of profit were not misplaced, just mistimed, and had they been able to hold out longer, many of their investments would have paid off handsomely. For all the fears Madison expressed in 1829 that large-scale capitalism would destroy the nation, conservatives maintained their faith that this unwieldy engine of economic growth and destruction would ultimately make America not only more prosperous but also the most powerful nation on earth.

Nor did the downfall of the Federalist Party destroy the principles these men had fought for. Conservatism survived, altered but alive, for conservatism is an ideology larger than any single party. A number of the founding conservatives, in fact, joined the Democratic-Republicans, injecting into it an indelible strain of Federalism. For many entrepreneurs and merchants after 1800, Jefferson's party seemed to serve their interests better than Hamilton's. After helping Alexander Hamilton implement his economic plans at the Treasury Department, Tench Coxe, for example, switched parties, positioning himself to continue influencing national economic policy during the Jefferson administration. In a report to Congress in 1804, he urged the government to help America move to a "new and more exalted stage of industry." He was able to convince many Democratic-Republicans that "complex manufactures," were crucial for taking the nation to a higher "state of civil society."[34] As the first person to understand the importance of promoting the cotton industry and of smuggling British manufacturing technology into the United States, Coxe played a crucial role in the development of America's economy.

Robert Livingston too joined the Democratic-Republicans and became by the end of his life one of the most successful entrepreneurs and industrialists in American history. In March 1802 at a dinner party in Paris, where President Jefferson had sent him as the American minister plenipotentiary, Livingston met the American inventor Robert Fulton, who dazzled him with his ideas for building steamships. Livingston had already dabbled with steam-powered travel on the Hudson, only to be labeled an eccentric. But he had not given up his dreams. After negotiating the Louisiana Purchase with Napoleon, doubling the size of the United States, Livingston returned triumphantly to New York, where he launched a new steamship enterprise. The partnership he formed with Fulton soon turned into one of the most profitable monopolies in the nation, and the technology he owned transformed the vast new territory he had helped acquire.

Livingston did more, however, than just make money. He also showed conservatives the only path to electoral victory in a democratic society. As he wrote back in 1777 while trying to prevent a radical takeover of New York State, conservatives had to accept the "propriety of swimming with a stream which it is impossible to stem." They needed to "yield to the torrent if they hope to direct its course." Though he never sought higher office again, Livingston recognized that he owed much of his later success to this insight.

Last, none other than John Dickinson became a Democratic-Republican. After leading Delaware to become the first state to ratify the Constitution, he penned a series of essays supporting the Federalist cause. Named *Letters of Fabius,* after the Farmer's favorite Roman general, the essays had a greater impact in their day than the *Federalist Papers.* What made them so effective was that Dickinson was able to write in an idiom that appealed to ordinary Americans: he used the language of classical Country Whig republicanism while advancing Court Whig ideas. Writing of "vice," "corruption," and "tyranny," Dickinson convinced Americans to support a far more powerful, centralized government. As great politicians throughout American history have understood, the vocabulary of revolution is the key to electoral success. Yet Dickinson's arguments remained essentially conservative. He alluded to Burke, describing the Constitution as "ever new, and always the same," and extolling it as full of "animated moderation."[35] Most important, he emphasized that the Constitution was a natural outgrowth of history, not of theory.

Following the ratification of the Constitution, Dickinson was largely absent from politics. He was often tired and his health had never been good. He did become increasingly active in abolition, fearing that the extension of slavery into the Louisiana Territory would divide the nation but he refused offers of appointment to the U.S. Senate and the governorship of Delaware. Nonetheless, he continued to wield his pen in the service of his country, composing countless addresses and letters and corresponding frequently with President Jefferson on the pressing issues of the day.

Dickinson was especially discouraged by the Federalists' antagonism toward Jefferson, lamenting the fact that they were "incessantly agitated by a spirit of hostility" toward anyone who disagreed with them.[36] The Democratic-Republicans, Dickinson told Jefferson, had produced "peace and liberty."[37] America, to his great satisfaction, was becoming exactly the sort of nation he had envisioned four decades earlier in his Farmer's *Letters*—a land, as the Bible describes, where every man "should sit . . . under his vine, and under his fig tree, and none should make them afraid."

Dickinson only appeared to switch philosophies in the last years of his life. Once again, he stood firm, while America's political firmament wheeled around him. And though he and his fellow conservatives disagreed at times, all of them stayed true to their principles to the end, bending when they needed to but pursuing their greater goals steadfastly, with moral courage and physical valor. Together they founded a uniquely American type of conservatism, one that balanced respect for liberty and for property. Far from being monolithic in nature, their ideology was an amalgam of Court and Country ideas, embodying rich and variegated strands of political thought and containing within itself both the seeds of revolution and the strictures of order. Like Dickinson, their philosophy stands firm, an ever-faithful guide to the American right, a fixed point of wisdom and prudence for us all.

Acknowledgments

I feel immense gratitude to the many people who inspired, exhorted, and sustained me throughout the years I worked on this book: Bernadette Serton for her relentless encouragement and probing questions; Brooke Carey and Adrian Zackheim for their endless patience; Larry Kirshbaum for getting me started; Meg Thompson for picking up the torch; John Jay Iselin, who embodied the principles of his forebears; Jenny Corbett, whose question sent me to the library; Ruth Lim for moving to Australia; Iraj Kalkhoran; Holly Halmo; Erich Kunhardt; Kevin Baker; Gail Buckland; Tania Wildbill; David Hsu; David Wang; Maura McDermott; Jonathan Funke; Kelly Macmanus Funke; Doug McClellan; Priya Wadhera; Francis Lui; Livia Wan; Lawrence Lui; Anne Griffin; Jay Lefer; Ted Lefer; Connie Farmer; and of course Yvonne and Hugo, who make everything worth it. Thank you all.

NOTES

INTRODUCTION

1. "Copy of paper drawn up by Joseph Reed for W. Henry Drayton," n.d., in Maria Dickinson Logan Collection, Historical Society of Pennsylvania.
2. Moses Coit Tyler, *The Literary History of the American Revolution* (New York: G.P. Putnam's Sons, 1897), p. 2:24. The epithet was probably first used by the historian George Bancroft.
3. Richard Hofstadter to Jack Pole, April 30, 1962, quoted in Robert Allen Rutland, ed., *Clio's Favorites: Leading Historians of the United States, 1945–2000* (Columbia: University of Missouri Press, 2000), p. 74.
4. David Hackett Fischer notes the first American usage of *conservative* in *The Revolution of American Conservatism: The Federalist Party in the Age of Jeffersonian Democracy.* According to the OED, the word was first used in England in an article by J. Wilson Croker on January 1, 1830, in which he replaced the word *Tory,* which had then been in use for 150 years.
5. As Dickinson put it in 1775, "My principles were formed very early in the course of this unhappy controversy. I have not yet found cause to change a single iota of my political creed." "Notes for a Speech in Congress," May 23, 1775, in *Letters of Delegates to Congress, 1774–1789,* ed. Paul H. Smith et al. (Washington, D.C.: Library of Congress, 1976–2000), p. 1:378.
6. Quoted in H. Trevor Colbourn, "A Pennsylvania Farmer at the Court of King George: John Dickinson's London Letters, 1754–1756," *Pennsylvania Magazine of History and Biography* 86, no. 3 (July 1962), p. 449.

CHAPTER I: COURT AND COUNTRY

1. Edward Sheppard, *The Old Royal Palace of Whitehall* (London: Longmans, Green, 1902), p. 210.
2. Gordon S. Wood, *The Creation of the American Republic, 1776–1787* (Chapel Hill: University of North Carolina Press, 1969), p. 49.
3. Quentin Skinner, "The Republican Ideal of Political Liberty," in Gisela Bock, Quentin Skinner, and Maurizio Viroli, eds., *Machiavelli and Republicanism* (Cambridge: Cambridge University Press, 1990), p. 302.

4. John Milton, "A Defense of the People of England" (1651), in Steve Pincus, "Neither Machiavellian Moment nor Possessive Individualism: Commercial Society and the Defenders of the English Commonwealth," *American Historical Review* 103, no. 3 (1998), p. 710.
5. H. Trevor Colbourn, *The Lamp of Experience: Whig History and the Intellectual Origins of the American Revolution* (Chapel Hill: University of North Carolina Press, 1965), p. 26.
6. The Saxon myth, as it is now called, proved remarkably long-lived. As late as 1902, Woodrow Wilson said that the only examples of democracy he knew of existed in governments "begotten of English race" or where "the old Teutonic habit has had the same persistency as in England." Woodrow Wilson, "Democracy," in *Harper's Encyclopedia of United States History* (New York: Harper Bros., 1902), p. 3:73.
7. Three historians stand out as the founding fathers of the study of republicanism during the American Revolution: Bernard Bailyn, Gordon Wood, and J.G.A. Pocock, whose work in the 1960s and 1970s transformed the field.
8. The writings of Plato, Aristotle, Cicero, and Polybius were among those that described the revolutionary cycle of governments.
9. The political philosopher Harvey Mansfield describes this sense of virtue in his book *Manliness* (New Haven: Yale University Press, 2006).
10. J. G. A. Pocock, *Virtue, Commerce, and History: Essays on Political Thought and History, Chiefly in the Eighteenth Century* (Cambridge: Cambridge University Press, 1985), p. 48.
11. Jerry Z. Muller, *The Mind and the Market: Capitalism in Modern European Thought* (New York: Alfred A. Knopf, 2002), p. 15.
12. The most authoritative account of the birth of radicalism can be found in Michael Walzer's *The Revolution of the Saints: A Study in the Origins of Radical Politics* (Cambridge, Mass.: Harvard University Press, 1982).
13. *Correspondence of King George III,* ed. Sir John Fortescue (London: Macmillan, 1928), vol. 5, no. 2991, quoted in G. H. Guttridge, *English Whiggism and the American Revolution* (Berkeley and Los Angeles: University of California Press, 1942), p. 17.
14. One of the best summaries of the origins of capitalism can be found in George David Rappaport, *Stability and Change in Revolutionary Pennsylvania: Banking, Politics, and Social Structure* (University Park: Pennsylvania State University Press, 1996).
15. Public debt was invented in Venice and Florence during the Renaissance, but the interest-bearing *monti* created by these city-states operated on a far smaller scale.
16. J. G. A. Pocock, ed., *Three British Revolutions, 1641, 1688, 1776* (Princeton, N.J.: Princeton University Press, 1980), p. 270.
17. *The Works of Voltaire. A Contemporary Version,* trans. William F. Fleming (New York: E. R. DuMont, 1901), p. 11:155.
18. Adam Smith, *Theory of Moral Sentiments,* p. 3:456, in Susan E. Gallagher, *The Rule of the Rich? Adam Smith's Argument Against Political Power* (University Park: Pennsylvania State University Press, 1998), p. 84.
19. Quoted in Reed Browning, *Political and Constitutional Ideas of the Court Whigs* (Baton Rouge: Louisiana State University Press, 1982), p. 41.
20. Ibid., p. 176.

21. Thomas Horne, "Politics in a Corrupt Society: William Arnall's Defense of Robert Walpole," *Journal of the History of Ideas* 41, no. 4 (October–December 1980), p. 607.
22. Henry St. John, Viscount Bolingbroke, *A Dissertation upon Parties: In Several Letters to Caleb D'Anvers, Esq.*, 10th ed. (London: T. Davies, 1775), p. 275.
23. With literary giants like Alexander Pope and Jonathan Swift writing on its behalf, the Country usually won the rhetorical battles.
24. Edmund Burke, "Speech on Conciliation with the Colonies," March 22, 1775, in *The Works of the Right Honourable Edmund Burke* (London: Henry G. Bohn, 1854–56), p.1:467, online at http://press-pubs.uchicago.edu/founders.documents.vachas2.html.
25. Lance Banning, *The Jeffersonian Persuasion: Evolution of a Party Ideology* (Ithaca, N.Y.: Cornell University Press, 1978), p. 72.
26. Stanley Elkins and Eric McKitrick, *The Age of Federalism: The Early American Republic, 1788–1800* (New York: Oxford University Press, 1995), p. 14.
27. See Colbourn, *Lamp of Experience.*
28. Banning, *Jeffersonian Persuasion,* p. 138.

CHAPTER 2: NONE SHALL MAKE THEM AFRAID

1. John Dickinson, *Letters from a Farmer in Pennsylvania: To the Inhabitants of the British Colonies,* in *The Writings of John Dickinson: Political Writings, 1764–1774,* ed. Paul Leicester Ford (Philadelphia: Historical Society of Pennsylvania, 1895), p. 1:307.
2. Quoted in Milton E. Flower, *John Dickinson: Conservative Revolutionary* (Charlottesville: University of Virginia Press, 1983), p. 25.
3. Described in detail by F. P. Lock, *Edmund Burke* (Oxford: Oxford University Press, 1998), p. 1:67.
4. Dickinson quoted in H. Trevor Colbourn, "A Pennsylvania Farmer at the Court of King George: John Dickinson's London Letters, 1754–1756," [part 1], *Pennsylvania Magazine of History and Biography* 86, no. 3 (July 1962), p. 245.
5. Quoted in K. M. Rowland, *Life of Charles Carroll of Carrollton, 1737–1832, with his Correspondence and Public Papers* (New York: G. P. Putnam's Sons, 1898), pp. 1:53–54.
6. John Dickinson to his father, March 8, 1754, in Colbourn, "Pennsylvania Farmer," [part 1], p. 262.
7. Alexander Bregman, *Reading Under the Folds: John Dickinson, Gordon's Tacitus, and the American Revolution,* senior honors thesis, University of Pennsylvania, 2008, unpublished, http://repository.upenn.edu/hist_honors/16/.
8. John Dickinson to his father, March 8, 1754, in Colbourn, "Pennsylvania Farmer," [part 1], p. 257.
9. Quoted ibid.
10. Quoted in H. Trevor Colbourn, "A Pennsylvania Farmer at the Court of King George: John Dickinson's London Letters, 1754–1756," [part 2], *Pennsylvania Magazine of History and Biography* 86, no. 4 (October 1962), pp. 421–22.
11. John Dickinson to his father, June 6, 1756, ibid., p. 445.
12. John Dickinson to his mother, May 25, 1754, in Colbourn, "Pennsylvania Farmer," [part 1], p. 274.
13. John Dickinson to his father, May 25, 1754, ibid., p. 269.
14. John Dickinson to his mother, May 25, 1754, ibid., pp. 274–75.

15. Ibid., p. 274.
16. John Dickinson to his mother, September 14, 1763, quoted in Flower, *John Dickinson*, p. 25.
17. Edward Countryman, *The American Revolution* (New York: Hill & Wang, 2003), p. 61.
18. Quoted in Flower, *John Dickinson*, p. 38.
19. James E. Hutson, "The Campaign to Make Pennsylvania a Royal Province, 1764–1770, Part I," *Pennsylvania Magazine of History and Biography* 94, no. 4 (1970), p. 443.
20. Quoted in Flower, *John Dickinson*, p. 42.
21. Samuel Powel to George Roberts, November 24, 1764, in "Powel-Roberts Correspondence, 1761–1765," *The Pennsylvania Magazine of History and Biography* 18, no. 1 (1894), p. 40.
22. Quoted in Flower, *John Dickinson*, p. 44.
23. Edmund S. Morgan and Helen M. Morgan, *The Stamp Act Crisis: Prologue to Revolution* (Chapel Hill: University of North Carolina Press, 1995).
24. John E. Ferling, *The Loyalist Mind: Joseph Galloway and the American Revolution* (University Park: Pennsylvania State University Press, 1977), p. 23.
25. Caesar Rodney to Thomas Rodney, October 20, 1765, in *Letters to and from Caesar Rodney, 1756–1784*, ed. George W. Ryden (Philadelphia: Historical Society of Delaware, 1933), p. 26.
26. Quoted in Ross J. S. Hoffman, *Edmund Burke: New York Agent* (Philadelphia: American Philosophical Society, 1956), p. 34.
27. Quoted in Hutson, "Campaign to Make Pennsylvania a Royal Province," p. 41.
28. Quoted in Ferling, *Loyalist Mind*, p. 20.
29. John Dickinson, in *Writings of Dickinson*, p. 1:307.
30. Quoted in Moses Coit Tyler, *The Literary History of the American Revolution, 1763-1783* (New York: G.P. Putnam's Sons, 1897), p. 1:237.
31. John Dickinson, in *Writings of Dickinson*, p. 1:324.
32. John Dickinson to Arthur Lee, October 31, 1770, quoted in Richard Henry Lee, *Life of Arthur Lee* (Boston: Wells & Lilly, 1829), pp. 2:302–3.
33. John Dickinson to Thomas McKean, October 20, 1757, quoted in Flower, *John Dickinson*, p. 27.
34. John Dickinson, in *Writings of Dickinson*, p. 1:400.
35. John Dickinson, ibid., p. 1:338.
36. Forrest McDonald and Ellen Shapiro McDonald, *Requiem: Variations on Eighteenth-Century Themes* (Lawrence: University Press of Kansas, 1988), pp. 25-26.
37. Flower, *John Dickinson*, p. 76.
38. McDonald and McDonald, *Requiem*, p. 94.
39. John Dickinson, in *Writings of Dickinson*, p. 1:399.
40. John Dickinson to Arthur Lee, October 31, 1770, in Lee, *Life of Arthur Lee*, pp. 2:302–3.

CHAPTER 3: THE RISE OF RADICALISM

1. Edwin G. Burrows and Mike Wallace, *Gotham: A History of New York City to 1898* (New York: Oxford University Press, 1998), p. 202.

2. E. P. Thompson. "The Moral Economy of the English Crowd in the Eighteenth Century," *Past and Present* 50, no. 1 (1971), p. 76–136.
3. The historian Pauline Maier has done extensive research on the "quasi-institutional" nature of colonial rioting. See Maier, *From Resistance to Revolution: Colonial Radicals and the Development of American Opposition to Britain, 1765–1776* (New York: Alfred A. Knopf, 1972).
4. Quoted ibid., p. 24.
5. Gary J. Kornbluth and John M. Murrin, "The Making and Unmaking of an American Ruling Class," in Alfred F. Young, ed., *Beyond the American Revolution: Explorations in the History of American Radicalism* (DeKalb: Northern Illinois University Press, 1993), p. 28.
6. Alfred F. Young, ed., *The American Revolution: Explorations in the History of American Radicalism* (DeKalb: Northern Illinois University Press, 1976), p. x.
7. Young, *Beyond the American Revolution,* p. 134.
8. Burrows and Wallace, *Gotham,* p. 203.
9. Quoted in Allan Kulikoff, "The Revolution, Capitalism, and Formation of the Yeoman Classes," in Young, *Beyond the American Revolution,* p. 91.
10. "A Tradesman," in *Pennsylvania Packet,* April 1775, in Margaret Jacob and James Jacob, eds., *The Origins of Anglo-American Radicalism* (Winchester, Mass.: Allen & Unwin, 1983), p. 176.
11. Quoted in Moses Coit Tyler, *Patrick Henry* (Boston: Houghton Mifflin, 1899), p. 207.
12. Gordon S. Wood, *The Radicalism of the American Revolution* (New York: Alfred A. Knopf, 1992), p. 232.
13. Carl Becker, *The History of Political Parties in the Province of New York, 1760–1776* (Madison: University of Wisconsin Press, 1909), pp. 5, 22.
14. Merrill Jensen, *The Articles of Confederation: An Interpretation of the Social-Constitutional History of the American Revolution, 1774–1781* (Madison: University of Wisconsin Press, 1940), p. xxvii.
15. Young, *American Revolution;* Wood, *Radicalism of American Revolution;* and Gary B. Nash, *The Unknown American Revolution: The Unruly Birth of Democracy and the Struggle to Create America* (New York: Penguin Books, 2006).
16. Staughton Lynd, *Intellectual Origins of American Radicalism* (New York: Pantheon, 1968), and Michael Walzer *The Revolution of the Saints: A Study in the Origins of Radical Politics* (Cambridge, Mass.: Harvard University Press, 1982).
17. John R. Alden, *A History of the American Revolution* (New York: Alfred A. Knopf, 1969).
18. Sir Francis Bernard quoted in Moses Coit Tyler, *The Literary History of the American Revolution* (New York: G. P. Putnam's Sons, 1897), p. 2:3.
19. Samuel Adams to John Scollay, December 30, 1780, in *The Writings of Samuel Adams,* ed. Harry Alonzo Cushing (New York: G. P. Putnam's Sons, 1904–8), p. 4:238. See John K. Alexander, *Samuel Adams: America's Revolutionary Politician* (London: Rowman & Littlefield, 2002), p. 177.
20. *The Letters of John and Abigail Adams,* ed. Frank Shuffelton (New York: Penguin, 2004), p. xv; Benjamin Franklin to Samuel Adams, February 2, 1774, in Adams Papers, New York Public Library, quoted in *Bulletin of the New York Public Library* 1, no. 9 (September 1897), p. 244.

21. Quoted in John Ferling, *A Leap in the Dark: The Struggle to Create the American Republic* (New York: Oxford University Press, 2004), p. 107.
22. Benjamin Franklin to Samuel Adams, February 2, 1774, in *Bulletin of the New York Public Library* 1, no. 9 (September 1897), p. 244.
23. John Dickinson, *The Writings of John Dickinson: Political Writings, 1764–1774* (Philadelphia: Historical Society of Pennsylvania, 1895), p. 1:462.
24. Quoted in Milton E. Flower, *John Dickinson: Conservative Revolutionary* (Charlottesville: University of Virginia Press, 1983), p. 98.
25. Burrows and Wallace, *Gotham,* p. 215.
26. Quoted in Ron Chernow, *Alexander Hamilton* (New York: Penguin, 2005), p. 241.
27. "Copy of paper drawn up by Joseph Reed for W. Henry Drayton," n.d., in Maria Dickinson Logan Collection, Historical Society of Pennsylvania.
28. Described in Mark Reinberger and Elizabeth McLean, "Isaac Norris's Fairhill: Architecture, Landscape, and Quaker Ideals in a Philadelphia Colonial Country Seat," *Winterthur Portfolio* 32, no. 4 (1997), pp. 243–74.
29. Quoted in J. H. Battle, ed., *History of Columbia and Montour Counties, Pennsylvania* (Chicago: A. Warner & Co., 1887), p. 16.
30. "Journal of Josiah Quincy, Junior, 1773," *Proceedings of the Massachusetts Historical Society,* 2d ser., vol. 49 (June 1916), p. 73.
31. Silas Deane to Elizabeth Deane, September 6, 1774, in *The Deane Papers,* ed. Charles Isham (New York: New-York Historical Society, 1886), p. 19:11.
32. Quoted in Arthur Meier Schlesinger, *The Colonial Merchants and the American Revolution, 1763–1776* (New York: Columbia University Press, 1918), p. 343.

CHAPTER 4: THE VIEW FROM ABOVE

1. Gouverneur Morris to John Penn, May 30, 1774, in Merrill Jensen, *The Articles of Confederation: An Interpretation of the Social-Constitutional History of the American Revolution, 1774–1781* (Madison: University of Wisconsin Press, 1940), p. 34.
2. Alfred F. Young, *The Democratic Republicans of New York: The Origins, 1763–1797* (Chapel Hill: University of North Carolina Press, 1967), p. 11.
3. Morris to Penn, May 30, 1774, in Jensen, *Articles of Confederation,* p. 34.
4. Quoted in Richard Brookhiser, *Gentleman Revolutionary: Gouverneur Morris, the Rake Who Wrote the Constitution* (New York: Free Press, 2003), p. *xv*.
5. Quoted in Max M. Mintz, *Gouverneur Morris and the American Revolution* (Norman: University of Oklahoma Press, 1970), p. 15.
6. Quoted in James Kirschke, *Gouverneur Morris: Author, Statesman, and Man of the World* (New York: Thomas Dunne, 2005), p. 24.
7. Quoted in Jared Sparks, *The Life of Gouverneur Morris* (Boston: Gray & Bowen, 1832), p. 1:25.
8. Morris to Penn, May 30, 1774, in Jensen, *Articles of Confederation,* p. 34.
9. Edward Countryman, *A People in Revolution: The American Revolution and Political Society in New York, 1760–1790* (New York: W. W. Norton, 1989), p. 115.
10. Quoted in Edwin G. Burrows and Mike Wallace, *Gotham: A History of New York City to 1898* (New York: Oxford University Press, 1998), p. 217.
11. Quoted ibid., p. 216.

12. Quoted ibid.
13. Quoted in Gordon S. Wood, *The Creation of the American Republic, 1776–1787* (Chapel Hill: University of North Carolina Press, 1969), p. 94.
14. Quoted ibid., p. 95.
15. Burrows and Wallace, *Gotham,* p. 221.
16. Quoted in George Pellew, *John Jay: American Statesman* (Boston: Houghton Mifflin, 1898), p. 10.
17. Carl Becker, *The History of Political Parties in the Province of New York, 1760–1776* (Madison: University of Wisconsin Press, 1909), p. 266.
18. Quoted in Frank Monaghan, *John Jay: Defender of Liberty* (New York: Bobbs-Merrill, 1935), p. 323.
19. Quoted in George Dangerfield, *Chancellor Robert R. Livingston of New York, 1746-1813* (New York: Harcourt Brace, 1960), p. 46.
20. Quoted in Edward P. Alexander, *Revolutionary Conservative: James Duane of New York* (New York: AMS Press, 1978), p. 97.
21. Quoted ibid., p. 46.
22. Quoted ibid., p. 97.
23. "Letter to the Boston Committee," May 23, 1774, in *American Archives*, ed. Peter Force, 5th ser. (Washington, D.C.: M. St. Clair Clarke and Peter Force, 1848), p. 1:297. Attributed to James Duane, in McDougall Papers, New-York Historical Society.
24. John Jay et al. to Boston Committee of Correspondence, May 23, 1774, in *The Correspondence and Public Papers of John Jay,* ed. Henry P. Johnston (New York: G. P. Putnam's Sons, 1890), pp. 1:13–15.
25. Alexander, *Revolutionary Conservative,* p. 99.
26. Quoted in Brookhiser, *Gentleman Revolutionary,* p. 47.
27. Quoted in Frank Gaylord Cook, "John Dickinson," *Atlantic Monthly* 65 (January 1890), p. 76.
28. "Address of the Mechanics to John Dickinson," June 27, 1774, quoted in Milton E. Flower, *John Dickinson: Conservative Revolutionary* (Charlottesville: University of Virginia Press, 1983), p. 109.
29. John Dickinson to Charles Morrison, May 1774, New York Public Library, quoted ibid., p. 108.
30. *The Political Writings of John Dickinson, Esquire, Late President of the State of Delaware, and of the Commonwealth of Pennsylvania* (Wilmington, Del.: Bonsal & Niles, 1801), p. 1:289.

CHAPTER 5: DELICACY AND CAUTION

1. John Adams, August 31, 1774, *Diary and Autobiography of John Adams,* ed. L. H. Butterfield (Cambridge, Mass.: Harvard University Press, 1961–62), p. 3:308.
2. *Life and Correspondence of George Reed, Signer of the Declaration of Independence,* ed. William Thompson Read (Philadelphia: J. B. Lippincott, 1870), p. 570.
3. Deborah Logan quoted in Charles Janeway Stillé, *The Life and Times of John Dickinson* (Philadelphia: Historical Society of Pennsylvania, 1891), p. 3:334.
4. John Adams, in *The Works of John Adams, Second President of the United States,* ed. Charles F. Adams (Boston: Little, Brown, 1850–56), p. 2:360.

5. John Adams, ibid., p. 2:338.
6. John Adams, in *Diary and Autobiography,* p. 1:95.
7. Edmund S. Morgan, *The Meaning of Independence: John Adams, George Washington, and Thomas Jefferson* (Charlottesville: University of Virginia Press, 1976), p. 9.
8. Benjamin Franklin to Robert R. Livingston, July 22, 1783, in *The Works of Benjamin Franklin,* ed. John Bigelow (New York: G. P. Putnam's Sons, 1904), p. 10:134.
9. Bernard Bailyn, *Faces of Revolution: Personalities and Themes in the Struggle for American Independence* (New York: Vintage, 1992), p. 7.
10. John Adams to William Tudor, March 29, 1817, in *Works of John Adams,* p. 10:245.
11. John Adams to William Tudor, September 29, 1774, ibid., *pp. 1*:153–54.
12. Ibid.
13. Quoted in Richard Brookhiser, *Gentleman Revolutionary: Gouverneur Morris, the Rake Who Wrote the Constitution* (New York: Free Press, 2003), p. 47.
14. Joseph Galloway to William Franklin, September 5, 1774, in *Letters of Delegates to Congress, 1774–1789,* ed. Paul H. Smith et al. (Washington, D.C.: Library of Congress, 1976–2000), p. 1:27.
15. Joseph Galloway, *Historical and Political Reflections on the Rise and Progress of the American Rebellion* (London, 1780), p. 66, quoted in Merrill Jensen, *The Articles of Confederation: An Interpretation of the Social-Constitutional History of the American Revolution, 1774–1781* (Madison: University of Wisconsin Press, 1940), p. 59.
16. Garry Wills, *Inventing America: Jefferson's Declaration of Independence* (Boston: Houghton Mifflin, 1978), p. 3.
17. Quoted in Jensen, *Articles of Confederation,* p. 59.
18. Patrick Henry, September 6, 1774, quoted in Neil L. York, "The First Continental Congress and the Problem of American Rights," *Pennsylvania Magazine of History and Biography* 122, no. 4 (1998), p. 360.
19. John Jay to Congress, September 5, 1774, in *Works of John Adams,* p. 2:368.
20. H. James Henderson, *Party Politics in the Continental Congress* (New York: McGraw-Hill, 1974), passim.
21. York, "First Continental Congress and Problem of Rights," p. 372n.
22. John Adams, in *Works of John Adams,* p. 2:374.
23. John Adams, diary entry for September 8, 1774, in *Diary and Autobiography,* pp. 2:128–30.
24. Quoted in James Haw, *John and Edward Rutledge of South Carolina* (Athens: University of Georgia Press, 1997), p. 59.
25. Ibid., p. 277.
26. Ibid., p. 60.
27. Ibid., p. 58.
28. Ibid.
29. Quoted in Edward P. Alexander, *Revolutionary Conservative: James Duane of New York* (New York: AMS Press, 1978), p. 100.
30. James Duane, "Address Before the Committee to State the Rights of the Colonies," September 8, 1774, in *Letters of Members of the Continental Congress,* ed. Edmund Cody Burnett (Washington, D.C.: Carnegie Institution, 1921), pp. 1:23–25.
31. John Adams, diary entry for September 8, 1774, in *Diary and Autobiography,* pp. 2:128–30.

32. October 14, 1774, in *Journals of the Continental Congress, 1774–1789,* ed. Worthington C. Ford et al. (Washington, D.C., 1904–37), p. 1:66–67.
33. Suffolk Resolves, September 17, 1774, ibid., p. 1:39.
34. John Adams, September 17, 1774, in *Works of John Adams,* p. 2:380.
35. Jack N. Rakove, *The Beginnings of National Politics: An Interpretive History of the Continental Congress* (Baltimore: Johns Hopkins University Press, 1979), p. 57.
36. *Pennsylvania Journal,* February 8, 1775, in Frank Moore, *Diary of the American Revolution: From Newspapers and Original Documents* (New York: Charles Scribner, 1860), p. 1:16.
37. John Jay to John Vardill, September 24, 1774, in *Letters of Delegates to Congress,* p. 1:95.
38. James Duane to Samuel Chase, December 29, 1774, in Alexander, *Revolutionary Conservative,* p. 102.
39. John Adams, diary entry for September 28, 1774, in *Diary and Autobiography,* p. 2:143.
40. John Adams, diary entry for September 28, 1774, in *Works of John Adams,* p. 2:387.
41. Ibid.
42. Quoted in James Kendall Hosmer, *Samuel Adams: American Statesman* (Edinburgh: David Douglas, 1886), p. 344.
43. John Adams, in *Works of John Adams,* p. 2:379.
44. Rakove, *Beginnings of National Politics,* p. 53.
45. John Adams to Abigail Adams, in *Letters of John Adams, Addressed to his Wife,* ed. Charles F. Adams (Boston: Charles C. Little and James Brown, 1841), p. 1:33.
46. Bernard Knollenberg, "John Dickinson vs. John Adams, 1774–1776," *Proceedings of the American Philosophical Society* 107, no. 2 (April 15, 1963), p. 140.
47. *The Political Writings of John Dickinson, Esquire, Late President of the State of Delaware, and of the Commonwealth of Pennsylvania* (Wilmington, Del.: Bonsal & Niles, 1801), p. 2:25.
48. "Annapolis Merchant to a Philadelphia Friend," January 28, 1775, in Jensen, *Articles of Confederation,* p. 73.
49. John Adams, in *Diary and Autobiography,* p. 3:313.
50. John Adams, October 24, 1774, in *Journals of the Continental Congress,* p. 1:103n.
51. John Dickinson to Josiah Quincy, October 28, 1774, in *Letters of Delegates to Congress,* p. 1:251.

CHAPTER 6: THE OLIVE BRANCH AND THE LIGHTNING BOLT

1. James Duane, "Notes on the State of the Colonies." May 15, 1775, in *Letters of Members of the Continental Congress,* ed. Edmund C. Burnett (Washington, D.C.: Carnegie Institution, 1921), pp. 1:98–100.
2. Ibid.
3. John Adams to Abigail Adams, May 8, 1775, in *The Letters of John and Abigail Adams,* ed. Frank Shuffelton (New York: Penguin, 2004), p. 51.
4. John Adams to Abigail Adams, May 29, 1775, ibid., p. 56.
5. John Adams, *Autobiography,* in *The Works of John Adams, Second President of the United States,* ed. Charles F. Adams (Boston: Little, Brown, 1850–56), p. 3:17.

6. John Dickinson, undated notes, John Dickinson Correspondence, 1775–98, in Simon Gatz Autograph Collection, Historical Society of Pennsylvania.
7. John Rutledge, in Silas Deane Diary, May 16, 1775, in *Letters of Delegates to Congress, 1774–1789,* ed. Paul H. Smith et al. (Washington, D.C.: Library of Congress, 1976–2000), p. 1:351.
8. H. James Henderson, *Party Politics in the Continental Congress* (New York: McGraw-Hill, 1974), p. 44.
9. John Adams to James Warren, July 6, 1775, in *Letters of Members of the Continental Congress,* p. 1:52.
10. Quoted in David McCullough, *John Adams* (New York: Simon & Schuster, 2002), p. 95.
11. Quoted in Jack N. Rakove, *The Beginnings of National Politics: An Interpretive History of the Continental Congress* (Baltimore: Johns Hopkins University Press, 1979), p. 73.
12. John Adams to Moses Gill, June 10, 1775, in *Works of John Adams,* p. 9:356.
13. Quoted in Henderson, *Party Politics in the Continental Congress,* p. 81.
14. John Dickinson, *Letters from a Farmer in Pennsylvania,* in *The Writings of John Dickinson: Political Writings, 1764–1774,* ed. Paul Leicester Ford (Philadelphia: Historical Society of Philadelphia, 1895), p. 1:327.
15. Quoted in William Cabell Rives, *History of the Life and Times of James Madison* (Boston: Little Brown, 1859–68), p. 1:105.
16. Charles Janeway Stillé, *The Life and Times of John Dickinson* (Philadelphia: Historical Society of Pennsylvania, 1891), p. 167.
17. John Adams, diary entry for November 9, 1775, in *Works of John Adams,* p. 2:409.
18. See *The Works of Benjamin Franklin,* ed. Jared Sparks (Boston: Hilliard Gray, 1840), p. 1:395.
19. John Adams, diary entry for November 9, 1775, *Works of John Adams,* p. 2:410.
20. *The Writings of Thomas Jefferson,* ed. Paul Leicester Ford (New York: G. P. Putnam's Sons, 1892), p. 1:17.
21. John Adams, diary entry for November 9, 1775, in *Works of John Adams,* p. 2:408.
22. "The Petition of Congress to the King's Most Excellent Majesty," July 8, 1775, in *Journals of the Continental Congress, 1774–1789,* ed. Worthington C. Ford et al. (Washington, D.C., 1904–37), pp. 2:158–60.
23. John Dickinson to Thomas Cushing, December 11, 1774, quoted in Milton E. Flower, *John Dickinson: Conservative Revolutionary* (Charlottesville: University of Virginia Press, 1983), p. 122.
24. John Dickinson to Arthur Lee, July 7, 1775, in *Letters of Members of the Continental Congress,* p. 1:157.
25. John Adams to James Warren, July 24, 1775, in *Works of John Adams,* pp. 2:410, 411.
26. John Adams to Abigail Adams, July 23, 1775, in *Letters of Members of the Continental Congress,* p. 1:175.
27. Quoted in Flower, *John Dickinson,* p. 137.
28. Quoted ibid.
29. David Freeman Hawke, *Benjamin Rush: Revolutionary Gadfly* (New York: Bobbs-Merrill, 1971), p. 131.
30. John Adams, diary entry for November 9, 1775, in *Works of John Adams,* p. 2:412.
31. John Adams, diary entry for September 15, 1775, ibid., p. 2:423.

32. John Adams, *Works of John Adams,* p. 2:408.
33. See Jane E. Calvert, *Quaker Constitutionalism and the Political Thought of John Dickinson* (Cambridge: Cambridge University Press, 2008).
34. John Dickinson to Tench Coxe, January 24, 1807, quoted in Flower, *John Dickinson,* p. 301.
35. John Dickinson to Arthur Lee, April 29, 1775, quoted in Calvert, *Quaker Constitutionalism,* p. 222.
36. Julian P. Boyd, "The Disputed Authorship of the Declaration on the Causes and Necessity of Taking Up Arms, 1775," *Pennsylvania Magazine of History and Biography* 74, no. 1 (January 1950), p. 70.
37. G. H. Hollister, *The History of Connecticut* (Hartford: Case Tiffany, 1857).

CHAPTER 7: PATRIOTISM AND PROFIT

1. Robert Morris to Samuel Inglis, January 30, 1776, in *Letters of Delegates to Congress, 1774–1789,* ed. Paul H. Smith et al. (Washington, D.C.: Library of Congress, 1976–2000), p. 3:170.
2. Robert Morris to Benjamin Harrison, December 29, 1776, in *American Archives,* ed. Peter Force, 5th ser. (Washington, D.C.: M. St. Clair Clarke and Peter Force, 1848), p. 3:1471.
3. Robert Morris to the Philadelphia Committee, August 5, 1779, in *The Deane Papers,* ed. Charles Isham (New York: New-York Historical Society, 1890), p. 4:34.
4. Robert Morris to Silas Deane, August 11, 1776, in *Letters of Delegates to Congress,* p. 4:657.
5. Quoted in Ellis Paxson Oberholtzer, *Robert Morris, Patriot and Financier* (New York: Macmillan, 1903), p. 18.
6. Quoted in John Adams, Notes of Debates, September 24, 1775, in *Letters of Delegates to Congress,* p. 2:53.
7. Richard Henry Lee to unknown, October 10, 1785, in *The Letters of Richard Henry Lee,* ed. James Curtis Ballagh (New York: Macmillan, 1911–14), p. 2:389.
8. Quoted in Gordon S. Wood, *The Creation of the American Republic, 1776–1787* (Chapel Hill: University of North Carolina Press, 1969), p. 96.
9. Henry Laurens to William Livingston, April 19, 1779, in *The Papers of Henry Laurens,* ed. David R. Chesnutt (Columbia: University of South Carolina Press, 1968–2002), p. 15:88.
10. Quoted in Wood, *Creation of American Republic,* p. 96.
11. Carter Braxton, May 1776, quoted in Robert L. Scribner and Brent Tarter, eds., *Revolutionary Virginia: The Road to Independence* (Charlottesville: University of Virginia Press, 1981), pp. 6:518, 520–23.
12. Quoted in Wood, *Creation of American Republic,* p. 97.
13. Robert Morris to William Hooper, January 18, 1777, in Clarence L. Ver Steeg, *Robert Morris, Revolutionary Financier* (Philadelphia: University of Pennsylvania Press, 1954), p. 38.
14. John Langdon to Robert Morris, February 18, 1777, quoted in E. James Ferguson, *The Power of the Purse: A History of American Public Finance, 1776–1790* (Chapel Hill: University of North Carolina Press, 1961), p. 77.
15. Robert Morris to William Bingham, June 20, 1777, in *Letters of Delegates to Congress,* p. 7:206.

16. Robert Morris to John Bradford, October 8, 1776, ibid., p. 5:321.
17. Robert Morris to Jonathan Hudson, May 20, 1777, and June 17, 1777, ibid., pp. 7:97, 206.
18. Robert Morris to Jonathan Hudson, August 19, 1777, ibid., p. 4:155.
19. R. H. Lee to Patrick Henry, April 15, 1777, ibid., p. 6:583.
20. Arthur Lee, in Secret Committee Minutes of Proceedings, May 1, 1777, ibid., p. 4:657.
21. Robert Morris to Silas Deane, June 29, 1777, in *Deane Papers,* pp. 2:77–84.
22. Robert Morris to Charles Lee, February 17, 1776, in *Letters of Delegates to Congress,* p. 3:268.
23. John Adams to Horatio Gates, April 27, 1776, ibid., p. 3:587.
24. King George III, "Proclamation of Rebellion," in *Select Charters and Other Documents Illustrative of American History, 1606-1775,* ed. William MacDonald (New York: Macmillan, 1899), p. 390.
25. In Merrill Jensen, ed., *American Colonial Documents to 1776* (London: Eyre & Spottiswoode, 1955), pp. 850–51.
26. Robert Alexander to Maryland Council of Safety, February 27, 1776, in *Letters of Delegates to Congress,* p. 3:168.
27. John Adams to Horatio Gates, March 23, 1776, ibid., p. 3:430.
28. Richard Smith's Diary, February 27, 1776, ibid., p. 3:307.

CHAPTER 8: YIELDING TO THE TORRENT

1. Quoted in David Freeman Hawke, *Benjamin Rush: Revolutionary Gadfly* (New York: Bobbs-Merrill, 1971), p. 137.
2. Thomas Paine, *Common Sense* (Philadelphia: W. and T. Bradford, 1776), p. 31.
3. Quoted in Merrill Jensen, *The Articles of Confederation: An Interpretation of the Social-Constitutional History of the American Revolution, 1774–1781* (Madison: University of Wisconsin Press, 1940), p. 94.
4. Quoted ibid.
5. James Duane to Robert Livingston, June 7, 1775, in *Letters of Delegates to Congress, 1774–1789,* ed. Paul H. Smith et al. (Washington, D.C.: Library of Congress, 1976–2000), p. 1:454.
6. Robert Livingston to Edward Rutledge, October 10, 1776, in Bancroft Transcripts, Robert R. Livingston Papers, New York Public Library, p. 1:229, quoted in George Dangerfield, *Chancellor Robert R. Livingston, 1746–1813* (New York: Harcourt Brace, 1960), p. 87.
7. Robert Livingston to William Duer, July 12, 1777, in Robert R. Livingston Papers, New-York Historical Society.
8. Charles Page Smith, *James Wilson: Founding Father, 1742–1798* (Chapel Hill: University of North Carolina Press, 1956), p. 63.
9. John Adams, *Autobiography,* in *The Works of John Adams, Second President of the United States,* ed. Charles F. Adams (Boston: Little, Brown, 1850–56), p. 2:510.
10. Robert Morris to Benjamin Franklin, November 27, 1781, in *The Revolutionary Diplomatic Correspondence of the United States,* ed. Francis Wharton (Washington, D.C.: Government Printing Office, 1888), p. 5:15.

11. Carter Braxton to Landon Carter, April 14, 1776, in *Letters of Members of the Continental Congress,* ed. Edmund C. Burnett (Washington, D.C.: Carnegie Institution, 1921), pp. 1:420–21.
12. Many conservatives held this view. In May 1776, Thomas Stone noted, "Upon their deceitful show of reconciliation being detected and open & exposed, the general and unanimous voice of America would have been for separation." Quoted in Jack Rakove, *The Beginnings of National Politics: An Interpretive History of the Continental Congress* (Baltimore: Johns Hopkins University Press, 1982), p. 100.
13. Quoted in Coy Hilton James, *Silas Deane: Patriot or Traitor?* (East Lansing: Michigan State University Press, 1975), p. 10.
14. New Jersey Archives, 1st ser., p. 10:691, quoted in Richard B. Morris, *Seven Who Shaped Our Destiny: The Founding Fathers as Revolutionaries* (New York: Harper & Row, 1973), p. 178; Governor William Franklin to the Earl of Dartmouth, January 5, 1776, in *American Archives,* ed. Peter Force, 4th ser. (Washington, D.C.: M. St. Clair Clarke and Peter Force, 1837), p. 3:1871.
15. Carter Braxton to Landon Carter, April 14, 1776, in *Letters of Members of the Continental Congress,* pp. 1:420–21.
16. Samuel Adams to Benjamin Kent, July 27, 1776, in *The Writings of Samuel Adams,* ed. Harry Alonzo Cushing (New York: G. P. Putnam's Sons, 1907), pp. 3:304–5.
17. John Adams to Richard Henry Lee, November 15, 1775, in *Works of John Adams,* p. 4:187.
18. Edward Tilghman, February 4, 1776, quoted in Charles Janeway Stillé, *The Life and Times of John Dickinson* (Philadelphia: Historical Society of Pennsylvania, 1891), p. 174.
19. Arthur Lee to Benjamin Franklin, February 13, 1776, in John Jay Papers, Columbia University Libraries.
20. John Adams to Abigail Adams, February 13, 1776, in *The Letters of John and Abigail Adams,* ed. Frank Shuffelton (New York: Penguin, 2004), p. 133.
21. Gardner Weld Allen, *A Naval History of the American Revolution* (Boston: Houghton Mifflin, 1913), p. 141.
22. John Adams, diary entry for May 10, 1776, *Works of John Adams,* p. 3:45.
23. Quoted in Smith, p. 81.
24. Quoted ibid., p. 82.
25. Quoted in Edmund C. Burnett, *The Continental Congress: A Definitive History of the Continental Congress from Its Inception in 1774 to March 1789* (New York: Macmillan, 1941), p. 157.
26. May 15, 1776, in *Journals of the Continental Congress, 1774–1789,* ed. Worthington C. Ford et al. (Washington, D.C., 1904–37), pp. 4:357–58.
27. Quoted in Merrill Jensen, *The Founding of a Nation: A History of the American Revolution, 1763–1776* (Oxford: Oxford University Press, 1968), p. 685.
28. Quoted ibid.
29. Quoted in Smith, *James Wilson,* p. 83.
30. Quoted ibid.
31. Quoted in Hawke, *Benjamin Rush,* p. 152.
32. *The Pennsylvania Gazette,* May 22, 1776.
33. Quoted in Smith, *James Wilson,* p. 85.

34. Undated note in the hand of Benjamin Rush among the Lee Family Papers, May 22, 1776.
35. Quoted in Charles Rappleye, *Robert Morris: Financier of the American Revolution* (New York: Simon & Schuster, 2010), p. 70.
36. John Adams to James Warren, May 20, 1776, in *Warren-Adams Letters* (Boston: Massachusetts Historical Society, 1917), p. 1:249.

CHAPTER 9: THE CRUCIBLE OF CONSERVATISM

1. John Adams to Patrick Henry, in *The Works of John Adams, Second President of the United States,* ed. Charles F. Adams (Boston: Little, Brown, 1850–56), p. 1:214.
2. *Memoirs, Correspondence, and Private Papers of Thomas Jefferson, Late President of the United States,* ed. Thomas Jefferson Randolph (London: Henry Colburn and Richard Bentley, 1829), p. 1:11.
3. Ibid.
4. Ibid., p. 1:13.
5. Ibid., p. 1:14.
6. Edward Rutledge to John Jay, June 8, 1776, in John Jay Papers, Columbia University Libraries.
7. James Duane to John Jay, May 18, 1776, ibid., quoted in George Pellew, *John Jay: American Statesman* (Boston: Houghton Mifflin, 1898), p. 9:49.
8. John Jay to George Alexander Otis, January 13, 1821, in John Jay Papers, Columbia University Libraries.
9. Edward Rutledge to John Jay, June 8, 1776, ibid.
10. Edward Rutledge to John Jay, June 29, 1776, ibid.
11. John Adams Diary, October 11, 24, 1774, in *Letters of Delegates to Congress, 1774–1789,* ed. Paul H. Smith et al. (Washington, D.C.: Library of Congress, 1976–2000), p. 1:173, 236; John Adams, diary entry for September 15, 1775, ibid., p. 1:401.
12. Edward Rutledge to John Jay, June 8, 1776, in John Jay Papers.
13. Edward Rutledge to John Jay June 29, 1776, ibid.
14. John Jay to Edward Rutledge, July 6, 1776, in Richard Morris, *Seven Who Shaped Our Destiny: The Founding Fathers as Revolutionaries* (New York: Harper & Row, 1973), p. 181.
15. Robert Morris to Horatio Gates, April 6, 1776, in *Letters of Delegates to Congress,* p. 3:495.
16. Quoted in Mark David Hall, *The Political and Legal Philosophy of James Wilson, 1742–1798* (Columbia: University of Missouri Press, 1997), p. 129.
17. Quoted in Charles Page Smith, *James Wilson: Founding Father, 1742–1798* (Chapel Hill: University of North Carolina Press, 1956), p. 25.
18. Quoted ibid., p. 42.
19. Quoted ibid., p. 67.
20. James Madison to Andrew Stevenson, November 17, 1839, in *The Records of the Federal Convention of 1787,* ed. Max Farrand (New Haven: Yale University Press, 1911), pp. 3:487–88.

21. Alexander Graydon, *Memoirs of a Life Chiefly Passed in Pennsylvania* (Harrisburg: John Wyeth, 1811), p. 327.
22. John Adams to Archibald Bulloch, July 1, 1776, quoted in Jane E. Calvert, *Quaker Constitutionalism and the Political Thought of John Dickinson* (Cambridge: Cambridge University Press, 2008), p. 241.
23. Dickinson's notes for his final speech were lost for more than a century and a half, until 1941, when the historian J. H. Powell discovered a draft among private family papers. Dickinson's small, cramped handwriting was unmistakable.
24. John Dickinson, speech opposing the Declaration of Independence, July 1, 1776, in "Notes and Documents," *Pennsylvania Magazine of History and Biography* 65, no. 4 (October 1941), p. 468.
25. Ibid., p. 470.
26. Ibid., p. 476.
27. John Adams, diary entry for July 1, 1776, in *Works of John Adams*, p. 3:54.
28. No transcriptions of Adams's rebuttal were made at the time. All that is left are accounts from other congressmen and Adams's own later, somewhat inconsistent recollections of the day.
29. Quoted in David Ramsay, *The History of the American Revolution* (1789), p. 1:341.
30. *Memoirs, Correspondence, of Jefferson*, p. 1:16.
31. Quoted in Ellis Paxson Oberholtzer, *Robert Morris, Patriot and Financier* (New York: Macmillan, 1903), pp. 20–21.
32. Charles Janeway Stillé, *The Life and Times of John Dickinson* (Philadelphia: Historical Society of Pennsylvania, 1891), pp. 196–97.
33. Forrest McDonald and Ellen Shapiro McDonald, *Requiem: Variations on Eighteenth-Century Themes* (Lawrence: University Press of Kansas, 1988), p. 89.
34. John Adams to Abigail Adams, July 3, 1776, in *Familiar Letters of John Adams and His Wife Abigail Adams During the Revolution*, ed. Charles F. Adams (New York: Hurd & Houghton, 1875), p. 193.
35. John Adams to Thomas Jefferson, November 12, 1813, in *Works of John Adams*, pp. 10:78–80.
36. *The Literary Diary of Ezra Stiles*, ed. Franklin B. Dexter (New York: Charles Scribner's Sons, 1901), p. 2:182.
37. John Dickinson to unknown, August 25, 1776, in John Dickinson Papers, ser. I. a., Correspondence, 1762–1808, R. R. Logan Collection, Historical Society of Pennsylvania.
38. Charles Stillé and Paul Leicester Ford, *The Life and Writings of John Dickinson* (Philadelphia: Historical Society of Pennsylvania, 1891–95), p. 1:204.

CHAPTER 10: THE PHILOSOPHER IN ACTION

1. Earl of Buckinghamshire to George Grenville, June 11, 1766, British Library, Add. MS 22358, fo. 35.
2. Samuel Johnson to Bennet Langton, March 8, 1766, in *The Letters of Samuel Johnson*, ed. Bruce Redford (Princeton, N.J.: Princeton University Press, 1992–94), pp. 1:264–65.

3. *The Writings and Speeches of Edmund Burke,* ed. Paul Langford et al. (Oxford: Oxford University Press, 1981), p. 2:423.
4. Quoted in Conor Cruise O'Brien, *The Great Melody: A Thematic Biography and Commented Anthology of Edmund Burke* (Chicago: University of Chicago Press, 1992), p. 139.
5. *Writings and Speeches of Burke,* p. 2:458.
6. *The Works and Correspondence of the Right Honourable Edmund Burke* (London: Francis & John Rivington, 1852), pp. 1:224.
7. Ibid., p. 3:252.
8. Ibid., p. 3:291.
9. Ibid., p. 3:290.
10. Ibid., p. 3:288.
11. Burke quoted in O'Brien, *Great Melody,* p. 155.
12. Ibid.
13. Edmund Burke, "Speech at Bristol, Previous to the Election," quoted in Jeff Spinner, "Constructing Communities: Edmund Burke on Revolution," *Polity* 23, no. 3 (1991), p. 399.
14. Quoted in F. P. Lock, *Edmund Burke* (Oxford: Clarendon Press of Oxford University Press, 1998), p. 1:350.
15. Quoted in O'Brien, *Great Melody,* p. 159.
16. Quoted ibid., p. 137
17. Edmund Burke, "Letter to the Sheriffs of the City of Bristol," quoted in Russell Kirk, *Edmund Burke: A Genius Reconsidered* (Wilmington, Del.: ISI Books, 1997), p. 64.
18. Edmund Burke, "Thoughts on the Cause of the Present Discontents," in *Works of Burke,* p. 3:170.
19. Ibid, p. 3:164.
20. Reed Browning, "The Origin of Burke's Ideas Revisited," *Eighteenth-Century Studies* 18 (1984), p. 71.
21. O'Brien, *Great Melody,* p. 153.
22. Browning, "Origin of Burke's Ideas," p. 60.
23. Quoted in *Selected Letters of Edmund Burke,* ed. Harvey Mansfield (Chicago: University of Chicago Press, 1984), p. 8.
24. Quoted in Russell Kirk, *The Conservative Mind: From Burke to Santayana* (Chicago: Henry Regnery, 1953), p. 19.
25. *Selected Letters of Burke,* p. 16.
26. Ibid., p. 11.
27. *Works of Burke,* p. 6:130.
28. Ibid.
29. Ibid., p. 4:177.
30. Ibid., p. 4:222.
31. Ibid., p. 5:300.
32. "Thoughts and Details on Scarcity," ibid., p. 5:189.
33. Ibid., p. 5:202.
34. Ibid., p. 5:192.
35. Quoted in Jerry Z. Muller, *The Mind and the Market: Capitalism in Modern European Thought* (New York: Alfred A. Knopf, 2002), p. 118.

36. "Tracts Relative to the Laws Against Popery in Ireland," *Works of Burke,* p. 6:16.
37. "A Letter to Sir Hercules Langrishe, M. P. on the Subject of the Roman Catholics of Ireland and the Propriety of Admitting them to the Elective Franchise, Consistently with the Principles of the Constitution as Established at the Revolution" (1792), ibid., pp. 4:544–45.
38. *The Works of the Honorable James Wilson, L.L.D,* ed. Bird Wilson (Philadelphia: Lorenzo Press, 1804), p. 2:458.
39. Ibid., p. 2:456.
40. Ibid., p. 2:460.
41. Ibid., p. 2:497.
42. The conservative commentator David Brooks, for example, noted in his column in *The New York Times,* "Modern conservatism begins with Edmund Burke." See "The Republican Collapse," October 5, 2007.
43. Edmund Burke, "Reflections on the Revolution in France" (1790), in *Works of Burke* p. 4:176.

CHAPTER II: ON THE BRINK OF A PRECIPICE

1. Broadside, June 26, 1776, in Broadside Collection, Historical Society of Pennsylvania.
2. Quoted in Eric Foner, "Tom Paine's Republic: Radical Ideology and Social Change," in Alfred F. Young, ed., *The American Revolution: Explorations in the History of American Radicalism* (DeKalb: Northern Illinois University Press, 1976), p. 208.
3. Quoted in Charles Page Smith, *James Wilson: Founding Father, 1742–1798* (Chapel Hill: University of North Carolina Press, 1956), p. 108.
4. Thomas Young to John Wendell, December 15, 1766, quoted in Foner, "Tom Paine's Republic," p. 208.
5. Quoted in Pauline Maier, "Reason and Revolution: The Radicalism of Dr. Thomas Young," *American Quarterly* 28, no. 2 (1976), p. 230.
6. Smith, *James Wilson,* p. 108.
7. Edward Countryman, *The American Revolution* (New York: Hill & Wang, 2003), p. 128.
8. Robert L. Brunhouse, *The Counter-Revolution in Pennsylvania, 1776–1790* (Harrisburg: Pennsylvania Historical Commission, 1942), p. 15.
9. Quoted in Edmund S. Morgan, *Benjamin Franklin* (New Haven: Yale University Press, 2002), pp. 307–8.
10. Quoted in Paul Leicester Ford, "The Adoption of the Pennsylvania Constitution of 1776," *Political Science Quarterly* 10, no. 3 (1895), p. 455.
11. Quoted in Brunhouse, *Counter-Revolution in Pennsylvania,* p. 20.
12. Thomas Young, "To the Inhabitants of Vermont, A Free and Independent State, Bounding on the River Connecticut and Lake Champlain," April 11, 1777, in Edward Countryman, *A People in Revolution: The American Revolution and Political Society in New York, 1760–1790* (New York: W. W. Norton, 1989), p. 158.
13. Quoted ibid., p. 158.
14. Quoted in George R. Lamplugh, "'To Check and Discourage the Wicked and Design-

ing': John Wereat and the Revolution in Georgia," *Georgia Historical Quarterly* 6, no. 4 (1977), p. 297.

15. Ibid., p. 304.
16. James Wilson, September 19, 1787, in *Pennsylvania Gazette,* quoted in Mark David Hall, *The Political and Legal Philosophy of James Wilson, 1742–1798* (Columbia: University of Missouri Press, 1997), p. 139.
17. *Collected Works of the Honorable James Wilson, L.L.D.,* ed. Bird Wilson (Philadelphia: Lorenzo Press, 1804), p. 3:207.
18. Benjamin Rush to Charles Lee, October 24, 1779, in *The Letters of Benjamin Rush,* ed. L. H. Butterfield (Princeton, N.J.: Princeton University Press, 1951), pp. 1:243–44.
19. Benjamin Rush to "Citizens of Pennsylvania of German Birth . . ." August 31, 1785, in *Letters of Rush,* p. 2:367.
20. Benjamin Rush, *Observations Upon the Present Government of Pennsylvania: In Four Letters to the People of Pennsylvania* (Philadelphia: Styner & Cist, 1777), pp. 13–16.
21. Ibid., pp. 8–9.
22. Ibid., pp. 13–16.
23. Gordon S. Wood, *The Creation of the American Republic, 1776–1787* (Chapel Hill: University of North Carolina Press, 1969), p. 374.
24. *Pennsylvania Gazette,* May 22, 1776.
25. Quoted in *Letters of Rush,* p. 1:240.
26. Quoted in Smith, *James Wilson,* p. 111.
27. Brunhouse, *Counter-Revolution in Pennsylvania,* p. 20.
28. Smith, *James Wilson,* p. 113.
29. Quoted in Charles J. Stillé, *The Life and Times of John Dickinson, 1732-1808* (New York: Burt Franklin, 1969), pp. 208–9.
30. Ibid.
31. Benjamin Rush to John Dickinson, December 1, 1776, in *Letters of Rush,* p. 1:119.
32. Robert Morris to the Commissioners in France, December, 21, 1776, in *American Archives,* ed. Peter Force, 5th ser. (Washington, D.C.: M. St. Clair Clarke and Peter Force, 1848), p. 3:1334.
33. "Diary of James Allen, Esq. of Philadelphia Counsellor-At-Law, 1770–1778," *Pennsylvania Magazine of History and Biography* 9, no. 1 (1885), p. 189.
34. April 15, 1777, in *Journals of the Continental Congress, 1774–1789,* ed. Worthington C. Ford et al. (Washington, D.C.: Government Printing Office, 1904–37), p. 7:268.
35. Brunhouse, *Counter-Revolution in Pennsylvania,* p. 32.
36. Memorial, in *Pennsylvania Packet,* May 20, 1777.
37. Quoted in Brunhouse, *Counter-Revolution in Pennsylvania,* p. 25.
38. Quoted in Stillé, *Life and Times of John Dickinson,* p. 392.
39. Ibid., pp. 214–15.
40. Ibid., p. 315.

CHAPTER 12: COOL AND DO MISCHIEF

1. George C. Rogers, Jr., "The Charleston Tea Party: The Significance of December 3, 1773," *South Carolina Historical Magazine* 75, no. 3 (1974), p. 154.

2. David Ramsay, *The History of South-Carolina from Its First Settlement in 1670, to the Year 1808* (Charleston, S.C.: David Longworth, 1809), pp. 2:511.
3. [John Rutledge], original draft of preamble, March 26, 1776, in William Edwin Hemphill and Wylma Anne Waites, eds., *Extracts from the Journals of the Provincial Congresses of South-Carolina* (Columbia: South Carolina Archives Department, 1960), pp. 256–58, quoted in James Haw, *John and Edward Rutledge of South Carolina* (Athens: University of Georgia Press, 1997), p. 81.
4. John Drayton, *Memoirs of the American Revolution, From its Commencement to the Year 1776, Inclusive; as Relating to the State of South-Carolina; and Occasionally Relating to the States of North-Carolina and Georgia* (Charleston: A. E. Miller, 1821), pp. 2:171–72.
5. Ibid., pp. 2:172–73.
6. "A Constitution, or form of Government, agreed to, and resolved upon, by the Representatives of SOUTH-CAROLINA," *American Archives,* ed. Peter Force, 4th ser. (Washington, D.C.: M. St. Clair Clarke and Peter Force, 1837), p. 5:614.
7. Ramsay, *South-Carolina,* p. 1:151.
8. Henry Flanders, *Lives and Times of the Chief Justices of the Supreme Court of the United States* (Philadelphia: J. B. Lippincott, 1874), p. 531.
9. Drayton, *Memoirs of the Revolution,* p. 2:243.
10. William Moultrie, *Memoirs of the American Revolution* (New York: David Longworth, 1802), p. 1:140.
11. Henry Laurens to J. Laurens, August 14, 1776, in *The Papers of Henry Laurens,* ed. David R. Chesnutt (Columbia: University of South Carolina Press, 1968-2002), p. 11:226.
12. George Washington to John Augustine Washington, March 31, 1776, in *American Archives,* ed. Peter Force, 5th ser., p. 5:561.
13. John Rutledge to Charles Lee, June 4, 1776, in *American Archives,* ed. Peter Force, 4th ser., p. 6:720.
14. Ibid.
15. Quoted in Flanders, *Lives of the Chief Justices,* p. 540.
16. Moultrie, *Memoirs of the Revolution,* p. 2:238.
17. Ibid., p. 2:248.
18. Drayton, *Memoirs of the Revolution,* pp. 2:298, 312.
19. Charles Lee to George Washington, July 1, 1776, in *American Archives,* ed. Peter Force, 4th ser., p. 4:1183.
20. Ibid.
21. Moultrie, *Memoirs of the Revolution,* p. 2:300.
22. July 7, 1776, in *American Archives,* ed. Peter Force, 5th ser., p. 1:611.
23. Quoted in Raymond Gale Starr, *The Conservative Revolution: South Carolina Public Affairs, 1775–1790,* unpublished Ph.D. diss., University of Texas, 1964.
24. Ibid.
25. Ibid., p. 65.
26. John Lewis Gervais to Henry Laurens, March 16, 1778, ibid., p. 66.
27. John Rutledge to Henry Laurens, March 8, 1778, in *Correspondence of Henry Laurens, of South Carolina* (New York: Printed for the Zenger Club, 1861), pp. 103–6.

28. John Rutledge, "Address to the General Assembly and Legislative Council, March 5, 1778," in David Ramsay, ed., *The History of the Revolution of South-Carolina, from a British Province to an Independent State* (Trenton, N.J., 1785), pp. 1:132–38.
29. Ibid.
30. John Lewis Gervais to Henry Laurens, March 16, 1778, in Starr, *Conservative Revolution,* p. 66.
31. John Rutledge to Henry Laurens, March 8, 1778, in *Correspondence of Laurens,* pp. 103–6.

CHAPTER 13: THE TURNING POINT

1. Philip Schuyler, Orderbook, p. 131, in Don Gerlach, *Proud Patriot: Philip Schuyler and the War of Independence, 1775–1783* (Syracuse, N.Y.: Syracuse University Press, 1987), p. 66.
2. Jacob Ten Eyck and Philip Schuyler to the Mayor, Recorder, Aldermen, and Commonality of the City of Albany, March 10, 1775, quoted ibid., p. 7.
3. Silas Deane to Elizabeth Deane, June 18, 1775, in *The Deane Papers,* ed. Charles Isham (New York: New-York Historical Society, 1887), p. 1:61.
4. Quoted in Gerlach, *Proud Patriot,* p. 8.
5. National Park Service, brochure, Schuyler Mansion, Schuylerville, New York.
6. George Clinton to James Duane, August 27, 1777, in Jared Sparks Papers, Harvard College Library.
7. Philip Schuyler to Gouverneur Morris, September 7, 1777, in Gouverneur Morris Collection, Columbia University Libraries.
8. *Diary and Autobiography of John Adams,* ed. L. H. Butterfield (Cambridge, Mass.: Belknap Press of Harvard University Press, 1961), pp. 3:386–87.
9. Philip Schuyler to Horatio Gates, June 25, 1776, in *American Archives,* ed. Peter Force, 5th ser. (Washington, D.C.: M. St. Clair Clarke and Peter Force, 1848), p. 6:1071.
10. Philip Schuyler to Benedict Arnold, August 17, 1776, quoted in Gerlach, *Proud Patriot,* p. 194.
11. *The Writings of Samuel Adams,* ed. Harry A. Cushing (New York: G. P. Putnam's Sons, 1904–8), p. 9:449.
12. March 15, 1777, in *Journals of the Continental Congress,* pp. 7:180–81.
13. Edward Rutledge to John Jay, November 24, 1776, in John Jay Papers, Columbia University Libraries.
14. James Duane to Robert Livingston, June 24, 1777, and William Duer to Robert Livingston, May 28, 1777, in *Letters of Members of the Continental Congress,* ed. Edmund C. Burnett (Washington, D.C.: Carnegie Institution, 1921), pp. 2:387, 377.
15. Alfred F. Young, *The Democratic-Republicans of New York: The Origins, 1763–1797* (Chapel Hill: University of North Carolina Press, 1967), p. 18.
16. "The Interest of America," *New York-Journal; or General Advertiser,* June 6–20, 1776.
17. "The Respectful Address of the Mechanicks in Union, for the City and Country of New York, represented by their General Committee," quoted in Edward Countryman, *A People in Revolution: The American Revolution and Political Society in New York, 1760–1790* (New York: W. W. Norton, 1989), p. 163.

18. Robert Livingston to William Duer, July 12, 1777, in R. R. Livingston Papers, New-York Historical Society.
19. Countryman, *People in Revolution,* p. 167.
20. Edward Rutledge to John Jay, November 24, 1776, in John Jay Papers, Columbia University Libraries.
21. Quoted in Young, *Democratic Republicans of New York,* p. 20.
22. Robert Troup to John Jay, May 15, 1777, quoted ibid., p. 21.
23. "A True Patriot," no. 7, *Pennsylvania Gazette,* June 16, 1779.
24. Young, *Democratic Republicans of New York,* p. 23.
25. John Jay to John Ten Broeck, June 6, 1777, quoted in Countryman, *People in Revolution,* p. 196.
26. Quoted in Countryman, *People in Revolution,* p. 197.
27. *Historical Memoirs of William Smith,* ed. William H. W. Sabine (New York: *New York Times* and Arno Press, 1971), p. 2:236.
28. William Duer to Philip Schuyler, July 3–5, 1777, in Schuyler Papers, New York Public Library.
29. Philip Schuyler to John Jay, June 30, 1777, in Young, *Democratic Republicans of New York,* p. 24.
30. Philip Schuyler to John Jay, July 14, 1777, ibid., p. 25.
31. *Correspondence and Public Papers of John Jay,* ed. Henry P. Johnston (New York: G. P. Putnam's Sons, 1890–93), pp. 1:146–47.
32. James Lovell to William Whipple, August 11, 1777, in *Letters of Members of the Continental Congress,* p. 2:425.
33. Philip Schuyler Letterbook, pp. 5: 295–98, 300–301, in Schuyler Papers, New York Public Library.
34. Quoted in Richard Brookhiser, *Gentleman Revolutionary: Gouverneur Morris, the Rake Who Wrote the Constitution* (New York: Free Press, 2003), p. 37.
35. Hoffman Nickerson, *The Turning Point of the Revolution, or Burgoyne in America* (Boston: Houghton Mifflin, 1928), pp. 276–77.
36. Quoted in Gerlach, *Proud Patriot,* p. 265.
37. *Familiar Letters of John Adams and his Wife Abigail Adams, During the Revolution,* ed. Charles F. Adams (New York: Hurd & Houghton, 1875), pp. 292–93.
38. Quoted in Gerlach, *Proud Patriot,* p. 264.
39. Thomas Burke to the governor of North Carolina, July 30, 1777, in *Letters of Members of the Continental Congress,* pp. 2:431–32.
40. Quoted in Gerlach, *Proud Patriot,* p. 286.
41. Thomas Anbury, *With Burgoyne from Quebec: An Account of the Life at Quebec and the Famous Battle of Saratoga,* ed. Sydney Jackman (Toronto: Macmillan of Canada, 1963), p. 170.
42. Quoted in Gerlach, *Proud Patriot,* p. 318.
43. Richard Varick to Philip Schuyler, October 13, 1777, in Schuyler Papers, New York Public Library; Schuyler to Varick, October 15, 1777, in Fort Ticonderoga Museum.
44. Gerlach, *Proud Patriot,* p. 260.
45. Quoted in Baroness Frederika von Riedesel, *Letters and Memoirs Relating to the American War of Independence* (New York: G. & C. Carvill, 1827), p. 191.
46. National Park Service, brochure, Schuyler Mansion, Schuylerville, New York.

CHAPTER 14: THE PLAYWRIGHT AND THE MERCHANT

1. Beaumarchais to Vergennes, August 13, 1776, *in Facsimiles of Manuscripts relating to America in the Archives of Europe, 1773–1788,* ed. Benjamin Franklin Stevens (London, 1870–1902), no. 889.
2. Silas Deane to Elizabeth Deane, March 3, 1775, in *The Deane Papers,* ed. Charles Isham (New York: New-York Historical Society, 1887), p. 1:122
3. Silas Deane to Elizabeth Deane, September 24, 1775, ibid., p. 1:80.
4. Silas Deane to Committee of Secret Correspondence, August 5, 1776, in *The Revolutionary Diplomatic Correspondence of the United States,* ed. Francis Wharton (Washington, D.C.: Government Printing Office, 1888), p. 2:123.
5. Silas Deane to C.W.F. Dumas, August 18, 1776, in *Deane Papers,* p. 1:219.
6. Silas Deane to Committee of Secret Correspondence, August 1, 1776, ibid., p. 1:214.
7. Beaumarchais to Silas Deane, July 14, 1776, ibid., pp. 1:145–46.
8. Silas Deane to Committee of Secret Correspondence, August 1, 1776, ibid., pp. 1:217.
9. Beaumarchais to Silas Deane, August 18, 1776, in *For the Good of Mankind: Pierre-Augustin de Beaumarchais: Political Correspondence Relative to the American Revolution,* ed. and trans. Antoinette Shewmake (Lanham, Md.: University Press of America, 1987), p. 157.
10. Silas Deane to Secret Committee, October 1, 1776, in *Deane Papers,* pp. 1:287–89.
11. Silas Deane to Secret Committee, November 9, 1776, ibid., p. 1:351.
12. CIA, Center for the Study of Intelligence, "Intelligence in the War of Independence: Intelligence Techniques," https://www.cia.gov/library/center-for-the-study-of-intelligence/csi-publications/books-and-monographs/intelligence/intelltech.html.
13. Beaumarchais to Silas Deane, October 14, 1776, quoted in Coy Hilton James, *Silas Deane: Patriot or Traitor?* (East Lansing: Michigan State University Press, 1975), p. 20.
14. Silas Deane to Secret Committee, October 8, 1776, in *Deane Papers,* p. 1:338.
15. "Memoirs of Silas Deane to French Foreign Office," September 24, 1776, ibid., p. 1:266.
16. Ibid., p. 1:281.
17. James, *Silas Deane,* p. 12.
18. Joel Richard Paul, *Unlikely Allies: How a Merchant, a Playwright, and a Spy Saved the American Revolution* (New York: Riverhead, 2009), p. 218.
19. Beaumarchais to Vergennes, December 7, 1777, in *Facsimiles of Manuscripts,* no. 1763.
20. John Adams to James Lovell, September 21, 1779, in *The Adams Family Correspondence,* ed. L. H. Butterfield (Cambridge, Mass.: Belknap Press of Harvard University Press, 1963–), p. 3:231n1.
21. *Revolutionary Diplomatic Correspondence,* p. 1:145.
22. Silas Deane to Arthur Lee, August 19, 1776, in *Deane Papers,* pp. 1:226–27.
23. Silas Deane to Jonathan Williams, January 13, 1778, ibid., p. 2:327.
24. Arthur Lee to R. H. Lee, October 4, 1777, in *Facsimiles of Manuscripts,* no. 269.
25. Arthur Lee to R. H. Lee, January 9, 1778, in Richard Henry Lee, *Life of Arthur Lee* (Boston: Wells & Lilly, 1829), pp. 2:127–28.
26. Silas Deane to Arthur Lee, December 13, 1777, in *Deane Papers,* pp. 2:272–73.
27. September 8, 1777, in *Journals of the Continental Congress, 1774–1789,* ed. Worthington C. Ford et al. (Washington, D.C., 1904–37), p. 8:721.

28. Beaumarchais to Silas Deane, February 19, 1777, in *For the Good of Mankind,* p. 200.
29. *Beaumarchais the Merchant: Letters of Theveneau de Francey, 1777–1780,* ed. John Bigelow, Theveneau de Francey, and New-York Historical Society (New York: Charles Scribner & Co., 1870), p. 4.
30. Robert Morris to Silas Deane, August 11, 1776, in *Letters of Delegates to Congress, 1774–1789,* ed. Paul H. Smith et al. (Washington, D.C.: Library of Congress, 1976–2000), p. 4:656.
31. Silas Deane to John Ross, March 23, 1778, in *Deane Papers,* p. 2:422.
32. Beaumarchais, "Memoir Secret Pour les Ministres du Roi, Seuls," March 13, 1778, ibid., pp. 2:420-21.
33. Beaumarchais to Congress, March 13, 1778, in *For the Good of Mankind,* pp. 298–300.
34. Vergennes to Louis XVI, January 7, 1778, in *Facsimiles of Manuscripts,* no. 1824.
35. Chaumont to Vergennes, April 18, 1778, in *Affaires Étrangeres Correspondence Politique, États-Unis,* Manuscript Division, Library of Congress, 1, no. 98.
36. Lord Stormont to Lord Weymouth, December 15, 1776, in Calendar of the Sparks Manuscripts in Harvard College Library, with an appendix showing other manuscripts, p. 10.
37. Vergennes to Silas Deane, March 1778, in *Deane Papers,* p. 2:436.

CHAPTER 15: THE SEED TIME OF GLORY

1. Washington described his men as "without clothes to cover their nakedness, without blankets to lay on, without shoes, by which their marches might be traced by the blood from their feet." George Washington to John Bannister, April 21, 1783, in *The Writings of George Washington, from the Original Manuscript Sources, 1745–1799,* ed. John C. Fitzpatrick (Washington, D.C., 1931–39), pp. 11:291–92.
2. George Washington to Nathanael Greene, February 6, 1783, ibid., p. 26:104.
3. Richard Brookhiser, *Gentleman Revolutionary: Gouverneur Morris, the Rake Who Wrote the Constitution* (New York: Free Press, 2003), p. 42.
4. Nathanael Greene to Alexander McDougall, February 11, 1779, in *The Papers of General Nathanael Greene,* ed. Roger N. Parks, Elizabeth C. Stevens, and Dennis M. Conrad (Chapel Hill: University of North Carolina Press, 1984), p. 235.
5. George Washington to Henry Laurens, December 13, 1777, in *Writings of Washington from the Original Sources,* p. 12:683.
6. Brookhiser, *Gentleman Revolutionary,* p. 42.
7. Gouverneur Morris to Sarah Gouverneur, 1778, in *The Diary and Letters of Gouverneur Morris, Minister of the United States to France, Member of the Constitutional Convention,* ed. Anne Cary Morris (New York: Charles Scribner's Sons, 1888), p. 1:9.
8. Gouverneur Morris to Robert Livingston, February 5, 1778, in Robert Livingston Papers, New-York Historical Society.
9. Gouverneur Morris quoted in James J. Kirschke, *Gouverneur Morris: Author, Statesman, and Man of the World* (New York: St. Martin's Press, 2005), pp. 70–71.
10. Quoted in Jared Sparks, *The Life of Gouverneur Morris* (Boston: Gray & Bowen, 1832), p. 1:154.
11. Quoted in Brookhiser, *Gentleman Revolutionary,* p. 45.
12. Quoted in Sparks, *Life of Gouverneur Morris,* p. 1:176.

13. Quoted ibid., p. 1:151.
14. John Adams to Joseph Warren, January 7, 1776, in *Warren-Adams Letters* (Boston: Massachusetts Historical Society, 1917–25), pp. 1:197–98, quoted in Richard H. Kohn, *Eagle and Sword: The Beginnings of the Military Establishment in America* (New York: Free Press, 1975), p. 2.
15. Joseph Warren to James Lovell, January 26, 1778, in Samuel Adams Papers, New York Public Library.
16. James Lovell to Sam Adams, January 13, 1778, in *Letters of Members of the Continental Congress,* ed. Edmund C. Burnett (Washington, D.C.: Carnegie Institution, 1921), p. 3:32.
17. Henry Laurens to James Duane, April 7, 1778, in *Letters of Members of the Continental Congress,* p. 3:154.
18. Quoted in Joseph Ellis, *His Excellency: George Washington* (New York: Vintage, 2005), p. 113.
19. Quoted in Sparks, *Life of Gouverneur Morris,* p. 1:151.
20. George Washington to the president of Congress, December 20, 1776, in *Writings of Washington from the Original Sources,* p. 6:403.
21. John Hancock, Boston Massacre Oration, March 5, 1774, in *Orations Delivered at the Request of the Inhabitants . . . to Commemorate the [Boston Massacre]* (Boston: Peter Edes, 1785), p. 51.
22. Henry Knox to Gouverneur Morris, February 21, 1783, quoted in Kohn, *Eagle and Sword,* p. 9.
23. August 20, 1776, *Journals of the Continental Congress,* p. 5:675.
24. Edward Rutledge to John Jay, June 29, 1776, in *Letters of Members of the Continental Congress,* p. 1:517.
25. H. James Henderson, *Party Politics in the Continental Congress* (New York: McGraw-Hill, 1974), p. 136.
26. Quoted in Charles Page Smith, *James Wilson: Founding Father, 1742–1798* (Chapel Hill: University of North Carolina Press, 1956), p. 104.
27. Thomas Burke, "Notes on the Articles of Confederation," November 15, 1777, in *Letters of Members of the Continental Congress,* p. 2:553.
28. Thomas Burke, November 15, 1777, ibid., p. 2:555.
29. Thomas Burke to Governor Richard Caswell, April 29, 1777, *ibid.,* pp. 2:345–46.
30. Gouverneur Morris quoted in William C. Banks and Peter Raven-Hansen, *National Security Law and the Power of the Purse* (Oxford: Oxford University Press, 1994), p. 26.
31. Philip Schuyler quoted in John Chester Miller, *Alexander Hamilton and the Growth of the New Nation* (New York: Transaction, 2003), p. 52.
32. Gouverneur Morris to John Jay, February 1, 1778, quoted in Sparks, *Life of Gouverneur Morris,* p. 1:154
33. Gouverneur Morris to George Clinton, March 16, 1778, quoted in William Howard Adams, *Gouverneur Morris: An Independent Life* (New Haven: Yale University Press, 2003), p. 100.
34. Quoted in Sparks, *Life of Gouverneur Morris,* p. 1:220.
35. Gouverneur Morris to Sarah Gouverneur, in *Diary and Letters of Gouverneur Morris,* p. 1:9.

36. Gouverneur Morris to Robert Morris, August 17, 1778, in *Letters of Members of the Continental Congress,* 3:376–77.
37. Adams, *Gouverneur Morris,* p. 103.
38. *Diary and Letters of Gouverneur Morris,* p. 1:12.
39. George Washington to Henry Laurens, April 10, 1778, in *Letters of the Members of the Continental Congress,* p. 3:xiv.
40. Gouverneur Morris to Robert Morris, May 11, 1778, ibid., p. 3:230.
41. John Adams to Abigail Adams, October 26, 1777, in *The Letters of John and Abigail Adams,* ed. Frank Shuffelton (New York: Penguin, 2004), p. 322.
42. James Lovell to Horatio Gates, November 27, 1777, in George W. Greene, *Life of Nathanael Greene* (New York: G. P. Putnam & Son, 1867), p. 2:8.
43. John Adams to Abigail Adams, September 2, 1777, *Letters of John and Abigail Adams,* p. 307.
44. Quoted in Adams, *Gouverneur Morris,* p. 89.
45. John Dickinson Sergeant to James Lovell, November 20, 1777, in Samuel Adams Papers, New York Public Library.
46. *The Writings of Samuel Adams,* ed. Harry A. Cushing (New York: G. P. Putnam's Sons, 1904–8), p. 4:1.
47. Henry Laurens to John Laurens, January 8, 1778, in Preston Russell, "The Conway Cabal," *American Heritage* 46, no. 1 (February–March 1995); see also David Duncan Wallace, *The Life Henry Laurens: With a Sketch of the Life of Lieutenant-Colonel John Laurens* (New York: G. P. Putnam's Sons, 1915), p. 268.
48. Marquis de Lafayette to George Washington, December 30, 1777, in *Memoirs, Correspondence, and Manuscripts of General Lafayette* (New York: Craighead and Allen, 1837), p. 1:136.
49. Edward Rutledge to George Washington, December 18, 1778, in James Haw, *John and Edward Rutledge of South Carolina* (Athens: University of Georgia Press, 1997), p. 114.
50. George Washington to Thomas Conway, January 4, 1778, in *The Writings of George Washington,* ed. Worthington C. Ford (New York: G. P. Putnam's Sons, 1890), p. 6:180.
51. John Laurens to Henry Laurens, in *The Army Correspondence of Colonel John Laurens in the Years 1777–1778,* ed. William Gilmore Simms (New York: Bradford Club, 1867), p. 104.
52. John Adams to Abigail Adams, May 22, 1777, in *Letters of John and Abigail Adams,* p. 279.
53. George Washington to Henry Laurens, January 31, 1778, in *Writings of Washington,* ed. Ford, p. 6:353.

CHAPTER 16: THE RUIN OF MR. DEANE

1. Henry Laurens to Rawlins Lowndes, August 18, 1778, in *Journals of the Continental Congress, 1774–1789,* ed. Worthington C. Ford et al. (Washington, D.C., 1904–37), p. 11:787.
2. Gouverneur Morris to John Jay, August 16, 1778, in *Letters of Delegates to Congress,*

1774–1789, ed. Paul H. Smith et al. (Washington, D.C.: Library of Congress, 1976–2000), p. 3:376.

3. Quoted in Elmer Bendiner, *The Virgin Diplomats* (New York: Alfred A. Knopf, 1976), p. 116.
4. Samuel Adams to Samuel Cooper, January 3, 1779, in *The Writings of Samuel Adams,* ed. Harry Alonzo Cushing (New York: G. P. Putnam's Sons, 1904–8), p. 4:112.
5. Arthur Lee to Samuel Adams, March 6, 1779, in Samuel Adams Papers, New York Public Library.
6. Samuel Adams to John Winthrop, December 21, 1779, in *Letters of Delegates to Congress, 1774–1789,* ed. Paul H. Smith et al. (Washington, D.C.: Library of Congress, 1976–2000), p. 11:363.
7. Samuel Adams to John Winthrop, December 21, 1778, in *Writings of Samuel Adams,* p. 4:123–24.
8. H. James Henderson, *Party Politics in the Continental Congress* (New York: McGraw-Hill, 1974), p. 193.
9. Richard Henry Lee to Arthur Lee, September 16, 1778, in *Letters of Delegates to Congress,* p. 10:132.
10. Robert Morris to John Jay, September 8, 1778, ibid., p. 10:609.
11. September 18, 1778, in *Journals of the Continental Congress,* p. 12:927.
12. James Lovell to John Adams, October 24, 1778, in *Letters of Delegates to Congress,* p. 11:114.
13. Silas Deane to Henry Laurens, October 12, 1778, in *The Diplomatic Correspondence of the American Revolution,* ed. Jared Sparks (Boston: N. Hale and Gray & Bowen, 1829), p. 1:129.
14. Silas Deane to Henry Laurens, November 1, 1778, ibid.
15. Silas Deane to the president of Congress, November 19, 1778, in Coy Hilton James, *Silas Deane: Patriot or Traitor?* (East Lansing: Michigan State University Press, 1975), p. 75.
16. Cyrus Griffin to Thomas Jefferson, October 6, 1778, in *Letters of Delegates to Congress,* p. 11:33.
17. Silas Deane to Barnabas Deane, November 23, 1778, in *The Deane Papers,* ed. Charles Isham (New York: New-York Historical Society, 1887), pp. 3:59–61.
18. "Address of Silas Deane," *Pennsylvania Packet,* December 5, 1778, reprinted ibid., pp. 3:66–70.
19. John Adams, diary entry for February 8, 1779, in *The Works of John Adams, Second President of the United States,* ed. Charles F. Adams (Boston: Little, Brown 1850–56), p. 3:187.
20. George Washington to Benjamin Harrison, December 18, 1778, in *The Writings of George Washington,* ed. Lawrence B. Evans (New York: G.P. Putnam's Sons, 1908), p. 133.
21. Robert Morris, "Statement of Robert Morris," January 16, 1779, in *Deane Papers,* p. 3:260.
22. Ibid.
23. "Thomas Paine's Reply to Robert Morris," January 11, 1779, in *Deane Papers,* p. 3:269.
24. Quoted in Jared Sparks, *The Life of Gouverneur Morris* (Boston: Gray & Bowen, 1832), p. 1:200.

25. "Silas Deane's Narrative," December 21, 1778, in *Deane Papers,* pp. 3:197–98.
26. Francis Lightfoot Lee to Richard Henry Lee, quoted in Joel Richard Paul, *Unlikely Allies: How a Merchant, a Playwright, and a Spy Saved the American Revolution* (New York: Riverhead, 2009), p. 298.
27. "Proceedings in Congress upon the Memorial of Minister Gerard Respecting the Publications of Thomas Paine," January 7, 1779, in *Deane Papers,* pp. 3:249.
28. *Quoted in* Robert L. Brunhouse, *The Counter-Revolution in Pennsylvania, 1776–1790* (Harrisburg: Pennsylvania Historical Commission, 1942), p. 62.
29. Robert Morris to Horatio Gates, February 5, 177, in Charles Rappleye, *Robert Morris: Financier of the American Revolution* (New York: Simon & Schuster, 2010), p. 171.
30. Silas Deane to the president of Congress, April 2, 1779, in *Diplomatic Correspondence of the American Revolution,* p. 3:109.
31. Silas Deane to John Jay, March 15, 1779, ibid., p. 1:403.
32. Henry Laurens, "Note to the Above by Henry Laurens," June 10, 1779, in *Deane Papers,* p. 3:484.
33. Report by the Committee on the Treasury, August 6, 1779, in *Journals of the Continental Congress,* pp. 14:929.
34. Paul, *Unlikely Allies,* p. 304.
35. Silas Deane to Barnabas Deane, April 20, 1780, in *Deane Papers,* p. 4:130.
36. Robert Morris to Benjamin Franklin, August 4, 1780, ibid., pp. 4:120–21.
37. Silas Deane to James Wilson, September 19, 1781, in James Wilson Papers, Historical Society of Pennsylvania.
38. Quoted in *John Jay: The Winning of the Peace: Unpublished Papers, 1780–1784,* ed. Richard B. Morris (New York: Harper & Row, 1975), p. 2:55.
39. Silas Deane to Simeon Deane, May 16, 1781, in *Deane Papers,* pp. 4:340, 343–44.
40. Henderson, *Party Politics,* p. 190.
41. Silas Deane to Barnabas Deane, January 31, 1782, in *Deane Papers,* p. 5:34.
42. George III to Lord North, July 19, 1781, ibid., p. 4:503.
43. Benjamin Franklin to Robert Morris, March 30, 1782, in *The Papers of Benjamin Franklin,* ed. Ellen R. Cohn (New Haven: Yale University Press, 2006), p. 37:365–66.
44. Dennis Kent Anderson and Godfrey Tryggve Anderson, "The Death of Silas Deane: Another Opinion," *New England Quarterly* 57, no. 1. (1984), p. 105.
45. Report on the Committee on Revolutionary Claims, 27th 2d, H.H. 952, p. 4.

CHAPTER 17: FORT WILSON

1. James Wilson, *The American Museum, or Repository of Ancient and Modern Fugitive Pieces, Prose and Poetical* (Philadelphia: Mathew Carey, 1789), p. 5:391.
2. Come on Coolly, in *Life in Early Philadelphia: Documents from the Revolutionary and Early National Periods,* ed. Billy Gordon Smith (University Park: Pennsylvania State University Press, 1995), p. 258.
3. Greer to Davis, March 29, 1779, in E. Wayne Carp, *To Starve the Army at Pleasure: Continental Army Administration and American Political Culture, 1775–1783* (Chapel Hill: University of North Carolina Press, 1984), p. 72.
4. Edward Countryman, *The American Revolution* (New York: Hill & Wang, 2003), p. 146.

5. *Pennsylvania Evening Post* (Philadelphia), May 29, 1779, quoted in John K. Alexander, "The Fort Wilson Incident of 1779: A Case Study of the Revolutionary Crowd," in *William and Mary Quarterly,* 3rd ser., 31, no. 4 (1974), p. 596.
6. *The Pennsylvania Packet,* September 10, 1779.
7. The power of the mob increased in stages, as the historian Robert Brunhouse describes. First, radical leaders began demanding that the Assembly punish monopolizers. Then extralegal committees created courts to try those it opposed. In the final stage, armed men roamed the city with guns and clubs to drive out their enemies. See Robert L. Brunhouse, *The Counter-Revolution in Pennsylvania, 1776–1790* (Harrisburg: Pennsylvania Historical Commission, 1942).
8. Countryman, *American Revolution,* p. 144.
9. Edward Countryman, *A People in Revolution: The American Revolution and Political Society in New York, 1760–1790* (New York: W. W. Norton, 1989), p. 183.
10. Egbert Benson to John Jay, July 6, 1779, in *The Correspondence and Public Papers of John Jay,* ed. Henry Phelps Johnston (New York: G. P. Putnam's Sons, 1891), p. 1:213.
11. Countryman, *American Revolution,* p. 146.
12. Charles Rappleye, *Robert Morris: Financier of the American Revolution* (New York: Simon & Schuster, 2010), p. 187.
13. James Read to George Read, August 7, 1779, in *Life and Correspondence of George Read,* ed. William Thompson Read (Philadelphia: J. P. Lippincott, 1870), pp. 350–51.
14. "To the Committee of the City," *Pennsylvania Packet,* July 1, 1779.
15. *Gazette,* October 18, 1779, in Brunhouse, *Counter-Revolution in Pennsylvania,* p. 89.
16. "Attack on Fort Wilson," *Pennsylvania Magazine of History and Biography* 5 (1881), p. 475.
17. Charles Willson Peale, "Statement of Peale," in *Life and Correspondence of Joseph Reed,* ed. William Bradford Reed (Philadelphia: Lindsay & Blakiston, 1847), p. 2:424.
18. Benjamin Rush to Charles Nisbet, August 27, 1784, in *The Letters of Benjamin Rush,* ed. L. H. Butterfield (Princeton, N.J.: Princeton University Press, 1951), p. 1:337.
19. Joseph Reed to Assembly, November 13, 1779, in Brunhouse, *Counter-Revolution in Pennsylvania,* p. 76.
20. Samuel Patterson to Caesar Rodney, October 6, 1779, in *Letters to and from Caesar Rodney, 1756–1784,* ed. George Herbert Ryden (Philadelphia: Historical Society of Delaware, 1933), p. 323.
21. Quoted in Charles Page Smith, *James Wilson: Founding Father, 1742–1798* (Chapel Hill: University of North Carolina Press, 1956), p. 137.
22. Morris to James Wilson, October 6, 1779, in Robert Morris Papers, Historical Society of Pennsylvania.
23. Benjamin Rush to Charles Lee, October 24, 1779, in *Letters of Rush,* pp. 1:243–44.
24. Quoted in Countryman, *American Revolution,* p. 143.
25. Henry Laurens to John Adams, October 4 1779, in *The Works of John Adams, Second President of the United States,* ed. Charles F. Adams (Boston: Little, Brown, 1850–56), p. 9:499.
26. Thomas Paine to Georges Danton, May 6, 1793, in *Life and Writings of Thomas Paine,* ed. Daniel Edwin Wheeler (New York: Vincent Prake & Co., 1908), p. 9:97.

27. *The Freeman's Journal: or, the North-American Intelligencer* (Philadelphia), April 7, 1784.
28. Smith, *James Wilson,* p. 139.

CHAPTER 18: AMERICAN DICTATORS

1. Christopher Gadsden to Timothy, June 8, 1778, in *The Writings of Christopher Gadsden,* ed. Richard Walsh (Columbia: University of South Carolina Press, 1966), pp. 130–31.
2. James Haw, *John and Edward Rutledge of South Carolina* (Athens: University of Georgia Press, 1997), p. 115.
3. John Wells to Henry Laurens, September 6, 1778, in *The Papers of Henry Laurens,* ed. David R. Chesnutt and C. James Taylor (Columbia: University of South Carolina Press, 1968–2002), p. 13:440.
4. *The South Carolina and American General Gazette,* February 11, 1779.
5. John Rutledge to Pierce Butler, February 17, 1779, in Haw, *John and Edward Rutledge,* p. 121.
6. John Rutledge to South Carolina delegates in Congress, March 18, 1779, ibid., p. 123.
7. William Moultrie, *Memoirs of the American Revolution* (New York: David Longworth, 1802), p. 1:426.
8. Joseph Johnson, *Traditions and Reminiscences Chiefly of the American Revolution in the South* (Charleston, S.C., 1851), p. 224.
9. Robert Barnwell, Jr., "Rutledge, 'The Dictator,'" *Journal of Southern History* 7, no. 2 (May 1941), p. 219.
10. Quoted in Charles W. Meister, *The Founding Fathers* (Jefferson, N.C.: McFarland, 1987), p. 282.
11. Barnwell, "Rutledge, 'The Dictator,'" p. 224.
12. John Rutledge to Horatio Gates, July 4, 1780, Horatio Gates Papers, New-York Historical Society.
13. Quoted in Haw, *John and Edward Rutledge,* p. 142.
14. Richard Barry, *Mr. Rutledge of South Carolina* (New York: Duell, Sloan & Pearce, 1942), p. 290.
15. John Rutledge to Thomas Sumter, October 6, 1780, in Haw, *John and Edward Rutledge,* p. 143.
16. Meister, *Founding Fathers,* p. 283.
17. Quoted in Barry, *Mr. Rutledge,* p. 291.
18. Edward McCrady, *The History of South Carolina in the Revolution, 1775–1780* (1901; reprint New York: Russell & Russell, 1969), p. 564.
19. John Rutledge to South Carolina delegates in Congress, January 24, 1781, in Joseph W. Barnwell, ed., "Letters of John Rutledge," *South Carolina Historical and Genealogical Magazine* 18, no. 3 (1917), pp. 131–32.
20. Philip Schuyler to Alexander Hamilton, September 10, 1780, in *Letters of Members of the Continental Congress,* ed. Edmund C. Burnett (Washington, D.C.: Carnegie Institution, 1921), p. 5:62.
21. Philip Schuyler to James Duane, October 4, 1778, in Duane Papers, New-York Historical Society.

22. *The Diplomatic Correspondence of the American Revolution,* ed. Jared Sparks (Boston: N. Hale and Gray & Bowen, 1829), pp. 3:212–14.
23. Nathanael Greene, October 29, 1779, in William Johnson, *Sketches of the Life and Correspondence of Nathanael Greene* (Charleston, S.C., 1822), p. 1:144.
24. George Washington to Joseph Jones, May 31, 1780, in *The Writings of George Washington from the Original Manuscript Sources, 1745–1799,* ed. John C. Fitzpatrick (Washington, D.C., 1931–44), p. 20:242.
25. Ibid., p. 18:453.
26. James Wilson, August 8, 1780, quoted in Charles Page Smith, *James Wilson: Founding Father, 1742–1798* (Chapel Hill: University of North Carolina Press, 1956), p. 141.
27. Edmund C. Burnett, in *Letters of Members of the Continental Congress,* p. 5:ix.
28. "Letter from the Committee of Congress at Head Quarters," May 10, 1780, ibid., pp. 5:132–34.
29. Philip Schuyler to James Duane, May 13, 1780, in *Letters of Delegates to Congress, 1774–1789,* ed. Paul H. Smith et al. (Washington, D.C.: Library of Congress, 1976–2000), p. 15:123.
30. E. Wayne Carp, "The Origins of the Nationalist Movement of 1780–1783: Congressional Administration and the Continental Army," *Pennsylvania Magazine of History and Biography* 107, no. 3 (1983), p. 374; Alexander Hamilton to James Duane, September 3, 1780, in *The Works of Alexander Hamilton: Comprising His Correspondence and His Political and Official Writings,* ed. John C. Hamilton (New York: John F. Trow, 1850), p. 1:150.
31. Alexander Hamilton to James Duane, September 3, 1780, in *Works of Hamilton,* p. 1:158.
32. *Writings of Washington from the Original Sources,* pp. 18:356–58.
33. John Sullivan to the president of New Hampshire, October 2, 1780, in *Letters of Members of the Continental Congress,* p. 5:397.
34. John Witherspoon to the governor of New Jersey, December 16, 1780, ibid., p. 5:487.
35. Ibid., pp. 5:134–39.
36. Quoted in Don Gerlach, *Proud Patriot: Philip Schuyler and the War of Independence, 1775–1783* (Syracuse, N.Y.: Syracuse University Press, 1987), p. 408.
37. Quoted in Edmund C. Burnett, *The Continental Congress: A Definitive History of the Continental Congress from its inception in 1774 to March 1789* (New York: W.W. Norton, 1964), p. 452.
38. Philip Schuyler to Governor Robert Livingston, June 12, 1780, ibid., pp. 5:207–8, 211–13.
39. Philip Schuyler to Major C. Carleton, November 10, 1780, in Gerlach, *Proud Patriot,* p. 433.
40. Alexander Hamilton to Margarita Schuyler, February 1780, in *Works of Hamilton,* pp. 2:269–71.

CHAPTER 19: POWER, CONSEQUENCE, AND GRANDEUR

1. Quoted in George Dangerfield, *Chancellor Robert R. Livingston of New York, 1746–1813* (New York: Harcourt Brace, 1960), p. 138.
2. Quoted ibid.

3. Arthur Lee to Francis Dana, July 6, 1782, in *Letters of Members of the Continental Congress,* ed. Edmund C. Burnett (Washington, D.C.: Carnegie Institution, 1921), p. 7:380.
4. James Wilson to Silas Deane, January 1, 1781, in *The Deane Papers,* ed. Charles Isham (New York: New-York Historical Society, 1890), 4:270.
5. *Freeman's Journal* (Philadelphia), June 27, 1781.
6. E. James Ferguson, *The Power of the Purse: A History of American Public Finance, 1776–1790* (Chapel Hill: University of North Carolina Press, 1961), p. 113.
7. Jared Sparks, *The Life of Gouverneur Morris* (Boston: Gray & Bowen, 1832), p. 1:27.
8. James Wilson, "Debates of Continental Congress," July 25, 1776, in *The Works of John Adams, Second President of the United States,* ed. Charles F. Adams (Boston: Little, Brown, 1850–56), p. 2:493.
9. Joseph Jones to Thomas Jefferson, June 30, 1780, in *Letters of Members of the Continental Congress,* p. 5:245.
10. Robert Morris to John Jay, July 4, 1781, in *The Papers of Robert Morris, 1781–1784,* ed. James Ferguson (Pittsburgh: University of Pittsburgh Press, 1978), p. 1:222.
11. Alexander Hamilton to Robert Morris, April 30, 1781, ibid., p. 1:32.
12. Nathanael Greene, 1778, in Charles Rappleye, *Robert Morris: Financier of the American Revolution* (New York: Simon & Schuster, 2010), p. 214.
13. Joseph Reed to Nathanael Greene, November 1781, in *The Life and Correspondence of Joseph Reed,* ed. William Bradford Reed (Philadelphia: Lindsay & Blakiston, 1847), pp. 2:374–75.
14. Ferguson, *Power of the Purse,* p. 119.
15. General William Irvine to Colonel Walter Stewart, August 26, 1781, in Colonel Walter Stewart Papers, New-York Historical Society.
16. Robert Morris to Committee of Congress, March 26, 1781, in *Papers of Robert Morris,* p. 1:20.
17. Robert Morris, "Circular to the Governors of the States," July 25, 1781, in *The Revolutionary Diplomatic Correspondence of the United States,* ed. Francis Wharton (Washington, D.C.: Government Printing Office, 1888), pp. 4:601–4.
18. Gouverneur Morris to Matthew Ridley, August 6, 1782, in Mathew Ridley Papers, Box 1, Massachusetts Historical Society.
19. *Revolutionary Diplomatic Correspondence,* pp. 5:56–59.
20. Lance Banning, "James Madison and the Nationalists, 1780–1783," *William and Mary Quarterly,* 3rd ser., vol. 40, no. 2 (1983), pp. 227–55.
21. George Washington to Joseph Reed, May 28, 1780, in *Life and Correspondence of Joseph Reed,* p. 2:200.
22. Robert Morris to Silas Deane, July 3, 1780, in *The Deane Papers* (New York: New-York Historical Society, 1890), p. 4:172.
23. Robert Morris to Philip Schuyler, May 12, 1781, *Papers of Robert Morris,* p. 1:93.
24. James Madison to Thomas Jefferson, June 23, 1780, in *The Writings of James Madison, Comprising His Public Papers and His Private Correspondence,* ed. Gaillard Hunt (New York: G. P. Putnam's Sons, 1900), p. 1:66.
25. Quoted in F. Cyril James, "The Bank of North America and the Financial History of Philadelphia," *Pennsylvania Magazine of History and Biography* 64, no. 1 (1940), p. 61.
26. Morris to the Governor of Virginia (Benjamin Harrison), January 15, 1782, *Papers of Robert Morris,* pp. 4:46–47.

27. Robert Morris to John Jay, July 4, 1781, ibid., p. 1:222.
28. Robert Morris to Benjamin Franklin, July 13, 1781, ibid., p. 1:283.
29. Robert Morris, *A Statement of the Accounts of the United States During the Administration of the Superintendent of Finance, 1781–1784* (Philadelphia, 1785), p. ix.
30. Robert Morris to John Jay, July 13, 1781, in *Papers of Robert Morris,* p. 1:287.
31. Robert Morris, "Circular to the Governors," July 28, 1781, ibid., p. 1:396.
32. Ibid.
33. Quoted in Rappleye, *Robert Morris,* p. 239.
34. Robert Morris to Thomas Lowrey, May 29, 1781, in *Papers of Robert Morris,* p. 1:91.
35. Robert Morris to Benjamin Harrison, January 15, 1782, ibid., p. 4:45.
36. Quoted in David Freeman Hawke, *Benjamin Rush: Revolutionary Gadfly* (New York: Bobbs-Merrill, 1971), p. 248.
37. Robert Morris to Joseph Reed, September 20, 1781, in *Papers of Robert Morris,* p. 2:309.
38. E. Wayne Carp, "The Origins of the Nationalist Movement of 1780–1783: Congressional Administration and the Continental Army," *Pennsylvania Magazine of History and Biography* 107, no. 3 (1983), p. 388.
39. Benjamin Rush, "The French Fête in Philadelphia in Honor of the Dauphin's Birthday, 1782," *Pennsylvania Magazine of History and Biography* 21, no. 2 (1897), p. 258.
40. Ibid., p. 259.
41. Ibid., p. 260.

CHAPTER 20: THE PAUSE THAT SAVED THE REVOLUTION

1. Philip Schuyler to George Washington, July 15, 1781, in Don Gerlach, *Proud Patriot: Philip Schuyler and the War of Independence, 1775–1783* (Syracuse, N.Y.: Syracuse University Press, 1987), p. 453.
2. Philip Schuyler to George Washington, January 15, 1782, in *Correspondence of the American Revolution,* ed. Jared Sparks (Boston: Little, Brown, 1853), pp. 3:462–63.
3. Colonel B. St. Leger to Captain Mathews, August 17, 1781, in Gerlach, *Proud Patriot,* p. 460.
4. Philip Schuyler to George Washington, August 8, 1781 (draft), Manuscripts Division, New York State Library.
5. Connor Cruise O'Brien, *The Great Melody: A Thematic Biography and Commented Anthology of Edmund Burke* (Chicago: University of Chicago Press, 1992), p. 202.
6. John Jay to Robert R. Livingston, September 18, 1782, in *The Revolutionary Diplomatic Correspondence of the United States,* ed. Francis Wharton (Washington, D.C.: Government Printing Office, 1888), p. 5:740.
7. George Washington to Robert R. Livingston, September 19, 1782, in *The Writings of George Washington from the Original Manuscript Sources, 1745–1799,* ed. John C. Fitzpatrick (Washington, D.C., 1931–39), p. 10:180.
8. Robert Morris to General Nathanael Greene, December 24, 1781, in Jared Sparks, *The Life of Gouverneur Morris* (Boston: Gray & Bowen, 1832), pp. 1:239–40.
9. Quoted in Charles Rappleye, *Robert Morris: Financier of the American Revolution* (New York: Simon & Schuster, 2010), p. 320.
10. Rhode Island Delegates to the Governor of Rhode Island, October 15, 1782, in *Letters*

of Members of the Continental Congress, ed. Edmund C. Burnett (Washington, D.C.: Carnegie Institution, 1921), pp. 6:503–7.

11. Edmund Randolph to James Madison, July 7, 1783, ibid., p. 7:21n2.
12. Gouverneur Morris to John Jay, January 1, 1783, in *The Papers of Robert Morris, 1781–1784,* ed. James Ferguson (Pittsburgh: University of Pittsburgh Press, 1978), p. 7:256.
13. Robert Morris to the president of Congress, January 24, 1783, in *Revolutionary Diplomatic Correspondence,* pp. 6:228–29.
14. Quoted in *The Writings of James Madison, Comprising His Public Papers and His Private Correspondence,* ed. Gaillard Hunt (New York: G.P. Putnam's Sons, 1900), pp. 1:328–30.
15. Ibid., pp. 1:334–36.
16. Ibid., p. 1:373.
17. John Jay to Robert Morris, July 20, 1783, quoted in Rappleye, *Robert Morris,* p. 345.
18. James Madison's notes, in John P. Kaminski, ed. *Founders on the Founders: Word Portraits from the Revolutionary Era* (Charlottesville: University of Virginia Press, 2008), p. 464.
19. Gouverneur Morris to Henry Knox, February 7, 1783, in *Papers of Robert Morris,* p. 7:417.
20. James Madison to Edmund Randolph, February 13 and 25, 1783, in *Letters of Delegates to Congress, 1774–1789,* ed. Paul H. Smith et al. (Washington, D.C.: Library of Congress, 1976–2000), pp. 19:693, 734.
21. Arthur Lee to Samuel Adams, January 29, 1783, in *Letters of Delegates to Congress,* p. 19:639.
22. Quoted in E. James Ferguson, *The Power of the Purse: A History of American Public Finance, 1776–1790* (Chapel Hill: University of North Carolina Press, 1961), p. 159.
23. George Washington, March 11, 12, 15, and 18, 1783, in *Journals of the Continental Congress, 1774–1789,* ed. Worthington C. Ford et al. (Washington, D.C., 1904–37), pp. 24:294–311.
24. See C. Edward Skeen, with a rebuttal by Richard H. Kohn, "The Newburgh Conspiracy Reconsidered," *William and Mary Quarterly,* 3rd ser., vol. 31, no. 2 (1974), pp. 273–98.
25. March 15, 1783, in *Journals of the Continental Congress,* pp. 24:306–10. For much of this account, I am indebted to Richard H. Kohn, *Eagle and Sword: The Beginnings of the Military Establishment in America* (New York: Free Press, 1975), pp. 24–32.
26. Philip Schuyler to Stephen Van Rensselaer, March 17, 1783, in Gerlach, *Proud Patriot,* p. 496.
27. Ibid.
28. George Washington to Alexander Hamilton, April 16, 1783, in *The Writings of George Washington from the Original Manuscript Sources, 1745–1799,* ed. John C. Fitzpatrick (Washington, D.C., 1931–44), p. 26:291.
29. Alexander Hamilton to George Washington, March 17 and April 11, 1783, in *The Works of Alexander Hamilton: Comprising His Correspondence and His Political and Official Writings,* ed. John C. Hamilton (New York: John F. Trow, 1850), pp. 1:345–49, 355–59.
30. Quoted in Karl-Friedrich Walling, *Republican Empire: Alexander Hamilton on War and Free Government* (Lawrence: University Press of Kansas, 1999), p. 62.

31. Alexander Hamilton to George Washington, February 13, 1783, *Letters of Delegates to Congress,* p. 19:690.
32. George Washington to Alexander Hamilton, March 4, 1783, in *Writings of Washington,* p. 26:277.
33. George Washington to Alexander Hamilton, April 16, 1783, in *The Papers of Alexander Hamilton,* ed. Harold C. Syrett and Jacob Ernest Cooke (New York: Columbia University Press, 1962), pp. 3:329–30.
34. George Washington to Alexander Hamilton, March 4, 1783, in *Writings of Washington,* p. 26:277.

CHAPTER 21: OUR AMERICAN TUMULTS

1. John Dickinson to Mary Dickinson, September 30, 1780, in John Dickinson Papers, Historical Society of Pennsylvania.
2. Milton E. Flower, *John Dickinson: Conservative Revolutionary* (Charlottesville: University of Virginia Press, 1983), p. 200.
3. Benjamin Rush to John Dickinson, March 20, 1778, in John Dickinson Papers, Historical Society of Pennsylvania.
4. Benjamin Rush, quoted in Forrest McDonald and Ellen Shapiro McDonald, *Requiem: Variations on Eighteenth-Century Themes* (Lawrence: University Press of Kansas, 1988), p. 95.
5. John Dickinson to Mary Dickinson, November 7, 1781, in John Dickinson Papers, Historical Society of Pennsylvania.
6. Quoted in Flower, *John Dickinson,* pp. 210–11.
7. Benjamin Franklin to Hopkinson, December 24, 1782, in *The Writings of Benjamin Franklin,* ed. Albert Henry Smyth (New York: Macmillan, 1905–7), p. 8:647.
8. Joseph Reed, December 3, 1782, in *Life and Correspondence of Joseph Reed,* ed. William Bradford Reed (Philadelphia: Lindsay & Blakiston, 1847), pp. 2:388–89.
9. Quoted in Charles Page Smith, *James Wilson: Founding Father, 1742–1798* (Chapel Hill: University of North Carolina Press, 1956), p. 174.
10. February 16, 1784, *Pennsylvania Archives,* ed. John B. Linn and William H. Egle (Harrisburg: B. F. Meyers, 1876), 1st ser., pp. 10:204–5.
11. Charles Rappleye, *Robert Morris: Financier of the American Revolution* (New York: Simon & Schuster, 2010), p. 358.
12. Robert Morris to unknown, April 18, 1783, in *The Papers of Robert Morris, 1781–1784,* ed. James Ferguson (Pittsburgh: University of Pittsburgh Press, 1978), p. 7:693.
13. George Washington to Alexander Hamilton, March 4, 1783, in *The Writings of George Washington from the Original Manuscript Sources, 1745–1799,* ed. John C. Fitzpatrick (Washington, D.C., 1931–44), p. 26:277.
14. James Madison, Notes of Debates, March 17, 1783, in *Journals of the Continental Congress, 1774–1789,* ed. Worthington C. Ford et al. (Washington, D.C., 1904–37), p. 25:926.
15. Private Bernardus Swartout quoted in Rappleye, *Robert Morris,* p. 374.
16. Minutes of Supreme Executive Council, June 21, 1783, in *Colonial Records of Pennsylvania* (Harrisburg: Theo. Fenn & Co., 1853), p. 13:605.
17. John Montgomery quoted in Charles Page Smith, *James Wilson: Founding Father, 1742–1798* (Chapel Hill: University of North Carolina Press, 1956), p. 191.

18. John Dickinson consultation with field officers, June 24, 1783, in *Minutes of the Supreme Executive Council of Pennsylvania, From Its Organization to the Termination of the Revolution* (Harrisburg: Theo. Fenn & Co., 1853), p. 13:610.
19. Quoted in Robert L. Brunhouse, *The Counter-Revolution in Pennsylvania, 1776–1790* (Harrisburg: Pennsylvania Historical Commission, 1942), p. 137.
20. Quoted in Rappleye, *Robert Morris,* p. 363.
21. Quoted in Flower, *John Dickinson,* p. 224.
22. Benjamin Rush to John Adams, April 1812, copy, in Benjamin Rush Papers, Library Company of Philadelphia.
23. *The Pennsylvania Packet,* June 28, 1783.
24. *The Pennsylvania Gazette,* June 25, 1783.
25. David Howell to the governor of Rhode Island, December 24, 1783, in *Letters of Delegates to Congress, 1774–1789,* ed. Paul H. Smith et al. (Washington, D.C.: Library of Congress, 1976–2000), pp. 21:226.
26. Samuel Osgood to John Adams, December 7, 1783, ibid., pp. 21:185.
27. January 19, 1784, in *Journal of the Council of Censors, Convened at Philadelphia on Monday, the Tenth Day of November, One Thousand Seven Hundred Eighty and Three* (Philadelphia: Hall & Sellers, 1784), p. 75.
28. Brunhouse, *Counter-Revolution in Pennsylvania,* p. 164.
29. William Binham to Cadwalader Morris, November 6, 1783, quoted ibid., p. 143.
30. Robert Morris to the president of Congress, June 30, 1783, in *Papers of Robert Morris,* p. 8:228.
31. Arthur Lee to St. George Tucker, October 23, 1783, ibid., p. 8:663.
32. Arthur Lee to John Adams, May 11, 1784, ibid., p. 9:585.
33. Robert Morris to Arthur Lee, October 11, 1783, ibid., p. 8:614.
34. Robert Morris, diary entries for July 10, 1784, August 28, 1784, ibid., pp. 9:450, 507.

CHAPTER 22: CAPITALIST INDUCEMENTS

1. *The Gazette of the State of South Carolina,* April 15, 1784; *Journals of the House of Representatives, 1783–84,* ed. Theodora J. Thompson and Rosa S. Lumpkin (Columbia: University of South Carolina Press, 1977), pp. 578–84.
2. Ibid.
3. *The Gazette of the State of South Carolina,* April 29, 1784.
4. Henry Peronneau, Jr., ibid., April 1, 1784.
5. Richard R. Beeman, "Deference, Republicanism, and the Emergence of Popular Politics in Eighteenth-Century America," *William and Mary Quarterly,* 3rd ser., vol. 49, no. 3 (1992), pp. 401–30.
6. Edward Rutledge to John Jay, May 21, 1789, in *Correspondence and Public Papers of John Jay,* ed. Henry P. Johnston (New York: G. P. Putnam's Sons, 1890–93), p. 3:368.
7. John Jay to Alexander Hamilton, September 28, 1783, in *The Papers of Alexander Hamilton,* ed. Harold C. Syrett and Jacob Ernest Cooke (New York: Columbia University Press, 1962), pp. 3:459–60.
8. Robert Livingston to Alexander Hamilton, August 30, 1783, ibid., p. 3:431.
9. Alexander Hamilton to Robert Livingston, April 25, 1785, ibid., pp. 3:608–9.

10. Henry Livingston to Walter Livingston, April 24, 1785, in Robert R. Livingston Papers, New-York Historical Society.
11. Robert Livingston, Jr., to Alexander Hamilton, June 13, 1785, in *Papers of Hamilton,* pp. 3:614–16.
12. Quoted in Clarence L. Ver Steeg, *Robert Morris, Revolutionary Financier* (Philadelphia: University of Pennsylvania Press, 1954), pp. 166–67.
13. *The Records of the Federal Convention of 1787,* ed. Max Farrand (New Haven: Yale University Press, 1911), p. 2:201ff.
14. Jared Sparks, *The Life of Gouverneur Morris* (Boston: Gray & Bowen, 1832), pp. 1:220–21.
15. Quoted in James Haw, *John and Edward Rutledge of South Carolina* (Athens: University of Georgia Press, 1997), p. 188.
16. National Park Service, brochure, Schuyler Mansion, Schuylerville, New York.
17. James Wilson, May 12, 1785, in Charles Page Smith, *James Wilson: Founding Father, 1742–1798* (Chapel Hill: University of North Carolina Press, 1956), p. 161.
18. John Ledyard to Isaac Ledyard, July 1783, in *The Papers of Robert Morris, 1781–1784,* ed. James Ferguson (Pittsburgh: University of Pittsburgh Press, 1978), p. 8:865.
19. Merrill Jensen, *The New Nation: A History of the United States During the Confederation, 1781–1789* (New York: Alfred A. Knopf, 1950), p. 225.
20. John Adams to Benjamin Franklin, August 17, 1780, in *The Works of John Adams, Second President of the United States,* ed. Charles F. Adams (Boston: Little, Brown, 1850–56), p. 7:247.
21. Quoted in Bray Hammond, *Banks and Politics in America: From the Revolution to the Civil War* (Princeton, N.J.: Princeton University Press, 1957), p. 116.
22. Thomas Jefferson to Mr. Lithson, January 4, 1805, in *The Writings of Thomas Jefferson,* ed. Paul Leicester Ford (New York: G. P. Putnam's Sons, 1892), p. 3:269n, quoted in Leo Marx, *The Machine in the Garden: Technology and the Pastoral Ideal in America* (New York: Oxford University Press, 1954), p. 159.
23. Quoted in J. G. A. Pocock, *The Machiavellian Moment: Florentine Political Thought and the Atlantic Republican Tradition* (Princeton, N.J.: Princeton University Press, 1975), p. 536.
24. *The Independent Chronicle* (Boston), November 24, 1785.
25. Drew McCoy, *The Elusive Republic: Political Economy in Jeffersonian America* (Chapel Hill: University of North Carolina Press, 1980), p. 164.
26. Quoted ibid., p. 127.
27. Smith, *James Wilson,* p. 159.
28. Ibid., p. 402n11
29. Quoted ibid., p. 164.
30. James Wilson, *On the Improvement and Settlement of Lands in the United States* (mid-1790s; reprint Philadelphia: Free Library of Philadelphia, 1946), p. 11.
31. Ibid., p. 20.
32. Circular to the Governors of the States, January 8, 1782, in *Papers of Robert Morris,* pp. 3:507–11.
33. George David Rappaport, *Stability and Change in Revolutionary Pennsylvania: Banking, Politics, and Social Structure* (University Park: Pennsylvania State University Press, 1996), p. 162.

34. Ibid., p. 158.
35. Quoted ibid., p. 183.
36. James Wilson, "Considerations," in *The Works of the Honorable James Wilson, L.L.D,* ed. Bird Wilson (Philadelphia: Lorenzo Press, 1804), p: 3:406.
37. Robert L. Brunhouse, *The Counter-Revolution in Pennsylvania, 1776–1790* (Harrisburg: Pennsylvania Historical Commission, 1942), p. 175.
38. *The Pennsylvania Gazette,* December 21, 1786.
39. Stockholder minutes, Bank of North America, November 23, 1786.
40. Benjamin Rush to Price, October 27, 1786, in *The Letters of Benjamin Rush,* ed. L. H. Butterfield (Princeton, N.J.: Princeton University Press, 1951), p. 1:408.
41. Quoted in Forrest McDonald and Ellen Shapiro McDonald, *Requiem: Variations on Eighteenth-Century Themes* (Lawrence: University Press of Kansas, 1988), p. 32.
42. "Proceedings of Commissioners to Remedy Defects of the Federal Government," September 14, 1786, in *The Debates in the Several State Conventions on the Adoption of the Federal Constitution, as Recommended by the General Convention at Philadelphia in 1787,* ed. Jonathan Elliot (Washington: Jonathan Elliot, 1836), p. 1:153.
43. George Washington to James Madison, November 5, 1786, in *The Writings of George Washington from the Original Manuscript Sources, 1745–1799,* ed. John C. Fitzpatrick (Washington, D.C., 1931–44), p. 29:51.

CHAPTER 23: EXPERIENCE MUST BE OUR GUIDE

1. George Washington to Henry Knox, March 8, 1787, and Henry Knox to George Washington, March 19, 1787, in *The Papers of George Washington: Confederation Series,* ed. W. W. Abbot et al. (Charlottesville: University of Virginia Press, 1992–97), pp. 5:74–75.
2. Ibid., pp. 5:95–98.
3. Quoted in Ralph Louis Ketcham, *James Madison: A Biography* (New York: Macmillan, 1971), p. 190.
4. George Washington, May 20, 1787, in *The Records of the Federal Convention of 1787,* ed. Max Farrand (New Haven: Yale University Press, 1911), p. 3:22.
5. Thomas Jefferson to John Adams, August 30, 1787, in *Memoirs, Correspondence, and Private Papers of Thomas Jefferson,* ed. Thomas Jefferson Randolph (London: Henry Colburn and Richard Bentley, 1829), p. 2:228.
6. Gouverneur Morris, July 21, 1788, in Morris-Croxall Papers, Library of Congress.
7. John Dickinson to Polly Dickinson, in *Supplement to Max Farrand's The Records of the Federal Convention of 1787* (New Haven: Yale University Press, 1987), p. 75.
8. William Pierce in *Records of the Federal Convention,* p. 3:89.
9. Edward Rutledge to Jeremiah Wadsworth, October 21, 1786, in Miscellaneous Manuscripts, Amherst College Library, Amherst, Mass., in James Haw, *John and Edward Rutledge of South Carolina* (Athens: University of Georgia Press, 1997), p. 201.
10. *Records of the Federal Convention,* p. 3:93.
11. Quoted in Jared Sparks, *The Life of Gouverneur Morris* (Boston: Gray & Bowen, 1832), p. 1:286.
12. *Records of the Federal Convention,* p. 1:48.

13. Ibid., pp. 1:86–87.
14. Ibid., p. 1:37.
15. Ibid., p. 1:483.
16. Mark David Hall, *The Political and Legal Philosophy of James Wilson, 1742–1798* (Columbia: University of Missouri Press, 1997), p. 151.
17. Quoted ibid., p. 154.
18. Mark David Hall describes Wilson's reliance on a Christian conception of natural law in *Political and Legal Philosophy of James Wilson,* p. 67.
19. *Records of the Federal Convention,* p. 1:49.
20. *The Works of James Wilson,* ed. James De Witt Andrews (Chicago: Callaghan & Co., 1896), p. 1:374.
21. Ibid., p. 1:545.
22. Quoted in Hall, *Political and Legal Philosophy of Wilson,* p. 50; *Records of the Federal Convention,* p. 1:605.
23. *Records of the Federal Convention,* p. 1:605.
24. Ibid., p. 2:201
25. Ibid., p. 1:53.
26. Ibid., pp. 1:86–87.
27. Ibid., p. 1:136.
28. Ibid., p. 1:156.
29. Ibid., p. 1:157.
30. Ibid., p. 1:153.
31. Ibid., pp. 1:153–54.
32. Forrest McDonald and Ellen Shapiro McDonald, *Requiem: Variations on Eighteenth-Century Themes* (Lawrence: University Press of Kansas, 1988), p. 91.
33. Quoted in J. G. A. Pocock, ed., *Three British Revolutions: 1641, 1688, 1776* (Princeton, N.J.: Princeton University Press, 1980), p. 75.
34. *Records of the Federal Convention,* p. 2:278.
35. Ibid., p. 1:183.
36. Ibid., p. 1:242.
37. Ibid., p. 1:259.
38. John Adams, *Novanglus,* in *The Works of John Adams, Second President of the United States,* ed. Charles F. Adams (Boston: Little, Brown, 1850–56), p. 4:8.
39. *Records of the Federal Convention,* p. 1:254.
40. Ibid., p. 1:327.
41. Ibid., p. 1:492.
42. Ibid., p. 2:218.
43. Quoted in Charles Page Smith, *James Wilson: Founding Father, 1742–1798* (Chapel Hill: University of North Carolina Press, 1956), p. 244.
44. See McDonald and McDonald, *Requiem,* p. 98, for an excellent analysis of Dickinson's contribution.
45. George Washington, diary entry for July 30, 1787, in *The Writings of George Washington,* ed. Worthington C. Ford (New York: G. P. Putnam's Sons, 1891), p. 11:150.

CHAPTER 24: WE THE PEOPLE

1. Quoted in Harold Evans with Gail Buckland and David Lefer, *They Made America: From the Steam Engine to the Search Engine, Two Centuries of Innovators* (New York: Little, Brown, 2004), p. 23.
2. Quoted ibid., p. 24.
3. See Edward C. Walterscheid, "To Promote the Progress of Science and Useful Arts; The Background and Origin of the Intellectual Property Clause of the United States Constitution," *Journal of Intellectual Property Law* 2, no. 1 (1994), pp. 4–9.
4. Quoted in Stephen P. Halbrook and David B. Kopel, "Tench Coxe and the Right to Keep and Bear Arms, 1787–1823," *William and Mary Bill of Rights Journal* 7 (February 1999), p. 226.
5. Quoted in Leo Marx, *The Machine in the Garden: Technology and the Pastoral Ideal in America* (New York: Oxford University Press, 1964), pp. 152–53.
6. Quoted ibid., p. 152.
7. Tench Coxe, "An Address to an Assembly of the Friends of American Manufactures, Convened for the Purpose of Establishing a Society for the Encouragement of Manufactures and the Useful Arts" (August 9, 1787), *American Museum* 2 (1965), pp. 248, 253.
8. Ibid.
9. Quoted in Marx, *Machine in the Garden,* pp. 153–54.
10. *The Records of the Federal Convention of 1787,* ed. Max Farrand (New Haven: Yale University Press, 1911), p. 2:322.
11. Ibid., pp. 2:129–75.
12. Ibid., pp. 1:108, 110.
13. Ibid., pp. 1:95, 98, 2:73, 391, 429.
14. *The Works of the Honorable James Wilson, L.L.D.*, ed. Bird Wilson (Philadelphia: Lorenzo Press, 1804), pp. 1:460–61.
15. *Records of the Federal Convention,* p. 2:73.
16. Ibid., p. 2:74.
17. Ibid., p. 2:75.
18. *Works of Wilson,* p. 2:303.
19. *Records of the Federal Convention,* p. 2:73.
20. Ibid., p. 2:501.
21. Ibid., pp. 1:65–66.
22. Ibid., p. 1:254.
23. Ibid., p. 1:96.
24. Ibid., p. 1:99.
25. Ibid.
26. Ibid., pp. 3:450–51.
27. Ibid., p. 1:68.
28. Ibid., p. 2:52.
29. Ibid., p. 2:523.
30. Ibid., p. 2:54.
31. *Works of Wilson,* p. 67.
32. *Records of the Federal Convention,* p. 2:222.

33. Ibid., pp. 2:364, 373.
34. Ibid., p. 3:275.
35. Quoted in Mark David Hall, *The Political and Legal Philosophy of James Wilson, 1742–1798* (Columbia: University of Missouri Press, 1997), p. 60.
36. Quoted in Forrest McDonald and Ellen Shapiro McDonald, *Requiem: Variations on Eighteenth-Century Themes* (Lawrence: University Press of Kansas, 1988), p. 101.
37. *Records of the Federal Convention,* pp. 2:9–10.
38. Ibid., p. 1:534.
39. Ibid., p. 3:392.
40. Quoted in Edward Countryman, *The American Revolution* (New York: Hill & Wang, 2003), p. 190.
41. Gouverneur Morris to Thomas Pickering, in *The Diary and Letters of Gouverneur Morris,* ed. Anne Cary Morris (New York: Charles Scribner's Sons, 1888), p. 2:574.
42. Ibid.
43. *Records of the Federal Convention,* p. 2:569.
44. Quoted in Richard Brookhiser, *Gentleman Revolutionary: Gouverneur Morris, the Rake Who Wrote the Constitution* (New York: Free Press, 2003), p. 90.
45. *Records of the Federal Convention,* p. 2:657.
46. Ibid., p. 2:565.
47. Ibid., p. 2:632.
48. George Washington, *The Writings of George Washington, Being His Correspondence, Addresses, Messages, and Other Papers, Official and Private,* ed. Jared Sparks (Boston: Ferdinand Andrews, 1839), p. 9:541.

EPILOGUE

1. James Madison, "Note During the Convention for Amending the Constitution of Virginia," in *The Writings of James Madison,* ed. Gailland Hunt (New York: G. P. Putnam's Sons, 1910), pp. 9:358n–360n.
2. These quotations are from notes Madison made in 1821, ibid., p. 4:121n.
3. For an in-depth discussion of Madison's thought, see Drew McCoy, *The Elusive Republic: Political Economy in Jeffersonian America* (Chapel Hill: University of North Carolina Press, 1980), pp. 255–56.
4. Madison, "Note During the Convention," pp. 9:358n–360n.
5. James Madison, "Parties," *National Gazette,* January 23, 1792, quoted in Ruth Bogin, "Petitioning and the New Moral Economy of Post-Revolutionary America," *William and Mary Quarterly,* 3rd ser., vol. 45, no. 3 (1988), p. 403.
6. John M. Murrin, "The Great Inversion, or Court versus Country: A Comparison of the Revolution Settlements in England (1688–1721) and America (1776–1816)," in J. G. A. Pocock, ed., *Three British Revolutions 1641, 1688, 1776* (Princeton, N.J.: Princeton University Press, 1980), p. 404.
7. George Washington Parke Custis, *Recollections and Private Memoirs of Washington* (Washington, D.C.: William H. Moore, 1859), p. 55.
8. J. G. A. Pocock, *The Machiavellian Moment: Florentine Political Thought and the Atlantic Republican Tradition* (Princeton, N.J.: Princeton University Press, 1975), p. 143.
9. "Atticus," *American Remembrancer,* p. 68, quoted in McCoy, *Elusive Republic,* p. 164.

10. The historian James Hutson traces these similarities back to the fight between the Federalists and the anti-Federalists over the ratification of the Constitution but does not go earlier. See James H. Hutson, "Country, Court, and Constitution: Antifederalism and the Historians," *William and Mary Quarterly,* 3rd ser., vol. 38, no. 3 (1981), pp. 338–68.
11. See David Hackett Fischer, *The Revolution of American Conservatism: The Federalist Party in the Era of Jeffersonian Democracy* (New York: Harper & Row, 1965), passim.
12. Benjamin Franklin quoted in Forrest McDonald, *Alexander Hamilton: A Biography* (New York: W. W. Norton, 1979), p. 329.
13. *The Diary and Letters of Gouverneur Morris: Minister of the United States to France, Member of the Constitutional Convention, etc.,* ed. Anne Cary Morris (New York: Charles Scribner's Sons: 1888), p. 2:456.
14. Quoted in George Washington Parke Custis, *Recollections and Private Memoirs of Washington* (Washington, D.C.: William H. Moore, 1859), p. 326.
15. Robert Morris to John Nicholson, quoted in Ellis Paxson Oberholtzer, *Robert Morris: Patriot and Financier* (New York: Macmillan, 1903), p. 348.
16. Robert Morris to Thomas Morris, December 5, 1801, quoted ibid., p. 354.
17. Robert Morris to Thomas Morris, January 31, 1802, quoted in Charles Rappleye, *Robert Morris: Financier of the American Revolution* (New York: Simon & Schuster, 2010), p. 514.
18. Robert Morris, Will, June 13, 1804, in Charles Henry Hard, "Mary White—Mrs. Robert Morris," *Pennsylvania Magazine of History and Biography* 2, no. 2 (1878), p. 182.
19. Quoted in Richard Brookhiser, *Gentleman Revolutionary: Gouverneur Morris, the Rake Who Wrote the Constitution* (New York: Free Press, 2003), p. 129.
20. George Pellew, *John Jay: American Statesman* (Boston: Houghton Mifflin, 1898), p. 282.
21. John Jay to Richard Peters, August 30, 1808, quoted in Henry Flanders, *Lives and Times of the Chief Justices of the Supreme Court of the United States* (Philadelphia: J. B. Lippincott, 1874), p. 426.
22. Quoted in Don Gerlach, *Philip Schuyler and the Growth of New York, 1733–1804* (Albany: Office of State History, 1968), pp. 45–47.
23. Quoted in Richard Barry, *Mr. Rutledge of South Carolina* (New York: Duell, Sloan & Pearce, 1942), p. 352.
24. John Rutledge to George Washington, October 27, 1789, in *The Documentary History of the Supreme Court of the United States, 1789–1800,* ed. Maeva Marcus and James R. Perry (New York: Columbia University Press, 1989), p. 1:22.
25. William Read to J. Read, July 21, 1795, quoted in James Haw, *John and Edward Rutledge of South Carolina* (Athens: University of Georgia Press, 1997), p. 249.
26. *The South Carolina Gazette,* July 17, 1795, in *Documentary History of the Supreme Court,* pp. 1:765–67.
27. Haw, *John and Edward Rutledge,* p. 250.
28. John Adams to Abigail Adams, December 16, 17, 1795, in *Documentary History of the Supreme Court,* pp. 1:813–14.
29. Jacob Read to Ralph Izard, December 19, 1795, ibid., p. 1:814.
30. W. Read to Jacob Read, December 29, 1795, ibid, pp. 1:820–21.
31. Haw, *John and Edward Rutledge,* p. 274.

32. See Adam L. Tate, *Conservatism and Southern Intellectuals, 1789–1861: Liberty, Tradition, and the Good Society* (Columbia: University of Missouri Press, 2005), passim.
33. Quoted in Robert L. Brunhouse, *The Counter-Revolution in Pennsylvania, 1776–1790* (Harrisburg: Pennsylvania Historical Commission, 1942), p. 222.
34. Quoted in McCoy, *Elusive Republic,* p. 226.
35. John Dickinson, *Letters of Fabius,* quoted in Forrest McDonald and Ellen Shapiro McDonald, *Requiem: Variations on Eighteenth-Century Themes* (Lawrence: University Press of Kansas, 1988), p. 102. Forrest McDonald, as usual, provides insightful commentary on Dickinson's conservative outlook.
36. John Dickinson to Thomas Jefferson, January 22, 1806, quoted in Milton E. Flower, *John Dickinson: Conservative Revolutionary* (Charlottesville: University of Virginia Press, 1983), p. 296.
37. Ibid.

Index